Pos

FRON

Gar

A

GamaNetwork
RESOURCES FOR GAME DEVELOPMENT

Books

rk, NY • Lawrence, KS

Published by CMP Books
an imprint of CMP Media LLC
Main office: 600 Harrison Street, San Francisco, CA 94107 USA
Tel: 415-947-6615; fax: 415-947-6015
Editorial office: 1601 West 23rd Street, Suite 200, Lawrence, KS 66046 USA
www.cmpbooks.com
email: books@cmp.com

Acquisitions editor:	Dorothy Cox
Managing editor:	Michelle O'Neal
Copyeditor:	Madeleine Reardon Dimond
Layout design:	Justin Fulmer
Cover design:	Damien Castaneda

Distributed to the book trade in the U.S. by:
Publishers Group West
1700 Fourth Street
Berkeley, CA 94710
1-800-788-3123

Distributed in Canada by:
Jaguar Book Group
100 Armstrong Avenue
Georgetown, Ontario M6K 3E7 Canada
905-877-4483

For individual orders and for information on special discounts for quantity orders, please contact:
CMP Books Distribution Center, 6600 Silacci Way, Gilroy, CA 95020
Tel: 1-800-500-6875 or 408-848-3854; fax: 408-848-5784
email: cmp@rushorder.com; Web: www.cmpbooks.com

Library of Congress Cataloging-in-Publication Data
Postmortems from Game Developer / [edited by] Austin Grossman.
p. cm.
ISBN 1-57820-214-0 (softcover)
1. Computer games—Design. 2. Computer games—Programming. 3. Electronic games industry—United States. I. Grossman, Austin, 1969– II. Game developer.
QA76.76.C672P67 2003
794.8'151—dc21 2003041466

Printed in the United States of America
03 04 05 06 07 5 4 3 2 1

ISBN: 1-57820-214-0

CMP Books

TABLE OF CONTENTS

INTRODUCTION

Tales from the Front Line

We are only beginning to understand how to make video games.

A couple of years ago I was working at a computer game company in Los Angeles, and one afternoon I took a walk through Universal Studios' nearby lot. I was new to the West Coast, so it was a big thrill knowing that I was standing at the physical place where movies were made. I roamed around and peered in open doorways at the cavernous sound stages stacked with pipes and lumber.

I had no idea what any of it was, but two things were immediately clear: (a) whatever they were doing was enormously complicated and expensive, and (b) they knew exactly how to do it.

Universal Studios was founded in 1912, and after 90 years of filmmaking, they have it down to something like a science. Every single item, down to the orange cones, had a name or number stenciled onto it. Somewhere someone with a clipboard knew what everyone on the project was doing that day and every day until the red-carpet premiere, and how much every minute was costing the studio. If the movie runs over time and budget, they know it and they know what to do to minimize losses and get it in the can and out the door. They have put their production techniques through more-than-complete shakedown.

Compare this to making a video game. This is another enormously complicated and expensive enterprise, but one much less clearly understood. Schedules, staffing, and budget are routinely inaccurate, if not vastly overoptimistic. Projects routinely run months and millions of dollars over what was initially projected. Job descriptions are vague and changeable. No universal vocabulary of design and production terminologies exists. Individual jargons are ad-hoc inventions, varying from company to company and project to project.

Every year new technologies for both production and display are introduced, and every year audience expectations change and the scale of the enterprise goes up. During the two years a project is in production, the whole medium evolves. The product quality in the game industry is immensely variable. Only a relatively small percentage of video and computer games are substantially profitable and many lose money. What's going on?

The game industry is in its shakedown phase. We have a loose set of procedures, methodologies, heuristics, and advice about how to make games, but judging by the rate at which projects go seriously off-track, it's not enough.

One reason for this is that the medium itself is still changing rapidly—in form, in content, and in scale. Computer games began as one-person projects, a single person doing code, design, art, and possibly marketing and distribution. The whole thing could be around 100 kilobytes, something like 50 typewritten pages of data. In the year 2000, an average game published by a major game publisher cost $5–10 million to develop, required 1–3 years in development time and a team of 10–50 developers and artists producing 500 megabytes of data, comparable to a 10-volume encyclopedia set.

Organizing the creation of this much data is daunting, to say nothing of shaping it into a functional software application that produces the delicate, ephemeral quantity known as "fun." To compound this, we have the industry's collective lack of experience. The entire industry is only 25–30 years old, and for the first 20 years of that it was relatively tiny. According to a survey by the IDSA, the average game programmer has 1–2 years experience; other game development staff, including technical directors, lead artists, and designers have on average 3–5 years' experience. So only half of the people in the industry have been there long enough to have shipped more than 2.5 games.

Our collective inability to complete projects smoothly is damaging on a number of fronts. Budget overruns and delayed product releases are obviously costly and make it much harder for companies to stay in business. This has indirect effects as well, as small companies without financial resources can go under even if they have strong, original game ideas. It suppresses creativity—with smaller profit margins and tight schedules, there is increased pressure to stick to proven formulae and reliable money-makers, rather than to experiment.

Too many games are released before they are actually complete, because they have to be shipped in order to balance the quarterly budget. The pressure to sign off on a game is enormous. This is clear from the number of games that require patches, meaning that they weren't ready to ship at all. Game companies operate so close to the margin that almost no one has the luxury of shipping a game "when it's ready."

When projects go bad, the first casualty is quality of life. Many products are shipped only at a grueling cost of lost sleep, strained relationships, weekends away from family and friends. There is such a thing as hard-core dedication, where you work long hours for the tremendous thrill of getting paid for what you love, of staying up until 3 A.M. to get a key feature up and running, and watching the game come alive before your eyes. But too many of us have experienced the agony of being stuck in a morass of a project, missing milestone after milestone with no end in sight, flinching and growling when innocent bystanders ask us how "that game thing is going." This has become an accepted part of the industry, rather than a symptom of project mismanagement.

As an industry, we are gradually becoming aware of this. Grim experience tells us that no matter how good your idea or how brilliant and dedicated your team, project mismanagement can wreck things. Project management is a complex subject worth studying—a collection of skills and knowledge as difficult and important to game production as art, programming, and design. While it is generally becoming accepted that the simple "waterfall" model of software development isn't enough, flexible development models are harder to implement than they look, and require daily courage, patience, and good judgment.

What this book hopes to do is speed up the game industry's shakedown process. The postmortems in this book are the next best thing to actual game development experience. They follow projects from start to finish, talking about mistakes as well as good decisions, giving candid accounts, rather than just trying to abstract general guidelines. They record the experiences of average game developers as well as high-ranking producers.

Each article is written in the same simple format. A member of the development team writes down how the game got made, starting from the initial vision and the starting goals, what kind of company and project team was involved, what tools were used, and any major events along the way. The author then lists five successes, five things that Went Right and conspicuously contributed to the project's success. This is followed by What Went Wrong, a list of five misjudgments, failures, or missed opportunities.

The postmortems in this book are grouped into five sections:

- Startups,
- Sequels and Sophomore Outings,
- Managing Innovation,
- Building on a License, and
- The Online Frontier.

These categories are designed to group games by factors relevant to production, rather than (for instance) gameplay or technology issues. They don't function with true Aristotelian purity, however, so some of the postmortems concern games that belong to more than one category—some of the online games were also made by startup companies, and so on.

The *Game Developer* postmortems have gradually become an industry institution, and deservedly so. The honesty, thoroughness, and specificity of these accounts make them a unique resource. One of the great strengths of the game industry is its ethic of cooperation and communication, and the belief that our identity as a community of passionate creators is more important than edging each other out for more money. This has created an atmosphere where we can share information about our successes and failures and help each other make better games.

This is part of the reason that games as a medium has come so far, so fast. This book will, I hope, be a part of that process, the candid exchange of experiences as we all struggle up the learning curve together.

SECTION I

Startups

The startup company is truly the heroic myth of the game industry. It's the young success story of a new generation, like a garage band getting a big record contract, or a goateed 22-year-old writing the latest Great American Novel. We know it by heart already: a collection of dedicated twentysomethings (the genius hacker, the visionary designer, the gifted artist), college buddies or the remnants of someone's high school D&D campaign; the brilliant concept, the next DOOM or TETRIS, neon lightning caught in a bottle; the cluster of PCs set up in low-rent office space or someone's living room; the late nights, the pizza boxes, the copy of *Business Plans for Dummies*. And of course the happy ending: killer demo for an industry publisher, a distribution deal, internet buzz, and the private dream is now a number-one seller. Fame and fortune, not to mention royalties and stock options, ensue. And above all, a true passion for the work, the holy fire.

And it happens, too. Look at the game industry's premier development houses, and you'll see garage companies started by hobbyists and amateurs who worked out a way to package and sell what they love. Even as the industry matures, there is still a niche for startups, as larger companies sometimes fail to keep pace with street-level innovation.

The realities of the startup company are often hard work, long odds, endless delays and hassle and frustration. The postmortems collected here are the rare success stories—we don't chronicle the hundreds (thousands?) of startup efforts that broke apart when money ran out, enthusiasm flagged, schedules slipped, or law school beckoned. Startup companies tank far more often than they succeed, and in the end the deal doesn't get made, the product never ships, and people go their separate ways. What makes the difference?

The postmortems in this section were all written by developers who succeeded. They all shipped great games their first time out, and were willing to share what went right and what went wrong. If you're working on a startup game company, none of their situations will be exactly the same as yours, but chances are much of it will have a familiar ring.

Startups typically have a few enormous advantages, which we'll see repeated in the pages to come:

Youth. Young, enthusiastic teams, willing to work long hours for low salaries.

No bureaucracy. When the whole company fits into one office and your CEO is also your lead programmer, communication happens faster.

Low overhead. Lean and mean companies have a low burn rate, especially when you're working out of someone's parents' living room.

Freedom. Until you've made a distribution deal, you call the shots—you can make the game you want to make, not the one you got handed because upper management managed to score the interactive licensing rights to a 70s TV show.

New company culture. It's a chance to form your own company culture and try out new models of game development, instead of inheriting them from an older company's bureaucracy. You design the work pipeline, organizational chart, greenlight process yourself, and change them right away if they don't work out.

There are also some perilous downsides:

Rookie management. Software development is an enormously complex task, almost a discipline in itself. Screwing it up can have grievous costs in time, money, and quality.

No money. Unless you have a sweetheart deal from the start, you'll be running on a shoestring budget, conceivably angsting about making payroll.

Overtasking. Everyone seems to be in agreement that small teams work better for many projects, but this can mean team members wear multiple hats. The problem is compounded when the same people are running the business and administration of a small company.

Overambition. Sometimes total freedom can be too much of a good thing. Big-company structures that force you to make milestones and ship product can be necessary discipline, ensuring that you cut unnecessary features and that someday you actually put the product in a box and ship it.

New company culture. A project being run at an existing firm already has guidelines and an outline of how to build a game. These can be a hindrance, but they can also be the road map that gets you through unknown territory.

Here are a few of the lessons that can be drawn from them:

- There's more than one way to form a startup.

  Bohemia Interactive and Surreal Software both took the traditional garage-band route, but there are other models. Some development houses start small, just doing ports of existing games, or add-on packs—you don't necessarily have to reinvent the wheel. Maybe someone has a gee-whiz piece of technology that needs a game built around it. Maybe a project team detaches from an existing company, then contracts with the parent firm—this is a model that gives you some of the freedom of a startup, but with an experienced team and a useful relationship to a larger company.

- **Publishers aren't necessarily the enemy.**

  It's easy to adopt a siege mentality when you're a small developer: your publisher is The Man, and he's going to stifle your creativity, make you jump through bureaucratic hoops, and then take the lion's share of the profits. Occasionally there's a grain of truth to this picture… but it's also possible for the publisher to be a partner. A truthful, realistic relationship may serve both parties better than the usual adversarial one—the publisher is putting up the money, and if they understand what the product is and when it's actually shipping, they can market it more effectively and everyone can benefit. If they're an established game publisher, they may actually be able to help manage the project or put you in touch with reliable contractors to help finish the game on time.

- **Perseverance counts.**

  None of these projects shipped without difficulties, and part of the reason they did ship is that the developers didn't give up, even when they lost their publisher, or key technologies didn't work out, or they ran years longer than they had expected, or they had to slash key features to keep their budget and schedule realistic. It was hard, but there isn't much glory in the making the Greatest Game That Never Shipped.

- **Hire the right people.**

  Startups are almost always small operations, which means every employee has to be someone you can work with and rely upon, and a good team dynamic is absolutely essential. Also, in a small company you probably won't have every single one of the skill-sets needed to make a game, so very likely you'll have to contract out certain elements of the game, like animation or some modular part of the engine. This means finding reliable contractors and managing them carefully, giving them a clear idea of how their work fits into the game you're making.

The grand tradition of the garage startup company is changing. Over the last decade there has been a trend toward consolidation, larger companies buying up smaller development houses, companies with deep pockets that could survive lean fiscal quarters while smaller companies went bankrupt. It's a high-risk industry, and diversified product lines mean you don't have to craft a hit every time out, especially if you have a few regular sellers to keep you in the black.

The scale of game production is also changing—consumers are expecting higher and higher production values, up-to-date technology, and Hollywood-quality art and animation. These are things that require multimillion-dollar budgets and bigger teams. It may become harder and harder to write a hit game with five people and a brilliant idea.

There may be a valid analogy with the film or music industry, with the way independent film and grassroots music movements feed their influences in to the more commercial scene. As id Software's Jay Wilbur once told *Wired* magazine, "People ask me who I fear, which of our competition—LucasArts, Microsoft, any of the big companies. They don't frighten me. What I'm afraid of is two guys in a garage, working in total obscurity. That's where the heart and soul of this business is at. Those are the guys who are going to come up with the stuff that blows us out of the water."

5

Irrational Games' SYSTEM SHOCK 2

by jonathan chey

This is the story of a young and inexperienced company that was given the chance to develop the sequel to one of the top ten games of all time. The sequel was allotted roughly one year of development with its full team. To make up for the short development cycle and correspondingly small budget, the project was supposed to reuse technology. Not technology in the sense of a stand-alone engine from another game, but individual components that were spun off from yet another game, THIEF: THE DARK PROJECT. The THIEF technology was still under development and months away from completion when our team started working with it. To cap everything off, the project was a collaborative effort between two companies based on a contract that only loosely defined the responsibilities of each organization.

Back-Story

SYSTEM SHOCK 2 came out in 1999, as the sequel to SYSTEM SHOCK, the critically acclaimed action/role-playing game released in 1994 by Looking Glass Studios. Like its predecessor, SYSTEM SHOCK 2 is an action game shown in first-person perspective but with a richer narrative and game-system than most shooters—players could hack into computers and access psychic abilities. It also tells a complex story—the player explores a derelict spacecraft after something has gone wrong with humankind's first interstellar colony mission. These elements blend in a marriage of design and technology—the rich level design and complex character-creation never get in the way of the storytelling and suspenseful action gameplay. SYSTEM SHOCK 2 is part of a wave of deeper, more story-oriented action games that began appearing in the late 90s (starting with UNREAL and HALF-LIFE), a change from the stripped-down, all-action approach of DOOM and QUAKE.

Add to these gloomy initial conditions the fact that the game from which our shared technology was derived slipped more than six months from the initially estimated date, that several developers quit during the project, that we didn't bring the full team up to strength until six months from the final ship date, and that we struggled with financial and business problems during the entire project. Having learned this, you might anticipate the worst. Strangely, SYSTEM SHOCK 2 shipped within two months of its targeted date and will, I hope, be recognized as a sequel worthy of its esteemed ancestor.

Let's step back and trace the origins of the companies and the project. Looking Glass Studios is familiar to many as the creator of a series of highly innovative titles including the original SYSTEM SHOCK, the ULTIMA UNDERWORLD series, the FLIGHT UNLIMITED line and TERRA

NOVA, among others. Three years ago, Ken Levine, Rob Fermier and I were developers at Looking Glass, struggling with the aftermath of VOYAGER, an aborted *Star Trek*™: *Voyager*™–licensed project. At the time, Looking Glass was in financial and creative disarray after a series of titles that, though critically acclaimed, had failed to meet sales expectations, the latest being TERRA NOVA and BRITISH OPEN CHAMPIONSHIP GOLF.

Game Data

Release date: August 1999

Publisher: Electronic Arts

Genre: 1st-person science fiction action-adventure

Intended platform: Windows 95/98

Project budget: $1.7 million

Project length: 18 months

Team size: 15 full-time developers, 10–15 part-time developers

Critical development hardware: Pentium II machines, 200MHz to 450MHz with 64MB to 128MB RAM, Nvidia Riva 128, Voodoo, Voodoo 2, TNT cards, Creative Labs' sound cards, Wacom tablets, Windows 95/98. Also used SGI Indigo workstations.

Critical development software: Microsoft Visual C++ 5.0, Opus Make, 3D Studio Max, Adobe Photoshop, Alias|Wavefront Power Animator, DeBabelizer Pro, RCS, Filemaker Pro, and Adaptive Optics motion capture software.

Frustration with the 18 months wasted on VOYAGER and a certain amount of hubris prompted three of us to strike out on our own to test our game design and management ideas. We wanted to nail down a rigorous and technologically feasible design, focus on gameplay, and force ourselves to make decisions rather than allow ourselves to stagnate in indecision. We wanted to run a project. So we formed Irrational Games.

After some misadventures with other development contracts, we unexpectedly found ourselves back at work with Looking Glass as a company rather than as employees. Initially, our brief was to prepare a prototype based on the still-in-development THIEF technology recast as a science-fiction game. The scope of the project was very wide, but we quickly decided to follow in the footsteps of the original SYSTEM SHOCK. Our initial design problem was how to construct such a game without the luxury of the actual SYSTEM SHOCK license, since no publisher had yet been signed.

Our initial prototype was developed by the three of us working with a series of contract artists. Our focus was on the core game-play elements: an object-rich world containing lots of interactive items, a story conveyed through recorded logs (not interaction with living NPCs), and gameplay realized through simple, reusable elements. This focus enticed Electronic Arts into signing on as our publisher early in 1998—a fantastic break for us. It meant we could now utilize the real SYSTEM SHOCK name and characters.

Immediately, we went back to our original design, threw away some of the crazier ideas that had been percolating and began integrating more of the rich SYSTEM SHOCK universe into the title. That was the point at which the real development began.

It's the Engine, Stupid

Nothing impacted the development of SYSTEM SHOCK as much as the existing technology we got from Looking Glass. This fact cannot be classified monolithically under the heading of "what went wrong" or "what went right," however, because it went both wrong and right. The technology we used was the so-called "Dark Engine," which was essentially technology developed as a result of Looking Glass's THIEF: THE DARK PROJECT (for more about its development, see "Looking Glass's THIEF: THE DARK PROJECT," Postmortem on page 171).

The THIEF technology was developed with an eye toward reuse, and I will refer to it in this article as an "engine." However, it is not an engine in the same sense as QUAKE's, UNREAL's, and LithTech. The Dark Engine was never delivered to the SYSTEM SHOCK team as a finished piece of code, nor were we ever presented with a final set of APIs that the engine was to implement. Instead, we worked with the same code base as the THIEF team for most of the project (excluding a brief window of time when we made a copy of the source code while the THIEF team prepared to ship the game). Remarkably, it is still possible to compile a hybrid executable out of this tree that can play both THIEF and SYSTEM SHOCK 2 based on a variable in a configuration file.

This intimate sharing of code both helped and hurt us. We had direct access to the ongoing bug-fixes and engine enhancements flowing from the THIEF team. It exposed us to bugs that the THIEF team introduced, but it also gave us the ability to fix bugs and add new features to the engine. Because we had this power, we were sometimes expected to fix engine problems ourselves rather than turning them over to Looking Glass programmers, which wasn't always to our benefit. At times we longed for a finished and frozen engine with an unalterable API that was rigidly defined and implemented—the perfect black box. But being able to tamper with the engine allowed us to change it to support SYSTEM SHOCK–specific features in ways that a general engine never could.

What Went Right

1. The irrational development model

In our hubris after leaving Looking Glass, we formulated several informal approaches to development that we intended to test out on our projects. Most of these approaches proved to be successful and, I think, formed the basis of our ability to complete the project to our satisfaction.

First, we designed to our technology rather than building technology to fit our design. Under this model, we first analyzed our technological capabilities and then decided on a design that would work with it. This process is almost mandatory when reusing an engine. Sometimes it can be difficult to stick with this when a great design idea doesn't fit the technology, but we applied the principal pretty ruthlessly. And many of the times when we did deviate, we had problems.

Another feature of our development philosophy is that everyone participates in game design. Why? Because all three of the Irrational founders wanted to set the design direction of our products, programmers were able to resolve design issues without having to stick to a design spec, and we strongly emphasized game design skills when hiring all of our employees and contractors. In all our interviews, one of our most pressing questions to ourselves was "Does this person get games?" Failure to "get" them was a definite strike against any prospective employee. Ultimately, the team's passion for and understanding of games was a major contributor to the design of the final product.

The final goal of our development process was to make decisions and hit deadlines. We focused on moving forward, and we didn't allow ourselves to be bogged down. We desperately wanted to ship a game and believed that the discipline imposed by the rule of forward motion would ultimately pay off in terms of the final product quality as well as delivery date. While there are features in SYSTEM SHOCK 2 that could have been better if we had not rushed them (the character portraits for example), we still firmly believe that the game as a whole was made better by our resolve to finish it on time.

2. Use of simple, reusable game-play elements

The field of companies developing first-person shooters like id and Valve, among others, is impressive. It would be a futile attempt to create scarier monsters, bigger guns, or higher-polygon environments. Additionally, we realized that our design time and budget were very tight and that we would not have time to carefully hand-script complicated game-play sequences in the engine.

Xerxes, central computer of the Von Braun.

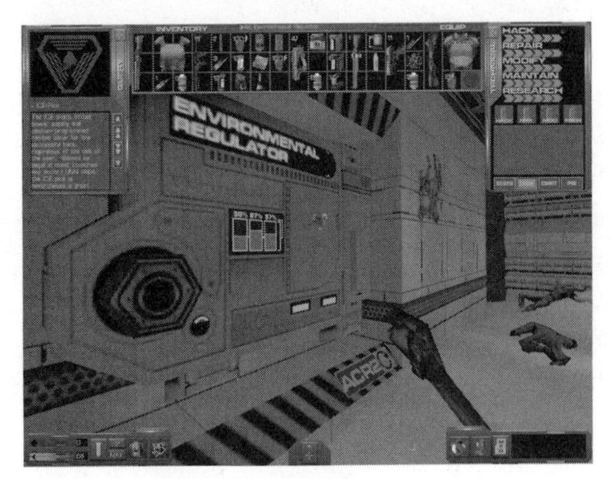

Cold comfort in Hydroponics.

Instead, in an attempt to shift the battlefield, we chose to focus on simple, reusable game-play elements. The success of HALF-LIFE, which launched while we were in the middle of SYSTEM SHOCK 2 confirmed our intuitions in this respect. We simply didn't have the time, resources or technology to develop the scripted cinematic sequences used by HALF-LIFE. We consoled ourselves with the knowledge that we were not even trying to do so. This strategy melded very well with our acquisition of the SYSTEM SHOCK license, as the original SYSTEM SHOCK had already been down this road. We decided to expand on elements that we liked in SYSTEM SHOCK and then add similar new systems. Each such new system was evaluated rigorously in terms of game-play benefits, underlying technology, and design-time requirements.

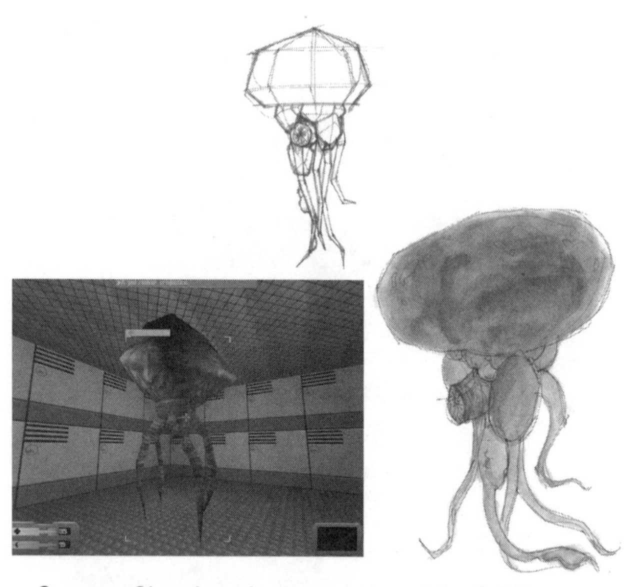

Concept Sketch and game version of the Psi Reaver.

For example, take the ship's security system. Early on we decided that we wanted to continue the surveillance theme from SYSTEM SHOCK, which we could leverage throughout the game to provide lots of gameplay for very little implementation cost. We realized that security cameras would be trivial to implement using existing AI systems (they are just AIs pruned of many of their normal abilities) and that once we had cameras that could spot and track the player, we would be able to build several gameplay elements out of them. Cameras could summon monsters to the player, so much of the gameplay consisted of avoiding detection by security cameras and destroying cameras before you were seen. Because cameras scan fixed arcs, the player can utilize timing to sneak by cameras, pop out and shoot them at the right moment, or get underneath them and bash them with a melee weapon. Once a player is spotted, monsters flood the area until the player is able to shut off the security system somehow or the system times out. This introduces the need to deactivate security systems via security computers that are scattered throughout the level.

This type of system was technologically simple to implement and required minimal design effort. While not completely formulaic, the basic procedure to set up a camera and security system could be shown to designers quickly using a few simple rules. From this one system and a couple of associated subsystems, we derived a large amount of gameplay without having designers create and implement complicated scripted sequences and story elements. When you throw together many such systems (as we did), you end up with a lot of gameplay.

3. Cooperative development

SYSTEM SHOCK 2 was truly a cooperative development between Irrational and Looking Glass. Looking Glass provided the engine and a lot of infrastructure support (such as quality assurance), while Irrational handled the design, project leadership, and the responsibility for marshaling resources into the final product. Both entities contributed personnel to the development team. Inevitably, some friction arose from this process while we sorted out who was responsible for what. However, this cooperation was ultimately successful because both sides were interested in developing a great product, and we were able to compromise on most issues. (On the most mundane level, Irrational ended up providing late-night, weekend meals for its development team and for Looking Glass on some days during the week.) Our cooperative arrangement was founded on a contractual agreement, but we avoided falling back on this contract in most cases. We preferred to resolve issues through informal discussions. Conceptually, Irrational was to be responsible for the development of the product and Looking Glass was to provide A/V content and quality assurance services.

During the early stages of the project, a deal was worked out whereby a small number of Looking Glass personnel were subcontracted to Irrational when it was determined that Irrational's development budget could not cover all the SYSTEM SHOCK 2 development costs, and as compensation for the late delivery of the THIEF technology. Unfortunately, these personnel were not always available on time—a situation which caused us much concern. We knew that this "resource debt" could never really be paid off until THIEF shipped—nothing is so difficult as prying resources away from a team that is trying to ship a product before Christmas. It wasn't until December 1998 that we first began to see some of these promised resources. However, these "resources"—real people—had just finished up THIEF and were totally fried following the grueling crunch to ship THIEF. The saving grace and reason that this arrangement was ultimately successful was that these developers were all talented and experienced and already knew the technology. Their addition to the team gave us a solid boost during the final months in our ship cycle.

The other benefit of the cooperative development agreement between Irrational and Looking Glass was that our respective engine programmers could share knowledge. The ability to walk over and quiz engine programmers about systems proved to be an invaluable benefit that more than compensated for the lack of a rigorously specified and documented engine. Without a formal understanding of the engine, we had to resolve engine issues in a personal and informal manner. This process relied on the personalities of the responsible individuals on the engine team. Thus, the Irrational programmers balanced their time not only according to the complexity of their tasks but also according to how much support was available from the engine side. Overall, Irrational's relationship with Looking Glass was an unusually close one and ultimately successful as a result of our mutual respect and willingness to work with each other. Despite our partnership being based on a formal contractual arrangement, it was our ability to work flexibly above this legal level that enabled the development to proceed smoothly.

4. Design lessons from SYSTEM SHOCK

Though the SYSTEM SHOCK license was wonderful, there were some problems. The biggest was simply the challenge of living up to the original. Fortunately, we had the freedom to pay homage to SYSTEM SHOCK legitimately by reusing elements from it. Additionally, we had access to some of the original developers, including our own lead programmer Rob Fermier.

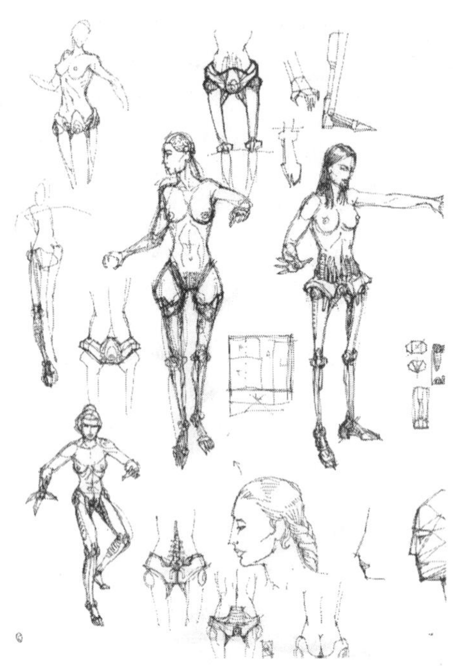

Concept sketches of the Cyborg Midwife.

As with most sequels, we faced the challenge of keeping the good elements of the original game while not blindly copying them. We knew that most players would want a new story set in the same world, with the same basic flavor as the original game, yet we also wanted to reach out to a broader audience. We resolved these issues by identifying the key elements that made SYSTEM SHOCK so good and reinterpreting those elements using current technology. Some elements made it through largely unchanged (for example, the storytelling logs and e-mails, the übervillain Shodan and her close involvement with the player throughout the game, and the complexity of the world). Other elements were reinterpreted (such as the look of the environment, player interface, and techniques for interacting with the world). A small number of items were simply cut, most notably the cyberspace sequences—we were fairly united in our opinion that these just didn't work well in the original.

Notably, as with the original SYSTEM SHOCK, we opted to omit interactive NPCs in the game. SYSTEM SHOCK eschewed living NPCs because the technology of the day was simply inadequate to support believable and enjoyable interactions with them. It's been four years, and that technology is still not available. So we continued the tradition of SYSTEM SHOCK and provided players with background information using personal logs and e-mails gleaned from the bodies of dead NPCs.

Perhaps our biggest deviation from the original revolved around the player interface. It's commonly accepted that SYSTEM SHOCK's interface, while elegant and powerful once understood, presented a significant barrier to entry. Our primary goal was to simplify this interface without dumbing it down. We devoted more design effort to this task than to any other system in the game, and it required many iterations before we were happy with it. We adopted a bi-modal interface in which there are two distinct modes (inventory management and combat/exploration) between which the player can toggle. This was a risky decision. This bi-modal model was mandated by our desire to keep the familiar and powerful mouse-look metaphor common to first-person shooters while retaining cursor-based inventory management. How we switched between modes became our biggest design challenge. Sometimes these mode changes are explicitly requested through a mode change key, and sometimes they are invoked automatically by attempting to pick up an object in the world. So far this system seems to be working well, though only time and user feedback will tell whether we really got it right.

5. Working with a young team

The SYSTEM SHOCK team was frighteningly young and inexperienced, especially for such a high-profile title. Many of our team members were new to the industry or had only a few months' experience, including the majority of artists and all the level builders. Of the three principals, only Rob had previous experience in his role as lead programmer. Neither Ken, the lead designer, nor I, the project manager, had previously worked in these roles. It's not totally clear how we pulled off our project with our limited experience.

Partially, it must have been due to our ability to bond as a team and share knowledge in our communal work environment ("the pit"). To a certain extent, inexperience also bred enthusiasm and commitment that might not have been present with a more jaded set of developers. We also worked hard to transfer knowledge from the more experienced developers to the less seasoned individuals. Rob worked on an extremely comprehensive set of documentation for the functional object tools, as well as a set of exercises ("object school") to be worked on each week. These kinds of efforts paid back their investment many times over.

This is not to say that our progress was all sweetness and light. The art team, for example, floundered for a long time as we tried to integrate the junior artists and imbue a common art look in the team's psyche. We had a lot of very mediocre art midway through our project and the art team was stagnating. Ultimately, management had little to do with the art team's success—they were largely able to organize themselves and create a solid, original look. On the management front, our inexperience was apparent. We blundered through the early stages of development with scheduling and management issues. A large problem was our failure to assign specific areas of responsibility and authority early on. Bad feelings arose as a result, which could have been avoided if we had clearly delineated areas of responsibility from the start.

What Went Wrong

1. Poor level design process

Level design is a clearly defined professional activity in the game industry. It's a profession that mixes artistic and technical skills in equal measure, and the bar is raised on both fronts every year. Despite our understanding from the very beginning that the level building would be a problematic part of the SYSTEM SHOCK development process, we didn't quite grasp how difficult and time consuming it would be, nor did we expect that it would eventually block the shipment of the game.

In hindsight, our failure to understand the amount of work needed to design levels is reprehensible given that we had seen the same problems emerge on THIEF, and that SYSTEM SHOCK 2 levels involved substantially more complex object placement than THIEF. I attribute this error mostly to our denial of the problem—we had a limited budget for level designers and there is a long training time required to get designers familiar with the complex Dark Editor. So we locked ourselves into working with the resources we had.

Hacking the security system.

Since each individual task required from the designer (apart from initial architectural work) was relatively simple, it was easy to believe that the sum total of work was also relatively small. What we overlooked was the fact that SYSTEM SHOCK 2 involves so many objects, scripts and parameters. As such, the work load on level designers was excessively large. In addition, we made a classic beginner's mistake and failed to provide adequate time for tuning in response to playtesting feedback. In SYSTEM SHOCK 2 this was particularly important because the ability of the player to reenter levels means that the difficulty of a level cannot be adjusted in isolation from the rest of the game. Often we had to impose global changes across all levels, which could be very expensive even when the change was relatively minor.

We took a novel approach to the level building process by attempting to design levels using a production-line method. Using this metaphor, we attempted to divorce the different stages of work on the level: rough architecture, decorative and functional objects, architectural polish, and lighting. It was not considered necessary for the same individual to be involved in all stages of this production process. This approach had positive and negative consequences. The advantages were that we could track progress on levels, we could "bootstrap" levels fairly quickly, and we could (in theory) swap individuals in and out of different tasks. The disadvantages are fairly obvious, and most stem from the fact that the various stages of level design are clearly not independent (for example, architecture is ideally built with an understanding of the functional objects that are to be used in the level).

Although I think our process was necessary in order to get the game out on time, it probably detracted from the quality of some of the levels. In addition, psychological factors, such as lack of ownership and training issues (stemming from unfamiliarity with levels) speak very strongly against transferring people from one task or level to another. Nevertheless, there were several benefits of our procedure—mostly the ability to employ particularly talented individuals to pinch hit on particular levels, and the psychological benefits of completing architectural work early in the schedule.

Perhaps the rudest shock in our level building process came from our misunderstanding of what part of the process would prove to be most difficult. Architectural work was actually fairly simple, because we intentionally kept our spaces fairly clean and did not attempt anything too unusual. However, placing and implementing our objects was far more complex and involved than we expected. One difficulty that we encountered was educating our designers in what was expected from them in terms of gameplay implementation. Most of our level builders had previously built QUAKE or UNREAL levels and were not familiar with the style of gameplay that we were trying to build in SYSTEM SHOCK 2. Partially this was because we were simply exploring a style of gameplay that we did not entirely understand ourselves. But it reflected a failure on our part to properly educate the designers. Building prototypical spaces, looking at past games, and conducting more intensive discussions about gameplay will all be part of our future projects.

2. Motion capture difficulties

The Dark Engine has a complex creature animation playback system and deformable mesh renderer. We encountered many problems with this piece of technology along our data integration path, and found quirks in the playback systems as well. Primarily, the system was hampered by the fact that data frequently had to be modified by hand, that mysterious bugs would appear in motions during playback which had not been present in the source data, and that few tools were available for debugging and analysis. We were ill-equipped to deal with these kinds of problems, having devoted few resources to dealing with the technology problems.

Our primary animation source was motion capture data. We were nervous about the technology from the start and attempted to minimize our risk by concentrating primarily on humanoid creatures with a small number of interesting variants such as spiders and floating boss monsters. In retrospect, this was a very wise decision, as we had a lot of trouble even with this simple set of creatures.

Motion capture technology and capture services were contracted from a local company, but unfortunately this company viewed its motion capture work primarily as a side business and did not display much interest in it. In fact, they cancelled this sector of their business during our project, and we had to fight hard to complete the sessions that we had already scheduled with them.

Our capture sessions were hampered by our inexperience with the technology and by the fact that we did not plan properly for the sessions. We hadn't defined key poses, rehearsed the motions, or ensured that our motions were compatible with the technology. Optical capture technology, the technology that we used, can be glitchy and has difficulty with motions that have obscured markers, as in the death motions that were necessary for SYSTEM SHOCK 2. Over the course of three sessions, we gradually refined our motions, but we spent a lot of time reshooting failed captures from earlier sessions. Even in the best cases, most of our captures exhibit strange artifacts (feet pointing down through the ground, hands improperly aligned, and so on), whose causes are still unknown to us. In future projects we will hand-animate almost all of the data, and we will need to understand better what aspect of the conversion process introduced these artifacts into our final game animations, although the irregularities never appeared in our raw data. Motion capture technology, while highly efficient compared to hand animation, must be approached carefully to obtain good results.

3. Implementing scripted sequences

Motivated by the dramatic scripted sequences in HALF-LIFE, we attempted to introduce similar elements into SYSTEM SHOCK 2. In doing so, we broke one of our rules: we tried to step outside the bounds of our technology. Although we attempted relatively simple sequences and ultimately got them working, they were time sinks, and the payback was relatively slight. For example, we scripted a hallucinatory sequence in which the player character rides through the interior of the alien boss-monster, known as the Many. This so-called "Many ride" was the source of innumerable bugs—the player would be thrown off the moving platform, manage to kill his projected self, bump into walls, and so on. We confirmed our intuition that the Dark Engine does not support complex scripted sequences well because the toolset (AI, moving terrain, and animation) is not optimized for this sort of behavior. The moral is, once again, to work with your technology, not against it.

4. Inexperience with multiplayer game development

Early in the project we were asked to identify the major risks associated with the project. Our number one candidate by far was the multiplayer component. This was the only new substantial engine feature that was to be added and it was a complicated piece of work. We were particularly nervous about this technology for a couple of reasons. First, it is usually much harder to make this kind of pervasive change to an existing piece of software than it is to build it in from scratch. Second, Looking Glass had no track record in shipping multiplayer technology, and we were not confident that the development was fully understood. Irrational did not want to introduce multiplayer support into SYSTEM SHOCK 2 because we considered it a tangential feature that did not contribute to our core strengths. However, marketing concerns dictated it, so ultimately we acquiesced. Our lack of enthusiasm for this feature contributed to its developmental problems because we failed to monitor its progress adequately or raise concerns when that progress fell behind schedule. Because this was the first multiplayer product developed by Irrational or Looking Glass, we did not properly estimate the time required for the multiplayer testing. We did not devote adequate quality assurance resources to this feature. Too much time was spent testing the multiplayer features over the LAN and not enough over the more demanding modem connections. Given the difficulties posed by the multiplayer technologies, the engine developers working on the task made great efforts, and their early results were promising. However, the early departure of one of the programmers, and the fact that he was not replaced, ultimately doomed any possibility of shipping the multiplayer technology with the initial SKU. Reluctantly, we opted for a patch that would be available at the same time as the single-player box reached shelves. Our cooperative multiplayer game will undoubtedly be fun and will probably be enjoyed immensely by a relatively small number of our customers. However, we wonder whether our failure to deliver a promised feature in the box will ultimately hurt us more than the absence of that feature from the start would have.

5. Running a company while building a game

As the principals of the company, Ken, Rob, and I didn't really understand what it took to run a business and simultaneously work in that business. None of the Irrational founders started the company to be businessmen, and we have always believed that the ultimate health of the company depended on us all staying involved in the development process, which is, after all, what each of us enjoys and wants to do. Unfortunately, as anyone who has run a business knows, there is a lot more to starting and maintaining a company than sitting around at board meetings smoking cigars. From the mundane matters of making payroll, organizing taxes and expense reports to business negotiations and contract disputes, there is substantial overhead involved in running even a small company such as Irrational.

In our naïveté, we did not factor these tasks into our schedules, and the result was that they mostly became extra tasks that kept us in the office late at night and on weekends. As a result of our misjudgment, we just had to work harder. Rather than enduring a crunch period of a few

The team at Irrational Games, from left to right: FIRST ROW: Steve Kimura/Artist, Jonathan Chey/Project Director, Justin Waks/Multiplayer Programmer, Mauricio Tejerina/Artist, Rob "Xemu" Fermier/Lead Programmer, Dorian Hart/Designer, Lulu Lamer/QA Lead. SECOND ROW: Ian Vogel/Level Designer, Scott Blinn/Level Designer, Michael Swiderek/Artist, Rob Caminos/Motion Editor, Nate Wells/Artist. THIRD ROW: Mike Ryan/Level Designer, Ken Levine/Lead Designer, Mathias Boynton/Level Designer. NOT SHOWN: Gareth Hinds/Lead Artist.

months, the entire last year of the project was our crunch time, as we struggled desperately to fulfill our jobs as programmers, designers, and managers as well as keep the money flowing in (and out) of the company.

Our tasks were complicated further by the need to reincorporate the company from an S-corporation to an LLC during the final two months of the project (a legal maneuver designed to allow me, an Australian national, to be allocated company stock). As well as destroying our personal lives, our failure to judge the magnitude of our task meant that we had to devote less time than we desired to every aspect of our work. My programming time was severely curtailed and I was able to spend far less time on SYSTEM SHOCK 2's AI than I wished. Simultaneously, I was unable to provide the level of direct management that I wanted, and I was forced to postpone company financial work until the end of the project or hurry it through. The results were less than optimal all around.

Ultimately, SYSTEM SHOCK 2 turned out better than I ever hoped it would. The final vindication for me was sitting in my office and playing the game in the final couple of weeks of the project, while waiting for EA to approve our final build. Despite the lack of sleep, the near-complete breakdown of my nervous system, and the 18 months of time I spent working on the project, it was still fun to play. I like to think that we have managed to capture the feel of the original game by putting more gameplay into what initially looks like a fairly straightforward first-person shooter. It's been a great first project for Irrational Games and we look forward to doing even better the next time around.

Bohemia Interactive Studios'

OPERATION FLASHPOINT

by marek spanel and ondrej spanel

The story of OPERATION FLASHPOINT's development is quite unusual in the game industry these days. For one thing, the team didn't start out as professionals; originally only the lead programmer was allowed to work on the game full-time. Switching publishers three times, starting a new company, growing the team from one to 12 full-time members, and moving offices five times during the game's development were just some of the hurdles we had to clear. Only the team's vision and obsession for the game remained consistent from the very first playable version until the end. It's not possible to describe whole story in the space given for this article, so let's just jump directly to the final moments.

Back-Story

OPERATION FLASHPOINT is one of the most realistic simulations yet made of modern infantry combat. Players assume the role of a Marine and progress from basic training to command roles, in a variety of real-world missions set against a background of 1980s central-European realpolitik. Bohemia Interactive accomplished the difficult task of adding realistic details, such as limited inventory and critical hits, without losing gameplay, raising the difficulty bar while substituting tension and immersion for the usual explosion-heavy killfest. OPERATION FLASHPOINT expands the standard formula with ground and air vehicles and squad-based combat, making this game as much a tactical simulator as first-person-shooter.

It was 8 P.M. on Friday, May 25, 2001. Our publisher's representative, who had been in Prague for the last few days to make sure everything was going OK as we were finalizing the gold master, left Prague feeling confident that things were going well—the disc was almost ready and could be sent to final testing and then to manufacturing after some weekend testing.

Meanwhile, our lead programmer (To make matters even more exciting, he was then working at his temporary home in France for couple of weeks.) was trying to resolve some serious graphical anomalies with the hardware transformation and lighting (HW T&L) rendering. If he were to fail, HW T&L would not be included in the final release. If he solved it, some data organization changes would be necessary to suit the needs of the HW T&L. He spent nearly the whole day resolving some random crashes that appeared in the game during the last day, going back and forth over e-mail with an Nvidia support engineer.

The crash was fixed by late afternoon, and by 10 P.M. it looked like the HW T&L problems were at an acceptable level. Around midnight, the tools that would perform the data format change were ready. On the other front, the team had received the final localized strings for the game. However, the file containing the core strings of the game that had been delivered by our publisher appeared to be untested and unusable. After spending a couple of hours dealing with it, most of the team had to go home to have some sleep. Still, the team leader stayed behind at the office, trying to use the new HW T&L data format, going over each step by phone or e-mail with the lead programmer (while also trying to implement new localized string tables and fix some problems in the campaign and missions). At 3 A.M. it looked like all the data had been converted—and both the lead programmer and the team leader could go have some sleep.

Saturday morning, our publisher realized that the gold master hadn't actually been delivered. Tensions rose even further, and nerves began to unravel. Only two days remained before mass production was scheduled to begin. Everyone on the team had been working since early Saturday morning, but at times a successful end to these last-minute crises seemed to be so far away. By around 5 P.M. on Saturday, most of the important issues in the code had been resolved, and the lead programmer decided to take another look at the HW T&L implementation. Luckily, within a few hours, he suddenly discovered the root of all of the HW T&L problems and fixed them.

The plan was to deliver the gold master to our publisher via FTP by that evening. Nobody expected that it would actually take until Sunday morning. After a long, sleepless night of playing through the game and fixing any problems that appeared, everything looked fine, and most of the team could finally go to sleep again. With some relief, we finally started the game upload on Sunday around 9 A.M. But were we done? Not yet. Suddenly, a seagull stopped flying in

Game Data

Release date: June 22 (worldwide except North America), August 29 (North America), 2001

Publisher: Codemasters

Genre: realistic first-person shooter

Platform: Windows 98/ME/2000

Full-time developers: 10

Part-time contractors: 3

Estimated budget: $600,000

Length of development: Over 4 years

Development hardware: Various PC systems from 266MHz Pentium IIs to 1GHz Pentium 4s and 1.2GHz Athlons with 20GB hard drives and Voodoo 2 or GeForce 2 graphics cards

Development software: Windows 98/2000, Linux servers, Visual C++ 6, SourceSafe, Adobe Photoshop 5.0, 3DS Max, Microsoft Office, TextAloud (for voice prototyping)

Proprietary software: Oxygen (3D low polygon modeling and texturing tool), Visitor (landscape editor), and some other proprietary tools

Notable technologies: DirectX, Vorbis Ogg, Vicon 8 motion capture system

Project size: 10,000+ files, 250,000 lines of C++ (some assembly), 5,000 textures, 800 3D models, 100,000 words (localized into six other languages), more than 60 single-player and multiplayer missions

some of the in-game cut-scenes. The team leader called to wake up the lead programmer in France: "The seagull is not flying. What should I do?" We had to stop the upload until the lead programmer delivered necessary code fix.

After the project leader received the updated files from the lead programmer, he started to rebuild the game in Visual Studio. It was Sunday around noon, and the game had finally gone to the publisher for final testing. The publisher's test staff started playing the game Sunday afternoon. Everything went smoothly at first, but later they discovered one serious scripting bug in one of the campaign missions that made it unplayable. Late in the evening, they called the team leader about the bug, and he had to drive to the office after sleeping just a couple of hours over the past three days to fix the bug as quickly as possible and then upload the fixed version to the publisher's server in the U.K. Around midnight Sunday night, the disc was finally ready to go.

Three weeks later, hundreds of thousands of copies of the game were available in stores worldwide. In the meantime, the development team was playing the game, terrified of finding a disastrous bug. Fortunately, no such critical bug appeared. Considering the amount of work we'd done on the game in those last couple of days and hours, the risk of finding some major problems was pretty high. On Friday, June 22, the game was released, and it immediately became the top-selling PC game in many countries. The team knew that their mission was successfully completed. The passion and hard work of every single member of the development and publishing teams started to pay off.

What Went Right

1. The team

Probably the most positive thing we encountered during development of this game was the people working on it. Almost all of the people who joined the team really helped to improve the game and remained fully dedicated to it from the first day until the final moments. While we were understaffed almost all the time, we are happy to say that while the team was growing steadily, it was very stable—almost all the people who participated in the development of OPERATION FLASHPOINT are still working at our studios now that the game is finished.

Another advantage was that the team was very cooperative. Some roles on the team were not demarcated very strictly. Still, between the programmers, designers, and artists, everyone could comment on any part of the game, and everyone's opinions were taken seriously. While this often made communication more difficult, it definitely helped the design and development process and enriched the game in many areas. One of the most powerful tools we used for internal communication was our intranet news server, which proved to be an invaluable tool during the whole design process. The game was mostly designed on the fly, and the newsgroups made the design process not only convenient, but really quite enjoyable.

2. The community

OPERATION FLASHPOINT's public following is incredible. We ourselves are surprised by the number of people creating fan sites, developing new content for the game, or just keeping in touch with the community by reading news and forums. Currently there are hundreds of different sites dedicated to FLASHPOINT, and dozens of them are of a truly professional quality with news updated almost hourly. Another great thing about the community is that some of the people have been following this game for years already, and they still carry a great deal of enthusiasm for it.

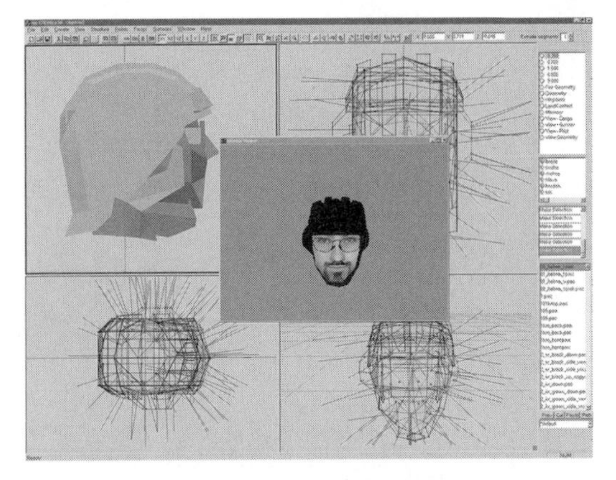

The Head of a tank crew in Oxygen. You can see face of Petr Pechar, one of the artists on OPERATION FLASHPOINT, under the helmet.

Some of the first great fan sites started out more than two years before the game was released, and we managed to keep people's excitement going with regular updates about the improvements we were making to the game throughout its development. We take it as a good sign that most of the sites are still online and updated regularly. About halfway through development, we invited some people from the community to participate in the design of the game directly, via external forums and newsgroups. Their skills in both military and gaming areas were invaluable, and we constantly used their feedback to improve the game.

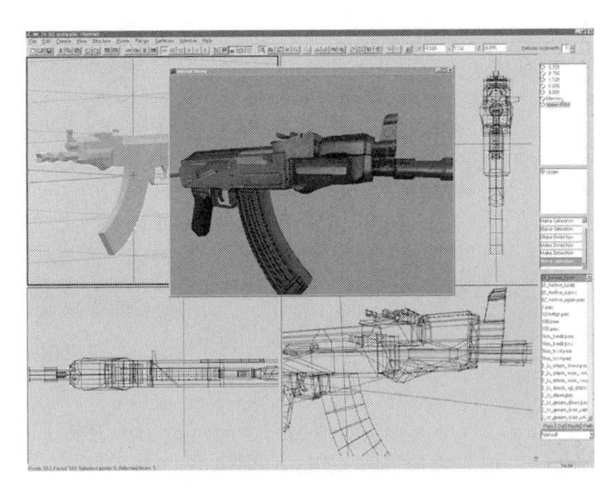

A Soviet AKSU rifle shown in Bohemia Interactive's proprietary modeling tool, Oxygen, with direct real-time previewing using the game's engine.

Since the release of the public demo version (around three months prior to the release of the final game), the community following has become much bigger. The only downside to the increase in the community base is that the community has become much less focused and less mature, as the average age of those visiting the Web sites has descended.

But the community still looks really vital and the most-visited fan site has counted millions of page views already. Recently, fans have been creating custom-made tools and enhancements to the game in addition to the various Web sites and services.

3. Open architecture

Since we know that plenty of players enjoy not just playing games but also providing their own content for them, we wanted to enable this extensibility as much as possible. Therefore, the game included exactly the same mission editor that we had used to design our missions. In addition, much of the game's functionality is data-driven instead of being hard-coded. This includes not only the mission files and world maps but also the capabilities and properties of units. The units are stored in a very powerful hierarchical configuration tree with inheritance capability, yet they are relatively easy to edit.

By using these configuration files, it is possible to add completely new units and worlds to the game or add modified versions of existing ones, which is what many players are doing to create their own content, thus lengthening the product's lifespan. We wanted to use configuration files to shorten coding time as well, because we figured that the fine-tuning of most values could be done by designers or testers instead of programmers. But this didn't work as we expected, mostly because only the programmers really knew meaning of the values.

Our scripting language also featured prominently in the game's development and extensibility. We started to build the mission editor as a visual tool, but we soon recognized its limitations in certain areas. Seeing this, we added an expression evaluator for trigger activation, which was surprisingly powerful, and a full scripting language soon followed. When the game was released, we knew immediately that scripting was a really good choice, as many user-made mission used scripts to implement specific new functionality. Looking back, we can say scripting proved to be much more powerful than we expected.

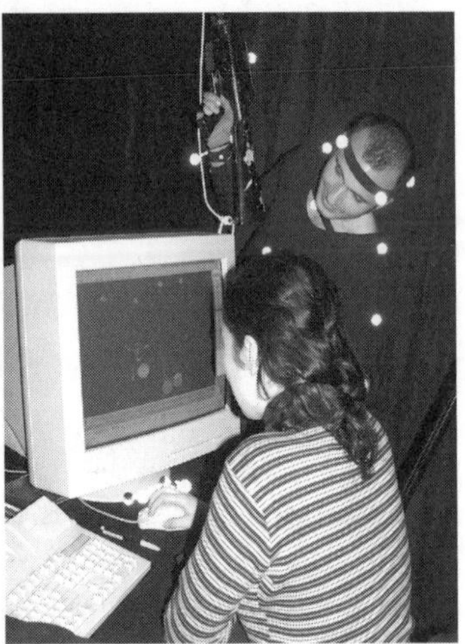

Bohemia Interactive's in-house motion capture facility has proven very beneficial in creation of lifelike human movement animations.

We only wish we had added it sooner in the development cycle, so that some of the functionality that we hard-coded into the game could have been scripted instead, including some AI behavior.

At a later stage of development (after the European release, in fact), we extended the game's ability to support add-on content. Single files stored in specific folders could add, for instance, new models, units, or islands. Besides some official add-ons that we have introduced since the game's release, there is already a massive number of user-made add-ons, all available for free on the Internet.

4. Creative freedom

From the very beginning of the project, we tried to create the game that we really wanted to play. We didn't look too much toward other games for inspiration, and we virtually ignored games that might be considered our competition. We also gave little regard to whether the market would like the game or not. Our relationships with publishers were never too strong (actually, we changed publishers several times), and all important decisions were made by the core development team, keeping us relatively independent throughout the game's development.

In fact, changing publishers so many times wasn't strictly a negative thing. Even though it led to some financial uncertainties, the creative freedom we enjoyed instead of some more money was more than worth it. The result of this creative freedom is a game that is really distinct. Our design-on-the-fly approach (or "design by playing," as we prefer to think of it) made the game very enjoyable and a different experience from any other.

Most design decisions were first discussed (mostly in newsgroups as mentioned earlier) and then tried out in the game. No matter how nice a design idea might have seemed at first, only the elements that worked well in the game ended up being included.

5. Long development cycle

The unusually long time that FLASHPOINT was in development was very beneficial. In terms of gameplay, the game is very mature, which would not have been possible in a shorter development cycle, especially because this was our first major game. Two or three years into development, the game started to be really enjoyable. In fact, it was polished enough then to suit our original plans for the release version. But due to various things (mainly on the publishing side), the game wasn't released at that point, which gave us more time to polish and improve it. We were able to incorporate various features that we originally hadn't planned to develop, either because they were too difficult or required excessive CPU or memory resources.

We were also able to incorporate feedback from various external testers—our friends as well as colleagues at well-known gaming companies who evaluated the game throughout its development. We refocused and redesigned the game a couple of times, always opting to keep everything that worked well and change the things we felt could work better.

What Went Wrong

1. Development cycle much longer than expected

Ironic as it is, we have to start What Went Wrong exactly where we left off with What Went Right. Despite some of the usefulness the extra development time offered us, in the end the cycle was probably too long, and in optimal conditions would have been at least 20 percent shorter. It may have been possible to shorten the cycle, but we experienced various external events or internal missteps that prevented us from accomplishing that.

First of all, some technologies in the game were a bit outdated after more than four years. We didn't know at the outset that the game would be still in development after so long, and we hadn't left time at the end to rework parts of the engine. Some of the criticism of OPERATION FLASHPOINT addresses the amount of detail in the textures and some models—and we have to admit that these could have been better.

OPERATION FLASHPOINT enables the player to use any vehicles, including gunships and planes.

Furthermore, the excessively long development cycle led to burnout and heavy exhaustion, particularly for the people who had been working on the game since very beginning (the lead programmer, lead artist Jan Hovora, and the team leader). In some cases, we weren't able to sustain some of the features we'd implemented two or more years prior. They just disappeared somehow in the process of reworking parts of the code, and we didn't even notice. Newcomers to the development and testing process never knew such features had ever existed.

The main problem wasn't that the development cycle was too long per se, but that the development was so much longer than we'd expected. Next time, we will work much more diligently to better estimate our development time—and we will probably try to aim higher with the detail of our artwork, even if it seems insanely detailed for present and predicted hardware capabilities.

2. Documentation

Lack of documentation is a common affliction among game developers, but some aspects of this problem were so severe in our case that they are worth mentioning. While we'd never believed too much in designing the game on paper, the real problem was that we never even had documentation of the things that we'd finished. This situation led to incredible problems in the final stages of development. Many tasks could only be done by one person on the whole team. In other cases, hours were spent trying to investigate how something had originally been meant to work.

We recognized these problems and tried to improve them, but apart from a few instances, our effort wasn't really successful. As the development team grew, the missing documentation was becoming a more serious problem. But the final project deadlines were getting closer as well, so it was nearly impossible to find the time to address the problem.

3. Quality assurance

We experienced various problems in communication and cooperation with our publisher. Generally, their focus and assistance in some areas of the production of the game (design suggestions, voice-overs, translation, scriptwriting) were really helpful. But in other areas, we experienced some events and circumstances that slowed down and complicated the game's development rather than moving things forward.

The combination of infantry combat with full simulation of vehicles is a crucial part of the design of OPERATION FLASHPOINT.

One of the most unsatisfactory areas was the way the QA procedures were managed and designed to work by the publisher. We never succeeded in achieving a common bug database, and the publisher enjoyed an illusory feeling that its QA database really covered the project. The truth was that such a database (even without any direct access for the development team) hardly said anything about the project's status because it covered just small fraction of all the problems we had tried to fix.

Even when the publisher dedicated a pretty big testing team to the game, it sometimes seemed something of a waste of time for everyone involved in it. In the end, we had to largely ignore the publisher's QA reports, because they contained too much useless information and very few real bugs. We tried to focus on very limited external testing managed directly in the very late stages of development to ameliorate this problem—but this approach could hardly replace real, full-time testing of the game.

We admit the situation was very difficult for the QA team as well—in no small part because of the lack of documentation on our side—but we still believe this process could have been handled much better. One of the mistakes we made was assuming that the publisher's QA would be sufficient, so we didn't build a strong testing team in-house. We definitely will find a solution for any future projects, because the way it was done for OPERATION FLASHPOINT wasn't satisfactory.

4. Some content was not under our full control

One area of concern thing was that our final CD was still manipulated by the publisher. The publisher applied SafeDisc protection to the final code, which caused some unexpected compatibility problems that we weren't able to control. The mixing of various SafeDisc versions and a serious compatibility problem with Windows 2000 that was present in the first European batch of CDs could have been avoided.

In addition, we weren't able to finalize the English language in the game because we didn't have a native English writer on the team. We also didn't oversee the voice recording and voice actor selection, which led to some results that were unsatisfactory to us.

Daytime and weather changes dynamically in the game so the area looks pretty different in various daytime and weather conditions.

5. Multiplayer API

From the very beginning we were aware that our game had huge multiplayer potential, especially if it were implemented as a massively multiplayer online game. But we knew we would be unable to deliver such experience.

Instead of aiming for such an unrealistically high goal, we decided to implement mission-based multiplayer that shared as much code as possible with single-player game. Even this effort proved to be extremely difficult.

OPERATION FLASHPOINT was always developed primarily as single-player game with a strong story, but for a very long time we were thinking about multiplayer functionality, and we tried to design the game code in such a way that it would help us incorporate multiplayer later. For implementation, we wanted to avoid low-level network coding and instead use a high-level API.

As we were already using Direct3D for graphics and DirectSound for audio, and both suited our needs quite well, we decided to use DirectPlay as our network API. DirectPlay offered high-level handling of all network communication, including Voice Over Net capabilities. Unfortunately, our experience with this API was extremely bad. Often when trying to get some high-level functionality working, we realized it contained bugs that rendered it almost unusable. We had to implement our custom code for things we thought DirectPlay would provide, but that was sometimes very hard, as we did not have the low-level control that we needed.

We also encountered many performance problems, some very strange, such as significant (particularly server-side) slowdown even with no traffic over the network. This along with the lack of documentation and a lack of stability resulted in many problems that were hard to debug. Another drawback that we didn't recognize beforehand is that DirectPlay is Windows-only, but many dedicated servers for games currently being played online run on Linux. Overall, selecting DirectPlay as our network API was one of the most unfortunate decisions in the whole game's development.

Future Dreaming

Most start-up game developers dream of developing a number-one title. We weren't any different. With OPERATION FLASHPOINT, this dream has come true for us. The game achieved the number-one position in sales charts of various countries and regions, including the U.S., Germany, the United Kingdom, Benelux, Scandinavia, and Australia. More than 500,000 copies sold worldwide in just three months, proving to us that our last four years of effort were worth something.

We always stayed focused on the game, and we didn't have too much regard for those who believe that the success of any game is mainly a question of marketing, securing a big license, or working on a sequel. We always believed that it's the game itself that makes the difference between success and failure. We're still playing the game and we still like it. After such a long time, it's hard to believe that OPERATION FLASHPOINT remains the favorite choice of games for most of the development team. We're still working on new content for FLASHPOINT out of pure enthusiasm. In the end, we don't feel ourselves to be anything more than proud members of a big and healthy FLASHPOINT fan community that has arisen around the world.

We know that someday we will have to leave FLASHPOINT to its own destiny. But currently, we still feel too involved in the game. We are already looking forward to future projects, but it will take months for us to start one. We consider the success of OPERATION FLASHPOINT as the pole position for our next race. We plan to use all the experience and resources that we have gained during the last couple of years to push gaming even further in the future.

Surreal Software's DRAKAN: ORDER OF THE FLAME

by stuart denman

Back-Story

DRAKAN: ORDER OF THE FLAME is a fantasy 3D action-adventure game on the TOMB RAIDER model with third-person perspective highlighting the iconic central characters: a beautiful woman with a sword teamed with a fire-breathing dragon. The different abilities of the protagonists combine to produce varied and new gameplay possibilities, with an aerial perspective unusual to the genre.

Origins of the Team

Because DRAKAN was Surreal's first product, the story of DRAKAN's development is also the story of Surreal's development as a company. Surreal's creation is the classic game development story in which four ambitious recent college graduates decided they had nothing to lose and formed a game company. These four founders contributed four critical skills to the team: art, programming, design, and business skills. None of us had ever run a company or managed schedules, but we all loved games, and we knew what it took to make a good one.

Lead designer Alan Patmore had always played games and had the business savvy to complement Nick Radovich's business experience and connections. I had been programming games and graphics since the age of ten, so even though I didn't have experience working at a game development company, I did have the skills and motivation. Mike Nichols, our creative director, came from within the industry and was the only member with any titles under his belt.

Our initial goal was to develop several game concepts and a solid technological foundation that we could pitch to game publishers. This would get us the funding we needed to pay ourselves and start hiring programmers and artists without having to involve venture capitalists. Once we got project funding, we were able to build a strong team of artists, programmers, and designers who all played games. Some of the team came from other game companies—lured by the informal atmosphere and the focus on games, not profit. Others were inexperienced with game development, but had the skills and fresh ideas we needed.

As the technology lead, I was determined to build Surreal's foundations on its technology. By retaining rights to our engine and tools, we always had something to fall back on if a game design was cancelled by the publisher. This also allowed us to develop multiple game titles from one generic technology and license the technology to other companies. Any investment in time that the programmers and I put into the engine could be quickly put to use on another project if anything went awry.

Game Data

Release date: August 1999

Developer: Surreal Software Inc., Seattle, Wash. http://www.surreal.com

Genre: 3rd-person fantasy action-adventure

Intended platform: Windows 95/98

Project budget: $2.5 million

Project length: 28 months

Team size: 23 full-time developers, 2 sound and music contractors

Critical development hardware: Pentium II and AMD K6-2 (3DNow!), 200 to 450MHz, 128MB RAM with Nvidia Riva 128 and TNT, 3dfx Voodoo 2 3D hardware. Artist workstations: Wacom tablets.

Critical development software: Windows software, Programming software: Microsoft Visual C++ 5.0 and 6.0, Visual SourceSafe 5.0, Intel VTune 2.5, InstallShield International 5.0. Art and animation software: Softimage, 3D Studio Max, Adobe Photoshop, In-house modeling and texturing tools. Sound and music: Sonic Foundry Soundforge, Emagic Logic Audio

We moved away from the popular DOOM-type engines toward a landscape-style rendering engine in order to set our games apart. There were many unique ideas that we could build from this: flying, underwater environments, outdoor deathmatch, and so on. But the technology was not only about rendering; the tools had to empower the designers and be general enough to support almost any game. So I designed a toolset in which every game-specific property and behavior would be provided by the game code itself, and the editor would be just a generic interface to the underlying game specifics.

Origins of the Beast

After pitching several game ideas to all the major publishers, we finally sold the first "dragon" concept to Virgin Interactive Entertainment (VIE) in the summer of 1996. The concept was very different from today's DRAKAN. The first concept was for a dragon RTS game in which the player's dragon could fly around taking over villages and forcing them to do their bidding. VIE wanted a more arcade-style shooter game to fill a slot in their product line, so we started developing a fast-paced, third-person dragon-flying game.

It was not until early 1997 (when VIE began cutting projects just prior to closing its doors) that Surreal sold the DRAKAN concept to Psygnosis. Psygnosis saw the strength in our team and gave us complete freedom to perfect the design. We wanted more of an RPG feel, but as a dragon, the player was limited in what he or she could carry or interact with. Adding a human rider was the best solution, and a female character was the natural choice since she would offset the dragon's immense size and power. With an increased budget under Psygnosis, we hired more team members and increased the art and game-play content to a level that the press called "ambitious" at our public debut at E3 in 1998.

The production under Psygnosis allowed us to expand the technology as well. We added real-time lighting effects and expanded the simple height-field landscape engine into our seamless indoor/outdoor layer technology. Critical to this technology was Psygnosis's willingness to drop support for software rendering (a risky marketing decision at the time). This allowed us unprecedented freedom. We switched over to true-color textures, increased the polygon counts throughout the game, and built arbitrary geometry for our worlds. The downside to relying on 3D hardware was that we faced serious compatibility challenges—the game would have to run on almost every 3D card. This also meant battling Direct3D driver bugs, and the possibility that we would be inundated with technical support calls, since people would not have software rendering to fall back on if the 3D hardware failed to work correctly.

What Went Right

1. Success with graphics

There's no doubt DRAKAN had an ambitious design, so the graphics had to be top-notch in order to make the game world believable. The amount of art and animation content we would need mandated careful planning, lest our schedule slip. The solution to the problem was what I call "flexible reuse." In addition to the sharing of texture and geometry data between objects, DRAKAN's engine (code-named the Riot engine) was programmed to allow arbitrary scaling and rotation of art content. By assigning different behaviors and combining multiple art components, we were also able to create totally new structures with minimal effort. Because we dropped 3D software rendering, we knew all of our textures could be created in true color. This vastly improved the look of DRAKAN, so much so that we decided to switch from using palette-based textures to true-color textures, which

A panoramic view of the first level in DRAKAN.

required quite a bit of reworking on most of the textures in the first few levels.

This decision is just one example of Surreal's aesthetic fussiness. Often if a few people thought that something within the game didn't look good enough, it would end up getting redone until everyone was satisfied. The benefits can be seen in the final product, but our schedule sometimes suffered as a result. Though the artists created the objects and buildings in the game, the designers were responsible for placing the objects into the game and gave immediate aesthetic and game-play feedback to the artists. They also were responsible for building the landscapes and caves, which defined the overall level flow. This process evened out the workload between artists and designers, but it required the designers to have a good artistic sense. This can be seen in the very fantastical landscape architectures that the designers constructed and then painted with tileable textures. The textures were drawn by the artists to have many variations and transitions, which added to the organic nature of the terrain.

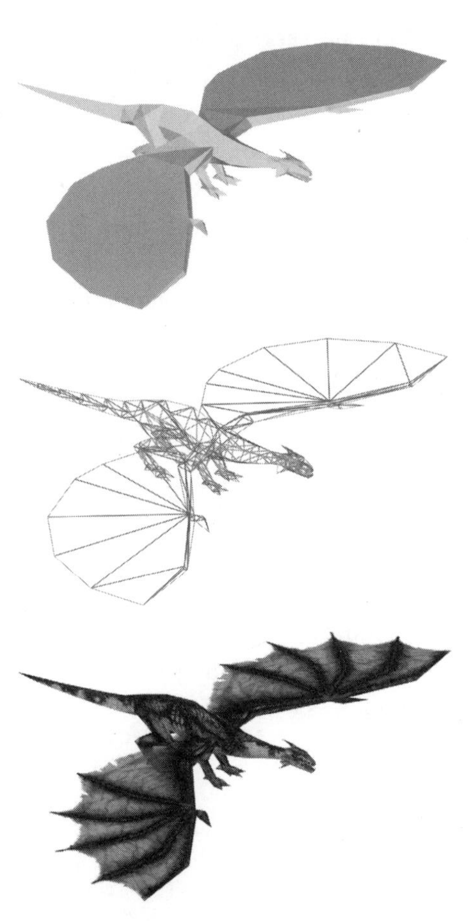

Arokh's polygon mesh and alpha-blended wings (above).

2. A green team with fresh ideas

DRAKAN had an advantage that many large game development companies sometimes overlook. It had a young team, highly motivated, bursting with ideas, and ready to take risks. The ideas were unique and motivated by the desire to set DRAKAN apart from the shooters and TOMB RAIDER clones (although this was still difficult, given the tendency of the gaming press to compare games to one another).

The most original idea in DRAKAN was the combination of dragon flight with sword and bow combat on the ground. This fundamental idea formed a developer's carnival for more innovative ideas and forced the player to strategize in a way not often seen in action games. The relative vulnerability of the female rider contrasted with the powerful dragon required careful thinking by the designers. Levels were created with restrictions on the dragon's ability to go places. Rynn could enter caves, but would come across areas where the dragon's flying abilities or strength would be necessary to proceed. The player (as Rynn) would then have to find a large door or other method to get the dragon inside the cave system. In this world of magic, creative ideas for special effects are very important, and these tasks were ideally suited to people who were not afraid to do things "outside the box."

3. Engine and tools

If ever there was an example to put the C vs. C++ argument to rest, it is DRAKAN. There simply are no performance reasons not to go with C++, as long as the programmers understand what is happening under the covers. Object-oriented code generates so many benefits, especially for an engine that you plan to build on for many years to come. In DRAKAN, the game-specific source code and engine source code were separated into different projects, so no game-specific code was allowed in the engine. The game-specific code included such features as the user interface, AI, and game entities, and contained no platform-specific code.

The engine is broken up into many classes that handle various engine tasks and are the interfaces by which the game code accesses the engine. For instance, there is a sound class for playing sounds, a texture class for working with textures, a sequencing class for playback of scripted cut-scenes, and numerous others. These also form a framework for future porting of the system-specific functions to other platforms. The stability of this system can be validated; we are currently creating additional games based on the DRAKAN engine with little or no code changes to the engine project. To further reduce the debugging time, we put coding guidelines in place to ensure the consistency of code between programmers, and created classes to catch array boundary violations and memory allocation problems.

DRAKAN has no scripting language. Instead, the programmers create modules that are visually connected by the designers to create scripted events in the game. Such modules include triggers, switches, timers, counters, and more complex modules such as doors, enemy creatures, and weapons. The modules have programmer-defined parameters associated with them. A parameter can be almost anything: a number, a list of options, a sound, a texture, another module, and so forth. The system meant designers could tweak parameters and combine modules in ways that the programmers never intended.

One particularly nice example was an effect that was originally created for the "ice sword." The effect was made up of a number of particles (originally snowflakes) that would collect for a certain amount of

Concept sketch of the Dark Union sailing ship.

time on the mesh of an affected object. After a time, the particles would fall to the ground and stick for a bit. All these properties, from the timings to the particle texture, are configurable. With this feature at their disposal, the designers created glowing auras around ghosts by increasing the particle size and making the stick-time infinite. They created snow that landed on invisible platforms to guide players across them. The snow effect was attached to arrows to drop ice behind them as they flew. All this from a small bit of programming.

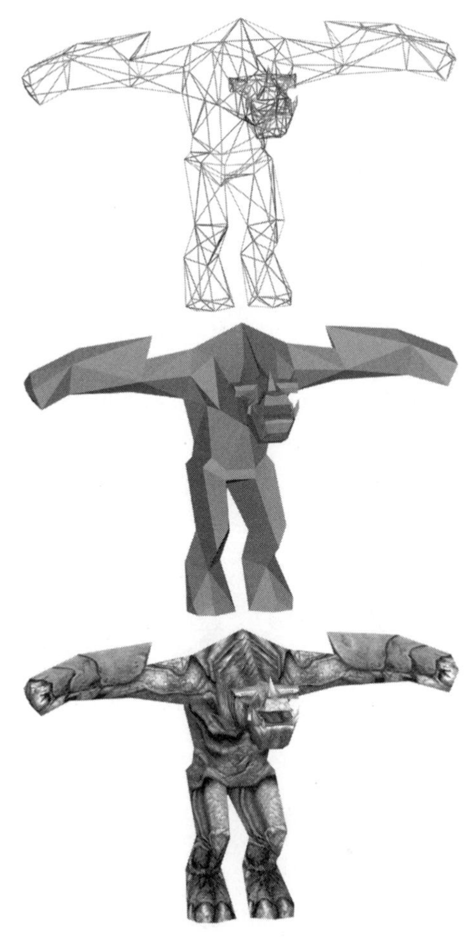

Colored conceptual sketch of a Wartok grunt.

The engine also has an efficient caching system, so it's able to handle hundreds of megabytes of data on our minimum system requirement of 32MB RAM. The two main characters, Rynn and Arokh, total more than 20MB of animations, plus 12MB of sounds (including in-game cut-scenes). To pull this off, the system keeps the most recently used sounds or animations in the cache and can flush memory that it hasn't used in a long time. Further reduction of memory usage is achieved by sharing animations between characters with the same skeleton, even if they have completely different skins. The system only loads the data that it needs, as it needs it. This is important during development, as artists and designers are prone to leave unused textures, sounds, and models in a database. The result is good engine performance during development, which is also representative of the final product.

We tried to ensure that the engine and tools always displayed to the artists and designers something that was representative of the final game (WYSIWYG). The best example of this was our real-time 3D editing system. The engine was integrated into the editor, so any geometry, texture mapping, or lighting changes made by the designer would be immediately reflected in the 3D view. The importance of this aspect of the tools should be emphasized because it gave the designers the ability to tune levels and game play very quickly and with a minimum of guesswork.

4. Compelling design

A good design will not only sell a game—it can also help smooth the development process. The DRAKAN world has immense possibilities, so new ideas were born easily within its scope. This kept the team highly motivated, as there were always innovative things to do with the genre. The varied environments gave a wealth of new things to work on for the art and design team, and were an ideal canvas for programmer invention. The design also kept Psygnosis very interested. DRAKAN became its top PC product, and it was comforting to us as developers to know that our publisher was behind the product.

Psygnosis saw the marketing potential in a beautiful female character combined with a fearsome, fire-breathing dragon and the press latched on to the concept with excitement. They could market it to TOMB RAIDER fans, AD&D fanatics, and even 3D shooter addicts.

Even the most brilliant design would be difficult to implement lacking a proper design document. The 175-page DRAKAN design document contained outlines for the entire game, including all AI behaviors, weapons, and level flows. It served its initial purpose well, and was a blueprint for our lead designer's vision. The document was vital to the development team, especially when it came to scheduling, creating tasks, and communicating with the publisher. But as you will read in the following "What Went Wrong" section, feature creep overtook the project halfway through, and the document never kept up with the changes. A design document should always be maintained throughout development to preserve it as a useful resource for the team. Fortunately, the team could always rely on Alan to explain anything or to fill in any holes in the design document.

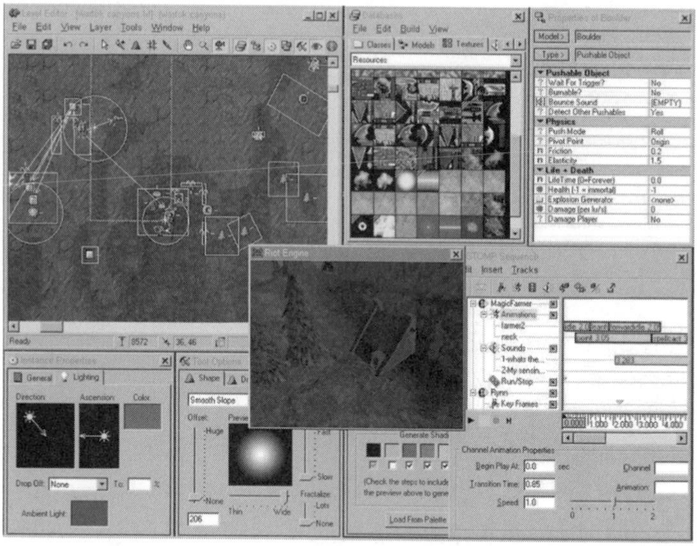

5. Indoor/outdoor environments

One of the major technologies that set the Riot engine apart from the other landscape engines was its ability to render both indoor and outdoor environments using the same engine. The benefits to game play were huge because we could do arbitrary cave systems, arches, overhangs, and other structures that were perfect for a fantasy game. The "layer" system that the landscape was created with was ideal for massive outdoor environments and allowed the designers to create very organic-looking worlds.

Rectilinear structures such as buildings and objects were created using arbitrary models imported from external 3D modeling programs.

Surreal's in-house level editing tool showing the real-time 3D editing window in the center and top-down layout view in the upper-left.

Although these models were not included in the visibility calculations, the layers were included and were nicely suited for use in the visibility culling of large environments. Because the layers were small height fields that made up the ceilings and floors of the surroundings, they took up very little space in memory. This meant that the levels could be vast, and it helped give the player a sense that there was a living world around them.

What Went Wrong

1. Staying on schedule

DRAKAN was originally slated for release in February 1999, but ended up being released six months later. Even with careful scheduling and task planning, we failed to meet the final deadlines. Part of the problem was that we didn't account for the time the team would spend creating versions of the game for E3 and for magazine and Internet demos. Each demo pulled nearly two weeks of time away from our normally scheduled tasks. The majority of the scheduling problems were due to feature creep and other improvements that were considered necessary during development.

In March 1998, the design team was faced with a mountain of work ahead in order to complete the 14 original levels as designed. After careful consideration, the designers decided to spend their efforts on enlarging and improving upon the ten best level designs. They also ended up cutting many features that did not show much game-play promise. The dart gun and the boomerang weapons were among those eliminated from the game. Even though these tasks had already been mostly completed (in terms of code) for several months, they had not yet been put into the game.

By the end of the project, the designers did not have adequate time left to work with programmers to play-balance those features, and the art staff had not done any work on them either. So they got cut. The decision allowed us to focus on improving the weapons that worked well, such as the bows and arrows. We now know that it's critical that programming tasks get put into the game and tested almost immediately so that their effectiveness can be realized early on. This lack of coordination between designers, artists, and programmers often caused problems during development. Some of this was because our design document wasn't updated when weapons, levels, or AI were redesigned.

The initial AI programming followed the original design document, but didn't work well when put into the game. It wasn't until our designers worked with the AI programmers to figure out exactly what they wanted for our combat system that the AI really came together. This kind of collaboration should have occurred at the beginning of the AI programming process and the lack of it caused moderate delays.

DRAKAN's art team often rebuilt geometry and model textures, sometimes up to three times before they were satisfactory. This may have been partially due to Surreal's high aesthetic standards, but a lack of consistent artistic vision is also to blame. DRAKAN had lots of character conceptual art, but no "art bible" to document all the models and environments for the game. This meant that if our art lead was not satisfied with work of another artist, he would often rebuild it himself. At various points during development his time was spread thin across many different tasks. In addition, the art team went through communication problems and power struggles that hampered the coordination of the team.

2. Inadequate testing

Although we tracked bugs internally before and during the alpha and beta releases, Psygnosis was responsible for the bulk of the testing after alpha. For a game as vast and ambitious as DRAKAN, the time that we allocated for testing was inadequate. Multiplayer and collision detection issues, in particular, were not given enough testing time.

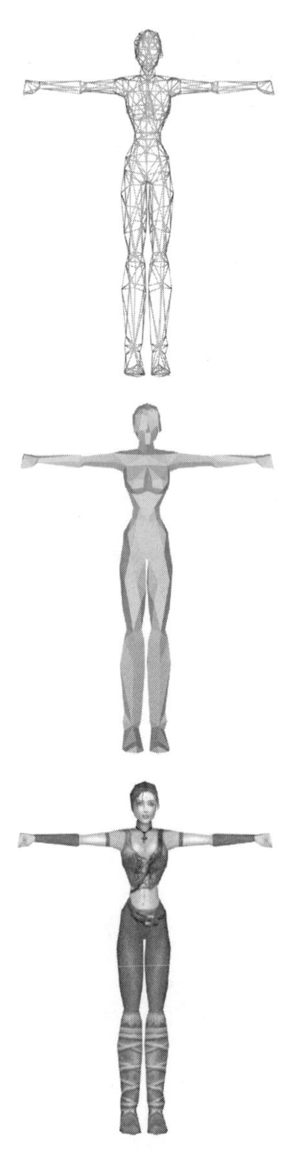

Rynn's highest polygon count was only 538.

When the final shipping date approached, we reluctantly agreed to allow some noncritical bugs to slip through to the gold master in the interest of meeting the deadline. A patch was inevitable.

Other testing complications added to the problems. As Psygnosis was being reorganized by its parent company, Sony Computer Entertainment Europe (SCEE), half the testing department was let go and merged with SCEE's U.K. testing group. This caused minor hiccups in tester allocations to DRAKAN. Since the testing team was located in Europe, communication was difficult, and often messages were delayed by a day or two. Bug reports were sent to us via Microsoft Excel worksheets, which were converted from an Oracle database that sat isolated on their LAN in the U.K. Often the Excel worksheets would come to us corrupted or would have incomplete bug descriptions. Bug responses from Surreal's programmers had to be tracked carefully and entered back into the Oracle database by hand.

We kept our own internal database at Surreal using Outlook forms in special public folders on our Exchange Server. We ended up generating almost 1,000 internal design, art, and programming bugs during the entire project. This rivaled the number of bugs generated by the testing team during alpha and beta. The internal system worked very well, but it could have been more useful if the Psygnosis testers had access to the system as well. We tried getting on-site testers, and some of the U.K. team did come to Surreal for about a week. But it was too late in the project and for too short a time to be effective.

3. Collision detection and response

One of the biggest chores for the testing team was to make sure that all of our hundreds of 3D models could not be penetrated by missiles, NPCs, or Rynn. Each model had to be properly bounded by the artist during the model's construction, a process which took about 20 percent of their modeling time to construct. Bounding was generated in our custom modeling tool and approximated the polygons of the model using a hierarchy (tree) of bounding spheres or oriented bounding boxes (OBBs). This made the collision detection system very fast and accurate, but it also meant that if an artist made a mistake in the bounding tree, collision detection might not work.

Lighting effects created varying moods. This bridge model was reused from the islands level.

To say this created a testing challenge would be an understatement. Even though the engine was capable of rendering arbitrary meshes, the collision detection system was not designed to handle some of the detailed meshes that the artists produced. Some of our AI used the bounding information at the lowest level, while Rynn's collision response system used a polygon-accurate analysis, which didn't work perfectly for some complex models. Frame-rate variations across machines also caused differing results, making it hard for programmers to reproduce the bugs and correct the problems. Finally, our indoor/outdoor landscape system created some challenging collision-detection problems that we hadn't anticipated when it was originally designed.

4. Multiplayer

Considered by some the Achilles' heel of DRAKAN, its multiplayer suffered from developmental neglect. For the game's multiplayer to have succeeded, the design, art, and programming teams would have had to spend at least twice as much time on it than they did. The two multiplayer designers did most of their level and weapon work during the alpha and beta periods. The same designers also created most of the artwork for the multiplayer effects and weapons. Any game-related bugs that came up were fixed by our single network programmer, who already had his hands full optimizing the underlying network engine.

Most of these game-related problems arose because the same weapons were used in both single and multiplayer games, but the original programmers were not careful to make them "network aware." Originally, we thought that DirectPlay was the easiest networking solution for us. But as the design got more complex, we found that DirectPlay just did not work well for us. DirectPlay was a debugging nightmare. The network programmer's machine crashed several times per day when debugging the networking code and we couldn't determine what was causing that to happen. It wasn't until we switched to Winsock that we discovered that the crashes were caused by DirectPlay.

DirectPlay also caused a serious problem for us while we debugged the game under the first release of Windows 98. DirectPlay actually caused the system clock to slow down. This caused the game to run slower and sucked up tons of CPU cycles, forcing a reboot. When put to the test, DirectPlay also had issues with firewalls, which we were not able to resolve. Under certain circumstances, the way DirectPlay handled the message queues sometimes caused messages to pile up until the application hung. Perhaps Microsoft will be addressing these issues in future releases.

It was clear even before alpha that the networking code would need to be rewritten. In the final design, we only used the TCP/IP portion of DirectPlay, and we used a Winsock front end to handle communication with the master server. We proposed to Psygnosis that they give us more time to convert the system over to Winsock, to which they replied yes—but only as a downloadable patch, since the additional work would have delayed the game's release. The Winsock conversion was not finished until a month after DRAKAN's release, and greatly stabilized the multiplayer experience. This, combined with the release of the level editor and mods, has created a resurgence in multiplayer support, but it will never be as good as it could have been.

5. Badly executed story

Although the overall story concept of DRAKAN was a great, the script and execution of the idea were lacking. We hired a movie scriptwriter to do the initial work on the script, but he was not familiar with the fantasy genre and did not have a firm grasp on Alan's vision for the design. From there, the script was edited and rewritten by several more people: members of Surreal, members of Psygnosis, even one of the voice actors. Under pressure to finish the script, it was completed with cheesy one-liners and other badly written dialog.

Once it had been recorded by the voice actors, it was very difficult to rerecord lines that were badly written or acted. Some were re-recorded, but that was a luxury we could only afford for the completely failed lines. The voice acting was difficult to get right, because just as some of the writers had almost no vision of the game, the voice actors likewise had little understanding of the characters they portrayed.

Another problem with the execution of the story was that most of the construction of the cut-scenes was left until the last minute, since all the levels had to be "geometry complete" before cut-scenes could be created. This meant that the scenes at the end of the game were hastily done, and some even had to be cut from the game.

The DRAKAN team: FRONT ROW, FROM LEFT TO RIGHT: Satish Bhatti (network programmer), Tim Ebling (programmer), Todd Andersen (designer), Susan Jessup (artist), Louise Smith (artist/animator), Andre Maguire (designer), Mel Guymon (lead animator), Tom Vykruta (programmer). MIDDLE ROW: Shaun Leach (programmer), Armen Levonian (programmer), John Whitmore (designer), Greg Alt (programmer), Heron Prior (animator), Tom Byrne (artist). BACK ROW: Stuart Denman (lead programmer), Scott Cummings (animator), Boyd Post (sound engineer), Alan Patmore (lead designer), Hugh Jamieson (character artist), Mike Nichols (lead artist), Hans Piwenitzky (artist), John McWilliams (designer), Nick Radovich (business/sound).

NOT PICTURED: Joe Olson (artist), Duncan (designer), Isaac Barry (designer), Ben Olson (artist).

Onward to the Next Project

DRAKAN's development was a bumpy ride, but it went suitably well considering it was the first game developed by an inexperienced team. Even with some of the schedule slips that occurred, the great design, art, and programming kept the project going strong. DRAKAN has been a great learning experience for the team, and the careful evaluation of our past mistakes has helped us in the development of our current projects. DRAKAN was recently named "PC Game of the Year" by several popular magazines, and it has sold very well. If DRAKAN showcases what this team is capable of in our first project, it will be very exciting to see what we are capable of in the future.

Pseudo Interactive's
CEL DAMAGE

by kevin barrett, john harley, rich hilmer, daniel posner, gary snyder, and david wu

Back-Story

CEL DAMAGE achieves an ambitious vision—to set a combat driving game in a universe with the look and feel of the golden age of cartoon violence. This feat is accomplished through a fusion of artistic vision with technical expertise—a renderer that mimics the look of cel animation and a cartoon physics engine that allows meshes to deform and bounce with the dynamic expressiveness of Warner Brothers mayhem. A range of entertaining cars and drivers contend in a variety death-match, capture-the-flag, and racing events. The action has an intuitive fast-paced arcade feel, and the range of powerups and characters give CEL DAMAGE depth and replayability. CEL DAMAGE is notable as part of a trend one could call post-realism—a high-tech tour de force whose aim is not just to mimic reality but to create a world with a particular feel and flavor.

The story behind CEL DAMAGE is long, winding, and harrowing, but ultimately uplifting. And because CEL DAMAGE is our first published title, its story is also the story of our company, Pseudo Interactive. Based in Toronto, we began work on the technological core of the game four years ago. A demo of our driving-combat physics engine at the Game Developers Conference in 1997, PI's first year of operations, received a warm reception. Shortly thereafter, PI struck up a relationship with Microsoft's Entertainment Business Unit (EBU). Over PI's first two years, we started up and killed a few projects. However, with the coming of Xbox, we found a proper niche for our emerging technology.

The physics engine that PI president and technology director David Wu was developing lent itself well to console applications. EBU recognized this, and an early alliance was formed between PI and the embryonic Xbox team. A high-profile Microsoft producer came to PI with a vision of where PI needed to take its game technology, and a new project was born. At that time, the project was called CARTOON MAYHEM and was primarily a car-based racing game with ancillary gag and weapon features. As we struggled with the demands of Microsoft's vision for IP development, rendering, and weapon effects, we realized that the game engine, which was a patchwork of two years' worth of diverging demands and evolution, would need a complete overhaul.

For better or for worse, we undertook that overhaul. So it was that just as we were getting into CARTOON MAYHEM's development, our engine, and our ability to iterate content in playable builds, went down for over eight months. This was a crucial time for Xbox and its first-party developers. Microsoft was allocating its resources to those teams with proven track records and those showing steady progress. We were obviously lacking in both areas. Microsoft cut PI, along with our Xbox title, at the end of 2000. Though this was a disheartening development for us, by this time we had the game engine back up and running, and we were suddenly able to produce good demo levels. It wasn't long before we drew interest from several other publishers. We had a quickly evolving technology and a ton of assets ready to go. The demos we put together enabled us to land a new publishing deal with Electronic Arts.

Switching publishers allowed us to prepare some great new material, including an internally developed IP, extra gameplay features, a new renderer, and a new title: CEL DAMAGE. We realized we were going to make the Xbox launch, and we were going to do it with our own property and the backing of the world's largest third-party publisher. These three facts alone made all the work of the previous several years worthwhile.

Game Data

Release date: November 1, 2001

Publisher: Electronic Arts

Genre: physics-based cartoon racing/combat

Platform: Microsoft XBox

Number of full-time developers: 16

Number of contractors: 12

Estimated budget: $2 million

Length of development: 2 years

Development hardware used: 600MHz Pentium IIIs with 256MB RAM, 30GB hard drives, and Nvidia GeForce cards

Development software used: Microsoft Visual Studio, 3DS Max, Photoshop, Illustrator, Winamp, SourceSafe

Notable technologies: pitaSim, Vtune, Microsoft Visual C++

Project size: 800,000 lines of code

What Went Right

1. Staffing

Two years ago, when we started work on our Xbox title, we had a core group of about eight people. It was apparent that if we wanted to develop a console game, whole cloth, in time for the Xbox launch, we would need more staff in every department. We hired more team members as we progressed through development. We were fortunate in that we were able to find very talented and motivated people who were also able to contribute to our corporate élan. We brought our staff in from all over North America, and although none of us had console development experience, each new member brought a rich skill set to the company.

The search and interview process for each team member was exhaustive. We would often see a candidate two or three times before rejecting him or her and moving on to someone else. Talent and experience were sought-after attributes, but not at the expense of team chemistry. In the end, our hiring methods were vindicated. We were able to create a group of friends who enjoyed working with one another and were deeply devoted to the project.

Our approach to team communication went hand in hand with our approach to staffing. We found that weekly full-staff meetings, individual weekly lectures or presentations to the entire staff, and regular departmental reviews greatly improved all team members' understanding of how their co-workers contributed to the project.

We also held an ace up our sleeve. We formed a strategic alliance with a local technical college that offered a diploma course in 3D visual arts. Through the school, we instituted an internship program in our art department. We integrated top students into our team, which was a very successful exercise that we will maintain during our next project.

Moral: Wait for the cream to rise, then scoop it off the top.

2. Early development with Xbox

As a new entrant in the highly competitive console market, the Xbox group was looking for game experiences that would make their console stand out. As Microsoft pointed out so often during the Xbox design period, "Great technology does not sell game systems, great games sell game systems." Picking up on that mantra, we started our development when the console was little more than an optimistic dream championed by a charismatic team of visionaries.

Chief among them was their bold Advanced Technology Group manager, Seamus Blackley. We were converts to his ambitious plans for the Xbox. With the promise of a stable, RAMpacked, hard-drive-enabled computational powerhouse, we were confident that we could deliver the breakthrough game experience that Microsoft was seeking.

Our game grew and achieved its focus as the Xbox did the same. Knowing that CEL DAMAGE would be held to standards set by second-generation Playstation 2 titles during the 2001 Christmas buying season, we were spurred on to utilize whatever technology the Xbox team was stuffing into the system. We believe that through this evolving relationship, we've managed to create an innovative and highly entertaining title. It's also worth noting that CEL DAMAGE probably would not exist today were it not for the support and inspiration provided by Seamus and the rest of the Xbox team. They stood up for our project and pushed as hard as any of us to make CEL DAMAGE a reality.

Moral: It's all about whom you know.

---

3. Synchronization tools

PI grew a great deal over the course of the project, and we knew it was important to keep everyone synchronized. The increasing size of the team, combined with the growing mountain of content and code, made regular updates more difficult and time consuming. The process of creating a build became a black art that only one or two people could do correctly.

The first step toward synchronization came fairly early on with the creation of an automated code-compilation process, dubbed AutoBuild. We investigated a few different automated build programs, but none was as flexible or complete as a home-brewed batch file (or rather, a collection of batch files and supplementary programs). Each night, or whenever necessary, AutoBuild could check out all source code to a clean directory tree. It then built and executed any code generators, built all binaries, copied the output to a shared directory, and generated an e-mail report containing a .ZIP file of all build output, along with a summary of errors and warnings. Whenever convenient, our programmers could run another batch file to synchronize completely.

Although we implemented AutoBuild with low-tech Windows commands and utilities, this one-button solution proved to be extremely valuable. Each build that the process generated served as the absolute point of reference for the current code base. Even with six people working simultaneously on the same source code, we were able to keep inconsistencies and problems to a minimum.

Another low-tech solution, MakeBuild, filled our largest gap in synchronization, though its implementation came quite late in the project. MakeBuild consisted of our source game content, automatically compiled into run-time format by adding a few simple commands to the game editor, and a few batch files. By automatically running MakeBuild after AutoBuild, we had a brand-new build waiting for us each morning. Our daily build process kept artists

Early in development, CEL DAMAGE was more race-themed. Here's an early concept for a loop-the-loop road gag in the desert theme.

and QA staff up to date without bogging down any individual with responsibility for creating the builds. MakeBuild accelerated the feedback cycle between content creation and gameplay review.

Of course, not all updates were visible in the build, and we made several other utilities to help keep everyone abreast of changes under the hood. Our CheckInReporter was a simple Visual Basic program that scanned the SourceSafe database for all check-ins over the previous 24 hours, and then created and e-mailed out an Excel spreadsheet report. These were especially helpful in tracking down regressions. We created another simple VB program that e-mailed out active bug lists to each team member once per day.

Moral: Spending a few days creating simple tools pays big dividends throughout the project.

4. Internal bug tracking and QA

We made sure that our daily build process was up and running before we built our internal QA department. The daily build mentality was instrumental in the iterative process and was QA's greatest ally. New art and game logic assets could be evaluated in-game within 24 hours of their creation, allowing broken assets and bad functionality to be identified immediately.

Asset pound-downs and targeted focus testing ran concurrently as soon as we had four functional game levels. As development progressed, focus testing generated reams of data, which was boiled down to nearly 400 gameplay and asset recommendations. This information provided an important perspective on what people were interpreting as fun and fair. This feedback was very valuable, since we'd lost all objectivity toward the game and its difficulty level once we'd mastered the various weapons and gags.

The bug-tracking software that our internal QA used for the duration of the project was called PI_Raid. This tool, designed and customized in-house, allowed us to stay on top of game defects, generate work items, and comment on evolving game features. We kept our bugs small and focused. While this approach often left each of us with a lot of bugs in our "bin," we were able to close out several per day, providing mini morale boosts throughout the project. Though some of the bugs that we logged might have been considered trivial, cumulatively tackling them had a dramatic, positive effect on the game and our level of polish.

Moral: Get fresh eyeballs on your game and efficiently iterate gameplay.

5. Coordinated schedule

One of the pleasures of working on CEL DAMAGE was the lack of a brutal crunch period in the final weeks of development. We also felt throughout the last year of the project that we'd be able to realize our desired feature set. A good schedule, coordinated with each department, helped us achieve this unique state. Our early work with Microsoft taught us the value of adhering to a schedule, and after we moved on from that relationship, we were able to maintain, and even improve, our scheduling skills. Our guess is that badly maintained and poorly enforced schedules are the primary cause of game projects missing their ship dates, dropping features, and winding up with morale-busting, project-end crunch periods. Following are some schedule-related factors that worked for us:

Some early desert environment renders made to test scale, detail, and color. Our tests included fog, vertex lighting, and gradations with the goal of evoking a classic Warner Brothers style. These elements were actually dropped as the vision of our own house style came into focus.

Estimating task duration. No one can estimate with 100 percent accuracy. However, our leads and staff communicated constantly to refine delivery date estimates. If an asset looked as though it was going to run overtime, we would cut it or some of that person's later deliverables, from the schedule. If such changes created holes in the game's design, we would be flexible and design around the holes.

Software. We used Microsoft Project. If you've used it, you know it's not great, but it gets the job done. That was all we needed. Once we got used to Project's idiosyncrasies, it was smooth sailing to the end of development.

Team-wide involvement. We periodically printed the master schedule and posted it on a wall where everyone could see it. This helped in many ways. First, it demonstrated the interdependence of the departments. Each staff member could see that an asset he or she was working on was needed by someone in another department. Second, missing items could be identified more easily, since more eyes were looking at the schedule. Third, seeing the schedule updated gave people a strong sense of making progress. This progress contributed to team confidence and morale.

Short, staggered crunches. We crunched, but we did it early in small, manageable, prescribed intervals, giving us a buffer at the end of the project, after our feature set was complete. People were then freed up to work on visual weapon enhancements and level polish. At the end of the project, the team was playing full- and split-screen CEL DAMAGE during and after business hours. This intense play period helped identify exploits and balance the gameplay. This data wouldn't have been available to us if we had crunched long and hard at the end of the project.

Moral: The schedule is your friend. Never let friends down.

What Went Wrong

1. Design on the fly

Once we got our technology back online in December 2000, it began evolving very quickly. Feature sets for weapon and death effects, driving behaviors, gag functionality, and animations were growing every day. Because we were designing a game to the technology (rather than the other way around), we were throwing out design documents as quickly as they could be written. Art assets had to be revised, retextured, discarded, and rebuilt from scratch several times. As most readers will know from experience, this is a scenario for feature creep, obsolete tool sets, and blown deadlines.

While we were able to nail down our feature set four months before shipping, our evolving engine did cause other problems. Essentially, our strategic preplanning was stillborn. Every week, we had to revise our perceptions of what the game would really be, which frustrated our attempts to describe the game to prospective publishers at the beginning of 2001. Different staff members had different ideas of what our game would finally end up looking and playing like.

Fortunately, once publishers and press played the game for themselves, the core of Cel Damage's identity as a cartoon-based vehicular combat game became self-evident.

Moral: It's OK to design to an evolving technology, but institute hard cut-off dates for code development and features.

---

2. Asset tracking and implementation

Our initial efforts produced large amounts of art content to show off the XBox's power. However, evolving performance specs for the Xbox and our game engine, along with a new IP introduced early in 2001, generated several massive content revisions. These revisions were necessary for level geometry, static world objects, gags, skyboxes, cars, characters, weapons—everything. In the worst cases, we saw at least 12 major revisions to individual assets.

A before and after shot using the desert theme's General Store. Cel-shading conventions were prototyped in 3DS Max using the Illustrate! plug-in.

While we had an established directory structure for storage at the beginning of the project, new workflows, staff, and management methods precipitated a patchwork of file-naming conventions and tracking methods. Final game meshes were

inadvertently overwritten with geometric primitives. We "lost" assets on the server for days at a time. Other tracking problems cropped up as well. A bug in our game engine created duplicate textures that were difficult to hunt down and eliminate. Also, we had a problem with texture revisions that got wiped out on import to the game editor. To compound our headaches, objects were often used in several different levels, but if an optimization was made to one, that change was not automatically propagated through all levels.

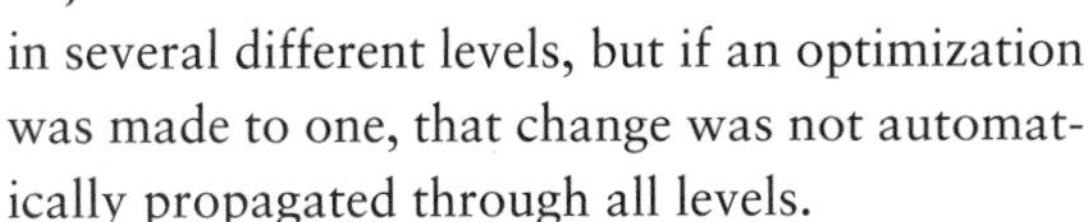

Obviously, we needed a tool to track our art assets and their properties and to update content in the game. We created the robust PI_Asset for just such a use. Unfortunately, it was introduced too late in the project for full implementation. As a stopgap measure, artists began sending out dailies through e-mail. These reports proved useful in tracking what had been accomplished in the course of a day and what should be updated in the build, but data management was still a problem. PI_Raid showed us just how many holes our pipeline had in it. While the primary purpose of PI_Raid was to track and resolve bugs, the artists and level builders found themselves using it as a means to provide a pathway to updated content. Through PI_Raid, a person could know when an asset had been updated, where it could be found, and what had changed in it. Using our bug reporter to track game assets was not an ideal solution, but it did serve us well in a pinch.

While the build-discard-rebuild process hit our staff pretty hard, it created a sturdy springboard for future asset-tracking methods, and it also reinforced a better mentality for thoroughness in our development procedures. Our next project will definitely see better tracking and implementation methods.

Moral: Don't overwrite finished, textured building models with spheres.

---

3. Single member over-tasking

Due to our relatively small staff, we had to put managers in the critical path of day-to-day asset delivery. These same people held crucial, unique skill sets. As you know, this is a recipe for bottlenecks that hamper development. One example among several was the role of our art director. We made this person responsible for overseeing the game art, scheduling his staff's workweeks while developing their technical expertise, modeling, creating the game's interface, producing our cut-scenes, overseeing interns, and distributing hundreds of art bugs. The time needed for one person to do all these things just wasn't available every day.

Fortunately, we were able to create an art lead position to handle the staff and bug tasks. However, not every instance of over-tasking could be fixed by adding a new body. We had one texture artist, but three or four art staff members were generating meshes. Add to this the frequent discarding of textures and rebuilding of models, and the amount of work crossing the texture desk became enormous. We also had a single staff member who was responsible for updating level content every day. If you consider that on some days we'd generate 100 updated assets, and each one had to be imported, adjusted, and hand-tweaked in the levels, you can gain an appreciation for the bottleneck occurring there.

With so many items funneling through one mouse, the balance between efficiency and human error was highly stressed. Ultimately we dealt with the regressions that cropped up, but it's clear that better integration tools for our next project will help a lot.

Moral: Spot bottlenecks early and divert the work as necessary.

---

4. Last-minute implementation of crucial elements

Our inexperience in console game development caught up with us about three months away from the end of the project. For the better part of two years, we had spent all of our efforts on developing in-game assets and gameplay. As our delivery date to EA came into focus, we realized that we still needed to get a fair bit of content underway, including a solid front-end interface, music, cut-scenes, voice acting, foley sound, and sound effects. Once we had our budget in place, we scrambled to pull together a stack of contracted, out-of-house assets.

We drew up a shopping list that looked something like this: 13 cut scene scripts and storyboards, 12 pieces of in-game music, a theme song, interface music, 450 sound effects, 1,000 lines of in-game dialogue and 200 lines of cut scene dialogue to be read by seven different voice actors, six minutes of foley sound and cut scene music, and six man-months of modeling and animation talent. We also realized we needed a way to play back our cut-scenes in real time through the game engine and renderer, even through these code elements were not designed to handle the task.

We took on the interface and playback tasks in-house, but farmed out everything else. Obviously, the work was finished on time, but to accomplish this we had to divert the attention of all of our in-house managers to get these items implemented. Spillover bottlenecking was unavoidable. Though we were ironing out implementation bugs until the day we shipped, the quality of the talent and assets we were able to find on short notice shone through in the finished product.

Moral: The last 5 percent of a game takes 50 percent of the effort.

---

5. Switching publishers

As we already mentioned, we switched to a new publisher halfway through development. Going from Microsoft to EA was a mixed blessing. While we were able to improve gameplay and develop our own IP, we lost both our financial backing and our internal focus at a crucial time in the project. We were also forced to reinvent all of our art assets to avoid an IP conflict with Microsoft.

However, what could have been a project-wide meltdown actually hardened our resolve to get CEL DAMAGE on store shelves. Once we realized that the CEL DAMAGE property would belong to us, and that our mistakes and successes would be our own, the training wheels came off. We became more determined and professional. As a rite of passage, this publishing switch might have been exactly what we needed. In the end, perseverance carried the day, and getting dropped as a first-party title was a black eye from which we recovered.

Moral: When life gives you lemons, start drinking hard lemonade.

Damage Control

Now that CEL DAMAGE is out the door, PI's last monkey is off its back. We are published and moving ahead. There is plenty for us to look forward to now, not the least of which is CEL DAMAGE 2. We are excited about the prospects for Xbox and hope to continue to exploit its strengths with network and team-based play in our next game. Fortunately, our experiences with CEL DAMAGE have shown us where we can improve our processes and strategic planning on our next venture.

Nihilistic Software's

VAMPIRE: THE MASQUERADE—REDEMPTION

by robert huebner

Back-Story

VAMPIRE: THE MASQUERADE—REDEMPTION successfully translates the popular paper-and-pencil role-playing system to the PC environment, bringing the lush, atmospheric Old-World mythos to digital life. Players take the part of Christof Romuald, a Christian knight turned vampire, in a lavish, complex storyline spanning 800 years, from Eastern Europe to London. The game plays through combat and the use of various disciplines, specialized vampire powers of mind and body. VAMPIRE is notable for its addition of Storyteller Mode, which allows players to fashion and run their own multiplayer campaigns in the engine, just as in paper-and-pencil gaming, a move that prefigures games, such as Neverwinter Nights, and might be a new direction for player-driven creativity.

When Nihilistic Software was founded in 1998, there were only two things we knew were certain. The first was that we wanted to form a company with a small number of very experienced game developers. The second was that we wanted to make a killer role-playing game. Nihilistic got started without much fanfare, just a few phone calls and e-mails. After finishing work on JEDI KNIGHT for LucasArts, the core team members had, for the most part, gone their separate ways and moved on to different teams or different companies. About eight months after JEDI KNIGHT shipped, various people on the original team began to gravitate together again, and eventually formed Nihilistic just a few exits down Highway 101 in Marin County, Calif., from our previous home.

Having moved into our new offices and bolted together a dozen desks from Ikea, our first project was to build a 3D RPG based on White Wolf's pen-and-paper franchise, *Vampire: The Masquerade*. Before linking up with Activision as our publisher, Nihilistic president Ray Gresko already had a rough design and story prepared for an RPG with similar themes and a dark, gothic feel. After Activision approached us about using the White Wolf license, we adapted parts of this design to fit the World of

Darkness universe presented in White Wolf's collection of source books, and this became the initial design for REDEMPTION.

Because of our transition from first- and third-person action games to RPGs, we approached our first design in some unique ways. Many features that are taken for granted in action games, such as a rich true 3D environment, 3D characters, and the ability for users to make add-ons or modifications, were reflected in our project proposal. We also adopted many conventions of the FPS genre such as free-form 3D environments, ubiquitous multiplayer support, and fast real-time pacing. To this we added the aspects of traditional role-playing games that we found most appealing: a mouse-driven point-and-click interface, character development, and a wide variety of characters, items, and environments for exploration.

Game Data

Release date: June 2000

Publisher: Activision

Genre: 3rd-person vampire role-playing game

Platform: Hardware-accelerated PC

Full-time developers: 12

Contractors: 8

Budget: $1.8 million

Length of development: 24 months

Hardware used: Intel and AMD PCs, Nvidia and 3dfx 3D accelerators

Software used: Alias|Wavefront Maya, Photoshop, QERadiant, Visual C++

Technologies: 3D skinned characters, continuous level-of-detail, custom-built 3D engine, MP3 audio compression, lip synching

Lines of code: 300,000 for game, 66,000 lines of Java for scripts.

Using the White Wolf license also meant that our users would have high expectations in terms of story, plot, and dialogue for the game. It's a role-playing license based heavily around dramatic storytelling, intense political struggles, and personal interaction. Fans of the license would not accept a game that was mere stat-building and gold-collecting.

In keeping with our basic philosophy, we built up a staff of 12 people over the course of the project's 24-month development cycle. The budget for the game was fairly modest by today's standards, about $1.8 million. The budget was intentionally kept low for the benefit of both Nihilistic and our publisher. We wanted our first project to be simple and manageable, rather than compounding the complexities of starting a company by doing a huge first project. Also, we were looking to maximize the potential benefits if the game proved successful. For its part, Activision was new to the RPG market and was testing the waters with RPGs and the White Wolf license in particular, so they probably considered the venture fairly high risk as well.

Development started around April 1998. When we began, we examined several engine technologies available, such as the Unreal engine and the Quake engine, but ultimately decided against licensing our engine technology. The game we envisioned, using a mouse-driven, point-and-click interface, had a lot more in common with games such as STARCRAFT than even the best first-person engines. We decided to create a new engine focused specifically on the type of game we wanted to create, and targeted 3D-accelerated hardware specifically—bypassing the tremendous amount of work required to support nonaccelerated PCs in a 3D engine. As an added benefit, the company would own the technology internally, allowing us to reuse the code base freely for future projects or license it to other developers.

What Went Right

1. Letting the artists and designers pick their tools

With such a small team and tight budget, boosting the team's efficiency was our primary focus. If bad tools or art paths slowed down progress in the art or level design departments, we would have no chance of hitting our milestones. When we started to map the development project, the programmers gravitated toward using a package such as 3D Studio Max for both art and level design. Our argument was that doing everything in a single package would increase portability of assets between levels and art, and save the company money by licensing a single, relatively inexpensive tool.

Thankfully, however, our leads in these areas strongly objected to this plan. They argued for allowing each department to use the tools that allowed them to do their work most efficiently. This single decision probably accounted for more time saved than any other. The level designers cited QERadiant as their tool of choice, since most of them had previously done work with id Software on QUAKE mission packs. id was generous in allowing us to license the QERadiant source code and modify it to make a tool customized to our 3D RPG environments.

Because QERadiant was a finished, functional tool even before we wrote our own export module, the level designers were able to create levels for the game immediately, even before an engine existed. And since QERadiant stores its data in generic files that store brush positions, the levels were easily tweaked and re-exported as the engine began to take shape. If the level designers had spent the first six months of the project waiting for the programmers to create a level editing tool or learning how to create levels in a 3D art tool, we would not have been able to complete the more than 100 level environments in 24 months with just three designers.

Locations included both interior and exterior cityscapes, allowing dramatic situations such as this battle atop a clock tower in medieval Prague.

On the art side, lead artist Maarten Kraaijvanger lobbied hard for the adoption of Alias|Wavefront tools for 3D art. We tried to convince him that a less expensive tool would work just as well, but in the end we decided to allow the art department to use what they felt would be the most efficient tool for the job. Since Maya was just being released for Windows NT at that time, the costs of using that toolset were not as great as we feared, and it allowed the artists the produce an incredible number of 3D art assets for the project. During the 24 months of the project, an art department of four people produced nearly 1,500 textured models, a mind-boggling figure using any tool.

2. Small team, one project, one room

When we started Nihilistic, we had a theory that a small number of highly experienced developers would be able to produce a title more efficiently than a larger team with fewer battle scars. In my experience, successfully delivering a game is less about what you do and more about what you choose not to do. Most games that ship late do so because the development team went down one or more "blind alleys"—development ideas or strategies that for whatever reason didn't pan out, and the work done in that direction is lost. As a small team on a tight budget, we could not afford to lose valuable time on these diversions. Experienced team members have the wisdom to look down a particular path and recognize when it's a likely dead end.

A set of four interactive 3D head models at the bottom of the screen are skinned and animated in real time to give lifelike status for each party member.

We also knew that we wanted an office environment where all the team members were in a single room without any walls, doors, or offices whatsoever. This didn't really seem like a radical decision—many of us got our start working for teams that operated like this—but it seems like these sorts of companies are becoming less and less common in today's industry. My first game job was working at Parallax (now Volition) software. We were eight people sitting along one wall of a narrow office space in Champaign, Ill. Even the original DARK FORCES development team was sequestered in a one-room studio in a building separate from most of the other LucasArts teams.

This type of environment doesn't just foster, but rather forces communication between all parts of the team. For instance, a programmer can overhear a discussion between two artists about how to proceed with something and be able to jump in with an answer that will save the project days or months of work. This sort of thing happens on a daily basis; artists correct missteps by the technology team before they are made, a level designer can immediately show a bug to a programmer, and so on. Each of these incidents represents hours or days of project time saved. In an office environment with walls and doors, most of these situations would go unnoticed or unaddressed.

3. Using Java as a scripting engine

We knew from the start that allowing the user community to edit the game was an important part of the design. After working in the first-person action-game market, we saw the benefits of supporting the user community and wanted to carry this idea over into role-playing games, where it is not the norm. A built-in scripting system makes a game engine much more extendable by fans. In JEDI KNIGHT, we created our own customized game language called COG. Creating COG took a lot of effort from the development team; several months of work went into creating the compiler, testing the generated code, and implementing the runtime kernel used to execute the scripts. The end result was worth it, but it cost a lot in terms of time and resources to pull it off.

Professional conceptual art, such as this rendering of Alessandro Giovanni by contractor Patrick Lambert, helped the characters evolve as the art design took shape.

When starting VAMPIRE, we looked for ways to incorporate a scripting engine more easily than creating our own from scratch yet again. There were several scripting systems we examined and tested. At about that time, another game development company, Rebel Boat Rocker software, was getting a lot of attention for its use of Java technology. After exchanging a few e-mails with lead programmer Billy Zelsnak, we decided to give Java a try. Up to this point I knew very little of Java, and had largely dismissed it as a language suitable only for making icons dance on a web page and the like.

After a crash course in Java, we did a few simple tests incorporating it into our game engine. It passed each one with flying colors. In a matter of a few weeks, we had solved the major challenges involved in interfacing a standard, freely distributable Java virtual machine to our 3D RPG engine. From that point on, the only maintenance required was to add new native functions to the scripting language, which we did whenever we added new engine functionality that we wanted exposed to the script writers.

We also trained several designers in the use of the scripting language, and they started creating the hundreds of small scripts that would eventually drive the storyline of the game. Ever since those initial tests, I kept waiting for the other shoe to drop, so to speak. I expected to come to work one day and find out that the Java thread was chewing up 100MB of RAM or eating 50 percent of the CPU time, but amazingly, the system was trouble-free throughout development and never became a significant resource drain. If for some reason we had hit a dead end with the Java system late in the project, it would have easily taken three to four months to get back on track using a different scripting technology. In the end, the gamble paid off. We saved months of programmer time that would have otherwise been devoted to creating a scripting environment, and the result was a system significantly more efficient and robust than any we could have created ourselves.

4. Storyteller mode

Throughout the project, the design slowly took shape through a series of meetings that involved the entire staff. Each new design element was presented to the group and subjected to a (sometimes heated) discussion. This process of open discussion and free exchange of ideas resulted in a lot of the most interesting design aspects of the game. It was in one of our earliest design meetings that we came up with the idea of developing the multiplayer aspect of the game not as a typical deathmatch or cooperative system, but rather to create a "storyteller" or "dungeon-master" system. The idea was inspired by the venerable text-based multi-user dungeon (MUD) games that date from a calmer time in the history of the Internet.

Many of us at Nihilistic had played MUDs in college, often to the detriment of our studies.

One thing that made MUDs so appealing was the ability for "wizards," high-ranking users of the MUDs, to manipulate the game environment and create virtual adventures for the players in real time. The Vampire license from White Wolf emphasizes the role of the "storyteller," or moderator, so we felt the time was right to take this style of play out of the college computer lab and into a commercial RPG. Implementing the storyteller system turned out to be fairly simple from a technology standpoint. Most of the basic functionality for a storyteller game is identical to what would be required in a traditional client/server multiplayer game.

The added cost was mostly in the area of design and the user interface. It took a bit of experimentation and redesign to arrive at an interface that was powerful enough to run games as a storyteller without being overly confusing to the novice player. The UI work included new interface panels with lists of objects, actors, and other resources, and a few buttons to manipulate the selected resources. Our overall design goal for the user interface was to ensure that important functionality was accessible using only the mouse, and all keyboard functionality represented only "advanced" controls such as hotkeys and shortcuts. Even though the storyteller system is something used primarily by advanced players, we wanted to preserve this design goal, which meant quite a bit of extra UI work to make a mouse-driven interface powerful enough to drive a storyteller game.

In the end, the storyteller feature ended up being one of the gems of the game design, and resonated with both the press and gamers alike. Activision made good use of the feature in their PR and marketing campaigns, and we hope the expandability and storyteller aspects of the game will give the game an increased shelf life.

The ambitious design included parties of up to four 3D characters, each with interchangeable weapons and armor.

5. Using experienced contractors

One problem with our strategy of using a small core team is that we couldn't possibly cover all the aspects of designing a commercial game with just 12 people. Instead, we relied heavily on external contractors for certain key aspects of the game. Sound was one area where we made use of external talent. Our colleagues from LucasArts referred Nick Peck to us, based on his excellent work on Tim Schafer's GRIM FANDANGO. Nick ended up not only supplying us with sound effects, but also working on some of the additional voice recording and ambient loops. For our music, we teamed up with Kevin Manthei who scored the Dark Ages portion of the game, and with Youth Engine, a local duo, for the modern-day tracks.

Even in the conceptual stages, we used external artists to help us sketch and visualize the game. Peter Chan was the lead conceptual artist for JEDI KNIGHT and had subsequently become an independent contractor. His work in the first months of the project was key in establishing the look of the game's environments. We also worked with Patrick Lambert for character concepts and he delivered incredibly detailed full-color drawings that really brought the characters to life for the modelers and animators.

Perhaps the most critical external relationship was with Oholoko, a small startup spun off from Cyclone Studios. We hired them to do our cinematic sequences that introduce the story and provide the endings. While starting the project, we met with several firms specializing in computer animation, but pretty much across the board their rates were well beyond our budgets for that part of the game. It seems that the high demand for computer animation from movies and television has driven the larger firms' prices beyond the reach of typical game budgets. By working with a smaller, less established company, we were able to get more bang for our buck in our cinematics, and the results proved to be of the highest quality.

All of the more than 100 3D characters, such as Lucretia, a Setite priestess, were modeled and animated by hand by a team of four artists using Maya.

What Went Wrong

1. Overly ambitious design

In retrospect, we were in some ways our own worst enemy. Many of the team members had wanted for some time to do a really huge, ambitious role-playing game. When we actually started the project and had a budget and schedule, we probably weren't realistic about how long RPGs typically take to develop, especially one that travels to four different cities across an 800-year timeframe. We were very reluctant to make big cuts in the design, such as cutting one of the two time periods or removing the multiplayer aspect. Because of this, we eventually had to make the decision to miss our first scheduled release date of March 2000. We also cut back on our plans to release an interactive demo some months before the game and scaled back the scope of the multiplayer beta.

Fortunately, by expanding the schedule a few months (from March to June), we were able to preserve almost all the elements from the initial design. But to accomplish this, the art and design departments really had to work above and beyond the call of duty for an extended period of time. We did cut back a bit in the area of multiplayer by removing the ability to play through the entire single-player scenario cooperatively as a team, and instead replaced that with two smaller, custom-made multiplayer scenarios using levels and art from the single-player game.

Part of this was because we did not plan properly for multiplayer when making some of the Java scripts that drive the single-player game. If the multiplayer game had been functional earlier in the schedule, the single-player game scripts might have been written from the start to be "multiplayer friendly" and we could have shipped more multiplayer content in the box.

2. Prototyping with a proprietary API

When we started developing the 3D engine for the game, which we named Nod, the 3D API landscape was quite a bit different from how it is now. We decided to use Glide as an initial prototyping API with the belief that it would be a more stable platform and avoid the complexities of supporting multiple hardware through a more general API until we had solidified the engine a bit. However, once we had a basic, functional engine running under Glide, the programmers' attentions turned toward game play and functionality rather than switching the graphics engine to a more general API such as Direct3D or OpenGL. Because of this "if it ain't broke" mindset, we expanded our support beyond Glide fairly late in development. At the first public showing of the game at E3 in 1999, we were still basically a Glide-only game, which meant we couldn't demonstrate the game in 32-bit modes or support some features not present in Glide at the time.

The extensive use of Glide also gave us some unrealistic performance estimates for other hardware. Since Glide allows low-level access to things like texture-memory management, we spent significant time writing our own optimized texture manager. When we switched to Direct3D, most of this work had to be discarded. Since Glide allows more flexible vertex formats than Direct3D, some of our underlying data structures needed to be changed, which meant re-exporting hundreds of levels and models. We were making low-level architectural engine changes at a stage when the engine should have been pretty much locked down.

Also, because we switched late in our development schedule, we probably didn't spend as much time as we should have on compatibility testing with a wide variety of hardware. In retrospect, we should have switched to Direct3D or OpenGL several months earlier in the development schedule.

3. Pathfinding difficulties

One problem we identified early in the development process was the problem of pathfinding. Navigation of variably-sized characters through a completely free-form 3D environment is one of the most difficult problems I've had to tackle as a game programmer. Unit navigation is hard enough when you have a flat 2D plane or restricted 3D environment, but in an environment where the level designers are free to make stairs, ramps, or any other 3D construct you can imagine, the problem becomes exponentially more difficult.

My natural tendency when presented with such a sticky problem is, unfortunately, to make it good enough for the early milestone and demo builds, and then just "deal with it later." Unfortunately, "later" quickly became "now," and "now" turned into "yesterday." We should have tackled this problem much earlier, before the levels were near completion. We should have worked with the level designers to come up with a set of restrictions for their levels, or some additional tagging in the editor to specify to the engine where characters should and should not move. Instead, the only hints from the level-design tool were "walkable" floor flags, but little or no special marking of walls, cliffs, and other pathing hazards.

Since we waited too long to address the problem, better solutions such as walk boxes or walk zones would have taken too long to retrofit into the more than 100 levels already in the can. Instead, we spent weeks making small iterative fixes to the system to hide the most extreme errors and turn what was an "A" bug into a "B" or "C" level problem.

4. Feature and data timing

This is a fairly common problem in games I've worked on, and VAMPIRE was no different. The technology team typically looks at the development schedule and schedules that entire block of time to achieve a certain feature set. Often, however, new engine features get added too late in the schedule to be utilized fully by the designers and artists.

This happened several times during VAMPIRE. Some of the more interesting special effects, for example, were added only a few weeks before the data was to be locked down for final testing. Other features that we added couldn't even be implemented extensively. For example, we added a more flexible shader language so late that only one to two percent of the surfaces in the game were able to take advantage of it. Some features that we had originally planned for the engine, like bump mapping and specular lighting, were cut completely from the initial release because there was insufficient time both to complete the feature and to create art to drive it.

We softened the blow somewhat by moving some of these features to a planned patch, which would add them later if the game proved successful. Unfortunately there are very few programming tasks that don't require some sort of artist or designer input to find their way into the finished product, so unless programmers spend the last six months of the project doing nothing but fixing bugs, some of this is inevitable. We can justify it to a degree by looking toward the likely sequel or add-on projects as a way to take advantage of some of the engine work that was underutilized in the original title.

5. Self-restraint

As the project was drawing to a close, we found that we ended up with a bit "too much game," as someone put it. From the start, we decided to author our data for a high end platform, so we'd have a good-looking game at the end of the 24-month schedule, and also because it's much easier to scale art down than up. Unfortunately, we never really started to rein in our art and design teams when we should have near the middle of the project. Instead, we continued to add more and more resources to the project, resulting in a minimum installation footprint of about 1GB.

We authored all our textures in 32-bit color and then scaled them down at load time for 16-bit cards. Our models were also extremely detailed

(1,000 to 2,000 triangles each, on average) and relied on automatic level-of-detail algorithms to scale them down for slower machines. We lit our levels with relatively high light-map resolutions. All of this made the game look great on high-end systems but it meant the game was fairly taxing on low- to midrange systems.

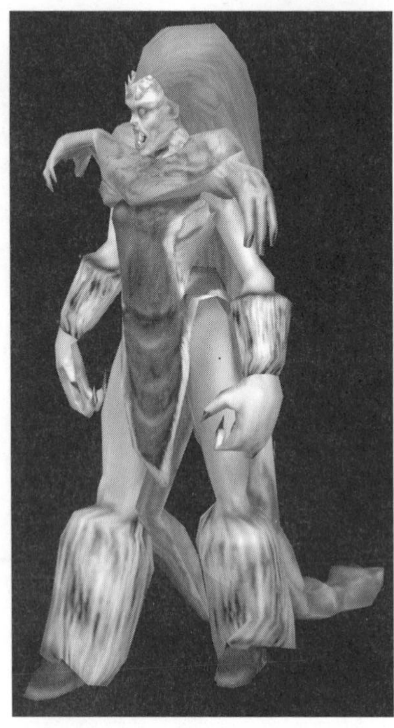

Characters were created with a budget of between 1,000 and 3,000 triangles. Boss characters, such as Ahzra the Tzimisce Elder were generally the most complex.

In the end, the game just barely fit on two CD-ROMs. We had originally planned to include both 16-bit and 32-bit versions of the game textures and allow players to choose which version to install, but after all the art was completed there was no room on the CD for more than one version. Likewise for sounds: we wanted to include multiple quality levels but space prevented this. We actually compressed most of the voice samples with MP3 and had to remove several sounds from the game in order to fit it on two CDs.

In the end, our game looked gorgeous but had difficulty running on machines with less than 128MB of RAM—and even then, it used a fair amount of space on a swap drive. This glut of resources will also make it more difficult if we choose to port the game to a more limited console environment.

At Last, Redemption

For the first project from a new development startup, I can't imagine how things could have gone much better than they did, except perhaps if we could have avoided shipping it the same year as DIABLO II. As a company, we managed to accomplish the three most important things in this business: not running out of money, not losing any team members, and actually shipping the product. Our publisher remained committed to the project throughout its life cycle, and even increased their support as the project continued to take shape.

The course of development was amazingly smooth, with very few surprises or conflicts along the way. In this industry, you can almost bet that at some point in a two-year development cycle something traumatic will happen to either the development team or its publisher, but for us the waters were remarkably calm. About the most exciting thing to happen during development was when we lost our entire RAID server while attempting to add drivers to it, resulting in the loss of a few months' worth of archived e-mails.

Our good fortune allowed the team to focus strictly on the game and prevented distractions from outside the company. Also, keeping our company focused on just one title and resisting the frequent temptation to take on more work and more staff allowed everyone to be on the same team with little or no secondary distractions. Hopefully, by avoiding feature creep and a four-year "death march" kind of ending to this saga, we can avoid a lot of the burnout that we have seen and often experienced on other teams. By maintaining links with both the fan community through our web board, and with the developer community at large by attending shows like GDC, E3, and Siggraph, our team was able to keep a positive attitude and high energy level throughout the schedule. We remain convinced that small development teams with a single-title focus are the best way to ship quality titles consistently, so our plans moving forward are to staff up gradually from 12 to perhaps 16 people over the next few months and embark on our next two-year ordeal a little older, a little wiser, and just a tiny bit larger.

63

Ensemble's

Age Of Empires

by matt pritchard

I had an experience in a local computer store recently that caused me to burst out laughing. I had stopped to self-indulgently admire the top-10 PC games display when I overheard the following exchange between two young men:

"What do you think about this one, Age Of Empires?" wondered the first.

His companion shot back, "Aww, the Borg at Microsoft just combined Warcraft and Civilization to cash in on these kind of games."

Always eager to boost our sales, I took this opportunity to tell the young men how AOE wasn't the creative product of a giant corporation, but of a small group of talented people living right in their own backyard. For us, Age Of Empires was not only a game of epic proportions, it was an epic journey for a small band of people determined to turn an idea into a real game company. Along the way, we laughed, we cried, we consumed pizza and caffeine, and we learned a great deal about making games.

Back-Story

Age of Empires gives a real-time-strategy treatment to early world history, from 5000 BC to 800 AD, in what many see as the real-time update to the classic Civilization. Players choose one of the major ancient peoples (each with their own characteristic strengths and weaknesses) and bring their nation from Stone-Age squalor up the cultural-technological ladder to the sprawling splendor of the empires of antiquity. The action unfolds in real time—players harvest grain, conduct diplomacy, marshal troops from the genre's godlike perspective, watching their shining white cities unfold across jewel-green landscapes. Strong play balance and beautiful presentation have made this game a pillar of the genre.

Designing the Past Perfect

Obviously, Age Of Empires didn't start out looking like the final product. Despite some accusations, Dawn Of Man (AOE's original title) wasn't created to be a Warcraft II clone. (In fact, Warcraft II wasn't released until after AOE's development was well underway.) Instead, the final design was evolved and refined over time, with a few significant design events along the way. One of the best things I think you can have in a game company is a staff that plays a lot of different games. This was true of our staff at Ensemble, and was helped in no small part by programmer Tim Deen's habit of buying and actually playing almost every new PC game as it came out.

It was Tim who brought WARCRAFT II to the attention of the rest of the Ensemble staff. At that time, many of AOE's game elements, such as resource management, empire building, and technology research, were taking clear shape. However, we didn't really know what to do about combat. WARCRAFT II was a splash of cold water in the face, waking us up to how much fun real-time combat could be. Several times a week, the staff would stay late to play multiplayer WARCRAFT. These impromptu events continued until AOE reached the point in development when it became more fun to play than WARCRAFT.

Game Data

Release Date: 1997

Publisher: Microsoft

Genre: Strategy

Platform: Windows 95 & Macintosh

Another major shift occurred a little over halfway through development, when the designers were looking at AOE's localization plans. They realized that AOE would be sold in Asia, but didn't include a single culture from that region. We held a company-wide meeting and decided to add early Asian civilizations to the early European, African, and Middle-Eastern tribes that we'd already developed. Though the addition would create more work for the artists and designers, the enhanced appeal that the game would have in Asia would make this a profitable decision.

All of these changes occurred because the game's designers weren't afraid of taking design input from the rest of the staff. Making a game that everyone would be proud of and would want to play was something that got more than just lip service at Ensemble.

Perhaps the best example of this core value is the Wonder, the penultimate building that a player can build and use to win the game. In early 1997, AOE was great for slugfests, but everyone felt that the game play needed to offer something more. Numerous ideas were tried and rejected. Then Mark Terrano, our communications programmer, hit upon the idea of building an "Armageddon Clock" that would force players to drop what they're doing and respond to the new challenge. AOE is chock full of little ideas and touches that were thought up by the artists and programmers. This participation tangibly increased the sense of ownership and pride that we all took in the game.

One of things that is truly underappreciated about the designer's job is play balancing. The designers spent months and months adjusting costs, strength, speed, and many other statistics in an effort to create a game that was fun to play and yet didn't offer any loopholes or cheats. At this point, I realized that Tim Deen was truly a gamer's gamer. During development, if any of the various iterations of AOE's design opened up a way for one player to take advantage of another player and thus make the game one-dimensional, Tim would find it. And when we didn't believe his assessments, he would promptly show us by using the loophole to kick our butts at the game. For the better part of a year, play balancing was a prominent task, and it paid off in giving AOE more staying power and better game play than many others in the recent crop of real-time strategy games.

Blazing the Multiplayer Path

Multiplayer support was an integral part of the early design, and AOE was structured in such a way that most of the game could not differentiate between human and computer players. When DirectX first came out, it appeared that DirectPlay would be the best choice for providing communications over the widest variety of connection types. To support a high number of moving units, we went with a modified game synchronous model, where the entire game is simultaneously run on all machines. Only moves, changes, and commands are communicated to other machines. This approach has the advantage of minimizing the amount of data that has to be sent. The unanticipated danger of using this model is that it can generate a condition where the game on one machine becomes out of sync with the game on other machines.

This caused some very hard-to-reproduce bugs with AOE. Load metering, the process of determining how much bandwidth the game updates required, was done before the computer AI was completed, and was based on the data flow model taken from human players. As a result, we initially missed the fact that computer players would sometimes issue large numbers of commands in quick bursts. We did, however, address this oversight with the first patch. An area where AOE's communications worked out better than expected was the game's ability to dynamically adapt to latency. A sliding window delays the actual game time when a command takes effect, so that all players receive the command and do not have to pause before executing it.

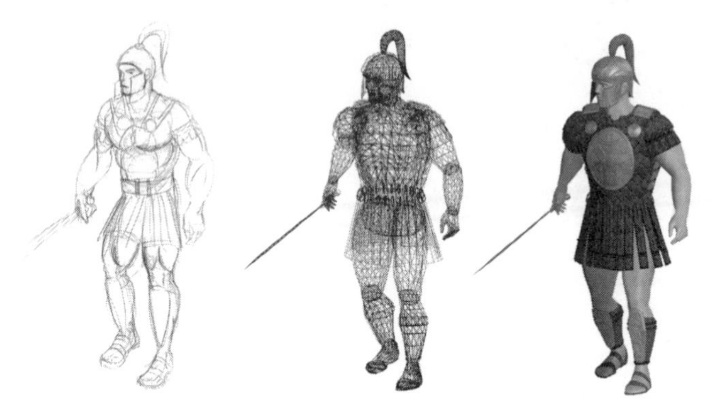
All of the 2D sprites in AOE began life as 3D models.

The problem of handling players who have dropped from a game presented Mark Terrano with difficult challenges. Since drops are unpredictable, usually there is no way to know what happened. The problem could be the game logic, Winsock, the physical connection, or the ISP, and could exist on either the sender's or receiver's side. Getting the game to handle drops by anyone at anytime required a great deal of work.

One of the lessons learned from the multiplayer experience was to make full use of communications testing tools, such as automated logs and checksums. Also, we discovered that creating a simple communications data flow simulator program can provide great benefits and isolate the communications code from the rest of the game.

DirectPlay also turned out to be problematical. Difficult-to-reproduce bugs, quirky behavior, and poor documentation made the going more difficult. Guaranteed packet delivery for IPX was one of the more notable examples. At the CGDC, Microsoft promised to deliver this feature with DirectX 5 and even included in the beta. However, when DirectX was actually released, this feature was nowhere to be found. The cost of that one missing item was the extra time we had to spend writing our own guaranteed delivery system and a bad packet generator program with which to test it.

Painting the Scene

AGE OF EMPIRES contains 20MB of in-game sprite graphics. Even though all of the displays are 2D, we decided early on that all of the graphics in the game would be taken from 3D models. We used 3D Studio and 3D Studio MAX for art production. Because 3D rendering is so time-consuming, each artist was issued two machines each, both usually 200MHz Pentium Pros with 128MB of RAM, which at the time was better equipment than the programmers were using. The objects in the game were created as 3D models that had anywhere from a couple thousand to 100,000 polygons. The models were then textured, animated, and rendered out to a .FLC (Autodesk Animator) file with a fixed 256-color palette.

So far, the process I've described is identical to that of many other games. At this point, however, the artists added another time-consuming step. The .FLC files were handed off to a 2D specialist, who took the animation apart frame by frame and "cleaned up" each image with Photoshop. The clean-up process involved sharpening detail and smoothing the edges of the irregular shapes. Since most of the sprites in AOE had screen dimensions of only 20 to 100 pixels in each direction, the visual quality improvement that we realized was significant. When AOE was shown at the 1997 E3, the artists received numerous compliments on their work from their peers at other companies.

The choice to go with 3D models for the in-game objects provided benefits for other art needs, as they were readily available for use in the static background scenes that appear on the menu, status screens, and the various cinematics. The cinematics, including the three-minute opener, were a fulltime project unto themselves.

The 256-color palette (actually 236) used in AOE was something of a problem. The palette was chosen and set in stone at the very beginning of the project, before most of the models and textures had been created. As a result, it turned out that some portions of the color spectrum, such as browns for wood textures, had too few available colors to get the best visual quality.

The palette wasn't revised during the development process because that would have required rerendering and touching up every image in the game—far too expensive time-wise. On the other hand, the palette did have a wide and balanced range of colors, which contributed to the overall bright and cheerful look of the game's graphics. If we do another 8-bit color game, we'll generate the palette at a point further along in the development process.

Early Asian civilizations had to be added when Microsoft announced plans to distribute AOE in Asia.

Going for Speed

Performance is an issue for all but the simplest of games, and it certainly was for AOE. When I joined Ensemble, the game was still in an early form and slow. The two biggest problems were the graphics engine (which was just plain slow) and various update procedures, which produced occasional pauses of up to a second in game play. If we were going to sell to anything but the most cutting-edge systems, some serious optimization was in order.

The story gets personal here, as I did a great deal of the work on this part of AOE. I started by trying to get a handle on what the over 100,000 lines of C++ code did (the source would rise to over 220,000 lines before it was finished). After spending a few weeks studying what we had, I proposed a major overhaul of the graphics engine structure, including writing a major portion in assembly. AOE's original design team asked if the frame rate of a benchmark scenario could be raised from its current 7–12 fps to 20 fps. I told them yes. Inside I was sweating bullets, hoping that I could deliver that much improvement.

I couldn't just go ahead and rip out the old graphics engine, as it would hold up everyone else, so I spent the next five months working mostly on the new engine. Along the way, I managed some incremental improvements that upped the frame rate to 10–14 fps, but the big breakthrough came during an all-nighter, when the last piece of the new design was put into place. Much to my surprise, the benchmark scenario was now running at 55 fps. It was exciting to come back into the offices the next day and see the formerly sluggish animation running silky smooth.

But my work was not all on the graphics engine. I also spent a great deal of time identifying and optimizing myriad processes in the game. Since the game was real-time, many improvements involved spreading out a process over several turns rather than of stopping the game until it completed. In the end, the optimizations paid off handsomely and allowed us to raise the default resolution from 640×480 to 800×600.

A practical lesson that I learned from this experience was how much additional overhead and slowdown a game can acquire as it approaches completion. Often, early in a game project the engine will show great performance—but the game's not finished. When you replace the simple test levels with the complex final levels, add all the AI, UI, and bells and whistles, you can find a world of difference in actual performance. This was true for AOE as well. As we approached completion and all of the loose ends were tied off, many of the performance gains were traded in for new features.

Things That Worked Out (S)well

1. The game was broken into separate engine and game components

About halfway through development, there was concern that the code base had expanded far enough beyond the initial design in some areas that every new change and addition would look like an ugly hack. Lead programmer Angelo Laudon and Tim Deen took two weeks and separated the code base into two separate sections, the general engine (Genie), and the game itself (Tribe). The conversion was very successful and allowed the AOE programmers to retain a nicely object-oriented design. The benefit here was that it made the code much easier to modify and extend, saving the programmers a great amount of development time.

2. We made the game database driven

Thanks to the object-oriented design, almost nothing about any object in AOE is hard-coded into the program. Instead, huge tables of information describe every characteristic of every object that appears in the game. The designers used a system of over forty Paradox tables to control and shape the game. As a result, they were able to constantly update and tweak the game, and then test their changes without having to involve a programmer.

3. We stayed in close contact and working together with the publisher

I can't say enough good things about how the close contact with our publisher, Microsoft, helped the development of AOE. By keeping them "in the loop" on our progress, they worked with us instead of against us as things happened. The best example of how this relationship aided development is the way we handled schedule slippage. Each time something took longer than expected or new problems cropped up, we effectively communicated the delay to Microsoft. With a clear understanding of what was happening and why, they reaffirmed their commitment to assist us in producing a quality game, whatever amount of time that would take. So instead of being panic-stricken and whacked out, we remained professional and focused on our goals.

4. We played our own game

While this may sound simple, it's very important. Throughout the development process, every person in the company not only playtested, but played AOE with the purpose of having fun. As a result, we were very in tune with why the game was fun, and what people were likely to get out of it. We had 20 guys who were determined not to let the game play be compromised or watered down.

5. Performance was good

Performance truly means a lot if you want your game to have broad appeal. AGE OF EMPIRES can adequately run an eight-player game in 16MB of RAM on a P120 system. Contrast that with TOTAL ANNIHILATION, which requires 32MB and at least a 200MHz CPU for an eight-player game. Achieving this level of performance required a group effort. The programmers expended extra energy on keeping memory consumption in check and identifying bottlenecks, while the artists culled extra animation frames and reorganized the graphics to maximize free memory.

6. The company respected its employees

I have to say something about the way Ensemble Studios treated its employees and their families. It is well-known that software development, especially game development, involves great sacrifices of time and can be hell on personal relationships. Ensemble's thoughtful management respected that by going out of their way to include families at numerous company dinners and other events, and to make them feel welcome to come by the offices at any time.

Additionally, after crunching hard to meet a milestone, they would insist that employees take a couple of days off to catch up with their families. People were allowed flexible schedules if they needed them, and flowers or other tokens of appreciation were sent to the families periodically. The result of this deliberate action by company management should be obvious; company morale and loyalty was higher than I have ever seen in fourteen years of software development. My wife loves my job as much as I do.

7. Localization really worked

From the beginning, we knew that Microsoft wanted to release AOE in six different languages, including Japanese. About halfway through development, we updated our code base to provide full localization support. This required stripping out and replacing all text references in the source code and maintaining all game text in an external resource file. It also placed severe restrictions on how we could draw and display the text. We had to use the Windows GDI exclusively, something most games shun like the plague. It also meant that interface items such as buttons had to be sized to hold the largest possible translated form of their captions, limiting the clever things one could do with the design of the user interface.

But we buckled down and did it, following the guidelines exactly. And to our pleasant surprise, the conversion was swift and painless. We felt even better when the translators at Microsoft told us that localizing AOE was the smoothest and most pain-free project they had ever done. The benefit to us was enormous in that we had a single executable program file that was the same for all translated versions of the game, thus avoiding the huge headache that comes with tracking bugs and releasing updates for multiple versions.

8. We worked as a team that respected all its members

A project of AOE's size required that we all work together in close quarters for extended periods of time. One of our expressed criteria in hiring new people is that we must be able to respect each other. This respect, complemented by the company's actions towards its employees, fostered an excellent sense of family and team spirit among everyone. We avoided having different groups develop a sense of isolation from the project, and as a result, attitudes and spirits remained high even during the worst crunch time. Had tempers flared and cliques developed, I honestly don't believe that AOE could have made it out the door in 1997.

Things That Went Wrong Or We Could Have Done Better

1. We held the beta test too late in the development cycle

A public beta test of AOE was held in August 1997, but we didn't come near to exploiting the full potential of it. We were too close to the end of the project to make any game play changes, despite the wealth of useful feedback we received. Manuals were already set to be printed, and most of the design had been set in stone. All we could really do was fix any bugs that were found. For any future projects, we vowed to hold the beta testing earlier.

2. There was inadequate communication with the QA people at Microsoft

For most of the project, bug reporting was handled through a database and developers didn't directly communicate with the testers. As a result many bugs wound up taking much longer to resolve, and new features went untested. An intermediate database was simply not enough to let testers and developers know what the other was really thinking. In future projects, we would like to assign a specific tester to each programmer and have them communicate by phone every couple of days. Near the end of development, this did happen for a couple people—for them productivity with testing and bug resolution was drastically improved.

3. We sometimes failed to coordinate development through the leads

Yet another area where personnel communication could have improved the development was among our own teams. Each team—Programming, Art, Game Design, and Sound—has a lead person who is responsible for keeping track of what each member of his or her team is doing. The lead is the go-to person when someone outside has new requests for the team. As the development of AOE progressed and the pressures rose, adherence to this system broke down as people went direct to get their needs filled quickly. We paid a price for it. People didn't know about programming changes or new art that was added to the game, and the level of confusion rose, creating a time drain and distraction. We all had to stop at times just to figure out what was going on.

4. We failed to adequately test multiplayer games with modem connections

One problem with our development environment is that it isn't comparable to the typical end user system. During the course of development, the multiplayer portions of AOE were tested extensively. When we played a game in the office, our fast machines, stuffed full of RAM, communicated with each other on our high-speed LAN. When we tested Internet play, our communications were handled through the company's T1 line. One thing that we failed to realize in our testing was the fact that most players would be using dial-up modem connections to commercial Internet service providers. And it wasn't just us; the same situation applied to the testing labs at Microsoft. As a result, modem connection games were undertested. Bugs that were harmless when ping times were low resulted in dropped games for users on slower Internet connections. And our high-speed network masked the fact that under certain not-so-uncommon circumstances, AOE could require 15K of network bandwidth per second—six times what even a 56K modem can provide on the uplink side. As a result, we were taken a bit by surprise when reports of multiplayer game problems rolled in. Though our first patch fixed this problem, the situation was unacceptable. Now, each developer has a modem and several different ISPs are used, as modem testing is a big part of our testing process.

5. Portions of development relied on products that were not delivered on time

There was a second reason that modem games were undertested: problems with the delivery and quality of DirectPlay from Microsoft. Features that were promised, and even included in beta releases, weren't present when the delayed final release was delivered. DirectX 5a wasn't available to us until a month before the game shipped. In the meantime, our communications programmer was burning the midnight oil writing the functionality that was expected but not delivered. Waiting on promised drivers and SDKs is one of the harder things that developers have to deal with; even those with Microsoft as a publisher have no control over them.

6. We did not plan for a patch

The version 1.0a patch, even though it was a success, was problematic in that as a company we had not planned for it. The general argument is that if you know you are going to need to release a patch, then you shouldn't be shipping the game in the first place. While one can take that stand, it's also a fact that no game developer's testing can match that of the first 50,000 people who buy and play the game. Your customers will do and try things that you never dreamed of, while running on hardware and drivers that you never heard of. Looking around, nearly every significant game released this year has had a patch or update released for it. Rather than deny this reality, we would like to allocate resources and expectations in the future so that we can release any necessary updates days or weeks after our games ship, rather than months.

7. We didn't manage "surprise" events as well as we could have

During the development period, we experienced several sudden events that caused us, as a company, to stop what we were doing. These events included the creation of a demo version of the game and materials for press coverage of AOE. While most of the events were beneficial to the company, we weren't very good at handling them, and they threw off our schedules. These disruptions mostly came late in development, when their impact was felt the most. One of our goals for future games is to minimize the impact of unplanned events by giving advance notice when possible and restricting them by minimizing the number of people that have to respond to them.

8. We didn't take enough advantage of automated testing

In the final weeks of development, we set up the game to automatically play up to eight computers against each other. Additionally, a second computer containing the development platform and debugger could monitor each computer that took part. These games, while randomly generated, were logged so that if anything happened, we could reproduce the exact game over and over until we isolated the problem. The games themselves were allowed to run at an accelerated speed and were left running overnight. This was a great success and helped us in isolating very hard to reproduce problems. Our failure was in not doing this earlier in development; it could have saved us a great deal of time and effort. All of our future production plans now include automated testing from Day One.

The AGE OF EMPIRES development team. The author is second from the right in the row of guys who are kneeling.

Patching It All Up

Once AOE was shipped off to production, we threw ourselves a big party to let off some stress. It turns out we were a bit premature in our revelry. Shortly after AOE arrived on store shelves we began receiving feedback on problems with the pathfinding, unit AI behaviors, population limits, and multiplayer play. Additionally, some bugs were found that a player could exploit to gain an unfair advantage in the game. Management was stirred to action at both Ensemble and Microsoft, and the decision to do a patch for AOE was made. Although time was taken away from other projects, and it took longer than desired, the patch was a success; it vastly improved the quality of multiplayer games, fixed the bugs, and addressed the game play concerns that had been raised. And that brings the development of AOE to where it is today, which I hope is somewhere on your hard drive...

SECTION II

Sequels and Sophomore Outings

A sequel project (and really any company's next game after producing a signature hit) marks a particular point in a company's life-cycle. You've made a game that sold, and maybe even made a profit. Your game idea is no longer a crazy experiment, it's a proven commodity. The fly-by-night startup is an actual business. People know your company's name, there are fans out there with Web sites and bulletin boards, talking about you. And your publisher is eager to make the next deal, in fact they've already penciled it in for Q4 of next fiscal year: the sequel.

There is, no question, a luxurious feeling to doing a sequel. It's a victory lap, an encore. So what if you're not blazing a trail into unknown territory—at least you get to travel in comfort. You don't have to explain your high concept to glassy-eyed listeners, waving your hands in the air to evoke an imaginary interface. Publishers love it. They know you're a bankable commodity now; they'll take your calls and return your e-mails. You are, to some extent, resting on your laurels, and a soft comfy perch it is.

At first glance it seems like easy money—if they bought the first one, they'll buy the next. But when you sit down to make a sequel, you realize it's not quite so simple. There are unique challenges involved. Sequels and follow-ups are harder than they look, as the postmortems in this section tell us.

It's true that any company making a sequel has several advantages. Obviously, name-recognition is one—there is a pool of people who bought the first game and presumably liked it, who will immediately be interested in the next one. Financially, there's a certain guaranteed level of sales. There is already a community of players out there who will buzz about it on gaming boards, and publicize details of the sequel on their Web sites. Game journalists will be more willing to write a preview, since the article has a ready-made hook. And, for better or for worse, you will have already have working code, proven game mechanics, and art assets to recycle or use for inspiration when you get down to work.

Crucially, the release of the first game has provided enormously rigorous testing of key technology and design elements. No amount of in-house quality assurance testing can replace hundreds of thousands of users out there in the real world installing your game on any and all machine types and display devices, now matter how inappropriate or unlikely. If it's for a gaming console, an army of twelve-year-old boys will have devoted weeks of their time to discovering any and all flaws in the design and technology. Any flaws in the renderer, any compatibility problems, will have been announced in magazine reviews, and shouted out in ALL CAPS on popular gaming forums. The almighty power of the Internet will leave no aspect of your game unmolested.

The feedback will also be about the design, and no matter how painful it is, it is worth listening to. Any imbalance in the gameplay and any exploitable bugs in the level design will have been thoroughly hashed over on half a dozen Web sites, most likely with illustrative screenshots. The judgment-calls you agonized over in design meetings will be re-argued endlessly in public, and it may be clear that you should reverse your decision in your next game, or at least try an alternate path. Regardless, you will know the public's opinion, most likely expressed in jauntily intercapped slang.

The advantages are obvious, but the difficulties of creating a sequel game are not always as apparent until you attempt to do it. The basic challenge of making a sequel is paradoxical—your job is to make exactly the same game, but more/different/better. Some things (graphics? story?) have to change, but others (audio? weapons?) must be exactly the same, yet somehow improved and more intense. You have to decide what the essence of the game is, what the fundamental thing about it that worked was, and then deliver it again in an improved package, with better graphics and a few new toys that extend the basic concept without deviating from it. The games discussed in this section all seemed to succeed by innovating on the small level, expanding and enhancing existing features rather than transforming them.

The first time the game shipped, it had nothing to live up to. This time, there will be a whole set of user expectations. Not everyone likes the same game in the same way, and some people will inevitably complain that what they liked about the original game is gone. Everyone will have some idea of what you should do, or should have done, with the sequel, how the basic formula can be improved. Not everyone will be pleased.

Also, as noted above, you will have existing assets to draw upon—code, design ideas, artwork. Again, you will have to decide what to keep, what to tinker with, and what to scrap wholesale. Sloppy hacks put in at the last minute to ship the first game can be rewritten cleanly or papered over and kept around for next time. The question of when to fix broken code and when to rewrite from scratch seems to be one of the most persistent and vexing in the whole field of software management. The arguments on both sides are endless—the pressure to reuse assets to save production time is balanced against the appeal of the clean slate.

It is worth noting, of course, that by the time the sequel ships, the entire industry will have moved forward. Any code you keep from the first game may be three or four years old by that time, an eternity in software years. The minimum acceptable standard for certain features may have changed utterly, and Moore's Law waits for no man.

On the production side, you will have a whole history of development processes to follow again, or change around—your own in-house postmortem of what you did right and wrong last time. Did weekly staff meetings work, or turn into an expensive waste of time? How bad was the crunch phase, and how can it be avoided? This can be difficult to evaluate, especially when it involves key personalities on the team. But a good, honest postmortem can save months of work and hassle and pain. Get it all out on the table, and the team will be stronger for it.

Finally, there is the issue of team fatigue. No one is more uniquely qualified to do a sequel than the existing team, but chances are they are ones most in need of a change. Unless they're very lucky or truly excited about the project, they'll be sick and tired of hockey or orcs or rabbits or whatever the first game was about and be aching to work on something new and completely different. Your hotshot renderer jockey may not feel like polishing up old code—he or she may only be interested in writing next-generation applications. After all (they may well argue), the team shipped a successful game, and their reward should be a chance to be creative again, not to grind out the same thing again.

Even if your company's second game is not a true sequel, many of the problems and opportunities are the same. If your first game was a success there are still challenges of continuity, because your company now has an identity, a vibe associated with it. It's a brand that you must now manage. You have a company culture and a set of production processes that have now shipped one game, and you have to make decisions about what to keep and change next time around.

Viewed in the wider context of the games industry, sequels are likewise a double-edged sword. In a sense, they help keep the industry alive by reducing risk, guaranteeing a certain amount of sales. This is incredibly important in an industry as expensive and as risky as the game industry. An average game published by a major game publisher costs $5–10 million to develop, and requires 1–3 years in development time and a team of 10–50 developers and artists. Anything that increases the odds of a decent return on this investment is important, especially since many, many games never make back their production costs, while a handful of hits take most of the profits. Sequels, and the brand name any studio represents, offer a modicum of stability in a desperately random industry. From the point of view of the consumer, buying a sequel means reducing their risk. They have a better sense of what's inside the box and whether it's worth investing their hard-earned $50.

The other side of the argument is that sequels and copycat titles lack innovation. The dull logic of capitalism supports design by formula—what sold before will sell again. The result is that the industry fails to move improve and invent as fast as it should, and the shelves of retail outlets are stacked with versions of the same title year in and year out. Clearly both sides of the argument contain an element of truth.

But sequels advance the field in their own way by refining existing styles of gameplay, innovating within known genres rather than creating new ones. As we can see in the following postmortems, sequels are a chance to use what has been learned in the first outing. Experimentation is useful, but only if we take the time to learn from the results, to build on the foundation. Someday the medium of digital games will mature, and we will have an established tradition and body of technique to build on when we make a game. In a sense, the sequels here are a glimpse of what that future will look like.

Blizzard Entertainment's
DIABLO II

by erich schaefer

The original DIABLO went gold on the day after Christmas in 1996, after a grueling four-month crunch period. We hadn't put any thought into what game to do next, but as most developers can probably relate to, we were pretty certain we weren't ready to return to the DIABLO world after such a long development cycle. The only thing we were certain of was that we wanted to avoid another crunch like we had just experienced. DIABLO II went gold on June 15, 2000, after a grueling 12-month crunch period. After DIABLO shipped, we spent about three months recovering and kicking around game ideas for our next project, but nothing really stuck.

Back-Story

The DIABLO series belongs to one of the oldest of all genres, the dungeon crawl—a lone adventurer exploring labyrinths full of monsters, traps, and treasure, accumulating experience, ability, and power. In their sequel to the original, Blizzard added a skill system to help differentiate characters and suit different playing styles and further polished the jewel-like simplicity of the game to refine the genre almost as far as it could go. DIABLO II's stripped-down one-click interface, online competition, and dynamically generated dungeons make for simple, addictive, endless exploration.

The idea of returning to DIABLO began to creep into the discussions, and after a couple of months of recuperation, we suddenly realized we weren't burned out on DIABLO anymore. We dusted off the reams of wish-list items we had remaining from the original, compiled criticisms from reviews and customers, and began brainstorming how we could make DIABLO II bigger and better in every way.

DIABLO II never had an official, complete design document. Of course, we had a rough plan, but for the most part we just started off making up new stuff: four towns instead of the original game's one; five character classes, all different from the previous three; and many new dungeons, vast wilderness tile-sets, and greatly expanded lists of items, magic, and skills. We wanted to improve upon every aspect of the original. Where DIABLO had three different armor "looks" for each character, DIABLO II would use a component system to generate hundreds of variations. Where DIABLO had "unique" boss monsters with special abilities, DIABLO II would have a system for randomly generating thousands of them. We would improve the graphics with true transparency, colored light sources, and a quasi-3D perspective mode. Level loads would be a thing of the past. The story would be factored in from the beginning and actually have some bearing on the quests.

We knew creating this opus would be a big job. Because we had the gameplay basics already polished, we figured we would hire some new employees, create some good tools, and essentially make four times the original game doing only two times the work. We estimated a two-year development schedule. The DIABLO II team comprised three main groups: programming, character art (everything that moves), and background art (everything that doesn't move), with roughly a dozen members each. Design was a largely open process, with members of all teams contributing. Blizzard Irvine helped out with network code and Battle.net support. The Blizzard film department (also in Irvine) contributed the cinematic sequences that bracket each of DIABLO's acts, and collaborated on the story line.

Game Data

Release date: June 28, 2000

Publisher: Blizzard Entertainment

Genre: dungeon crawl

Platforms: Windows and Macintosh

Full-time developers: 40

Length of development: more than 3 years

Development hardware used: Typical programmer workstation: 500 MHz Pentium II running Windows NT with 128MB RAM and 9GB hard drive. Typical artist workstation: dual 500 MHz Pentium IIs running Windows NT with 256MB RAM and 14GB hard drive.

Development software used: 3D Studio Max, Photoshop, Microsoft Developer Studio/Visual Studio and SourceSafe

Notable technologies used: Glide, Direct3D, RAD Game Tools' Bink, DirectSound3D, and Creative Labs' EAX.

Almost all of DIABLO II's in-game and cinematic art was constructed and rendered in 3D Studio Max, while textures and 2Dinterface elements were created primarily with Photoshop. The programmers wrote in C and some C++, using Visual Studio and SourceSafe for version control.

Blizzard North started out as Condor Games in September 1993. The first contracts we landed were ports of Acclaim's QUARTERBACK CLUB football games for handheld systems and, more significantly, a Sega Genesis version of JUSTICE LEAGUE TASK FORCE for Sunsoft. Silicon and Synapse, a developer that would later change its name to Blizzard Entertainment, was developing a Super Nintendo version of JUSTICE LEAGUE TASK FORCE. Condor ended up pitching the idea for DIABLO to Blizzard, and halfway through the resulting development process Blizzard's parent company acquired Condor, renaming us Blizzard North.

Throughout a tangled history of corporate juggling and ownership changes, Blizzard North has remained a very independent group. Our staff has grown steadily from about 12 at the start of DIABLO to 24 at the start of DIABLO II, and finally to our current group of more than 40. We concentrate 100 percent of our efforts on game development. To help keep this focus, Blizzard's headquarters in Irvine manages other functions, such as quality assurance, marketing, public relations, technical and customer support, as well as the operation of the Battle.net servers. Our parent company, Havas Interactive, deals with business functions such as sales, manufacturing, and accounting.

What Went Right

1. DIABLO II is still DIABLO

A constant theme in previews and reviews of DIABLO II was that we didn't change anything; it was more of the same. At first that struck us as odd. We kept less than one percent of the code and art from the first game. We rewrote the graphics engine, changed all the character classes and skills, shifted and expanded the setting, reworked and added to the magic items, brought back only a handful of our favorite monsters, and designed a ton of new gameplay elements, such as running, hirelings, left-click skills, and random unique monsters.

Why, then, did everyone think it was the same thing? In the end, we decided just to take it as a compliment. The play-testers and reviewers meant they were having exactly the same kind of fun that they had in the original game. Both DIABLO and DIABLO II provide a constant source of simple pleasures, many of which are perhaps too basic and obvious to mention in evaluations and reviews, but which are fundamental to their success.

We used the term "kill/reward" to describe our basic gameplay. Players continually kill monsters and get rewarded with treasure and experience. But the rewards don't stop there. We offer a steady stream of goals and accomplishments to entice the player to keep playing. There's always a quest that is almost finished, a waypoint almost reached, an experience level almost achieved, and a dungeon nearly cleared out.

On a smaller scale, we tried to make every single action fun. Moving around inventory items produces pleasing sounds. Monsters die in spectacular fashion, like piñatas exploding in a shower of goodies. We strove for overkill in this sense, in that players are constantly on the verge of something great—only a few mouse-clicks away from a dozen interesting things.

DIABLO II retained DIABLO's randomly generated levels, monsters, and treasure. This obviously allows for better replay potential, but also serves to make each player's game his or her own. Players feel an ownership of their own game experience in that they are actively generating a unique story. It's enjoyable to tell friends about what you have just done in the game, knowing for sure that they have not done the same thing. Simply following an online walkthrough won't help them accomplish goals without effort.

Finally, DIABLO and DIABLO II are easy to play. We used what we call the "Mom test"—could Mom figure this out without reading a manual? If we see new players struggling with how to sell items, we look at how they're trying to do it and make that way work too. We strove to make the interface as transparent as possible. You want to open a door? Left-click on it.

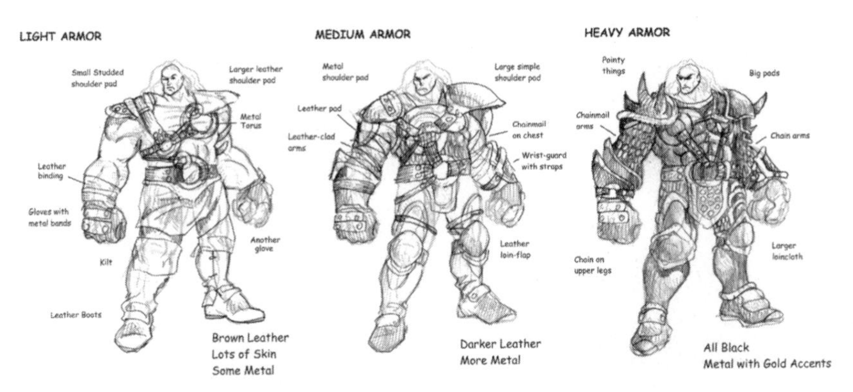

The player characters have modular armor of three varieties, light, medium, and heavy, which were mixed and matched to provide more individualized character appearances. "Paper dolls" created on paper and in Photoshop allowed mixing and matching of different pieces of armor to see how they worked together on the Barbarian.

Want to move to a target location? Left-click on it. Want to attack a monster, pick up an item, or talk to a non-player character? Well, you get the idea. It's amazing how many games have different controls and key combination for all these actions when simpler is always better.

2. Blizzard's development process

Blizzard's development process is designed to ensure that we make a great game. While our goal is to meet the milestones we set, our process, in terms of design and business, is structured to allow us to wait until the game is as good as it can be before we ship it. We recognize that not all developers have this same opportunity, but many of the methods we use along the way are applicable to any development environment.

First, we make the game playable as soon as possible in the development process. Our initial priority was to get a guy moving around on the screen and hacking monsters. This is what players would be doing most of the time, and it had to be fun. We were constantly able to hone the controls, pathfinding, and feedback mechanisms during the entire length of the game's development. Most importantly, it allowed us to determine what was fun to do, so we could provide more of it, and discover what was awkward or boring, so we could modify or remove it.

For instance, it became obvious very early that players would be killing large amounts of the same monsters, and those monsters would predominantly be attacking the players. This gave us the opportunity to plan for multiple death sound effects and additional attacking animations for each monster. If we hadn't experienced the core gameplay as early as we did, combat would have ended up feeling much more repetitive.

Also, we constantly reevaluate gameplay and features. Up until the very end, if we can make the game better we will, even if it means redoing big tasks. For instance, we decided that we didn't like the Bone Helmet graphics for the characters more than a year after having rendered them, but we went ahead and remade them, even though it took a couple of weeks and the collaboration of four artists. Only weeks away from scheduled beta testing, we scrapped our Act IV level layout schemes because they were just a bit too empty and similar. The last-minute fixes turned these levels into some of the best, befitting their climactic function. DIABLO II took more than 40 people and over three years, essentially because we made two or three games and pared them down to the best one.

Creating detailed sketches of settings, such as this hut in the Act III dock town of Kurast, preceded the actual modeling of background art. Much time was spent perfecting Act I since it would likely be used in a beta test or demo. The Amazon was the first character to be completed.

Another gigantic reason for our success is our open development process. We strive to hire people who love games, and we make games that we want to play. Every member of the team has input into all aspects of the game. Discussions around the halls and at lunch become the big ideas that shape the game. A programmer suggested to a designer the concept of gem-socketed, upgradeable weapons, which turned out to be a huge crowd-pleaser. A musician's dislike for the old frog-demon's animation inspired us to redo it. As a team, we don't have to wonder what our audience wants, because we are our audience.

If we like the game we are making—especially if, after two years of playing it, we are not bored to death—the game is clearly going to be a winner.

3. Character skill tree

Our most revolutionary new idea was the character skill tree. For a character to attain more powerful skills, he or she must master prerequisite skills. The ability for characters to branch into different areas of the skill tree, and to choose a level of specialization in each skill along the way, provides truly unique characters. At the start of development, we planned to use the model from the original DIABLO: characters would find and read books to learn spells and skills. Unlike DIABLO, which had 28 spells shared by all three characters, we wanted to create a separate group of 16 skills for each of our five new character classes. This would definitely have been an improvement, but every character of a given class would still end up knowing all the same skills as other members of their class.

Another problem was that players would likely be finding spell books for other character classes much more often than for their own. The skill tree solved these problems. The general idea was taken from the tech trees many strategy games employ. In strategy games, players advance by researching new technologies, which in turn open up further avenues of research. We adapted this to have our characters advance by choosing a new skill or strengthening an old skill every time they gain an experience level. Characters can generalize by choosing a wide variety of skills, or specialize by allocating many skill choices into a small group of skills.

We also created a strategy element of choosing skills you might not use, just so you can get to one further up the tree later.

The architecture in DIABLO combines aspects of many different cultures in order to arrive at an interesting mix that doesn't look too much like any single one. Here, the buildings of Travical from Act III are based on Mayan and Aztec references.

The end result of the skill tree is that one player can develop a Necromancer who kills monsters with a powerful poison dagger skill augmented by curses that cause monsters to fight each other, while his friend's Necromancer will summon hordes of skeletons to fight for him, and doesn't use any curses at all. The longevity of DIABLO II will be enhanced by the endless strategies that can be debated and experimented with.

4. Quality assurance

The task of testing a game of DIABLO II's scope, with its huge degree of randomness and its nearly infinite character skill and equipment paths, required a Herculean effort. We found we could not play-balance the climactic fight against Diablo without actually playing the entire game up to that point, because we could not predict what kinds of equipment a character might have, or what path through the skill tree he or she may have followed. This meant 20 or 30 hours of play for all the different characters, with a good variety of skill sets and equipment for each. Whenever we changed the game's treasure spawn rate or experience curve, we had to test it all again.

Further complicating matters were multiplayer and difficulty-mode balance. Would a party of five Paladins, each using a different defensive aura, be untouchable? After more than 100 hours of play, is a fire-based Sorceress unable to continue in "Hell mode"?

The QA team created a web-based bug-reporting database through which we categorized and tracked all bugs, balance issues, and gameplay suggestions. In the end, this list delineated more than 8,300 issues and suggestions. Well-organized teams of testers concentrated on different aspects of the game, divided into groups that would specifically test character skills, item functionality, monster types, and spawn rates, or explore the countless variations found in the random level generation system. The members of the QA team became very good players and astute observers of the progress of the game. Everything worked much more smoothly than our experiences with the original DIABLO.

While the player characters are only seen in the game as 75 pixels tall, all were modeled and rendered in high resolution for use on the character selection screen and in promotional materials. Here, the Paladin stands tall.

5. Simultaneous worldwide release

In the past, Blizzard's strategy for shipping its game has been to get games on North American retailers' shelves as quickly as possible after the English version of the game went gold. With the original DIABLO, we created our gold master on December 26, and some stores had it on the shelves by the 30th. Since DIABLO was released, the percentage of international customers had increased substantially, and with DIABLO II, we fully expect more than half of our sales to come from outside North America.

With such a large number of customers located outside the United States, for DIABLO II we decided that there would be significant advantages to coordinating the U.S. release to coincide with the rest of the world, not only to build anticipation for the product, but for the benefit and satisfaction of our customers as well. If we release a game in the United States first, customers in the rest of the world don't want to wait a few months while we translate and localize it for their country. Due in part to the international climate fostered by the Internet, players around the world all know about the game at the same time and want to get it while it's hot. They might buy the U.S. version under the table or search out a pirated copy. Worse, they might lose interest by the time we release a localized version.

DIABLO II's simultaneous worldwide release also allowed our marketing and PR departments to focus their efforts toward creating a frenzy of interest for the first week of sales. Although the simultaneous release was a logistical headache, it was all worth it in light of DIABLO II's superb success.

What Went Wrong

1. Developing the new Battle.net

We have always been very proud that our company launched Battle.net with the original DIABLO. Just a couple of months after DIABLO shipped, Battle.net was the largest online game service in the world. At DIABLO II's launch, Battle.net had more than 6 million unique active users. Despite the original DIABLO's success online, we knew as we began development that to create the type of multiplayer experience that we wanted to achieve in DIABLO II, we would need to fundamentally change the game network.

And, as we expected, this became one of our biggest challenges during development. We had to reinvent Battle.net's structure by melding existing technology with new programming and feature sets. This had implications across the board. We had to rethink everything—programming, hardware, bandwidth, staffing, online support, and how we could financially support this model while keeping it free.

Although the original Battle.net had been further modified to support STARCRAFT as a chat and matchmaking service, for DIABLO II we needed much more: game servers where the

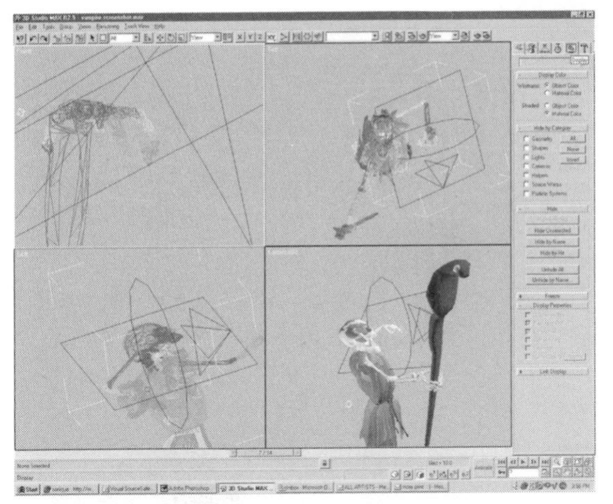

Characters and monsters, such as this Vampire, were created in 3D Studio Max. An in-house tool would render the files from many different angles (eight for all monsters, 16 for player characters), and export them in the file formats used in the game.

Realm games would actually be played, secure character-data servers, and game tracking systems. Trying to shoehorn these elements in the existing Battle.net system proved very difficult. For instance, we planned to have character names represent players in Battle.net, but it was designed to handle chatting between account names.

It took a lot of design and implementation time to arrive at our final system, where users see character names but have to send remote messages to account names. We initially believed that working with the existing Battle.net would save us time, but in retrospect, we learned that melding technologies is a difficult process, and in some cases, recoding instead of integrating is the better course of action.

2. Launching the new Battle.net

The success of Battle.net after DIABLO's launch created a new challenge for us. When DIABLO was released, Battle.net was a new online service. Basically, we were able to ramp up as more customers joined the service. When DIABLO II shipped, Battle.net had millions of users. The level of anticipation was higher than for any of our other games. We were well aware of the expectations, and we knew that no other company had ever attempted to create and sustain an online service that could support the type of usage DIABLO II would experience right out of the chute.

We spent countless hours preparing for Battle.net's DIABLO II debut. We teamed with the best ISPs in the word, and conducted months of internal and external beta testing. We ramped up bandwidth and hardware. We beefed up the Battle.net, quality assurance, and support service teams.

Although we had more than 100,000 people testing the DIABLO II Realms, having more than one million customers in just three weeks proved to be very different from beta testing. The beta test was very successful in uncovering many stability issues that were addressed before the launch. After the game shipped, we faced bugs that only appeared at much higher usage rates. The issues that we faced at launch were ones that could not have been simulated in a beta test of 100,000 people. It took a much larger influx of players to trigger certain situations.

Knowing the massive scope of what we were trying to achieve with Battle.net, we had measures in place at launch to help us deal with issues that arose as usage increased. For instance, we maintained both a team of programmers and the entire quality assurance department to solve problems as they appeared, and had our support team working overtime. We also had an action plan in place to increase hardware and bandwidth as needed. In some respects, we are victims of our own success. We underestimated sales, but we also underestimated the allure of playing on the Battle.net Realms. By solving the cheating problem in DIABLO and enhancing Battle.net with new features—such as the ability to see everyone's characters in the chat room—we seem to have attracted a larger share of Battle.net players than with any of our previous titles.

3. Graphics

Shortly before DIABLO II shipped, we began noticing some feedback from customers about the resolution of the graphics in the game. They were frequently labeled "outdated" or "pixelated." The shame is that the technology choices we made eclipsed the recognition of the fantastic job the artists did. We put a lot of effort into creating characters, monsters, and landscapes

The Barbarian, translated from the sketches into a full, high-polygon model. Each part of a character's armor (the head, the torso, the legs, each arm, a weapon, and a shield) was rendered separately with in-house tools.

with a lot of unique character. The game displays an incredible amount of action happening onscreen in an easy-to-follow manner. Still, with all the negative reaction, we probably should have done it differently. When we began producing art for DIABLO II in mid-1997, we investigated a lot of options. We mocked up a 3D engine and checked out voxel systems. It didn't take us long to go back to what we used in DIABLO: 2D graphics at 640×480 resolution with 8-bit color depth. At that time it was still the only way to get eight characters, upwards of 30 monsters, and upwards of 100 missiles all interacting on the screen at one time without sacrificing detail and atmosphere.

The graphics criticism caught us by surprise. We thought (and still think) that the game looked great. We probably should have built in a scaling technology to take advantage of hardware that could display the same graphics at higher resolutions. In any case, DIABLO II will probably be our last 2D game.

4. Tools

We developed the original DIABLO with almost no proprietary tools at all. We cut out all the background tiles by hand and used commercial software to process the character art. Spells and monsters were balanced by verbal estimates ("Hey, let's make the lightning about ten percent weaker.").

DIABLO II's vastly increased scale required much better tools, and we made some, but not enough. In many cases we created tools to speed up content creation, but then abandoned them. Too often, we decided to keep using inferior tools because we thought we were almost done with the game, and didn't want to take the time to improve them. Unfortunately, in most of these cases, we were not really almost done with the game, and in retrospect, a couple of weeks' worth of work would have helped in the year or more of development remaining.

The greatest deficiency of our tools was that they did not operate within our game engine. We could not preview how monsters would look in the environments they would inhabit. We couldn't even watch them move around until a programmer took the time to implement an AI. Even after that, an artist would have to hassle someone to get a current working build of the game to see his creation in action. Our sound effects engineers ended up painstakingly creating .AVI movie versions of animations in order to synch sounds with actions.

Our lack of tools created long turnaround times, where artists would end up having to re-animate monsters or make missing background tiles months after the initial work was completed. We should have made tools that let us create content within the game engine. Instead of just handing off a set of animations and hoping they looked all right when dropped into the game, artists should have had the ability to position and orchestrate their creations themselves. The extra tool development time would have been more than offset by increased efficiency and higher-quality work.

Some of the many locales in Act II: The Sand-Maggot lair (top), Jerhyn's Palace (middle), and the Sewers (bottom).

5. Save-game methodology

As much as we tried to make a frustration-free game, we seem to have failed some people with our save-game scheme.

Eschewing the common save-game feature we used in the original DIABLO's single player mode, where every facet of the game state can be saved to files and reloaded at will, we opted to make all modes behave more like DIABLO's multiplayer game. In DIABLO II, we do not save the world state. Reloading the game resets the location of monsters and treasures every time. The character is placed in the town he or she last visited, not in the wilderness or a dungeon.

Although this choice was slightly controversial around the office, it had a lot of advantages. For one, players could not get stuck, unable to progress further. At any time you can restart in town, refight the same monsters for more experience and loot, and return to a difficult area when ready. We created a waypoint system that allows characters in new games to return quickly somewhere close to where they quit the previous game. Finding new waypoints is a rewarding mini-goal during play. We also wanted to discourage the type of play where players feel they must always save the game right before a difficult section, then constantly die and reload until they get lucky and make it through. Finally, it was just easier to make single-player games and multiplayer games work the same way, and multiplayer requires the method we used.

A lot of players don't like our decision. They feel it is too inconvenient to have to fight their way back though the same areas and monsters. Many also want the opportunity to experiment with skill choices and equipment purchases, then later revert the game back to an earlier state if they don't like the results. There are good points on both sides, and we probably didn't spend enough time developing alternatives.

The Final Word

Many more things "went right" than could fit in that section. Our internally controversial plan to tell a separate but parallel story through our cinematic sequences seems to have succeeded, and the workmanship and quality of these sequences has set a new standard. Our marketing and PR departments did a fantastic job building customer awareness and creating a frenzy of interest. DIABLO II's music is outstanding, and along with an amazing array of sound effects, contributes hugely to the atmosphere of the game.

The development of DIABLO II is a remarkable success story. We got the opportunity to make the game we wanted to make—and the game we wanted to play. DIABLO II turned out to be a great game, one that many of us still play every day. Initial sales figures are phenomenal, and reviews have tended to be better than those of its predecessor. We have gained a lot of experience that should help us make even better games in the future. The only major downside to DIABLO II's development was the inhuman amount of work it required. A year-long crunch period puts a huge burden on people's relationships and quality of life.

Our biggest challenge for the future is figuring out how to keep making giant games like DIABLO II without burning out. As a start, we are hoping our experience will help us do a better job scheduling and managing the workload. We also believe that taking the time to make better tools will make things easier at the end of projects. Although I tried to avoid personalizing this article, I am extraordinarily proud of the entire development team. DIABLO II could not have happened without all the superb individual efforts, the incredible creativity, and the whole team's dedication to the project, for which they have earned my gratitude, and no doubt that of the legions of players who enjoy the game.

Epic Games' UNREAL TOURNAMENT

by brandon reinhart

UNREAL TOURNAMENT, released in November 1999, was, in a way, an accident. After the original UNREAL was completed, Epic wanted to follow up the project with some sort of add-on pack. UNREAL multiplayer code was very poor, so the team felt that an expansion that improved multiplayer would be ideal. As feature lists grew and patches to UNREAL were released, the add-on turned into a complete and independent game.

UNREAL TOURNAMENT has certainly seen a very nontraditional development cycle, one that I feel would not have succeeded in any other genre. Ultimately, our decisions paid off, because the game earned more than five "Game of the Year" awards and is consistently rated in the top ninetieth percentile in reviews. The online community is producing excellent expansions and modifications to the game and we feel that UNREAL TOURNAMENT will be around for a long time to come.

Back-Story

UNREAL TOURNAMENT is the sequel to one of the definitive first-person shooters, UNREAL. For UNREAL TOURNAMENT, Epic shifted from a hybrid of single-player exploration and multiplayer deathmatch to a purely gladiatorial format. UNREAL TOURNAMENT has no single defining innovation, but multiple game modes, inventive level design, and improved AI make it a solid incremental improvement to the genre.

Early Development

A proper look at the development of UNREAL TOURNAMENT begins with the completion of UNREAL. The Unreal engine was four years under development and the team was wearing down. When the game shipped, it met with a large amount of acclaim, but that positive image was tarnished over time as hardcore players began to complain about the terrible network support. The UNREAL team was now faced with several more months of work on the game, essentially to bring it to the point it should have been at when it was put on shelves.

Early in the process, plans were discussed to work on an official Epic add-on to UNREAL. The add-on would introduce much-improved network play, new maps, and probably some new game features. The original ideas for the add-on were never put on paper, and it never had a name. I was hired by Epic in August 1998 to assist with patching UNREAL. Eventually I started to write new code for the add-on with Steve Polge.

Initial work on the add-on in early summer 1998 was made difficult by the fact that Epic was a virtual company. The last year of UNREAL's development took place in Canada, with the U.S.-based Epic team flying back and forth to work with Digital Extremes in London, Ontario. When UNREAL was finished, no one at Epic wanted to travel anywhere, but at the same time the team recognized that they needed to move to a central location. The team decided to relocate all of its employees to Raleigh, N.C.

Game Data

Release date: November 1999

Publisher: Info Games

Genre: first-person shooter

Intended platform: Windows 95/98/NT, Linux

Project budget: $2 million

Project length: 18 months

Team size: approximately 16 developers

Code Length: 350,000 lines of C++ and UnrealScript

Critical development hardware: Pentium II 400s with 256MB RAM and Voodoo 2 or TNT-based cards

Critical development software: Microsoft Visual Studio, 3D Studio Max, UnrealEd

By September 1998 everyone was together or had a travel plan. Work started to come together rapidly on the add-on project. Steve Polge had laid the groundwork for several new game types, including Capture the Flag and Domination. The level designers had five or six good maps ready for testing. Throughout sporadic but intense meetings, the team agreed to focus the add-on entirely on improving the multiplayer aspect of the game with new features and better net code. The amount of content grew, and we soon realized we had a much larger project on our hands than we had originally thought. In November, after meetings with our publisher GT Interactive, Mark Rein suggested we turn the add-on into a separate game. Initially, the team opposed the idea. We wanted to finish the project quickly and move on to something fresh. The promise of a much higher profit potential, coupled with our recognition of the state of the project finally led us to agree with GT. In December, the name UNREAL: TOURNAMENT EDITION was chosen, with "Edition" subsequently dropped from the title.

A Game Takes Shape

Epic's internal structure is extremely liberal, probably the most liberal in the entire gaming industry. Programmers work on the projects they want to work on, with major features being assigned to whoever steps forward to take on the task. Artists work with level designers but are given significant design freedom. Level designers work on the kinds of maps they think would be cool. This design philosophy pervaded UNREAL TOURNAMENT's development. In December, I downloaded a sample of a new UNREAL mod under development by an Australian named Jack Porter. The mod, UBrowser, was a server browser using a Windows-like GUI. It was impressive, so I showed it to James Schmalz, lead designer at Digital Extremes, who said, "We need that, we need to hire this guy." A few weeks later Jack was a part of the team, expanding his UWindow GUI and reworking

UNREAL TOURNAMENT's menus to use the system.

Jack fit into the team perfectly, bringing a complete solution for the interface and menus as well as his own independent programming initiative. Weekly meetings infused order into our chaotic corporate structure. Everyone would debate and yell about what features were cool and what features sucked.

The assignment of major features was largely automatic. Tim Sweeney worked on improving net code and engine fixes. Steve Polge wrote the original AI code and focused on adding player orders and other improvements (in addition to filling out the new game types). Jack had the windowing system and a lot of menus to work on. Programmer Erik de Neve was in Europe putting together level-of-detail code as well as experimenting with next-generation technology. I worked on the single-player game, game-play features, scoreboards, HUDs, special level actors, tutorials, and wrote a lot of the game's story and character background content.

The characters in UNREAL TOURNAMENT were designed to be futuristic pit fighters. The selection of characters include ex-military specialists, criminals, and alien warriors such as the Necris Phayder Assassin pictured above.

The best features were added entirely by the initiative of individuals. Level designer Cedric "Inoxx" Fiorentino designed CTF-Face, an extremely popular Capture the Flag map. I added the Multi-Kill system after a short discussion with lead designer Cliff Bleszinski sparked the idea, and Jack implemented decals shortly before we shipped. It was this individual creativity that ultimately bound the team together. Each new feature infused everyone with the enthusiasm to add more.

Once the first batch of new player models, weapon models, and maps was completed we realized we had a game quite different from UNREAL. Feedback from the UNREAL deathmatch community (including the highly vocal QUAKE community's complaints) also drove our designs. Subtle alterations to player movement and control changed the feel of the game completely. Some changes in game play—such as whether to enable weapon-stay in single player—were controversial, so we held polls on popular UNREAL message boards.

Throughout the spring and summer of 1999, Epic was pursuing contract renegotiations with GT Interactive. Everyone believed the game could ship at any time, so development became stop-and-go. We would be in a code lockdown one week and adding major new features the next. The result of this jarring development cycle was good and bad. The periods of code lock-down allowed us more time to play-test and fix bugs, which contributed greatly to the game's overall polish. On the other hand, it prevented us from adding many features that would have otherwise been included, and it was detrimental to the morale of the team. We liked working on UNREAL TOURNAMENT, but it still felt like old technology to us. The world had seen the Unreal engine; we were ready to move on.

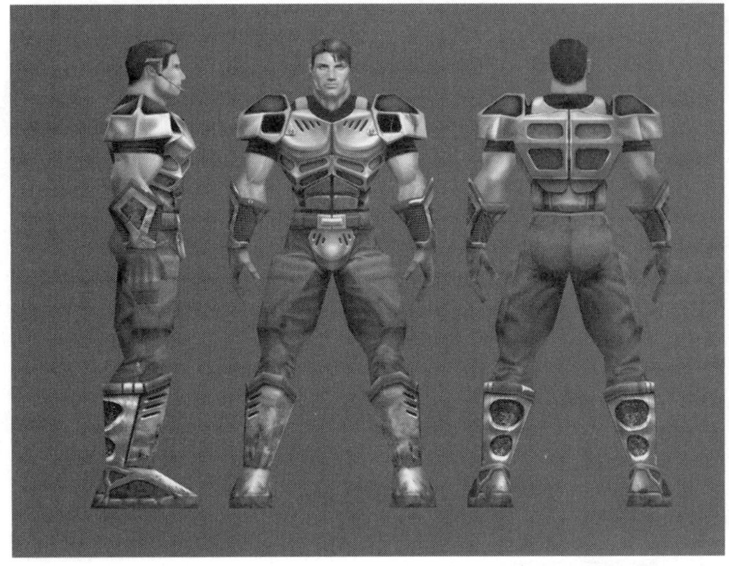

A close-up shot of the Black Thunder skin on Shane Caudle's Male1 model. This was one of the first new skins developed for UNREAL TOURNAMENT.

New Code, New Features

As it turned out, though, we had a lot of time to enhance the engine. UNREAL was before its time, and a lot of the content and code was rushed by the need to ship. With UNREAL TOURNAMENT, the team had a lot of time to use previously unexplored engine features. Erik de Neve's level-of-detail code ended up really speeding the game up, giving us room for beefier characters and more map decorations. Early on we experimented with using 16 256×256 textures per player, but opted for three or four 256×256 pieces out of memory considerations. This quadrupled the detail available to our skin artists for the player models. Reserving one of the 256×256 textures for the head alone allowed us to mix and match body skins with heads, yielding a massive amount of customization with only a small amount of work. Another one of the 256×256 textures was reserved for team color bits, so that a player skin could encompass all five possible team colors (none, red, blue, yellow, green) without too much memory use.

Level design didn't stand still either. Changing from single player to deathmatch-oriented design was refreshing for the designers, but not without its unique challenges. One issue was the task of balancing the number of "hardcore" maps with "theme" maps. A hardcore map focuses entirely on layout and game play, while the overall style of the map comes second. Theme maps, on the other hand, focus on a unifying idea or look and build from that. For example, the Koos Galleon, designed by Pancho Eekels of Digital Extremes, is a large sailing ship. It's a very beautiful level, but focuses on the theme of being a ship more than being a deathmatch map. The UNREAL TOURNAMENT team decided that mixing the two styles was the best approach.

While most magazine reviews have expressed frustration at the theme-oriented maps, we didn't want to appeal to only the hardcore crowd. Including maps that were designed for their look and feel increases the game's interest to average players who aren't skilled enough at the game to benefit from hardcore designs. Realism through textures and architecture is one of the Unreal engine's strengths and it was critical that we exploit that strength. Ultimately, we shipped UNREAL TOURNAMENT with somewhere around 45 to 50 maps, offering more than enough variety and replay value for everyone.

Epic hired several extremely skilled contractors to assist with art production. This is an extremely detailed female skin by Steve Garofalo.

Another task we faced was choosing which of UNREAL's weapons to keep and which to ditch. UNREAL TOURNAMENT has two firing modes, which makes designing a weapon like designing two weapons in one. UNREAL's stinger and dispersion pistol were not needed in UNREAL TOURNAMENT. Those weapons were good in UNREAL, because a player needed to start with simple, weak weapons and build up. In UNREAL TOURNAMENT, all the weapons had to be equally effective and carefully balanced. A player good with the minigun needed to be lethal with it. A player good with the pulse gun needed to be lethal with it. Eventually we settled on the current load-out, but made quite a few gameplay changes to the weapons that stayed from UNREAL. Each weapon was also given a much more beefed-up look and sound.

In the End, It All Worked Out

While the talents and devotion of individual team members created the content, the overall team spirit tied it together. UNREAL TOURNAMENT's design process was often reckless, but the game that resulted is nevertheless very polished and a hell of a lot of fun. The deathmatch-focused first-person shooter doesn't need a story, dialogue, or scripted sequences, which are all features that more or less require an organized design. Had we applied our hodgepodge design approach to a more focused genre, we probably would not have had such a successful game. UNREAL TOURNAMENT should not be seen as a lesson in how to design a game, but as a lesson on how to organize a small team of developers.

What Went Right

1. Smart internal marketing team

At the front of Epic's public relations were Mark Rein and Jay Wilbur. Their job was particularly difficult during the development of UNREAL TOURNAMENT. The media perceived us as impossible upstarts, taking an engine with terrible net-play and attempting to compete against id Software, the industry multiplayer champion. Both Mark and Jay fought hard to win over supporters in the online and magazine press. Mark made sure that the team stayed professional and that everyone was saying what he needed to be saying. Jay hunted down potential engine licensees, and helped establish a level of curiosity among the community and media.

UNREAL TOURNAMENT was able to garner significant magazine coverage because of the ongoing "QUAKE killer" debates. Mark and Jay worked to turn the initially negative public response into something positive. While we felt that our game would definitely stand on its own, we had to ensure that the positives were being clearly broadcast. Epic was very careful to avoid mentioning QUAKE 3: ARENA whenever possible, keeping the focus solely on UNREAL TOURNAMENT's features and staying away from comparative previews.

UNREAL TOURNAMENT's deathmatch maps were not constrained to any one particular theme or timeframe. Cliff Bleszinski's DM-Barricade, shown above, is a castle floating above a storm, while Pancho Eekels' DMGalleon is a massive ship sailing the ocean (bottom).

Most interviews and previews would ask us the inevitable "What about QUAKE 3?" question, to which we tried to answer with complete respect for id's project. Everyone knew that UNREAL TOURNAMENT and QUAKE 3 would be pitted against each other. Mark and Jay established very early on that the competition would be friendly.

2. Liberal internal structure, open design discussion

The laid-back environment that both Epic and Digital Extremes fostered greatly enhanced the quality of UNREAL TOURNAMENT. Everyone was free to suggest or implement an idea. Programmers had as much design freedom as anyone else on the team. Cliff Bleszinski (Epic) and James Schmalz (DE) were the lead designers of their respective companies and served as content filters. They worked towards focusing the ideas put forth in the meetings. In addition, both of them contributed significantly to the final game content. James designed two of the player models and created many skins and faces, while Cliff designed many of the game's best maps.

After the release of UNREAL TOURNAMENT, the Epic team started working on a free bonus pack containing additional models. These are concept drawings of the Skaarj Warrior model for the pack.

Team members were allowed to come into work when they wanted and stay however long they felt like being there. The only requirement was that every member attend a weekly design and focus meeting. This system worked because Epic was very careful to hire mature, dedicated employees and the core development team was kept small. The open hours often saw team members working a 24-hour day, sleeping on a couch for six hours, and then working another 24-hour day.

In addition to fostering a hardcore work ethic, the system created a sideways information flow. A programmer would go straight to the artist he needed something from, instead of through an art director. The fast communication allowed the programmers to stomp out bugs relatively quickly and the level designers to talk directly to the texture artists. An example of this was the single-player ladder system. Shane Caudle designed the art and I wrote the code. The fewer people we had to consult in order to complete the task meant a much faster turnaround. Everyone participated in giving the "coolness factor" thumbs-up or thumbs-down, but the actual development process was intentionally kept thin.

3. Direct communication with the gaming community

Nearly every Epic and Digital Extremes employee frequented message boards dedicated to the subject of UNREAL and UNREAL TOURNAMENT. The majority of Epic employees were drawn directly from the gaming community, either through mod projects or independent game work. Keeping in contact with the gaming community allowed Epic to focus on the target audience during the design process. Beyond our direct communication with the UNREAL community, we also trolled QUAKE 3 message boards, reading the discussions of the fans of our lead competitor's game. Learning what people liked in a first-person shooter and why they liked it helped us change the marginal multiplayer experience in UNREAL to the much faster paced gameplay in UNREAL TOURNAMENT.

In the Assault game type, players have to enter a heavily defended base and complete map-specific objectives to win. Assault was the most difficult UNREAL TOURNAMENT game type to design, balance, and play-test.

The gaming community can really help set the tone for your game. When UNREAL was released, the online community became extremely vocal and angry about the state of the net play. While most magazines had reported positive experiences with UNREAL's single-player mode (reflected in positive reviews), the media eventually came to reflect the cries of the hardcore gaming community. This was in part because the net play was poor, but also due to the fact that many members of the gaming media are themselves hardcore game players and visit those same message boards and community outlets.

We also learned that while the hardcore community is very vocal, it is also relatively small. Designing a game to appeal to that community alone is a critical mistake. Early in 1999 we started work on tutorials for each game type. The tutorials are far from definitive, but they did cover the basics of playing a 3D shooter. Testing on the parents and grandparents of team members demonstrated that the tutorials were useful for attracting and keeping new players.

This community-mindedness greatly contributed to the quality and completeness of UNREAL TOURNAMENT. We had a very good idea of what players wanted. As I mentioned earlier, we often posted controversial design questions on public message boards to gauge public reaction. The results of these polls were taken into consideration when the feature in question was implemented.

4. Strongly object-oriented engine design

The Unreal Tournament engine's strong object-oriented design makes it extremely modular. This modularity allowed our programmers to make massive changes to parts of the game without affecting other features. Each subsystem is connected to other subsystems through a clearly defined interface, and platform-specific code is consigned to separate libraries. Creating the Linux port, for example, was simply a matter of rewriting an input and sound device and writing a Linux version of the platform-specific library behavior.

Throughout UNREAL TOURNAMENT's development, Tim Sweeney and Steve Polge worked on improving the networking code. The modularity of the engine meant that their work didn't disturb anyone else's work. Some features, such as Jack's decal system, were added very late in the project. The decal system added a lot of depth and feedback to the game, and took less than a week to get working and fully debugged. Erik de Neve's mesh level-of-detail code touched only a handful of source files. This ease of use is also reflected in the engine's scripting language, UnrealScript. Calling it a scripting language is a misnomer; it's actually a lot like Java. Weapons, pickups, level events, AI nodes, and other world actors are all independent objects.

Steve Polge, our AI and game play programmer, made the bots understand the unique advantages and disadvantages of each weapon. Here a bot is moving in very close to use the powerful Flak Cannon.

A weapon can be added to the game without touching any source files but the new object definition. This highly extensible language meant that each programmer could add extensive new game-play features with a very limited set of potential side effects. In the end, 90 percent of UNREAL TOURNAMENT's game-play code was written in UnrealScript.

The Unreal Tournament engine's modular package system coupled with UnrealEd makes the game a mod-creation system out of the box. We designed a lot of our code with amateur extension in mind. Everyone at Epic recognized the value of the mod community and we wanted to make the game attractive to new artists and programmers. Constructing game code in this way made it much easier for us to prototype our own new features. Early UT weapons and pickups were child objects of UNREAL. The two games can easily coexist even now.

5. Good timing

As I said earlier, UNREAL TOURNAMENT was developed in the same time period as id Software's QUAKE 3: ARENA. The two games promised to be of the same genre and the two companies were known for a high level of competition. While we tried to avoid the "QUAKE 3 vs. UT" comparisons, they ultimately worked in our favor. The high level of public interest in the new engine war greatly increased our visibility. Magazines and Web sites often posted split previews instead of focusing on one game in particular. Interviews with id employees would always lead to UNREAL TOURNAMENT questions and vice versa.

UNREAL TOURNAMENT took almost exactly a year and a half to develop, giving the team a lot of time to pack in features. We didn't have to focus on writing an engine from scratch, so we were free to focus entirely on improvements. At this point, we've released three patches for

UNREAL TOURNAMENT that have solved a handful of relatively minor problems. The team has had a lot of time available to spend on adding even more features to the game since its release, instead of fixing outstanding issues. By the time this article hits the stands, we'll have released our first bonus pack: a free collection of new models, maps, and game-enhancing features.

What Went Wrong

1. Bad timing

Many aspects of the game's timing worked against us. While the QUAKE 3 vs. UT hype increased our exposure, it also set a very hard deadline for completion. It was critical that we complete the game before QUAKE 3 was released. The media advantage belonged to id and we believed that if UNREAL TOURNAMENT launched after QUAKE 3, we would be forgotten in the storm. At the same time, however, we were caught up in grueling contract renegotiations with GT Interactive. We did not want to deliver the completed game until we knew the contract would work in our favor. Many times during the development of the game we were promised that a resolution to the contract issue was close at hand.

The team would race to reach a point where the game could be shipped, only to have negotiations drag on. The gold master was delivered to GT days after a final contract was agreed upon. Unfortunately, the game hit shelves in November, pushing us very close to QUAKE 3's release date. While UNREAL TOURNAMENT often performed better than QUAKE 3 in reviews, we believe that sales would have been much higher still had we released in October. Word-of-mouth is a powerful force and the extra month would have given us time to build a larger community before Christmas.

2. No central design document

While I am a big supporter of open, cabal-style design, I have to stop and wonder how UNREAL TOURNAMENT would have turned out had we a strong initial design. It's quite possible that the game's weaker elements would have been much stronger if we had put together some concept art and focus material. In reviews, we have been criticized for not having enough variation in characters. If UNREAL TOURNAMENT had had a library of concept art to draw from, we might have had more interesting alien warriors. The story is more or less nonexistent in UNREAL TOURNAMENT, but at times we considered having in-game cut-scenes as rewards for a player's progress. The idea was dumped, but a design document might have made it easier to visualize those scenes.

I suppose this isn't really a "what went wrong." It's simply more of a "what we should have done." I think it's important to think about the game in that light. UNREAL TOURNAMENT is a very fun game with a lot of features packed into a short amount of development time. Those features were largely added through spur-of-the-moment decisions. A more unified approach to design would have allowed us to construct features that play on features, or even think of ideas we didn't have the perspective to realize.

Epic will always be a very open, liberal company when it comes to the design process. If we develop a design document, we'll use it with the understanding that it can be modified at any time. That having been said, I think there is a definite positive argument for having some sort of central guide to everyone's ideas. Having the ability to sit down and look over the big picture is very valuable.

3. Co-development across two countries

Epic Games and Digital Extremes co-developed UNREAL TOURNAMENT. The Digital Extremes team was located in Canada and Epic was located in the U.S. Epic supplied the programming team and a large group of content designers. Digital Extremes provided level designers, a sound guy, and texture artists. James Schmalz, the high-up man at Digital Extremes, contributed two of the game's player models and a lot of art. This co-development worked well for the most part, but near the end of the project it became very difficult. During UNREAL, Epic team members flew to Canada to work at Digital Extremes' offices. With UNREAL TOURNAMENT, it became Digital Extremes's turn to do the traveling. Unfortunately, flying and driving back and forth every couple of weeks is a very draining experience. Many of the Digital Extremes team members spent several weeks away from their wives and girlfriends. Near the end of the project, they grew increasingly frustrated with the situation.

To compound this problem further, Digital Extremes and Epic were attempting an expensive merger. As UNREAL TOURNAMENT came to a close, it became clear that the merger would not happen. It was prohibitively expensive for a small company to move across the border. Many Digital Extremes team members already had apartments and plans for living in Raleigh, and the news of the terminated merger process was devastating.

Much to Digital Extremes's credit, the company quickly recovered and moved to its backup plan of developing its own game with the Unreal Tournament engine. Nonetheless, the process of co-developing the game had taken its toll on everyone. The ups and downs of the merger process had a negative effect on team morale. Had the co-development happened between companies more closely situated, it would not have been a problem.

UNREAL TOURNAMENT used from three to four 256×256 textures per model. This allowed us to focus a lot of detail in the head and face area. Within the game a player can choose a skin and then swap through several different faces.

4. Not enough artists

On the content side, UNREAL TOURNAMENT was held back by the number of available artists. Epic's artist, Shane Caudle, is a supreme Jack-of-all-trades, creating skins, models, and levels of the highest quality. He spent most of his time working on new player models and skins for those models. Digital Extremes brought a few texture artists to the table, but not enough to create the huge libraries of new textures needed for the game. In order to supplement the skin and texture production, Epic turned to contract artist Steve Garofalo.

Even with the additional help from external sources, the team was unable to produce enough new textures. Level designers who wanted custom textures for their maps had to make do with their own texturing ability. While the final texture and level count in UNREAL TOURNAMENT is quite high, the levels would have been much more impressive had the team been able to act with full freedom. Since the completion of UNREAL TOURNAMENT, Epic has hired both Steve Garofalo and John Mueller to strengthen the art team for future projects.

5. Visual Basic editor interface

The Unreal Tournament engine uses UnrealEd as its level design and content management tool. For several years, UnrealEd has used a windowing interface written in Visual Basic. The VB code is fragile and very old. Add to this the fact that nobody at Epic except Tim Sweeney knows or cares about VB, and you have a level design team that is stuck with a tool that's not easily updated. Several interface bugs have plagued UnrealEd for some time and nobody on the team had the time or inclination to fix them. If we had a more easily extensible tool, the team would have been able to add extra features to the editor for level designers to use. As it stood, the editor was considered "off limits" for new features.

Where We Go from Here

The things that went wrong are, all in all, much less significant than what went right. UNREAL TOURNAMENT could have benefited from a more focused initial design and a more solid ship date, but it turned out to be very polished and a lot of fun. Many of the factors that worked in our favor, like timing, also worked against us to some extent. "What went wrong" is a good way of looking at what we could have done to make UNREAL TOURNAMENT even better.

UNREAL TOURNAMENT served as a good learning tool for the team. We have a good idea of what processes we need to adopt to produce larger, more story-driven games in the future. We see UNREAL TOURNAMENT as a good lesson in how to organize a team and produce a game in a short amount of time. The team has grown socially, and everyone is much more experienced in the process of game development. We feel very prepared to face the upcoming challenges and, hopefully, to continue to be seen as innovators in the industry.

Westwood Studios' TIBERIAN SUN

by rade stojsavljevic

Ever since the release of Westwood's DUNE 2 in 1992, real-time strategy (RTS) games have become the hottest-selling computer games around. Countless RTS games were released soon afterward including COMMAND & CONQUER (C&C), RED ALERT, WARCRAFT II, AGE OF EMPIRES, and TOTAL ANNIHILATION. These games have propelled the genre to new heights and have drawn an increasing number of fans.

After the success of C&C and RED ALERT, the team at Westwood Studios started work on TIBERIAN SUN, the sequel to C&C. To build the game, we assembled a team that consisted of veterans from C&C and RED ALERT along with a couple of new faces, including me. We started with the goal of taking what made C&C fun and expanding it even further. To begin the development process we reviewed what makes a great RTS game and came up with one answer: tactics. Westwood doesn't build games based on a specific technology and we never sell technology over the game play. We have a firm belief that a great strategy game must have interesting, fun, and new tactics that afford players a multitude of unique ways to play a game. We wanted TIBERIAN SUN to appeal to a broad audience, yet also appeal to core game players and fans of the series.

Back-Story

COMMAND AND CONQUER is one of the widest-selling series of all time for the PC, a real-time strategy game set in a future history of Western allied nations, terrorist cults, and rogue mutants. Like any good sequel, TIBERIAN SUN took the familiar formula up a notch with new units, improved AI, and cinematics starring big-money actors, such as James Earl Jones.

Towards this goal, we continued to apply a "wide and deep" approach to designing the tactics we created. Wide and deep essentially means a nice assortment of diverse yet readily apparent tactics that, under the surface, contain an even greater number of tactics. With this approach, you can provide first-time players with a number of different things to do while letting more experienced players discover new and advanced tactics on their own. These design goals made working on the game more challenging—as if being the biggest project in Westwood Studios' history wasn't enough.

Game Data

Release date: September 1999

Genre: real-time strategy; science fiction

Intended platform: Windows 95/98/NT 4.0

Project length: 36 months

Team size: 25 full-time, 15 part-time developers

Critical development hardware: Pentium Pro and Pentium II machines, 200 to 450MHz dual-processor with 128 to 256MB RAM,
Creative Labs sound cards, Windows 95/98/NT, SGI 02 workstations, BlueICE accelerators

Critical development software: Microsoft Visual C++, Lightwave, 3D Studio Max, Discreet Flint, Adobe Photoshop, Adobe After Effects, Adobe Illustrator, Avid Media Composer, Filemaker Pro, Deluxe Paint

What Went Right

1. Maintained C&C style of game play

One of the most difficult tasks we had to overcome during the development of TIBERIAN SUN was to maintain the feel of the original. When making a sequel, the question that always has to be answered first is, How far do you stray from the original game to make it compelling, yet still familiar? The intent with TIBERIAN SUN was to maintain, as much as possible, the feeling of the original while providing new and interesting tactics for players to master. To aid in this goal, when adding a new feature we asked the questions, "Is this consistent with COMMAND & CONQUER?" and "How can we make it easier and even more exciting?"

In this area, it really helped to have a development team that worked on the previous games. They were able to draw from previous experiences to create a consistency in the game dynamics. This gave the team a great deal of independence since everybody already had a good idea of how the game was supposed to look, play, and feel. The main areas we focused on in order to be consistent with previous games were the user interface and unit behavior. We knew we had to keep the sidebar metaphor for unit construction, but we wanted to update it to accommodate new features, such as unit queuing, waypoints, and power/energy control.

For unit behavior there was a set of rules that we had to conform to, specifically how a unit deals with player commands so that its internal logic never overrides a player's orders. One of the times we tried to change the rules was when harvester threat-avoidance logic was introduced. I remember hearing lead designer Adam Isgreen screaming at his computer when his harvesters refused to obey his orders to retreat. We decided to scrap that idea shortly afterward.

It was important for the overall visual presentation of the game to bear a resemblance to its predecessors in order to maintain a consistent artistic style. We decided to alter the perspective slightly, rotating the camera to create a three-fourths isometric perspective that afforded a better sense of depth and realism in a 3D perspective. It was at this point that we decided not to use a polygonal engine since it wouldn't be possible for us to keep the system requirements low enough to achieve the mass-market appeal that we wanted. Also, at the time we planned to release TIBERIAN SUN, 3D accelerator cards and systems weren't fast enough for us to maintain the visual detail we wanted for the hundreds of units and structures on-screen at once.

Concept sketch of an Orca bomber.

2. Working on a sequel to a successful franchise

Being the fourth RTS game Westwood has done, there were a lot of lessons learned that the team was able to carry forward into TIBERIAN SUN. First, we had an established and streamlined user interface. This user interface has been a cornerstone of Westwood RTS games since DUNE 2, and we've been gradually improving it ever since. Anyone who has ever played a Westwood RTS is immediately familiar with the controls and can jump right into the action. Additionally, the interface is simple and intuitive enough to let new users become comfortable with it in a short time. Another nice benefit of making a sequel is that we had a set of basic features we knew worked based on previous games. These provided a solid foundation that could be expanded upon and modified as needed.

We started with features from the previous games that we knew we wanted and updated them to fit a world that was 30 years in the future. Tanks evolved into two-legged mechanized walkers, soldiers could now use drop pods launched from space, and cloaking technology advanced to yield a stealth generator that hid many units and buildings at once. When it came time to create the story, we already had the basic framework in place. There was a very rich and fascinating world to draw upon when creating new characters for this story. The one difficulty encountered was making sure the story could stand up on its own and be accessible to new players without subjecting players familiar with previous games to mind-numbing exposition. To solve this problem, we set the story 30 years after the end of the original, which provided an opportunity to create an outstanding introduction that showed players what had been going on in the world.

3. Team experience and cohesion

The TIBERIAN SUN development team is one of the most experienced and professional teams

I've ever had the privilege of working with. For many of the team members, this was the fourth RTS game they had done (the previous being DUNE 2, C&C, and RED ALERT). This level of experience was key in allowing the team to conquer all the obstacles thrown in their path.

Concept sketch of a GDI Titan.

Even though I had worked on half a dozen titles before I started on TIBERIAN SUN, at first it was a little unnerving for me to be working with a team of this caliber. Several members of the programming team had worked together on previous Westwood RTS products and were accustomed to each other's coding styles. New programmers were quickly assimilated into the team and were able to adapt well. The coding rules and Westwood libraries allowed the programmers to familiarize themselves with each other's work with minimal difficulty.

The designers had worked on previous RTS games and were very familiar with the universe before we started the project. This saved several months since no one had to familiarize themselves with anything except the design for TIBERIAN SUN. The tools used were derivatives of the C&C and RED ALERT editors, which also minimized the ramp-up time required before they could produce missions. The designers worked well together and were friends; something that helped a lot when there were differences of opinion. It proved to be very beneficial to know that you could argue your point and not have to worry that the person you were arguing with would hold a grudge afterward.

Without the technical knowledge and creativity of the artists on the project, we would have suffered a great deal of pain when integrating artwork. Like most projects, TIBERIAN SUN had a specific set of technical criteria that had to be satisfied when creating art for the game engine. On this front, we reaped the rewards of having artists who had done it all before. They had worked with our programming team and knew the tools well enough that they were able to head off potential problems before they could get out of control.

The cinematic artists had much of the same experience; they didn't have as many technical restrictions as the in-game artists, which allowed them to be able to express unbridled creativity. The cinematic artists didn't have to deal with frame limitations or palettes. Also, compared to previous games, the movie player in TIBERIAN SUN allowed for full-resolution movies (as opposed to previous games where every other line was cut out) using 24-bit color depth and a 15FPS frame rate. I still remember the first time we saw the movie in which the Mammoth Mk. II laid waste to an entire Nod base by itself; it left everyone in the room speechless.

The final piece was the management team. Under executive producer Brett Sperry's strong leadership, we established systems to deal with routine tasks, facilitated communication between the teams, and were able to avoid a lot of problems early on. Brett has always been very protective of the C&C franchise and with TIBERIAN SUN, his clear and consistent vision of where the game should be was absolutely critical to the project.

4. Balancing process

Balance is one of the things that can make or break a RTS game. It's one of the hardest things to do on the design side of the product since you're essentially trying to optimize an equation with dozens of independent variables. If you get it wrong, you'll have a boring game and a horde of disgruntled fans cursing your name forever.

Nod bikes fire at an underground UFO. Nod bikes flee from the ensuing explosion.

When the issue of balancing comes up, you'll often hear about the "rock-paper-scissors" idea, but I like to think of it more in terms of a chess game. You've got a lot of different pieces, each with a unique function and set of strategies that takes a long time to master. Having made several RTS games before, the team knew how to balance a game. We started with two approaches: one scientific and one artistic. Using the scientific approach, we started with the relatively simple idea that in a steady state units with an equivalent cost should do equivalent damage to one another. The basic idea is that if I have $1,000 worth of units and you have $1,000 worth of units and they fight, the fight better be really close. From here, we kept adding variables until we had a relatively playable game.

The next step was a lot more artistic and was where experience really paid off, keeping the team from long periods of fumbling around blindly. We played countless games with each of us championing one side vs. the other, carefully noting how effective units and tactics felt against one another. We would get together after each game to compare notes, argue our points, get into fights, and then make one change at a time to the game and try it again until we were all satisfied with the results.

The whole process took about three months for TIBERIAN SUN, compared to six months for C&C and four months for RED ALERT. Even after the countless games we played against one another, we still got into shouting matches during close multiplayer games. When this happens, you know you've got a winner on your hands.

5. Mission design

Mission design is one of the most important elements of RTS games. Based on experience with previous games, Westwood has established a series of processes that are used whenever a mission is created. We've designed these processes to foster creativity, maximize efficiency, and promote communication between the design, programming, art, and management groups. This process has been refined on every project, and we've taken it to the next level with the upcoming FIRESTORM add-on.

A Nod obelisk of light incinerates its attackers.

The process begins with a mission design proposal submitted to the lead designer and producer. The proposal is a two- to three-page document that contains summary information about the mission such as name, side, difficulty, map size, mission type, and so on. The mission briefing is included along with a description of what the briefing movie should be and all of the critical information that must be revealed to the player. Mission objectives are listed as they would appear in the game, along with specific information on how to achieve the objectives. Win and lose conditions are created, as well as descriptions of the victory and defeat movies that play at the end of a mission. The last things included are all of the new voice and text messages used in the mission.

Once this proposal has been approved, the map for the mission is sketched out on paper. We've found that this process can save a great deal of time since it eliminates distractions and allows the designers to get an overall view of the map quickly. When the designers finish sketching their mission, they proceed to the editor and begin to create the basic battlefield. Terrain is laid down first, followed by buildings, roads, trees, and pavement. The final step to complete a mission is to take a map and add scripting, which takes approximately two-thirds of the time to create a mission. One of the great things about TIBERIAN SUN is that the editor is tied directly into the game, which allowed designers to switch rapidly between the editor and the game. This feature also proved to be a liability, however, because if a bug appeared that prevented the game from running, we couldn't run the editor, either.

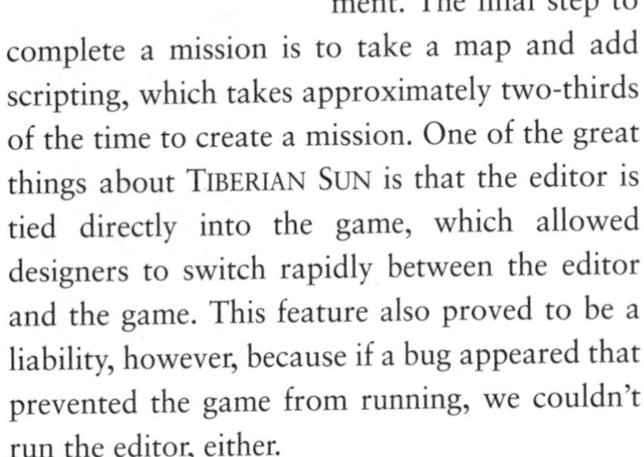

TIBERIAN SUN features a good blend of production (such as building bases) and nonproduction missions that keep the pace of the game interesting and challenging. We tried not to do the same mission twice and added variety by combining mission types into nonproduction/production missions that switch from one to the other when players reach specific objectives. Branching missions were added to give players the option of completing sub-missions before they tackled the main objective. By playing sub-missions first, the player makes the final objective easier and it gave the designers added granularity when creating the difficulty levels for the game.

What Went Wrong

1. Unrealistic expectations

The degree of hype and expectations that TIBERIAN SUN had to fulfill was staggering. We had a team of experienced developers who wanted to beat their own expectations while simultaneously building a game that would be everything the fans of the series expected and more. This was not a realistic goal since it's just not possible to make something that will meet everyone's expectations. One of the things that we did not do was explore all of the new features to their logical conclusions. This would have allowed us to do a lot more with a smaller feature set and provide an even better game.

On location at Red Rock, Nev. Chandra, McNeil, and Brink pose on the Kodiak Bridge.

A perfect example of a feature that was begging to be used more is the dynamic-battlefield concept. The basic idea behind the dynamic-battlefield concept is that players' actions alter the battlefield. For example, a player could set fire to trees to burn a path into an enemy's base. We wound up cutting this particular feature because it caused path-finding problems. Also, battles with heavy weapons would cause cratering of terrain which hindered unit movement. We could have used it to create more new strategies for players, and since it was one of the more expensive features in the game, we could have squeezed a lot more use out of it.

Trying to fill the shoes left behind by RED ALERT proved to be daunting. If you had asked a dozen people what they expected out of TIBERIAN SUN before it was released, you would have heard a dozen different answers. We devoted a lot of effort to add as many features into the game as possible instead of just trying to make the best game we could. Getting into a feature war is one of the worst things that can occur during development because it siphons effort away from adding the "fun" to the game.

2. Feature creep

TIBERIAN SUN started strong and we developed a robust and large feature set we intended to fulfill. The project started smoothly, but as we progressed, the temptation to add new features not included in the design document grew. These features arose out of shortfalls in the original design, omissions from the original design, and input from fans. Everybody stresses the importance of working off of a design document and not deviating from it. Unfortunately, this just isn't realistic since every product evolves during the course of development and sometimes the original design proves to be lacking. A team has to be able to incorporate new ideas during development if the final project is to be better. However, the flip side of this idea is that the team must be able to cut features diplomatically when it is in the best interest of the project.

Umagon prepares for a take.

TIBERIAN SUN's development had many challenging moments when features had to be cut for one reason or another. A perfect example of this was the ability to order a limited number of units through a drop-ship loading screen before a mission. This sounded like a great idea on paper and we had already coded it and incorporated it into the game. It wasn't until we actually played with it that we realized it just didn't fit and had to be removed.

Looking back at the project, I think we could have been more aggressive in cutting or changing certain features to make sure their returns were really worth the development investment. I'm a firm believer in the idea that less is more and that fewer but more fully developed features are the way to go. If a feature isn't amazing, you should cut it or make damn sure it becomes amazing before you ship the product.

3. Post-production complications, compositing woes

TIBERIAN SUN features the most complex and highest-quality cinematic sequences Westwood has ever done. These movies help drive the story elements forward. However, these movies came at a very high price. Westwood has a soundstage with a bluescreen and in-house post-production capability that allowed us to handle the entire production ourselves. We've done several different projects with video, including RED ALERT, DUNE 2000, and RED ALERT RETALIATION for the Playstation.

Based on these past experiences, it was decided that we would push the limits of what we could do in TIBERIAN SUN. We started by fully storyboarding every scene in the script. From the storyboards, we built concept sketches of the major sets to be constructed (practical as well as computer-generated) and proceeded to build the sets Before the shoot there was a three-month lead time for our team of six 3D artists to build the sets. We wanted to have the sets 100 percent complete so we would have camera and lighting information to match up with the live actors.

For various reasons, the pre-production for TIBERIAN SUN was much shorter than it should have been. If you've ever worked in film or television production, you've probably heard the phrase "we'll fix it in post." Believe me when I say there's a reason why this little phrase can spook even the most veteran members of any production crew. Anything you have to fix after the fact winds up being ten times as difficult and ten times more expensive than planning for it in the first place. Everybody on the team knew this, and we tried as hard as we could to work out all the details before we started the shoot. The problem was we didn't have enough time and couldn't change the date of the shoot because we wouldn't have been able to get our two main actors, James Earl Jones and Michael Biehn.

Concept sketch of a GDI carry-all.

Going into the shoot, we had a pretty good idea of how we were going to work out all of the technical details such as camera tracking on a bluescreen, matching lighting to computer graphics, compositing, and so on. However, we ran into difficulties because we didn't allow enough time for the more complex shots and were forced to edit on the fly during the shoot. An unforeseen problem during the post-production was that we dramatically underestimated the storage and network requirements of working with 60 minutes of digitized video. Westwood has a very robust and fast network with a large amount of storage space, but it was never designed to meet the needs of video post-operation. An amazing effort by the MIS staff and a couple of called-in favors got us enough storage space on the network to keep going.

From the start, the team struggled to get video from digital beta to the SGI– and PC–based compositing systems. Footage was digitized on an Avid system and copied to file servers for distribution to the PCs. The SGIs grabbed the footage directly from tape using built-in digitizing hardware. From the compositing stations, various shots were completed and transferred back to a file server to be compressed and put in the game. This, along with the fact that many individual scenes were worked on by several artists, multiplied the storage requirements several times over.

In the end, the video assets were spread across four separate file servers and took up well over 500GB of space. Not only was space a problem, but moving hundreds of megabytes of files a day from machine to machine became a bottleneck. A few minutes here and there to transfer files doesn't sound like much until you add it all up. If we had it to do over again, we could have alleviated the problem by building a very specialized (and expensive) network, by getting hardware that allowed artists to digitize their footage directly from tape, or by reducing the scope of the project and sidestepping the problem entirely.

4. Locked documents too early

One of the side effects of schedule slippage was that we locked our documents too early in order to achieve the localization plan. We knew this was going to wind up causing us significant pain, but at the time there was nothing we could do to avoid it. The result turned out well, but a lot of time and effort was spent to make everything work together. At the point when we locked the audio script, mission design and balancing were not complete. As we played through the missions, we realized that certain objectives were not clear and needed to be explained further.

The previous method for doing this was to have the in-game AI persona (Eva or Cabal) relay the information to the player through voice cues. This was not an option for TIBERIAN SUN, however, since we made the switch to professional voice talent for Eva and Cabal. Costs and scheduling didn't allow us to do as many pickup recording sessions as we wanted. Also, the locked audio scripts were already localized and recorded, which made recording additional lines out of the question.

The only option available was to redesign the missions or add text to the missions to make the objectives clearer. Redesigning the missions would have added at least a month to the already late schedule, so we quickly ruled that option out. We wound up going with text that popped up in the missions, although the original design called for all text in the game to be accompanied by a voice-over.

Nod laser turrets repel a GDI horde.

5. Scheduling problems

As with most projects in development today, TIBERIAN SUN suffered from scheduling problems; ours resulted in a nine-month delay. There wasn't a single reason that caused the product to be delayed, but rather a series of seemingly minor contributing factors. Brett Sperry has a rule of thumb that we often refer to when scheduling projects. When you add one fundamental new technology to a project, it can cause slippage up to 90 days. When you add two fundamental new technologies it can add a year to the anticipated release date. When you add three or more new technologies it becomes impossible to predict the release date of the project accurately.

TIBERIAN SUN features three new systems that resulted in an unpredictable schedule. First, we switched our core graphics engine to an isometric perspective in order to enhance the game's 3D look. This resulted in a cascade effect of broken systems that weren't anticipated. Bridges that could be destroyed and rebuilt, for example, wound up taking over ten times as long to program as we originally estimated. Adding bridges complicated systems such as path-finding, Z-buffering, rendering, unit behavior, and AI. Scripting was another area in which we added a slew of new functionality.

An Orca carry-all transports a hover MLRS.

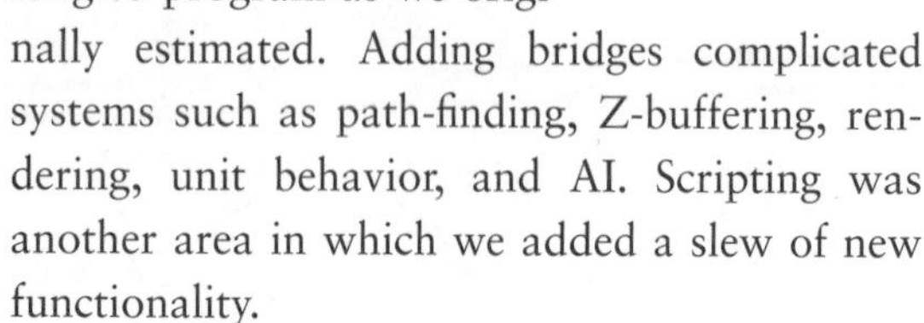

We added an increasing number of triggers to the game to allow the designers flexibility in creating the missions. Each new trigger added was more specific than the last and was used for increasingly rarer conditions. Since triggers could be used in combination, we ended up with an overwhelmingly large number of events that needed to be debugged. We would often fix one trigger to work in a specific situation and inadvertently break the same trigger in a different situation.

AI and unit behavior was the third main area that used new technology. We set out to create a challenging and fun AI that could react to the player's actions and change tactics to compensate. We should have focused on fewer areas of the AI instead of trying to redesign the whole package from the ground up.

Overall Tips

With TIBERIAN SUN, we built the game we originally set out to build over three years ago. Almost all of the new engine features we designed were implemented in the final product, and many more were added along the way. We built a game that is as easy to play as its predecessor while offering up lots of new units featuring interesting tactics. All of this was done while keeping the system requirements low enough to run on most systems: a 166MHz Pentium with 32MB RAM and a 2MB video card. We learned, or relearned actually, a few more things about making RTS games that weren't listed above.

They are:

- If the game has Internet or multiplayer capability, build this functionality as soon as possible since it will let you get into the game and balance it early.
- Don't shield yourself from reality. If your game supports Internet play as well as LAN play, don't play only LAN games and assume that Internet performance is acceptable.
- Keep the story tightly focused on players' actions and don't treat the story as a separate entity. Remember that the player is always the main character.

- Wherever possible, try not to mix disparate technologies (3D visual systems with 2D, for example) that have inherent problems working together. Instead, go back and modify the design.

After three years of working on TIBERIAN SUN, it was a great feeling to finally finish the game and see it on the shelves. No matter how many products you ship, that feeling never goes away. TIBERIAN SUN broke Electronic Arts' sales record for the fastest-selling computer game in the 17-year history of the company with more than 1.5 million units sold so far. But best of all, the team is proud of the product they created and can't wait to get started on the next one.

Ensemble Studios'

AGE OF EMPIRES II: THE AGE OF KINGS

by matt pritchard

Back-Story

AGE OF KINGS advances the historical timeline begun in the first AGE OF EMPIRES, encompassing the thousand years from the fall of Rome through the Middle Ages. Meanwhile nearly every aspect of the game was updated to deliver a worthy sequel—graphics and AI saw improvement, and new units, technologies, and game modes were added.

Catching Up

Two years ago in this very column (You can read the original AOE article on page 63.) I told you the story of Ensemble Studios, a scrappy upstart that overcame challenges to create the game AGE OF EMPIRES (AOE). Since its release two years ago in the great real-time strategy (RTS) wars of 1997, approximately three million copies of AOE have been sold worldwide, along with almost a million copes of the RISE OF ROME (ROR) expansion pack. The totals don't give the whole story, though. AOE proved to be a consistent seller, hanging around the top of the PC Data charts, and even re-entered the top ten a year-and-a-half after its release. The demographics of the buyers were another surprise. Sure, we had the sales to the 14- to 28-year-old male hard-core players, but we also had significant sales to older players, women of all ages, and casual game players of all sorts. That is to say, we had a crossover hit on our hands.

If you have ever watched the VH1 show *Behind the Music*, then you know the story of the upstart band that finds itself suddenly on top of the world—things change, and not always for the better. I wouldn't go so far as to say that we sank into a wild orgy of sex, fast cars, and money—despite the wishes of a couple of our guys—but this change along with the benefits of success brought us a whole new set of challenges, making our next game no easier than the first.

Designing a Sequel

It was a surprise to no one that Ensemble Studios' next game would be a sequel to AOE, although most people probably didn't know that we had a contract with our publisher for a sequel long before the original game was finished. Given our historically-based themes and time periods in AOE, the chosen time period for AGE OF EMPIRES II: THE AGE OF KINGS (AOK), the Middle Ages, practically picked itself. That was the only easy part, however.

Like a band going back into the studio after a hit record, there were differing opinions of what direction to take next. Do we play it safe and stick tightly to the AOE formula, or do we get bold and daring and take the whole game genre in new directions? This is the million-dollar question every successful game is faced with when the topic of a follow-up is raised. But the successful band I'm using as an analogy is fortunate. They don't have to contend with the unbelievably rapid pace of evolution in PC hardware and games.

Game Data

Release date: October 1999

Publisher: Microsoft

Genre: real-time strategy; historical

Intended platform: Windows 95/98/NT

Project length: 24 months

Team size: 40

Critical development hardware: Pentium II 450 128MB, Dual Xeon 450 512MB

Critical development software: Visual C++, 3D Studio Max

Improvements to the game in every area from graphics to user interface are expected in this business as a matter of fact. Expectations can be a bitch sometimes. Take the vast demographics of AOE players that I mentioned earlier—they are the largest group of people most likely to buy the sequel—and everyone is concerned about making sure that this huge and diverse group will like the next game so much they will run out and buy it. We'll just do more of what we did right in AOE, we said. That sounds great, but it's almost impossible to quantify in a meaningful, detailed way. The game business is brutal to those who fail to move forward with the times, but it's also equally brutal to those who experiment too much and stray from the expectations of the players.

When we started work on AOK, we thought that we could make use of our existing code and tools, and that this would make the sequel easier to create than the original. Filled with these optimistic thoughts, we concluded that we could develop AOK in a single year. This was also going to be our opportunity to add all those dream features and make our magnum opus of computer games. So we set about to do just that. To make enhancements for AOK, we had pulled together a giant wish list of features and ideas from inside and outside sources. To the game design we added all sorts of neat new features such as off-map trade, renewable resources, combat facings, sophisticated diplomacy and systems of religion, and so on. Of course, the art, sound, and game content were also going to be bigger and better and bolder and brighter and...well...you get the idea.

Several months down the road, reality reared its ugly head in big way: we had bitten off more than we could chew and the game's design was losing focus. Instead of sticking to the core of what makes an RTS game great, we had gone off in many contradictory directions. Along with that came the realization that there was no way that we were going to finish AOK in a single year and have it anywhere close to the quality of AOE. This was a sobering time for Ensemble Studios staff and our publisher, Microsoft. While the Ensemble Studios crew adjusted quickly, it caused a few problems for some of the people at Microsoft: "Uh, guys, we've already gone ahead and committed to our bosses that we would have another AGE OF EMPIRES game this year," is probably a good way to paraphrase it.

A Turkish mosque shows off the greater detail and improved skills of our art staff.

From this situation, a contingency plan was born. We were going to take another year to finish AOK, giving us time to get the game back on track and to create the ambitious content for it. We also had a plan to help our publisher out: we would create an in-house expansion pack for AOE. It would be a significant addition to the game, yet require only a small amount of our resources, and most importantly, it would be ready in time for Christmas 1998, taking the slot originally planned for AOK. Thus was born the ROR expansion pack. ROR helped, but it didn't take all the pressure off us. Unlike the latitude we had with AOE, which had also come out a year late, our new deadlines for AOK were very firm and hung over us the entire time. The pressure was very much on.

What Went Right

We did what it took to make AOK a triple-A game. While the decisions to take an extra year and reset the units to an AOE baseline were tough in the short term, they were the right decisions to make. The commitment of Ensemble Studios to exceed the quality of its prior games never wavered. To realize our goals, we added the additional programmers, artists, and designers that we needed. When we needed to stop, take a hard assessment of what we were doing, and kill our own children if need be, we did just that. We pushed ourselves hard and we came together as a team.

1. Addressed the major criticisms of the first game

Despite AOE's success and generally glowing reviews, there were two things about the game that were repeatedly criticized: the artificial intelligence of the computer players and the pathfinding and movement of units. And to be honest, they were right. Because these issues got

so much press, we knew going in that if we didn't address them in a visible and obvious way, AOK was going to be raked over the coals by reviewers and users. It didn't matter that other popular RTS games had pathfinding that was just as bad, or that our AIs didn't cheat and theirs did—we weren't going be judged against them, but rather against ourselves.

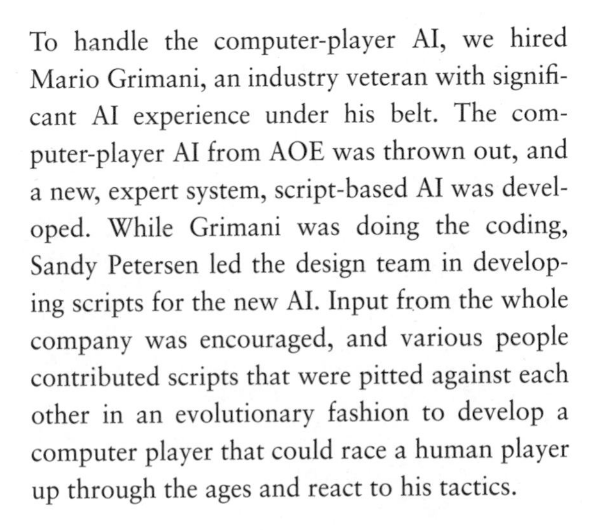

To handle the computer-player AI, we hired Mario Grimani, an industry veteran with significant AI experience under his belt. The computer-player AI from AOE was thrown out, and a new, expert system, script-based AI was developed. While Grimani was doing the coding, Sandy Petersen led the design team in developing scripts for the new AI. Input from the whole company was encouraged, and various people contributed scripts that were pitted against each other in an evolutionary fashion to develop a computer player that could race a human player up through the ages and react to his tactics.

For the pathfinding problems, nothing less than an all-out blitz was ordered up. The game engine's movement system was redesigned and no fewer than three separate pathfinding and two obstruction systems were developed, requiring five different people working on them at various times. A high-level pathfinder computes general routes across the world map, ignoring such trivial things as people walking, which were handled by lower-level pathfinders that could thread a path through a closely packed group of units. In the end, we were so successful in ridding the movement problems that hampered AOE that reviewers and players couldn't help but take notice and acknowledge the improvement.

2. We innovated within the genre

While in the end AOK stayed much closer to its AOE roots than we had initially envisioned, we pushed the RTS gaming experience forward with a host of improvements. Some of these were interface-only improvements, such as the "Find Next Idle Villager" command, completely customizable hot-keys, and the extensive rollover help. Other improvements changed the game play itself, such as the Town Bell (ring it and all your villagers run inside the Town Center to defend it), in-game technology tree, and of course, Automatic Formations.

One of the most praised features, Automatic Formations caused a group of selected units to automatically arrange themselves logically by putting the strongest units up front and the ones needing protection in the rear. They stay in formation while traveling, replacing the "random horde" that players had become accustomed to in RTS games. Programmer Dave Pottinger originally set out to create a formation system incorporating characteristics of a turn-based war game's formation system, but as the game progressed and our understanding and vision for the game matured, a complicated formation system gave way to a simpler system that better served the game.

When I wrote the graphics engine for AOE, I used a 166MHz Pentium at work and tested on my 486 at home. A 2MB video card was my target, but the game would run with only 1MB of video memory. Today I have a 32MB TNT2 card in my 500MHz Pentium III system. These changes in the typical game player's system are mirrored by the increase in player expectations for a great visual experience.

In AOK, I'm proud to say, we met and exceeded game players expectations. The first thing that you notice upon playing AOK is the scale. The units in the game are about the same size, but the buildings and trees are no longer iconic. They are large structures with a scale that looks as if the units could comfortably reside inside them. Castles and Wonders are now gigantic, imposing structures that fill the screen.

And the art itself is just so much better. Our entire art staff gained a great deal of experience and skill with AOE and ROR, and AOK became a showcase for their improved talent. It wasn't just the units and buildings, though. In AOE, the terrain had something of an Astroturf feel to it and the need to make transition tiles by hand limited the game to four terrain textures.

For AOK, a whole new terrain system was developed, allowing us to mix terrains together, shade elevation in 3D, greatly increase the number of textures, and even alpha-blend textures such as water. The highest compliments came at the 1999 E3 show when we were unable to convince people from some of our biggest competitors that AOK was still a 256-color game

3. Better use of bug tracking software and crunch-time management

A scene from one of the game scenarios. The updated graphics engine and building scale allowed us to create scenes much more impressive than in AOE.

During the development of AOE, we had a single machine in the office that would connect up to RAID, a remote bug database in Redmond, Wash., via an ISDN modem. This was used to handle bugs found by testers at Microsoft. Every so often someone would fire the connection up and, if the machine at the other end was in a good mood, make hard copies of new bug reports to pass around to people.

We also had a different software package for communicating bugs and issues among ourselves, but there were not enough users on the license for everyone. Suffice it to say, this system left something to be desired, but it was all we had. During the development of AOK, ThinRAID was made available to us, allowing everyone to access the bug database directly from their web browser. Having only one system on everyone's desktop, available whenever needed, that was always up-to-date made a huge improvement in our ability to track bugs, stay on top of things, avoid redundancies, and just plain save time.

The last six months of development on AOE were pretty much one continuous blur of people working nonstop. This took a heavy toll on people, sometimes even straining their health or marriages. As a company, we vowed to not let things get that bad again. To further underscore the need, the composition of Ensemble Studios had shifted dramatically away from being mostly young, single men (with presumably no life) to being dominated by married men with a growing number of children and babies on the way.

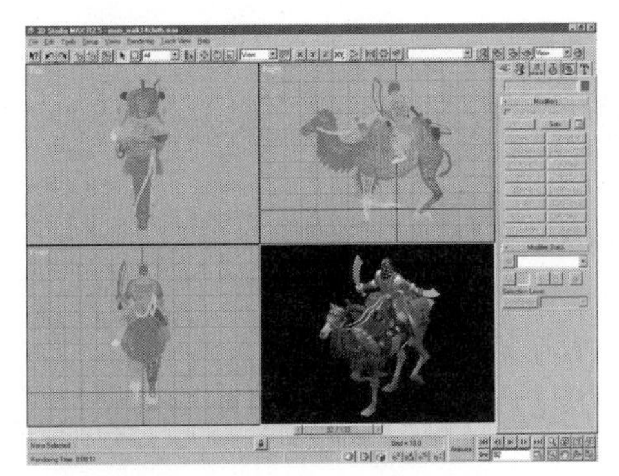

A 3D Studio Max model of the Mameluke character. Twenty thousand polygons got reduced down to several hundred pixels for the final game.

To protect ourselves, we scheduled crunch time well in advance at multiple points in the development process. The hours were 10 A.M. to midnight, Monday through Friday, with Wednesday nights ending at 7 P.M. so we could go home to our families. We had weekends off and meals were provided during the week. For the most part this worked very well, although having a "family night" where family members could join us for dinner once a week proved to be more of a distraction than we would have liked. Producer Harter Ryan deserves much credit for making crunch time so much easier on AOK.

4. Better use of tools and automated testing

After AOE was finished, we developed several in-house and in-game tools to make the job of development easier. The most-used tool was ArtDesk, a multipurpose program that converted graphics from standard formats to our proprietary formats, which allowed us to view and analyze the content of our graphics data, and generated many of the custom data files for the game. This easy-to-use GUI-based program replaced several antiquated DOS command-line utilities and automated many tasks, saving a huge amount of time over the development span.

In an effort led by Herb Marselas, programming tools such as Lint, BoundsChecker, and True-Time were used to a degree never approached during AOE's development and proved invaluable in improving the quality of our code. Finally, in-game utilities such the Unit Combat Comparison simulator allowed the designers to balance the game in a more scientific way. Every effort made in the tools area was rewarded with either time saved or significant improvements in the product. The only glaring omission in all this was the lack of an art asset management tool.

5. We met our system requirements

A game that's expected to sell in the millions needs to be able to run on most of the computers it will encounter. Requiring cutting-edge systems or specific video cards won't work. With AOK being an 8-bit 2D game, meeting video card requirements wasn't going to be very difficult. But memory and processor speed targets were another story. All the new systems in AOK would put their demands on the computer. Optimization issues were worked on hard for the last several months of development.

The eleventh-hour addition of some clever tricks and a variable graphics-detail switch allowed us to hit our CPU target of a Pentium 166MHz, MMX-supported CPU. The minimum memory requirement of 32MB was also met, but with some reservations. Large multiplayer games on huge maps would need an extra eight or 16MB to be really playable. All in all though, the minimum system requirements for AOK are some of the lowest for games released in the Christmas 1999 season, widening the game's potential audience.

What Went Wrong

I'd like to say that we had fewer problems developing AOK than we did for AOE, but it didn't turn out that way. Some problems listed in the AOE Postmortem were addressed in AOK and others weren't. And like that band going back into the studio to record a follow up to a hit album, we encountered a whole slew of brand new problems, many of which we found we were just as unprepared for as we were the first time around. I've tried to include some of the issues that became more important due to the fact that we were making a sequel to a successful game.

1. We still don't have a patch process

This was a problem area from the AOE Postmortem, and as of this writing it still has not been addressed. I outlined the reasons we needed a process to issue patches for our game in a timely manner in the AOE Postmortem. Additionally, a new reason reared its ugly head: cheating in multiplayer games. At first people found bugs in AOE and exploited them to win unfairly. Then it got even worse. Programs called "trainers" were developed that would actually modify the game's code while it was running to allow players to cheat.

Being the developer—not the publisher—of AOE, we don't have the final decision if or when a patch is to be released. As a result, all during 1999 our reputation as developers was assaulted by fans who saw us as uncaring about the problems that were driving people away from online play of our games. The topic of cheating in multiplayer games is so extensive I hope to do an article on it in the near future. We addressed this problem with our publisher and were promised a patch process.

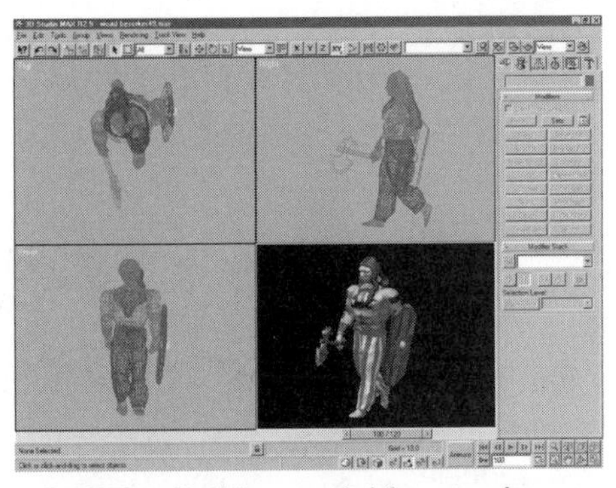

A 3D Studio Max model for a male villager. For AOK, female villagers were also added.

Unfortunately, AOK shipped with a couple bugs that seriously needed addressing in the short term. They're not show stoppers, but if not addressed soon, the game's (and our) reputation may suffer another black eye. If a patch for AOK is out by the time you read this, then you can conclude that we finally established our process.

2. Unfinished versions of the game got out

This is a problem that is born of success. Prerelease versions of nearly all games wind up circulating in pirate channels known as "warez." This happened with AOE. Imagine our surprise at reading an entire review of the game (an alpha version) eight months before it was released. Fortunately, almost no one bothered with it until the game was properly released because nobody knew much about it. AOK was a completely different story. It was a highly anticipated sequel to a very successful game, and the various warez sites were tripping all over themselves to get a copy of the latest build. And get a copy they did.

They were usually only one or two weeks behind our latest build. It seemed as though copies were leaking out from every imaginable source—play-testers at Microsoft, previews sent to magazines, even internal sources. Unfortunately, positively identifying and fingering the culprits was almost impossible.

There were hacking attempts on our FTP server and network, although the real rub came from the pirates in Hong Kong and Singapore. They took the warez versions of AOK, burned them onto CDs, added some cover art, and sold the game throughout the Pacific Rim. In Korea, the CD vendors operating in front of Microsoft's headquarters had a warez version of AOK for sale. Warez versions were even turning up on eBay.

Though we doubt bottom-line sales were hurt much, our pride certainly suffered. Any of our future games will probably require connecting to a secure server of our own design to operate, even for single-player games.

3. Play-testing had a lot of problems

This item is a catchall for several problems that we encountered. On the good news front, our new offices have a dedicated play-test area equipped with identically configured machines. The bad news is that we didn't make the best of it. Many of our play-tests were not organized and focused enough, seriously reducing the amount of new and meaningful feedback obtained. It wasn't always clear when we were testing for specific bugs and issues, and when we were testing for "fun."

We had a schedule of participants which drew upon the whole company, but schedule conflicts and lax enforcement resulted in the same people playing most of the games. We played too much multiplayer and not enough attention was given to the single-player game. And some people took it much too seriously, trash-talking other players, celebrating wins at the loser's expense and storming off when they were losing.

Play-test problems weren't confined to Ensemble, though. At Microsoft, it was discovered that a play-tester had turned cheats on, playing to win not to test, in almost every game for over a month, which invalidated all the feedback from that group for the prior two months.

4. Art asset management was nonexistent

The number of individual frames of graphics in AOK is in the tens of thousands, and we didn't do a good job managing it. The programmers had a source-control system to help coordinate their primary output of code and the designers had the game's database system, but no such equivalent existed for the game's art assets. Artists could be working on something with no idea that anyone else was also working on it. There was no way to get a momentary snapshot of who was working on what, other than going around from office to office. Plus, there was no way to tell which files were actually live and being used and which ones were just taking up space.

A bird's-eye view of the AOK game world. Compared to AOE, AOK has bigger worlds with more objects and richer graphics.

Also missing was a way to go back and find prior versions of art, or to guarantee that new versions wouldn't be overwritten. As we have grown as a company, this problem has grown even faster. To address this problem in the future, a source-control similar to the art asset management system is being developed for use in all future projects.

5. Problems with third-party APIs and software

Another one of the items from the AOE post-mortem returns again. Microsoft's DirectPlay API still has a number of issues that make it less than perfect. One of its biggest problems is documentation and testing of the lesser-used portions of the API, or rather the lack thereof. Late in the development of AOK, our communications programmer, Paul Bettner, was able to communicate with the DirectPlay developers and an interesting scenario played out several times: Paul would attempt to solve some problem and the developers would indicate that it wouldn't work because of bugs in DirectPlay that they knew about but that were not documented.

DirectPlay wasn't the only problem. We decided to use DirectShow to handle our cinematics. The short version of this story is that it just didn't work. And then there was the Zone software for Microsoft's online Gaming Zone. The Zone software was developed too late in the process and had a number of problems, due to a lack of time to test and correct. Unfortunately, this means that direct TCP/IP games are more reliable than those played over the Zone, which is disappointing. This was not all the Zone's fault because we did not get our requirements to them soon enough.

TOP ROW, from left to right: Jeff Goodsill (COO), Brad Crow (art lead), Brian Hehmann (artist), Angelo Laudon (lead programmer), Sandy Petersen (designer), Dave Pottinger (programmer), Ian Fisher (designer), Harter Ryan (producer), Duncan McKissick (artist), Trey Taylor (programmer), Mario Grimani (programmer), Paul Bettner (programmer), Chris Van Doren (artist), Jeff Dotson (artist), John Evanson (programmer), Doug Brucks (programmer), Roy Rabey (IS support), Paul Slusser (artist), Chea O'Neill (artist), Bob Wallace (strategic), Mike McCart (webmaster). BOTTOM ROW: Rob Fermier (programmer), Nellie Sherman (logistics), Stephen Rippy (music), Herb Marselas (programmer), Mark Terrano (lead designer), Chris Rippy (sound), Herb Ellwood (artist), Thonny Namounglo (artist), Duane Santos (artist), David Lewis (programmer), Sean Wolf (artist), Bruce Shelley (lead designer), Matt Pritchard (programmer), Brian Moon (CFO), Tony Goodman (CEO), Don Gagen (artist), Greg Street (designer). NOT PICTURED: Tim Deen (programmer) Brian Sullivan (strategic), Chad Walker (artist), Eric Walker (artist), Scott Winsett (lead artist).

The Show Goes On

One of the touchiest and most personal issues concerned letting success go to our heads. The success of AOE is something that a lot of people in this business have not experienced. It exceeded our wildest dreams and allowed our company to take charge of our destiny. I remember when we got our first AOE royalty check—I had never held a multimillion dollar check before. That was great. We all got caught up in how good we were doing. Over time an attitude of invincibility set in. With a success like AOE, it's easy to forget what it was like to wonder if we were going to be in business the next year.

At some of the industry events such as the Game Developers Conference and E3, some of our people behaved in ways that embarrassed us. With success comes a responsibility to behave appropriately—the game industry is a small and incestuous one, and nothing lasts forever. Behaving in an exemplary manner and being friends with the industry at large is far more important than chest-beating about our current success. Suffice it to say that people in the Ensemble Studios organization have stepped forward to address this and we have challenged ourselves to be better people.

All the early indications for AOK are that it's going to be a blockbuster on the order of its predecessor, and maybe even greater. The reviews from the press have been unbelievably positive. According to PC Data, AOK was the number-one selling game in October. The great success of AOE made it possible for us to go to the next level of making great games. Though it enabled us to grow and acquire greater resources, it also raised expectations for our next game and spawned a host of new challenges. Meeting these new expectations has proved to be just as tough and rewarding a journey as creating the first game. In the end we succeeded in creating a game to be proud of, and I feel privileged to have been part of it.

Presto Studios'

MYST III: EXILE

by greg uhler

"Hello?"

"Hi, Greg, this is Bret Berry from Mindscape. How ya doin'?"

"Just great, thanks. What can I help you with?"

"Well, I'm calling about a game proposal we'd like you guys at Presto to put together for us. We've contacted several developers about this. Whoever gives the best proposal will get the project."

"OK, what's the project?"

"MYST III."

Did he say MYST III? A new sequel in the MYST series that has sold almost 10 million copies worldwide? After picking the phone up off of the floor and closing my gaping mouth, I could only say, "Wow!"

"Yeah, I thought you'd be excited. The proposal we require needs to include some story concepts, an analysis of MYST and RIVEN, a technology discussion, and, if at all possible, a technology demonstration. Oh, and we need this in five weeks."

Back-Story

MYST 3 is the second sequel to MYST, the phenomenally successful work of the mid-90s, and the first MYST game to be produced outside the original development house, Cyan. The MYST games follow the model of some of the earliest text adventures, in which the players solve puzzles to find their way through beautiful static environments, revealing a story as they go. CD-ROM technology allowed these environments to be realized in splendid visual and auditory detail, and their serene beauty drew many PC owners to enjoy their first computer game ever.

Needless to say, we hit the ground running. Presto Studios has been in the computer game business for more than 10 years. We began as a group of friends working out of a home in San Diego on an interactive CD-ROM game called THE JOURNEYMAN PROJECT. Since that time, we've shipped six other products, grown to as many as 45 employees, and have enjoyed limited success with our games. MYST III: EXILE, however, had the potential to take Presto to a whole new level. Production of EXILE began with a very small team: a writer, a creative director, three conceptual designers, and me as producer.

The first subject we tackled was an analysis of MYST and RIVEN. What worked? What didn't?

Why were those particular games so phenomenally successful? And what did we want to do differently?

Our discussions eventually led to the formation of a few overriding goals for EXILE. First, we would strive for great visual variety in the game.

Game Data

Release date: May 7, 2001

Publisher: UBI Soft

Genre: adventure

Platforms: Macintosh and PC (hybrid)

Staff: 22 full-time employees, 1 full-time contractor, 2 part-time contractors

Budget: Multimillion-dollar budget

Length of development: Two and a half years

Development hardware: Mostly Dells, averaging dual 700MHz Pentium IIIs with 1GB RAM and 30GB hard drives

Development software: Discreet 3DS Max, Discreet Combustion, Apple Final Cut Pro, Adobe Photoshop, Metrowerks CodeWarrior, Microsoft Visual C++, Microsoft Word, Microsoft Excel, Microsoft Project, Digidesign Pro Tools.

Notable technologies: RAD Game Tools' Bink and Miles Sound System, Apple's QuickTime

Project size: A feature-length animated film like Toy Story uses 120,000 frames of animation; EXILE used more than 150,000

We much preferred the varied worlds of MYST over the more homogeneous chain of islands found in RIVEN. Second, we would need to provide a way in which players could gauge their progress throughout the game. Players who had failed to complete MYST or RIVEN did so because they were unsure of how much remained of the game and what their goals were. We didn't want that to happen with EXILE. Finally, we wanted an extremely satisfying ending to the game, one which drew upon all of the knowledge that players had acquired throughout their journey. With these goals in mind, we set out on a two-and-a-half-year journey to create a worthy sequel to MYST and RIVEN.

What Went Right

1. Identifying the customer

Who played MYST and RIVEN? What did they like and dislike? What type of computer do they own? We felt that answering these questions would be instrumental in shaping what a MYST sequel should be. So we obtained data from registered owners of the two products, read all of the reviews and articles we could get our hands on, and became active readers of the MYST-related Internet fan sites and web boards. All of the information we gathered was used by the preproduction team to evaluate every part of our game—the visuals, story, puzzles, music, and technology.

For example, the hottest debate in preproduction was whether or not EXILE should use prerendered or real-time 3D graphics. By using prerendered graphics, we felt that we could meet or exceed the visual quality that RIVEN had achieved, but our puzzles would be more limited

Spiney bridge in Voltaic.

than if we used real-time 3D, because we would need to precalculate all the possible states for each puzzle from every viewable location. Conversely, real-time 3D would allow us to make the worlds more active and constantly changing, but to achieve the graphic realism of the worlds, the customer would be required to have a very fast CPU and a high-end 3D card.

In the end, this debate was resolved by identifying the MYST consumer. Our research showed us that many MYST players only played a few games each year. They are not out buying new computer systems every few years, so they typically have a slightly older computer, one that would have a hard time keeping up with an advanced real-time 3D game. So, we decided to use prerendered visuals for EXILE, in order to give us the largest possible customer base.

2. Preproduction and planning

Having created adventure games for eight years, you'd think that we would have been able to skip a lot of preproduction and just get to the production of the game very quickly. Actually, the opposite was true. For EXILE, we wanted more preproduction and planning time than we'd had for any of our other products. We had been burned too many times in production, and didn't want that to happen again. There is nothing more disheartening for an artist than to see his or her work go down the drain because of last-minute changes or redesigns.

With this foresight in mind, we convinced our publisher that we required a full nine months to design EXILE on paper, before we would create a single graphic. Though I'm sure it made our publisher quite nervous, we knew that this amount of preproduction time would help ensure a smooth production phase. Preproduction of EXILE began with two teams, one working on story and the other on visuals. We didn't want either team constrained by the other, so we kept them separate for the first month or so. Then we met together and began bouncing ideas around. It was amazing to see the two teams inspire each other—concept sketches led our writer down new plot lines, while story ideas and characters caused our artists to break out their sketchbooks during the meeting. Gradually the two camps met more frequently until the story and visuals became inseparable, ensuring continuity between the final game's world, plot, and characters.

Once the overall story and visual ideas began coming together, we focused on what we call the gameplay structure. This refers to the puzzles or challenges and their accompanying solutions and rewards that the player experiences during the adventure. This gameplay structure needed to allow for the story to be revealed over the course of the entire game, the level of difficulty to increase during the course of the game, and nonlinear events to be employed. We created a flowchart of the game, listing all of the challenges along the way, what they reveal when solved, and any interdependencies between puzzles or areas of exploration. This flowchart was used as a tool to see the game at a glance and make sure that it met our goals of gradual story revelation, increasing difficulty level, and a nonlinear experience.

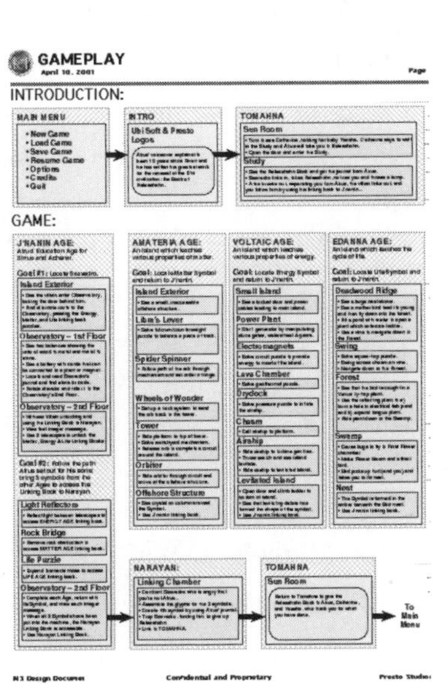

Gameplay flowchart.

When the gameplay flowchart, visual concept sketches, and story were complete, we had our blueprint for the game. This 160-page document was required reading for the entire team. But now it was time to put our money where our mouth was and develop the graphics for the game.

3. Using 3DS Max for art

To be honest, we were at a bit of a crossroads when it came to what 3D package to use for the art of EXILE. We had been using Electric Image on Macintoshes for many years, but had also recently been using Discreet's 3DS Max on PCs for our real-time 3D work. Could 3DS Max create the type of prerendered photo-realistic scenes we required for EXILE? And what else could it offer? Our lead animator, Mike Brown, was convinced that with the right finesse, 3DS Max could rival any high-end rendering package, so he set out to do a few tests. In about a week, he re-created one of the small islands in RIVEN and also built a prototype of one of our concept worlds. The results were very encouraging. We also explored the work flow of an artist using 3DS Max and discovered that the benefits of it being an integrated package were tremendous. The ability to model, texture, light, and animate in the same package solved a huge production nightmare for us. In the past, if an animator found something wrong while he was lighting a scene, he'd have to tell the modeler, who would fix the problem in a different package and send it to the animator, who would need to update his file with the fix. Talk about a recipe for disaster when you're dealing with tens of thousands of objects.

An example of EXILE'S Ocean water texture.

Our evaluation of 3DS Max proved that it was also the right choice for many practical reasons. First, we knew that we would need to hire many more artists to create EXILE. We found that there were many knowledgeable, talented 3DS Max artists available all over the world. Second, 3DS Max's open architecture and resulting litany of third-party plug-ins meant we could pick and choose additional features for the program at a very low cost. Why spend huge R&D costs to develop realistic ocean water when you can buy the plug-in for a few hundred dollars and have the same water that was used in Titanic? We took great advantage of this not only for water, fire, and hair, but also for production tools that helped us model, texture, light, and render much more quickly. 3DS Max proved to be a great choice—loved by the artists and indiscernible from more expensive packages by our customers.

4. Technology

Having decided to use prerendered graphics for EXILE, we were faced with the challenge of making these traditionally static images as immersive as possible. In one of our previous games, we had licensed a technology that displayed still images as 60-degree panoramic views (similar to QuickTime VR) but were unhappy with its performance and image quality. To overcome these deficiencies, we decided to write our own 360-degree technology. We developed a technique that took advantage of the speed and quality of real-time 3D cards. Quickly prototyping our idea with existing imagery, we realized that it worked flawlessly, allowing for very high frame rates without any degradation in image quality. We felt this was exactly the right technology to immerse a player in the worlds of EXILE.

With the basic technology complete, we pursued how to integrate animation, video, and water movement into the panoramic views. For animations and video, we wanted to avoid the QuickTime bounding-area rectangle and harsh compression artifacts that were typical of MYST and RIVEN. So we investigated several other compression algorithms and playback engines, finally deciding on RAD Game Tools' Bink technology. Bink provides fantastic compression and high image quality, playback engines for both Macintosh and PC, a fairly low processor speed requirement, and a host of special features. For instance, using the alpha channel support inherent in Bink, we were able to display animations and video in such a manner that only the changing pixels were drawn. This meant that the bounding box rectangle of the movie was gone and the compressed pixels were much less noticeable in the changing image.

Villian's costume concept sketch.

The last piece of the technology puzzle was the procedural effects, such as the moving ocean water. The waves needed to move realistically, look correct from altitudes ranging from five to 400 feet, and fade off into perspective toward the horizon.

To accomplish this, we first generated alpha channels of the ocean water for each panoramic image in the game. Next, we wrote an image manipulation algorithm (similar to a Photoshop filter) that properly bent and twisted the water pixels. The altered pixels were then applied to the ocean water texture (using the alpha channel) 15 or more times per second to give the water the illusion of movement. Variations of this technique were also used to simulate bubbling and ebbing lava as well as one puzzle's visible sound waves.

5. Web support and fan community

One of our early concerns for EXILE was that MYST fans seemed to believe that only Cyan (the creators of MYST and RIVEN) could create a great MYST game. We had to find a way to convince the MYST/RIVEN/D'ni fan community that even though Presto was creating the game, EXILE would meet or exceed their expectations. Our solution was the Internet. First, we identified two leading fan sites on the Internet, and in May 2000 (one year prior to shipping) invited their webmasters to come to Presto for a special sneak preview of EXILE. After viewing our teaser trailer, getting a hands-on demo, and browsing our concept sketches, both webmasters were sufficiently impressed and vowed to share their positive experience on their sites. Furthermore, we established such a good relationship with both webmasters that we coordinated with them over the next year and worked with one of them to create the official Myst3.com site.

Our second solution using the Internet was to release a teaser trailer and early screenshots. The trailer was intended to evoke the spirit of

MYST and RIVEN while providing a sneak peek at what EXILE had to offer visually. Supporting the trailer were numerous screenshots that showed the detail and beauty of the first world of EXILE. The trailer was downloaded more than half a million times in the first month, and the screenshots were posted on numerous Web sites and scrutinized by the diehard fans. In short, our underground public relations campaign was working well, and the fans were rejuvenated, eager to follow EXILE's progress over the next year, culminating with the game's launch.

What Went Wrong

1. Video quality

The live-action video shoot, and everything leading up to it, was probably the game's most important development milestone. It was an extremely hectic time. The scriptwriting had to be completed, the costumes designed and sewn, the props built, the CG backgrounds rendered, the actors hired and rehearsed, and the studio and personnel booked. All of these individual elements did come together, but one critical oversight prevented our resulting video from being crisp and perfect: we didn't use HDTV cameras.

Months after the video shoot was complete, we began compositing the video footage—removing the blue backgrounds from the live-action video and replacing them with our computer-generated worlds. After running a de-interlace filter on the footage (to remove the inherent NTSC scan lines), it quickly became evident that the lack of source video resolution (the number of pixels) was resulting in a blurry image. Even with image-sharpening tools and the latest filters in our compositing package, we were unable to achieve the crisp video that we had hoped for. This issue would have been avoided entirely if we had used the vastly superior image resolution of HDTV. We certainly now know the adage: Garbage in, garbage out.

2. Underestimating the budget

Having created many adventure games in the past, we had a reasonable estimation of how much it would cost to develop EXILE. However, what we didn't account for was how much extra effort it would take to reach the image quality level that was required. We were no longer working under our own quality levels, but rather ones that MYST and RIVEN had established. This mistake meant that we underestimated the cost of the game, though we had signed a contract to produce the game for that amount.

Underestimating the budget translated directly into not being able to hire enough team members, which translated into an insane schedule. It really was as simple as that. We all had to, and did, work our tails off, but this only resulted in a general feeling of "Whew! Glad that's over" rather than "That was a blast! Let's do another one!"

3. Sacrificing future projects

Undermanned and underfunded, everyone hunkered down and focused solely on EXILE. Not just the team, but the entire company. Personally, I was producing the game, prototyping puzzles, and programming many of our final worlds. Our president was executive producer for the title, technical director for the video shoot, and responsible for compositing all of the live-action footage. Clearly, we were wearing too many hats. So many, in fact, that we lost sight of some company goals and, most importantly, landing more projects. As a result, we only had one project in development after EXILE was complete, and we were forced to lay off staff. It was very disappointing to me personally to see people who had slaved over the project be "rewarded" with being laid off. The devotion that we all had to EXILE clearly had its cost.

4. So we've made another adventure game

Prior to EXILE, Presto was already known as an "adventure game company," having worked on six of these games in the past. We were eager to shake this image and prove that we could do much more. Obviously, the fantastic opportunity to create EXILE was something we could not resist. However, we are very concerned that the completion of EXILE will further brand us as an "adventure game only" company. Will EXILE's completion bring us many new opportunities? Or will we have to try even harder to avoid this moniker? Only time will tell.

Amateria world from wireframe to final image.

5. The launch: It's out of our hands now

The launch of any title is usually one of the most stressful times for the developer-publisher relationship. The developer is exhausted, having just crunched through several years of production, yet hopeful and full of expectations for the success of "their" product. However, the publisher then takes the reins, promoting the product, manufacturing the boxes, selling as many copies as possible, and handling customer support. But where does this leave the developer? In truth, the developer is still financially tied into the product but has absolutely no more control over it. That is why the launch is always so stressful, for it represents the transition of power that has taken place from the developer to the publisher.

Atrus' costume sketch.

This stressful launch period was no different for EXILE. We were exhausted. We obviously had high hopes for the game. We felt that if EXILE was promoted as being "big," it would be big. After all, MYST and RIVEN are the best-selling PC games of all time. Unfortunately, the purchase of our publisher by another publisher changed the decision-making process, the people in power, and the management approach. What we felt should have been a huge launch was, in our opinion, slightly disappointing. A great multilingual feature of the game was cancelled in the last few weeks. Our presence at E3 was minimal, due to our producer being taken out of the loop on the decision-making process. Advertisements were scarce and short-lived. And negotiations for a possible sequel ground to a halt.

Even with these occurrences, however, we believe that time will determine EXILE's success, not the minor setbacks from the launch period of the game. Going forward, we expect that the launch will only be a bump in the road, not a sign of things to come.

Closing Thoughts

As you've seen, some elements of our production worked out perfectly, and probably saved us months of time and tens of thousands of dollars. Others didn't go quite as well as we'd hoped, and parts of the product suffered because of them.

Throughout the process, we tried to appreciate the positives and learn from the negatives. I've heard it said that good judgment comes from experience, and experience—well, that comes from poor judgment. Here's hoping that we showed a lot of good judgment and that the "experience" wasn't too painful.

137

Poptop Software's **TROPICO**

by brent smith

Back-Story

Some games form their own mini-genre, and TROPICO is one. Players take the role of a petty dictator, el Presidente of a Caribbean island, with control of its political and economic development. Poptop's previous game was the economic strategy game RAILROAD TYCOON II, but TROPICO is a much deeper, broader simulation of an entire mini-republic, reaching down to the level of individual citizens and across the board from education to tourism. Despite its depth and complexity, TROPICO also manages to convey the quirky, cynical humor of its banana-republic material.

In the spring of 1999, Poptop had just wrapped up development on the successful RAILROAD TYCOON II (RT2) and its expansion, THE SECOND CENTURY. At the time, Poptop was staffed by the overwhelming count of four artists and two programmers. Being that small, we had had no time to think about anything other than the current project, and suddenly we found ourselves sitting around a table, eyes still slightly glazed from the inevitable project-end rush we had just gone through, looking for new ideas. These were uncharted waters for Poptop. RT2 had been based very closely on Sid Meier's classic RAILROAD TYCOON. The original RAILROAD TYCOON had been an inspiration, a design manual, a blueprint for making a good game, and a launching point for new ideas. The upside was that a good part of the design work had been done for us. The downside, as we were to find out on our next project, was that it left us a bit naïve about the effort it would take to create a new game from an original idea.

The almanac.

As we sat around our company card table, brainstorming ideas, one idea quickly jumped to the forefront. The idea of taking a building game and putting a political game on top of it had captured everyone's imagination. With our creative energies renewed by a fresh idea and the thrill of starting a new project in our hearts, we rushed off to create TROPICO—each of us in our own way. Actually, it wasn't that bad. We did discuss major elements of the game. We knew that it would have buildings and people that the player would not control directly. We knew it would use the RT2 engine but would be more ambitious than RT2 had been. As we rushed off to begin development, that was about all we knew—and, as we were to discover later, each person on the team didn't even share the same vision about the things we thought we did know.

Game Data

Release Date: April 2001

Publisher: Gathering of Developers

Genre: real-time strategy/"god game"

Platforms: Windows 95/98/ME/2000/NT 4, Mac

Number of Full-time Developers: 10 (7 artists, 3 programmers)

Number of Contractors: 1 musician

Estimated Budget: $1.5 million

Length of Development: 2 years

Development Hardware (average): 550MHz Pentium IIIs with 512MB RAM, 40GB hard drives, and a variety of 3D cards running Windows ME or 2000 (programmers) or Windows NT (artists)

Development Software: Visual C++ 6.0, Visual SourceSafe 6.0, 3DS Max 3.1, Character Studio 2.2, Photoshop 5.5, Tree Factory plug-in for 3DS Max

Notable Technologies: Bink Video, Miles Sound System

Project Size: Approx. 150,000 lines of code (plus 20,000 for tools)

During the project, Poptop grew to the bloated size of 10 employees—seven artists and three programmers. It is a testament to the talent and hard work of this team that we ended up with a strong, fun product in spite of the pitfalls that we encountered along the way.

What Went Right

1. Created "deep" character

It was obvious from the beginning that the most important aspect of TROPICO would be the people. If we intended to have a game in which the player didn't have direct control of the units on the map, then we had better make sure that the people acted in a reasonable and somewhat predictable fashion.

This was no trivial task. Each unit on the map (in the later stages of the game there can easily be more than 500 units) has more than 70 characteristics, which determine its actions and reactions to the player. This includes items as simple as name, age, and what part of the island the unit was "born" on, to things as complex as the unit's satisfaction with various aspects of the environment (religion, national pride, pay compared to others in the same situation, and so on). Additionally, as units live their sim lives—they are born, prance about as children, enter the workforce at a certain age, and eventually retire and die—we keep track of their families. Each unit potentially has a mother, father, spouse, and multiple children. Units also know about their grandparents, cousins, aunts, and uncles. What this means to the player is that the repercussions for treating one unit badly filter through their family tree much like you would expect in real life. Send Juan Pablo Ramirez to jail, and not only are his parents, wife, and children upset, so are his five siblings, their 18 children, and so on down the line. This added a lot to the political atmosphere of TROPICO.

Our second goal with this system was hiding its complexity from the player. Part of the fun of TROPICO is trying to see and understand what response your actions will evoke from the population of your island. Although we kept detailed information about each unit in the game, there was a balancing act in taking advantage of it without flooding the player with information. I think we succeeded here. Our interface provides the player with in-depth information about the people in the game—making them come alive—without overwhelming the player with having to know trivial details about them.

Unit development was not easy, but because we identified this as a critical area up front and spent a lot of time and manpower addressing it, it turned into one of the strengths of TROPICO.

Banker.

2. Small, streamlined, and talented team

Being as small as we are certainly has a downside, the most serious being that we are limited in the things we can do in a given amount of time by sheer lack of manpower. However, the advantages to a team this small, at least in terms of developing a project such as TROPICO, outweighed the disadvantages. Everybody at Pop-top knows everyone else. Not just knows them, but knows what they are working on, what their strengths and weaknesses are, the name of their significant other, and so on. There's no hiding here. If you screw up, people know it was you. If you do something brilliant, everyone knows that too.

This kind of intimacy makes us very streamlined. Everybody knows where he stands and what his job is. There is no middleman; if you need to talk to someone, you talk directly to him. There is no distraction of having team members pulled off to work on a different, behind-schedule project or promotional material. We did one thing, TROPICO, and that's all we did. Of course, this kind of team only works if every member is talented, and that is, without a doubt, the case at Pop-top. I see it every day, and I think the players of RT2 and now TROPICO have seen the result as well.

3. Homegrown tools

Upon the completion of RT2, we had accumulated a nice suite of tools for preprocessing and manipulating art assets and interface elements. With TROPICO, we continued this work, both improving the existing tools and developing new ones. Our most-used tool was a program written to preprocess art assets into our custom format. It also had the ability to clip and scale the art, and also reduce animations to a keyframe and delta information for efficient storage.

When TROPICO began, we further modified this tool to allow it do work with 24- and 32-bit

TIFF files. A palette reducer/optimizer was added to create 8-bit palettes from one or more higher color-depth images. We also included the ability to add parameters to the instruction set that the program used to process the files, allowing such things as tinting (which allowed us to construct placeholder art rapidly by simply taking an existing image and tinting it to another color), and lightening or darkening of the image.

Tourists relax and sunbathe on the beach.

Finally, we added support that allowed us to read image-depth information stored in RLA files and store it with the image. This information could then be used to tell us the Zorder information of the various parts of the image, which allowed us, for example, to handle units walking behind parts of a building while walking in front of others. Another tool that we inherited from RT2 and improved upon during the development of TROPICO allowed us to create, size, and position interface elements outside of the code. Using a simple scripting language, interfaces could be built and then compiled by this tool into a format that could be used by the TROPICO code.

A new type of tool that we developed and began using with TROPICO, and which turned out to be a real time-saver, was used for game data manipulation. Using MFC (which I'd never recommend for any software intended for release, but which is tremendous for quick development of tools such as these), we quickly built a very robust unit editor and building editor.

These editors allowed us to manage all the data associated with a particular type of building or unit outside of the program.

This capability was invaluable for balancing and tweaking the data, as it allowed us to change information in a relatively safe way while the game was running and see its effects immediately upon the game world.

4. Fun topic

Without a doubt, one of the key factors in the success of TROPICO was the topic. During our brainstorming sessions, a number of ideas were thrown on the table, but the idea that became TROPICO was the one that had everybody excited. While a lot of the elements of TROPICO can be found in other games, the mixture of those elements and the setting itself had everyone eager to see what we could make. This enthusiasm translated outside of the company, too. Nearly everyone to whom we showed the game voiced their enthusiasm about the freshness of the idea. Something about the idea of ruling an island full of sun-drenched beaches and tropical beauties strikes a chord in most people's hearts.

One of the most promising indicators late in the project that we had something special on our hands was that we were still eager to play the game, and were still throwing out new ideas, even after spending two long years developing it.

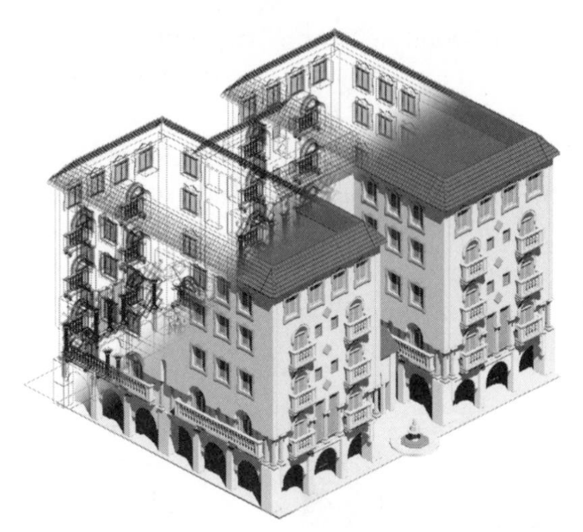

Wireframe and model of the hotel.

5. Localization

Having been involved in the translation of RT2 into a variety of different languages, including double-byte handling for Asian languages, we knew up front that this was something that we needed to be concerned with in TROPICO. Fortunately, a lot of the groundwork had been established during RT2's development. The code contained home-grown string manipulation functions, which allowed us to maintain tight control of many of the issues associated with localization. We also had a tool that allowed us to pull strings out of the code base for insertion into a string table near the end of the project. The tool was very useful in that it not only recognized strings within the code, but it was smart enough to disregard strings within comments and strings on lines which we tagged with a special comment telling the tool that it was O.K. for this string to remain in the code (format strings, for example).

This meant that for much of the project we didn't have to concern ourselves with trying to keep a string table up to date, but when the time came, we were able to do it quickly and efficiently. Overall, localization was a breeze. Having seen what a nightmare this step can be on other projects, we were dreading the work we thought we would have to do in this area, but the final tally was less than a man-week of work spent getting the game ready for foreign language translation.

What Went Wrong

1. Lack of up-front design work

Coming off the success of RAILROAD TYCOON II, we were excited to get the chance to work on something new and unique. A few company brainstorming sessions and a game or two of Junta, and we knew that we wanted to do a tongue-in-cheek political game. We couldn't jump into the project fast enough. Ideas were flying hot and heavy. Everyone was excited. Unfortunately, we failed to realize at the time that everybody was carrying a slightly different picture in his head of what the final game would be. Some were envisioning the stab-your-neighbor, laugh-a-second antics of the Junta board game. Others were seeing the close-up, detailed view of people in action that ROLLERCOASTER TYCOON had done so successfully. Most of us were somewhere in between.

Having come from RT2, we really found ourselves unprepared for this problem. With RT2, Poptop had the original as a blueprint and design document. Design was only an issue so far as how the original game could be improved upon and how current technology could be utilized to improve the game. The game could practically write itself, with Poptop's main concern being to re-create the magic of the original game while adding a few minor twists of our own. Now we found ourselves with a blank slate, an original idea where every gameplay detail had to be created from scratch.

Unfortunately, we approached this in much the same way as we had approached RT2. Rather than settling on a unified design, or even trying to create one, each of us ran back to his workstation and began to create what we thought the game would be.

It quickly became apparent that we were not all moving in the same direction. People had very different views of where the game should go. Decisions had to be made on the fly. Some people's visions were cut out entirely, while others had theirs altered to the point that it became something entirely different.

Luxury tourist.

A tourist.

This process was a very difficult growing pain for Poptop. People's feelings were hurt when they realized the idea that they were so excited about was not the idea that we were creating. The game lost "buy-in" from people in the company as it became something that they were less interested in or someone else's idea that they didn't really understand. During this time we struggled onward, trying to create this game that wasn't really what anyone had originally intended. Amazingly, we stubbornly refused to stop and consolidate our ideas in meetings or on paper so that the team could be unified in the idea and to rekindle the original excitement for the game.

Eventually, working on TROPICO stopped being a passion and became just a job for many on the team, leading to low morale and loss of productivity. Hopefully, we've learned from this mistake, and on our next idea (original or not) we will figure out what it is we are creating before we start to create it and try to keep everyone excited about the direction in which we are moving.

2. Modifying the existing code base

One of the givens, decided before any work was even begun on TROPICO, was that we would use the 3D engine from RT2. This would allow us to have working maps with many of the features we would need in TROPICO almost immediately, thereby giving us a huge jump start on development. The idea was a great one and paid huge dividends in getting us working almost immediately on the game itself rather than the engine. Unfortunately, in conjunction with this decision, we started from the existing RT2 code base—not only the engine, but all the game code from RT2 as well. We were trying to "morph" RT2 into TROPICO, which led to all kinds of problems and slow-downs.

An in-game overview of the island.

First of all, a single programmer had developed almost the entire RT2 code base. With TROPICO, the staff of Poptop had nearly doubled in size. Each new programmer immediately faced the daunting task of getting a grasp of the RT2 code before he could even begin to make the modifications necessary to create TROPICO. Second, there were huge chunks of the code base that became dead once TROPICO was started, such as the multiplayer code. (We had decided pretty early in TROPICO's development to scrap multiplayer and concentrate on the single-player experience.) Of course, multiplayer code was integrated very tightly into many areas of the RT2 code, and at first we tried to work around it. Eventually we tore it out, once we became frustrated trying to determine which areas of the code were dead and which were important.

Finally, the process of working off the original RT2 code base was inherently dangerous at best. We automatically inherited any bug that had managed to survive in RT2 and created quite a few more just going through the process of weeding out what code was unnecessary for TROPICO. We would have been much better off starting with a clean slate and then pulling over those sections of the RT2 code base that we could use. The RT2 code was not cleanly delineated between engine code and game code. However, the process of untangling the usable engine code and importing it into a clean code base would have been inherently more bug-free and more comprehensible to those unfamiliar with the RT2 code, and would have saved us time in the long run.

3. Fun factor versus gee-whiz factor

Because we started with an existing engine, one of the errors that we made during development was to see how far we could push the envelope with the engine, working on "gee whiz" enhancements that would improve the look and the technology of the game instead of features that would enhance gameplay.

The biggest example of this was what we dubbed "Zoom 0." As the graphics in TROPICO were much more detailed than RT2's, we looked for ways to show off these gorgeous images in the game. Allowing the engine to zoom in one level closer than it had previously been able to (Zoom 1) was one of the ways that we did this. In TROPICO, players can zoom in very close and get very detailed views of the people and the buildings. Unfortunately, Zoom 0 is not very useful for gameplay, as it is almost impossible to see enough of the map at that zoom level to get a feeling for how you should play. The majority of players tend to stay zoomed out about two levels, occasionally zooming in or out one level as the situation warrants.

OK, so we added a feature that allowed us to show off the graphics even if it didn't help gameplay. What's the big deal? The deal is that we pre-scaled all of the images for the various zooms beforehand and stored them in the data file, so these high-resolution close-up graphics ate up as much space as all the other zoom levels' graphics combined. We spent a full 50 percent of our graphics budget on this one feature. As we got deep into the project, it became apparent that memory and CD file space budgets were going to be tight, but we had invested too much into this feature to be comfortable with cutting it.

Ultimately, we had to cut other features to create space, features which would have improved

The dictator's mansion.

the game. Rotatable buildings, more unit animations, and repeating animations on the buildings (such as blinking lights and moving machinery) all had to be cut to make room. Looking back, it is apparent that tossing out Zoom 0 and putting in more gameplay-friendly features would have been a big net improvement to the overall game.

4. Waited too long for scenarios

After the scenario-intense RT2 and its add-ons, we were more than happy to try creating a game in which the strengths lay in randomly generated maps and sandbox-style open-ended play. From day one we worked on TROPICO with this goal in mind. A lot of effort went into creating a map generator that would create pleasing, logical, and most importantly playable maps. We modeled rainfall on what we knew and could find out about meteorology. We researched vegetation, not only to find flora indigenous to a

Caribbean setting but also to find out under what conditions a particular plant would thrive and how to represent that in the game.

A significant amount of time went into creating realistic mountains and series, even ranges, of mountains. We even went so far as to model the terrain under the water, so that shallow beach areas and deeper waters would be accurately created. As we neared the end of the project, we had no doubt that our map generator could create some fabulous-looking maps, and, given the number of factors we allowed the player to tweak during map generation, an endless supply of playable maps.

Pit boss.

However, the game was missing clearly defined goals. Using the map generator, there was no way to create a map that had a specific situation to solve, and only a very limited way to create maps with unique obstacles to overcome. In other words, the game and the maps were great for an open-ended, sandbox style of game, but were lacking in goal-oriented, problem-solving gameplay.

While the sandbox mode allows players to create a wide range of different maps, much more depth and many hours of play could have been added to the game if we had included a rich set of scenarios and the tools for the players to create even more.

As we realized this late in the project, we scrambled to create scenarios to include. Unfortunately, our tools in this area were underdeveloped, and time had to be squeezed out of people's schedules even to produce what we did. The result was that TROPICO included a very limited number of scenarios (eight with the game and two others included in some promotional CDs) that weren't nearly as involved as they could have been, and certainly weren't up to the standard that we had created in RT2.

Another by-product of this oversight was that we never spent time polishing the map editor tools that we used in development.

The original game design was oriented toward random-map play, so we never saw the need for a more sophisticated editor until late in the project. These tools ended up being disabled in the release version, disappointing many fans who were hoping to create their own maps. Fortunately for our fans, a map editor should be available in an upcoming patch.

5. Lack of unified artistic vision

As I mentioned, one of the effects of essentially bypassing the design phase of this project was that there was a lack of consistent vision among team members. One of the places that this became most apparent was in the game art. Almost all of the artists at one time or another during the project worked on creating buildings for the game. They were given only a vague notion of what type of building they were to create—a paper sketch or a very crude 3D mockup—and left on their own to move forward from there.

Halfway through the project, the problems with this became apparent. Scale varied wildly from artist to artist, as did level of detail. The same problems were occurring with the character animations, as the two artists working on those had taken different approaches. One artist was striving toward very lifelike figures with complex animations, while the other created more cartoonish parodies of TROPICO's inhabitants with more outlandish but less complex animations. Both artists had a clear idea of what they were trying to do, and both accomplished their respective goals brilliantly, but the difference in their approaches can still be seen in the release version of the game if you compare, for example, the banker to the female luxury tourist.

At this point we appointed a person to take on the role of art producer. His job was to try to coordinate the artists' efforts and make sure they shared more or less the same vision. But the damage had been done. Team members had to spend valuable time sifting through and reworking art. Frustrations mounted as artists who previously had been able to work toward their personal vision now found themselves having to compromise to a shared vision of the whole team. This problem could have been significantly reduced with more up-front planning and more ongoing feedback to the artists as they completed each task. We definitely learned from this process and will improve upon it in our next game.

In Hindsight

It's pretty much the experience with any game project, whether the developers will admit to it or not, that you look back and see mistakes that you made and bemoan the ways that the game could have been better if only those mistakes had been avoided. TROPICO is certainly no different in that regard. Every member of the TROPICO team felt the sting of loss at some point or another when a feature that they were particularly fond of was cut. Each of us can look back and think of a hundred ways that we could improve TROPICO. That, in itself, is a good sign. At the end of two years of development, we still cared about the game and wanted to make it better. Everyone was happy with what we had created, but no one was satisfied with the details. Art is never done.

We learned a lot individually and as a team about how to approach a project and how to manage it once it is underway. This was our first attempt at a completely original idea, and although we encountered a lot of pitfalls along the way and stumbled more than a few times, I think the end result is pretty amazing—something that we are proud of and that the game's fans will enjoy. Considering that TROPICO was done with a team of only 10 people—tiny by today's standards—the game's success is a testament to the Poptop team's talent, creativity, and hard work.

SECTION III

Managing Innovation

The great thing about an innovative game is that it starts with desire. A person or a development team comes up with an idea for a game no one has seen before, and they want to play it badly enough that they're willing to go through all the risk and work and inordinate hassle required to bring it into being.

Suppose you have an idea for a game, something no one has seen before. There are many forms this could take. It could be a clever piece of software you've been toying with, a graphic style, or a method of telling a story, or a haunting image. It could be an untried subject like haberdashery or whale-watching, or a dream you had (SPACE INVADERS, apocryphally, was based on a dream), or just a strange indescribable feeling. It could be anything.

This will not be easy. Someone has to fund the game, to be convinced that the vision you and your team share will one day be exchanged for hard cash. A marketing team has to understand what the game is, and why people will want it. The development team has to communicate effectively enough so that they can be sure that they all share the same idea. And no one can see this so-called "great idea"—it's still a thought in someone's brain. Of course, it's the very newness of the thing that makes this process so difficult. Any game starts this way, but in the innovative games, the radical departures, it's toughest—you have nothing you can point to and say, "it's going to be like this."

Over the next 18–36 months, there is the task of converting this invisible feeling, this hunch, into a functioning piece of software that runs on an actual machine. This is the process that is unbelievably subtle and difficult. It comes down to a series of tiny decisions made daily, about interface, art direction, technology. Should such-and-such a command be made with the right or left mouse button; should the heroine be blonde or brunette; should we invest CPU cycles in AI or in rendering? All with the looming, crushing knowledge that a factory in upstate New York is waiting to stamp your answer onto 400,000 CDs.

These are the kinds of choices that slowly convert the charged, elusive vision within you into an application on your desktop that anyone can run and experience. It's particularly difficult in this medium because you're part of a group of 8–40 people, practicing at least four different disciplines (programming, art, game design, audio, not to mention storytelling and project management) in an interdependent process that is supposed to yield one unified coherent whole that captures a feeling that 15 months into the project you may well be unable to recollect. All done on a tight schedule and budget, as every day and every penny cuts into the net profit.

(The crowning irony, of course, is that other people consider this a trivial amusement. When you tell them what you do for a living, the inevitable response is, "Oh, so you get to play games all day?" Yes. Yes, that's exactly right.)

There is an art to this process. In an ideal world, making an innovative game would be as simple as (a) getting a good idea, (b) writing a detailed technical and design document and making some concept art, and (c) getting a development team to make it (this is sometimes called the "waterfall" development model). Then you wait 24 months while they work, and on the last day the game is complete and you sit down and play it and voila...fun.

If this book teaches one lesson, it should be that this is not always possible. Game development is very complex, especially new kinds of games. Features take longer than expected, or interact in surprising ways, or suggest other exciting features that suddenly seem worth implementing two weeks before beta, and so on. Experienced teams expect surprises. They build something, play it, double back, rethink, cut features, hold meetings, and try again. Shipping a successful game usually involves this iterative cycle of building features, testing them, and then revising them, repeated several times over the development period.

Different games present different problems. Sometimes the initial idea proves too ambitious, and you have to decide which features to cut while keeping the core idea intact. Sometimes the initial idea proves too vague, and part the process of building the game is refining and tightening the focus. Sometimes it's a process of discovery. As the game becomes a concrete thing, as it encounters reality, it works a little differently than it did in your head. Games are very complex entities, and it's impossible to work out in advance how everything in them will behave. You may notice playtesters using some feature in ways you never imagined, to defeat obstacles or just as a kind of mini-game by itself. They're not playing the game you imagined, they're playing the game you actually made, which is slightly different but perhaps no less fun.

- **Define a high concept.**

  Have a clear sense of where you're trying to go, even if you don't know how to get there. Every week, you and the rest of your team will have to make decisions, you can use the high concept as a compass to check your bearings against. If you can ask of any given task, "does this bring us closer to our goal of creating the ultimate robot ninja jai-alai simulator," it's easier to make these judgment calls.

- **Know when to cut features.**

  A feature can be cool, but still not form an essential part of the game you're making.

- **Build good tools for creating and editing content.**

  It is essential to be able to test content in your game engine, and revise it if things don't work the way you plan. The easier it is to edit game data, the quicker you can react to testing feedback, and the more cycles of testing and revision you can go through.

- **Form a solid relationship with your publisher.**

  If the game needs revision, someone on the publishing side needs to understand why and how it's going to take place. If they can trust that your development process is under control, and have a sense of the goal you're working toward, things will go much more smoothly.

- **Create a clear chain of command, or some other protocol for tough decision-making.**

  Not every decision can be made as a group, especially when it comes to setting the vision for the game. If team members disagree on some point, it has to be resolved so development can continue.

- **Prototype early.**

  Get the game and its core features running and playable as soon as you can. Have people who haven't heard about the concept play it and tell you whether it's fun, and why or why not.

Why make innovative games? They take appalling chances with the time and money of the people who make them, all for the slim chance of becoming a breakaway win or at least a quirky cult hit.

There are large-scale reasons to make them. Most people agree that digital games are an immature phenomenon and that we are far from seeing what can be done in this medium. If sequels are the bankable projects that keep the industry alive from year to year, it is the radical departures that help it grow, that expand our sense of what the medium is. We are all waiting for better games, and innovation is the only way they get made. Of course, they play an economic role as well as a creative one—games like MYST, and, yes, BARBIE FASHION DESIGNER, changed the market as well as the medium, by bringing people who had never thought about it before to sit in front of a computer play games.

151

Lionhead Studios'

BLACK & WHITE

by peter molyneux

Back-Story

BLACK & WHITE belongs to the god-game genre popularized by Lionhead auteur Peter Molyneux in the POPULOUS series—the player is literally a god, helping his or her people prosper, through guidance and miracles. The showpiece is the Creature, which is a living animal avatar that the player raises from childhood, shaping its personality by reward and punishment. The Creature is a complex, semi-autonomous artificial intelligence, whose nature changes as it grows—like the player-god, the Creature can become good or evil, black or white. BLACK & WHITE is an ambitious accomplishment—apart from its originality, it features fluid, epic-scale storytelling, gorgeous graphic presentation, and an elegant, versatile mouse-based interface.

BLACK & WHITE is the game I always wanted to make. From the days of POPULOUS I had been fascinated by the idea of controlling and influencing people in an entire world. I was also interested in the concepts of good and evil as tools the player can use to rule or change the world. These themes crop up regularly in my games, but I realize now that with every game I was heading toward my ultimate goal—the god game BLACK & WHITE.

I wanted the game to be more flexible, more open, and more attractive than anything I'd ever played. I was determined that the player could do almost anything he or she wanted. Instead of leading players deeper into a world of levels and testing them with tougher and tougher monsters, I wanted players to be engaged by the story but to take it at their own pace and decide which bits to tackle and when to tackle them. More technically, I didn't want a panel of icons or a set of on-screen options. With DUNGEON KEEPER I felt we overdid the control panel, and, while it worked, it didn't add to the immersive sense of being this evil overlord deep underground. Frankly, it simply reminded you that you were playing a video game. Finally, I wanted to place into BLACK & WHITE the ability to select a creature (originally any creature from the landscape) and turn it into a huge, intelligent being which could learn, operate independently, and do your bidding when you wanted. I knew that this would require an artificial intelligence structure unlike any ever written. It had to be the best.

Of course, I needed a team for all this, but I wanted the right sort of team and so had to build it slowly. A core team of about six was formed, and at the start of Lionhead we worked at my house. Our first task was to create a library of tools, so we spent our time there doing boring foundation tool-building. We started work on the game proper when we moved into our offices in February 1998, at which time there were nine of us. By this time we had begun thinking about the game in general terms. We discussed what we could have in it, what we should have in it, and what, in a perfect world, we'd like to see. Funnily enough, much of the last category did in fact make it in, things such as the changing atmosphere and buildings if you change alignment between evil and good or vice versa. Also, ideas for some fully lip-synched characters were thrown around. At that time, we didn't seriously think it could be done.

Game Data

Release date: March 30, 2001

Publisher: Electronic Arts

Genre: real-time strategy/ "god game"

Platforms: Windows 95/98/2000/ME

Full-time developers: 25

Contractors: 3

Budget: Approx. £4 million (approx. $5.7 million)

Length of development: 3 years, 1 month, 10 days

Hardware used: 800MHz Pentium IIIs with 256MB RAM, 30GB hard drives, and Nvidia GeForce graphics cards

Software used: Microsoft Dev Studio, 3DS Max

Notable technologies: Bink for video playback, Immersion touch sense for force-feedback mouse

Project size: Approx. 2 million lines of code

During the first year of Lionhead we added people gradually, as I was very keen for the friendly, family-style atmosphere of Lionhead to remain, and it takes a certain sort of person to fit in and enjoy working with such a close-knit team. This policy of only recruiting people whom we felt had the talent and a way of working which fit in with Lionhead's existing members meant that our team had evolved their own way of working. They didn't just carry out their tasks but questioned, tested, and pushed both themselves and each other. It's labor-intensive, but you often end up with more than you expected. For example, the art team divided up the tribal styles for the villages and tried to outdo each other in terms of design and effort put in. The result was better design work than we thought we'd get.

At Lionhead Studios, we all knew that BLACK & WHITE was going to be something special. This belief became self-fulfilling as we were inspired by each new feature and every neat, innovative section of code. Naturally, this meant that everyone worked exceptionally hard. Over the course of the project the team did the work of a group twice their number. We regularly went home as dawn broke, and weekends became something other people did.

What Went Right

1. It got finished

This sounds stupid, but we encountered some big problems, and there were times when we doubted that the game (as it ultimately ended up) would get released. As a new company, we not only had to work out the game we were going to create, but we had to write the tools and libraries, create everything from scratch in software, and also gel together as a team. We couldn't have a dress rehearsal for this, so we learned by trying things and then changing them if they didn't work. As time rolled on, we couldn't afford to make any mistakes or pursue blind alleys.

For example, we talked about updating some of the graphics at one point. It didn't seem a big job, but once we'd changed some of the buildings in the tribal villages, they showed up any unchanged ones and made them look less impressive, so we had to assign time to do them all. We got a much better set of buildings out of this, but if we'd known that we'd have had to do all of them, we would have said, rightly, that there wasn't time.

Render of the evil cow Creature.

The programmers were likewise coming up with neater and neater ways of coding, and thus trying to do more and more with the code they had. It says a lot about the talented and single-minded development team at Lionhead that everybody always wanted to make every element that little bit better. And as we fixed the bugs and sent the game to QA, we felt like people who'd run a marathon and could see the finish line, but it didn't seem to be getting any closer. Perhaps this is a function of not getting enough sleep over a period of several months.

2. All the risks paid off

We wanted to do some pretty groundbreaking things in BLACK & WHITE. One example was doing away with the panel of controls and using the Gesture system for casting Miracles. We tried and tried to get this feeling just right, and if we'd had to dump it, I'd have been so disappointed. But after research, testing, and simple trial and error, we got it working beautifully, and we now have a feature no one else does.

Also, integrating the story line into such a free-flowing strategy game was a risk. We thought it would sit quietly behind the game, popping up to direct you if you hadn't moved on, but the story came alive and started to draw the player through the game in a way none of us, apart from perhaps scriptwriter James Leach, had envisaged. It also gave us characters such as Sable, the Creature trainer, and those advisors whom we hear people now quoting lines from, and who exist outside the game as recognizable characters.

The huge, learning, intelligent Creature was also more of a gamble than he now seems. To go into

AI in such an in-depth way required Richard Evans, our AI programmer, to consider what learning was, how practice works, and how the reinforcement of ideas comes about. Then he built all this into a character which appeared to live and learn like, say, a clever puppy. AI is always a minefield, and I'm always disappointed

Good ape.

by great strategy games which appear to have the most simple, easy-to-predict AI running your enemies. We just wanted to advance the technology to its extreme.

We also wanted to do more with graphics and animation blending. The world changes depending on whether you're playing as a good or an evil god, and things take on subtle new looks. The Creature, the player's hand, and many of the buildings change, and we used more animation blending to achieve smooth movement and changes than anyone else has ever done, I believe.

We're also the first game (apart from Microsoft's FLIGHT SIMULATOR) which enables you to import real weather in real time into the world. We are also the first to enable unified messaging, whereby you can send messages to the web from the game, or receive them, using e-mail and mobile phones. This integrated two-way messaging as well as the ability to take your Creature out of BLACK & WHITE and onto the web is brand-new. Also, the game can import names from your e-mail package and assign them to unique villagers in your tribe in the game. I expect lots of games to do similar things in the future, but we took massive risks and devoted huge amounts of effort to being the first and to making it work properly.

3. The game looks so stunning

When we started, we used a wireframe test bed and a couple of conceptual screenshots to provide some atmosphere. I first showed the test bed and these mocked-up screenshots to the press at E3 in Atlanta in 1998, and I could see on the assembled faces that nobody believed we could accomplish anything like it in the final game. I was complimented on the depth and beauty of preliminary efforts, but the compliments had a slightly hollow ring. I could almost hear people thinking, "Yeah, it looks great, but anyone can draw pretty screens using an art package. What's your game really going to look like?"

Not only did we manage to pull off the look we wanted, but we exceeded it by some margin. The sheer beauty of the lands is something I hope won't be matched for a while, and the fact that you can move, zoom, and rotate to view it from any angle, anywhere in the game, is again something we got spot-on. Looking back, I don't know whether we were insanely ambitious, because at the time we started, you couldn't have done what we did. We needed so much custom-written software, and we also needed the minimum specification of the PC community at large to get better before this would be viable. When we started BLACK & WHITE, most people had 32MB of RAM in their PCs. The game requires 64MB, but that's commonplace now. So, if you like, we aimed beyond the horizon, and the world rotated and caught up with us so we still hit our target.

4. The artificial intelligence

The Creature AI, as I have mentioned, is absolutely spot-on. Richard Evans worked tirelessly on this, and it became something that surprised even him with its flexibility and power. The AI isn't just restricted to the Creature. Every villager in the game has it as well, and they are all different in their wishes, desires, motivation, and personality. Because there is no upper limit to the number of villagers you can have, we had to cap the AI slightly by giving some of the villager control to the Village Center, which acts like a hive and farms out some of the cooperative elements to the people. We couldn't have them interrogating each other, so this central control means that they do work as a unit but can retain their individual characteristics. This makes the game much faster and still gives them minds of their own.

Concept drawing for the tortoise Creature.

The Creature himself is an astonishing piece of work. Once he starts learning, he forms his own personality as he goes, and no two players will ever have the same Creature. The complexity is kept to a minimum to keep him fast, but we managed to steer completely clear of using random elements to make him seem like he has a mind of his own. And there is nothing in the game that you can do which you can't teach your Creature to do. It's true to say that the Creature mirrors you and your actions, so in BLACK & WHITE we've got a game in which part of the game itself learns from everything you do and tailors itself to you.

5. The way the team came together to make BLACK & WHITE happen

This is Lionhead Studios' first project, and everything started from scratch. The people, the software, and the working environment were all new. Although this was exactly what we needed to do a game so fresh and diverse, it also created problems which I was delighted to overcome. The lack of any precedent meant that things took a lot longer than they should have, and the open-ended nature of the game throughout much of its development meant that team members were limited only by their own imagination.

But the nice thing is, every member of the Lionhead team gelled brilliantly, and although I know we picked the very best people, there is an element of luck in whether they can all work together so well. We certainly lucked out with the team, and every one of them contributed massively to making the game what it is. The last few months of the project were the hardest any of us has ever had to work, but thanks to the people, they were also some of the most fun months we ever had. If nothing else, we'll always remember the time we spent closeted together making BLACK & WHITE. And I'll never forget that without the right team, this game never would have happened. It's as simple as that.

The citadel.

What Went Wrong

1. Planning the story

We underestimated how long it would take to construct and write the story element of BLACK & WHITE. The free-form nature of the game required an unfolding tale to give it some structure and lead it to a conclusion, and in October 1999 we began to work on the story. We thought it would take no more than two months, but after a while we realized that we didn't have the skill set needed to take care of this vital aspect of the game. I contacted James Leach, who'd been the in-house games scriptwriter at Bullfrog and had worked on SYNDICATE WARS, DUNGEON KEEPER, THEME HOSPITAL, and many others. He was working as a freelance ad copywriter but gladly came on board, again in a freelance capacity, and turned our ideas into a fully plotted story line, wrote hundreds of challenges and quests, and wrote all the dialogue in the game. It ended up being more than 60,000 words, the size of a novel.

Hiring James meant that we got a sense of continuity, consistency, and style throughout the game. It also meant that we could describe what we wanted, or even write placeholder text, and he would rapidly turn it into finished work. Sections of the game that were still at an early stage seemed more easy to understand, get a feel for, and work on when we used dialogue and text which seemed, to us, finished. Of course, another pass was usually needed to make it accurate and sometimes to polish it, but having a dedicated scriptwriter made this a simple task.

Storytelling in games, as elsewhere, is an art. If a story line flows easily and naturally, that's because someone has worked incredibly hard at

Tortoise morphs from evil to good.

it. I'm a great believer in the emotion and immersion that can be added to a game through good story and dialogue. It can't make a bad game good, but it can make any game better. And when the script was looked at by Hollywood scriptwriters and film directors from the BBC, we knew we were on to a winner.

Another by-product of using a professional scriptwriter was that we morphed the in-game advisors, the good and evil guys, from being just sources of information and guidance into stylish, popular characters who are now bankable properties in their own right.

2. Fixing the bugs

After canceling our Christmas party on December 26, 2000, we managed to hit Alpha, which as any developer knows is a very loose definition, but at least we could say that all the game features were now locked. After a well-deserved Christmas break, we came back to find that we had more than 3,000 bugs. We had six weeks to reduce this to zero, but the thing about bug-fixing is that you can solve one problem but in doing so create three more. So although we worked as hard as we could, the overall figure crept down slowly rather than dropped at the rate at which we were actually sorting out the bugs.

By this stage the team was very tired. The only things that kept them going were the sense that the end was in sight and the fact that they could now play the game and actually experience what we had created. Bugs, of course, could have killed the game, so there was no way around it but to fix each and every one. We had bug lists circulated to every member of the staff, and we put up a chart on the wall which was updated daily. Some days we had more bugs than the day before, and that was like looking at a mountain which was growing quicker than we could climb it.

But there came a moment three weeks into this process when we felt we'd broken the back of the major bugs, and the numbers fell steadily. Of course, the irony was that the last 10 bugs were the hardest to fix, and with every one there were four more created. It was as if the game just didn't want to be finished and perfected.

3. The project was too big

BLACK & WHITE got to be so large that we almost felt lost within the code. In fact there are well over a million lines of code within the game. Loading up even the most simple of the smallest tools would take many minutes, and compiling the entire game took over an hour. This meant that toward the end of the development phase even a tiny change could take a whole day to implement. Checking in changes and rectifying errors was a nightmare. We eventually decided to limit the checking-in to one machine, and we implemented a buddy system whereby nothing was done without an onlooker checking it at every stage. This put a stop to tired people checking in changes at four in the morning and finding that, instead of fixing something, they'd actually caused further problems.

Concept sketch of the good Celt.

Another worry about the project's size was that we didn't think the game would fit on one CD, although we were desperate for it to. The audio files are immense. Music, dialogue, and effects are all compressed, but of sufficiently high quality that we refused to reduce them any further. And with 15 language versions to get translated and recorded, we had to do the biggest localization job I've ever seen. This landed on Lionhead Studios at the very busiest time, and although our publisher did an excellent job of handling it, we were needed to check and answer questions and to provide explanations for some of the more arcane elements of the game.

4. Leaving things out

The idea of the game didn't really change much over the course of its creation. But I do have some regrets that features we thought would be great proved unworkable. I expected this, as it happens with every project, but I thought the problems would be caused by software or even hardware limitations. In fact, it came down more to emotional issues.

For example, the original idea of the Creatures was that a player could choose to make any living thing a Creature. We wanted the player to be able to select an ant and grow that, or a human being from a tribe, and raise him or her. Christian Bravery, one of the artists, spent a long time drawing concept work and sketches depicting what the Creatures could look like at various stages of their development. This of course included humans.

We soon realized that people would have certain expectations from a human. Players wouldn't expect a turtle to learn as quickly as a man, but if we dumbed down the people, they'd seem like a proto-hominid race from eons ago, and we didn't want that. Also, discipline in the game involves slapping your Creature. We certainly couldn't have the player slapping a child or a woman or, really, even a grown man. The emotional feel of raising a human, teaching him or her to eat what you want, and leading him or her around in a speechless environment was all wrong. Christian's work in visualizing humans as player Creatures was all for nothing in the end, and we dropped the idea. We also dropped the notion of turning any living thing into a trainable Creature, as ants, butterflies, fish, and other non-mammals would have caused big problems. A flying Creature would change BLACK & WHITE into a totally different game.

Concept art of the evil Celt.

I also regret that we couldn't use color as a dynamic concept a little more. The landscapes in the game are gorgeous, and our sound and music man, Russell Shaw, suggested that various spells could drain the color out of areas, or spread different colors around. We liked this idea for its surrealism, and we thought about having color wars with other wizards (at this stage you weren't a god, you were a wizard battling others on a land). The idea lost momentum when we thought about how the land would actually look, and how it would seem like something drawn by a preschooler. I still like the idea of color wars, but I think children's TV has also cottoned on to the idea, which means we won't be going there.

5. Talking about release dates

I have to admit, ruefully, that I have a reputation for being, shall we say, optimistic about when the projects I'm working on will be completed. I opened my big mouth and announced that Lionhead Studios would finish BLACK & WHITE and get it released at the end of last year. I just can't resist talking about whatever I'm currently working on. This has been a problem I've experienced with every game I've ever developed.

But the thing is, when I think something is going to be finished in December, I really do believe it. People at Lionhead were telling me that we had to build in time for bug-fixing, and I knew this was true, but the truth is that there seems to be no formula for working out how long things will take. The best thing to do, I guess, is to take the finishing date I first think of and move it twice as far away—and then not announce it until we're halfway there.

It's a function of working on products which could literally be endless. Unlike a film, where once the footage is shot, you edit it with an idea of where you'll end up, you can add completely new features to a game and then balance it and change it radically right up until the last minute. I'm sure that there were many people who didn't believe me when I said we'd finished making BLACK & WHITE and were only convinced when they saw a box with a CD in it.

We tried to make the micromanagement of the villagers as user-friendly as possible.

"Just More"

BLACK & WHITE is unlike any other game ever written. That was our goal, and we achieved it. We wanted something more beautiful, more complex, more emotive, more innovative, more clever, and more, well, just more.

As you've read, it was beset by problems. We nearly drove ourselves crazy solving them. Nothing worthwhile is ever simple, though, and for every minute spent thinking up wonderful ideas to include in the game, there were probably 20 hours of sheer hard effort trying to get them to work.

People told Lionhead we were perfectionists, but if we were, the game would never have been finished. It's not a perfect game. Our next game won't be, either. But because there's no such thing as a perfect game, we'll just try to do something different, and do it as well as we possibly can. Someone asked me recently what drove us to work so hard on this and to spend so much time thinking outside the box. The simple truth of my answer only struck me afterwards. With BLACK & WHITE, we made the game that we wanted to play.

Bungie Software's

MYTH: THE FALLEN LORDS

by jason regier

Back-Story

MYTH: THE FALLEN LORDS uses the same overhead view as real-time strategy games, but brings the perspective lower to portray the bloody details of tactical conflict in a fantasy setting. The game follows the fortunes of one legion in an army of allied peoples fighting a desperate, losing war against the undead armies of the Fallen Lords. Well-balanced units and successful multiplayer make this a successful piece of game design, and the grim atmosphere of this well-executed fantasy tale leaves a lasting impression.

As the team at Bungie Software put the finishing touches on the MARATHON series of first-person action games, our thoughts drifted to bringing our 3D game experience to the real-time strategy game (RTSG) genre. We were inspired by movies such as *Braveheart,* with its close-up portrayal of bloody melees between large forces, and books such as Glen Cook's *The Black Company,* in which gruesome tales of battle contrast with engaging and intriguing characters. We envisioned a dark, amoral world where opposing sides are equally brutal and their unity is torn by power struggles within the ranks. We dreamed of game play that combined the realism and excitement of action games with the cunning and planning required by strategy games.

Our original design document, if you could call it that, was simply opposing lists of "Stuff that Rocks" and "Stuff that Sucks." Anything vaguely cliché, such as excessive references to Tolkien novels, Arthurian legend, or "little boys coming of age and saving the world," went in the "Sucks" category. The "Stuff that Rocks" list was filled with ideas that contributed to the visual realism of the game: a true 3D landscape, polygonal buildings, reflecting water, particle-based weather, "blood-spattered battlefields littered with limbs," explosions that send shock waves through the terrain, and "lightning frying guys and their friends."

Our goals for the product were lofty: simultaneous release on Windows 95 and Macintosh platforms, integrated Internet play, and a free online service to allow players from across the globe to battle one another. From this vision, MYTH: THE FALLEN LORDS was born.

The Making of a Legend, er, Myth

The project began in January 1996 with four programmers, two artists, and a product manager. Midway through development, one programmer dropped out and an artist was added. Music, sound effects, and cut scenes were done out-of-house, and a few artists were contracted to help with interface artwork. The roots of the MYTH programming team were on the Macintosh, so most initial coding was done on the Mac with Metrowerks CodeWarrior. When PC builds were required, though, we used Microsoft Visual C/C++. MYTH was written entirely in C.

Game Data

Release Date: November, 1997

Genre: 3D real-time strategy; fantasy

Publishers: Eidos, Pacific Coast

Platform: Windows and Macintosh

In addition to creating the shipping product, we developed four tools to aid in the construction of the game. One utility, the Extractor, handled the importing of sprites and the sequencing of their animations. Another tool, dubbed Fear, dealt with importing polygonal models such as houses, pillars, and walls. The Tag Editor was responsible for editing the constants stored in cross-platform data files, which we called tags. And finally, Loathing, our map editor, handled the rest. Loathing was built around the MYTH engine and allowed us to modify the landscape, apply lighting, set terrain types, script the AI, and place structures, scenery, and monsters.

The artists used Alias|Wavefront's PowerAnimator and StudioPaint on a single Silicon Graphics Indigo 2 to create polygonal models and render all the characters. At one point, the artists worked separate day and night shifts so that they could maximize their time on the SGI. Models were brought into the game using Fear, while the sprites were cleaned up in Adobe Photoshop and imported with the Extractor. To create the texture maps for the terrain, the artists used Photoshop to draw what looked like an aerial photo and applied it to a 3D landscape in Loathing.

If this sounds like a lot of work to you, you're right. Most maps took at least a week or two to create. We considered using fractal-generated landscapes, but we were worried that the inherent randomness of such terrain would make it extremely difficult to design good levels. As a result, all maps were painstakingly constructed by hand. As the artists put the finishing touches on the landscapes, the programmers, who doubled as level designers, scripted the AI for the levels.

MYTH took approximately two years from start to finish. It began as a six-degrees-of-freedom engine that allowed you to fly around a landscape. Soon, troops were added, heads started flying, blood was made to destructively alter the terrain's color map, and the network game was born. Most of the first year was spent developing the initial network/multiplayer game play. Almost the entire second year was spent developing the single-player game, refining the levels, and testing bungie.net, our free online service.

What Went Right

1. Bringing carnage to the masses

It's a real trick to create a simultaneous, identical-look-and-feel, cross-platform release. It's even harder to do so within the expected time frame with only three programmers. Our experience porting MARATHON, our popular Macintosh-only action game, to Windows 95 was a valuable learning experience, and we vowed when starting MYTH that, "This time, we're going to do it right."

Doing it "right" meant designing MYTH from the ground up to be cross-platform compatible. Ninety percent of the code in the game is platform independent; the other ten percent is split evenly between routines that handle PC- and Macintosh-specific functionality. It was a programmer's dream come true—we spent almost all our time implementing features and solving real problems, rather than wasting it fighting the OS.

All of the data for MYTH, from animated cut scenes to the percentage of warriors who are left-handed, is stored in platform-independent files called tags. Tags are automatically byte swapped when necessary and are accessed via a cross-platform file manager.

One of our programmers worked in conjunction with Apple Computer Inc. to develop a cross-platform networking library code-named Über. One of the greatest things about Über is that it supports plug-in modules for network protocols. Thus, although MYTH currently only allows games over TCP/IP, AppleTalk, and through TEN, it would be trivial to add support for new protocol modules. MYTH must provide a user interface to set up the connection, but once Über establishes that connection, game play over a LAN is the same as over the Internet.

To keep the game's appearance identical across platforms, we implemented our own dialog and font managers. This allowed us (actually, it required us) to use custom graphics for all interface items. We designed our font manager so that it supported anti-aliased, two-byte fonts, as well as a variety of text-parsing formats. Thus, our overseas publishers Eidos and Pacific Software Publishing were able to localize relatively painlessly. The German version of MYTH was finished only a couple of weeks after the English release, with Japanese and French versions close behind. The only game experience that is different for the two platforms is the installation, and two players on bungie.net have no idea whether their opponents are on Macintoshes or PCs.

2. bungie.net and beta testing

MYTH was also released with integrated support for our first online service, bungie.net. This service was designed specifically for MYTH and was developed simultaneously. Similar to online services for other games, it allows players to connect via the Internet to game rooms, where they can chat or play against one another. The Linux-based server that runs bungie.net keeps track of player statistics and gives everyone a score in our ranking system. The service's Web site (www.bungie.net) has access to this database and sports a leader board that lists the top players.

Our networking layer is based on a client/server model. Once you advertise a game on the network, you become a server, and other players join your game. Network traffic during a game is limited to the commands issued by the players. All copies of MYTH in a network game run deterministically and merely interpret the commands that they receive. This makes cheating difficult; if you hack the game to perform something illegal, such as making all your units invincible, you'll go out of sync with other players. When portions of the game data are periodically checksummed and compared, a message will indicate that you're out of sync (and out of luck). So far, the only form of cheating we've encountered is users trying to exploit the bungie.net ranking system.

To rigorously test our server load capacity and the bungie.net code, we released a public beta of the network game. Initially we were apprehensive because it was our first public beta test of a product, but it was an amazing success. When errors occur, MYTH alerts the player, logs the error messages, and usually allows the user to save a replay of the problem. Testers submitted these detailed bug reports via e-mail and chatted about features and improvements to levels on internal newsgroups.

Best of all, the testers used bungie.net to give instant feedback to the developers. This interaction allowed us to gather even more useful information about bugs, and it made the testers really feel involved in the final product. By the end of the beta-testing cycle, we not only had a clean product, but also had a loyal following of users who sang our praises when the NDAs were lifted.

3. 3D graphics acceleration

When the project started, 3D acceleration hardware was only just starting to become popular. Nevertheless, we tried to keep hardware acceleration in mind when designing our rendering pipeline. When the opportunity arose to add hardware acceleration, the implementation worked beautifully.

We worked closely with people from 3Dfx and Rendition and added support for their chipsets in about a week. It's amazing how much these accelerators add to the smoothness of the terrain, the fluidity of camera movement, and the realism of the units and effects. These chips rock, and great on-site developer assistance made them easy to support.

4. Getting back to the people

Once we had released MYTH, we definitely did the right thing by waiting for player feedback and then releasing a patch to address their issues. Since our public beta test caught most of the bugs in the shipping product, nearly all our post-shipping efforts were directed towards adding user-requested features. We scoured the newsgroups, read email, and talked to customers about their complaints. From these disparate sources, we compiled a list of improvements for our 1.1 patch.

All major user complaints were addressed in the patch. We added support for Rendition and Voodoo Rush cards. We extended the camera's maximum zoom for a better view of the battlefield. We made our easy difficulty levels even easier. And we improved the unit AI. By the time the early reviews came out, we'd already released a beta patch that addressed almost everything on the reviewers' lists of MYTH's failings.

5. Doing more with less

It doesn't take fifty people to create a major cross-platform software title. Period. Bungie Software has barely half that number of employees in the entire company, and we not only develop all our games, but publish and distribute them as well! Macintosh and PC versions of MYTH, all our internal tools, and our online service were essentially developed by only six people, and everything shipped on time with no major glitches. There's no big quality assurance department here at Bungie; the public did our testing for us, and we listened to them as seriously as if they were coworkers on the project.

We didn't hire any game designers, writers, or level designers to come up with our game concept and story line. MYTH truly is the combined vision of our team, and each of us feels that it was our game. We came to work each day excited about the project, and we're damn proud of what we managed to create.

What Went Wrong

1. Staffing problems

On the flip side, it became clear very early in the project that we were understaffed for such an ambitious undertaking. Success or failure rested with a handful of people, and that was extremely stressful. Losing a programmer halfway through development added still more pressure during the final push to get the game out the door. Additional programming tasks had to be shouldered by the remaining developers, who were already also responsible for level design. To alleviate the problem somewhat, we even found it necessary to ask our busy network administrator to aid in AI scripting and level design.

We did hire a third artist near the end of the project, but it was almost too late. While his contributions to the final product were by no means insignificant, it took a long time to get him up to speed. Similarly, when we dropped the services of our original sound guy late in the development cycle, a new sound team had to rush to redo all the work.

If you're looking for good anecdotes about how we blew off steam with wild weekend trips to Cancún, you won't get any. We all worked incredibly hard, and did so willingly because MYTH represented a two-year labor of love. All the great previews and supportive feedback from beta testers kept us excited and made us realize that we really did have something special on our hands. Nobody wanted to slack off and allow competing products to beat us to the shelves. The moral of the story: staff up as early as possible and plan to weather the unexpected.

2. Scripting

The biggest announced feature that didn't make it into the final version of MYTH was a scripting language that would allow the player to modify elements of the game. We had hoped that user scripts could be written for extensible artificial intelligence, as well as custom formations, net game rules, and map behaviors. We selected Java as a good basis for the MYTH scripting language because of its gaining popularity, good information-hiding capabilities, and relatively simple byte code interpretation.

After several months of work, early versions of the game loaded, compiled, and ran code from tag files. A few simple scripts worked for presentation purposes, including one that instructed a unit to search the battlefield for the heads of the enemy and collect them in a pile. Unfortunately, when the programmer responsible for the scripting language parted ways with Bungie, we were left with a number of features to implement and no library of user-friendly interfaces with the game code. Given its incomplete state at such a late stage of development, there was little choice but to drop this functionality.

3. More frames of animation

One of the complaints most often voiced by players is that the sprite-based units' animations are not fluid enough. At the start of the project, when we planned for the number of frames of animation per unit, there was a good deal of uncertainty regarding how much RAM would be consumed by large texture maps, sounds, and other resources. As things were, it was not uncommon for our landscape textures to reach 5MB in size, and certain animations already consumed close to 1MB—our uncertainties were not unfounded. We erred on the conservative side. Though we implemented caching schemes that greatly reduced our memory requirements, there wasn't enough time to rerender the units.

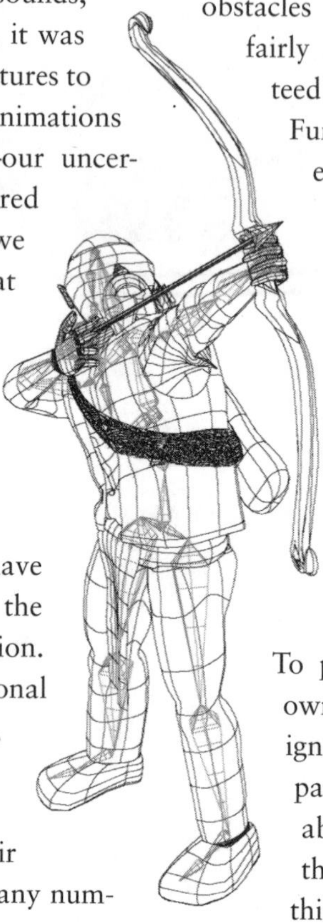

4. Pathfinding

Perfect pathfinding seems to have become the Holy Grail for games in the RTS genre, and MYTH is no exception. The game's terrain is a 3D polygonal mesh constructed from square cells, each of which is tessellated into two triangles. Cells have an associated terrain type that indicates their impassability, and they may contain any number of solid objects, including trees, fence posts, and units.

Ah! Square cells, you say? Having read previous *Game Developer* articles (Bryan Stout, "Smart Moves: Intelligent Pathfinding," *Game Developer*, October/November 1996; Swen Vincke, "Real-Time Pathfinding for Multiple Objects," *Game Developer*, June 1997), your first thought may be that the A* pathfinding should do the trick.

The first problem with a pure A* approach for MYTH is that impassable obstacles, such as troops and trees, may lie anywhere on the terrain. Penalizing the cells beneath impassable obstacles is a bad idea because the cells are fairly large and obstacles are not guaranteed to be aligned at the center of a cell. Furthermore, even if a tree did consume exactly one cell, the A* path to avoid it would make a unit walk up to the tree, turn, and continue around it. Units that bump into trees and walk between the centers of large cells appear extremely stupid; you really want your group of troops to avoid obstacles (including each other) ahead of time, and smoothly weave their way through a forest.

To produce this effect, we created our own pathfinding algorithm. First, we ignore all obstacles and calculate the A* path based solely on the terrain impassability. For all intents and purposes, the terrain in MYTH never changes, so this path can be calculated once and remembered. Now, we consider the arbitrarily placed obstacles and periodically refine our path using a vector-based scheme. If the planned path would cause us to hit an obstacle, we need to deviate our path. We recursively consider both left and right deviations, and choose the direction that causes us to deviate least from our A* path. Thus, we've considered terrain impassability information and we can avoid arbitrarily placed (or even moving) obstacles well before we bump into them.

For every game, pathfinding is a pretty complex and sensitive beast. This method worked well for 90 percent of our cases, but rigorous testing revealed certain cases that were not adequately handled. As the ship date drew near, we were forced to say "good enough" rather than handle these problem cases and risk introducing new bugs. Our current algorithm works pretty well and provides the effect we sought, but there's definitely room for improvement.

5. Features that missed the cut

With a few exceptions, everything from our list of "Stuff that Rocks" made it into the final product. Those features that didn't make it came so close and were so exciting that they definitely deserve mention.

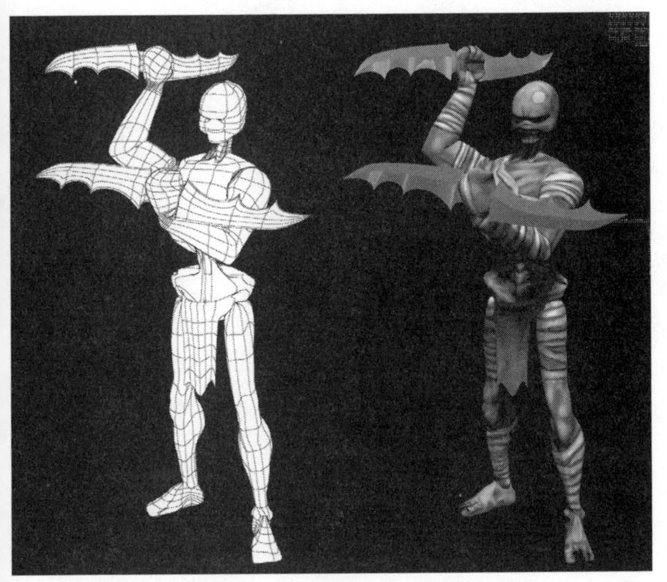

Near the end of the project, we started adding support for 3D fire, which would be ignited by explosions and flaming arrows. Our flames were sprite-based 3D particle effects, complete with translucent smoke. Fire could spread across the landscape and move at different rates over the various types of terrain. To our dismay, when a spark in the woods spread into a raging forest fire (as it should), all the translucent smoke sprites slowed even fast, 3Dfx-accelerated machines to a crawl. With little time to rectify the problem, we had to put out the fire, so to speak.

We had also planned for wildlife to scamper across the terrain and for birds to fly through the air, breathing life into our empty landscapes. Our attempt at ambient life started with a giant squirrel created by one of our artists. Unfortunately, due to time constraints, we didn't have a chance to create very interesting behaviors for it. Just about the only AI that we had a chance to code simply made the squirrels gravitate towards the player's units. We thought it best to drop ambient life rather than subject players to hordes of nuzzling squirrels.

Post-Release Reactions

With all the prerelease hype MYTH had received, we were very anxious to see how the public would receive the final version. The reactions from beta testers were phenomenally positive, as were the comments from customers and reviewers. Our swiftness in correcting problems and adding several user-requested features with a 1.1

patch only earned us more kudos from the press and public.

But possibly the most satisfying result of the game is the degree to which it lessens the appeal of playing with a traditional isometric perspective. Working on MYTH so consumed our time that we didn't get a chance to play anything else; we looked forward to playing some old favorites and the latest demos of our high-profile competition after we shipped. It was a real surprise to discover that once we were accustomed to MYTH's 3D camera and its associated freedom, playing isometric games was frustrating—the action seemed distant and unrealistic, while the view of the world was annoyingly rigid. This sentiment was echoed in both player comments and reviews of the game.

Since our MARATHON products were derided by some as DOOM rip-offs, it was especially satisfying to hear players say that MYTH pushes the genre in a new direction, from which there's no looking back. It remains to be seen whether MYTH will inspire other entries into the 3D real-time strategy game genre. But if nothing else, MYTH is proof that a very small team with a strong product vision can still make a very big game.

The MYTH development team. FROM LEFT to RIGHT: Mark Bernal (artist), Frank Pusateri (artist), Rob McLees (artist, holding statue of a Trow), Jason Regier (programmer), Jason Jones (programmer/project leader) Marcus Lehto (artist). NOT PICTURED: Ryan Martell (programmer), Tuncer Deniz (product manager), Jay Barry (level design).

Looking Glass's THIEF: THE DARK PROJECT

by tom leonard

THIEF: THE DARK PROJECT is one of those games that almost wasn't. During the long struggle to store shelves, the project faced the threat of cancellation twice. A fiscal crisis nearly closed the doors at Looking Glass. During one seven-month span, the producer, project director, lead programmer, lead artist, lead designer and the author of our renderer all left. Worse still, we felt a nagging fear that we might make a game that simply was not fun. But in the end, we shipped a relatively bug-free game that we had fun making, we were proud of, and that we hoped others would enjoy.

Back-Story

In the early 90s, Looking Glass Studios helped invent first-person 3D gaming with ULTIMA UNDERWORLD and SYSTEM SHOCK and, in the late 90s, reinvented the form with THIEF: THE DARK PROJECT. THIEF breaks out of the first-person shooter model and shifts the emphasis to stealth. Looking Glass developed lighting, AI, and audio technologies to allow players to use silence and shadow and sneak attacks rather than firepower to achieve their goals. In keeping with this new style of play, they gave the game a cynical thief for a hero and set it in a half-fantasy, half-Victorian steampunk world.

The Concept

The THIEF team wanted to create a first-person game that provided a totally different gaming experience, yet appealed to the existing first-person action market. THIEF was to present a lightly-scripted game world with levels of player interaction and improvisation exceeding our previous titles. The team hoped to entice the player into a deep engagement with the world by creating intelligible ways for the world to be impacted by the player. The central game mechanic of THIEF challenged the traditional form of the first-person 3D market. First-person shooters are fast-paced adrenaline rushes where the player possesses unusual speed and stamina, and an irresistible desire for conflict. The expert THIEF player moves slowly, avoids conflict, is penalized for killing people, and is entirely mortal. It is a game style that many observers were concerned might not appeal to players, and even those intimately involved with the game had doubts at times.

The project began in the spring of 1996 as DARK CAMELOT, a sword-combat action game with role-playing and adventure elements, based on an inversion of the Arthurian legend. Although development ostensibly had been in progress on paper for a year, THIEF realistically began early in 1997 after the game was repositioned as an action/adventure game of thievery in a grim fantasy setting. Up to that point we had only a small portion of the art, design, and code that would ultimately make it into the shipping game.

Game Data

Release date: December 1998

Publisher: Cyan

Genre: first-person stealth/action; fantasy

Intended platform: Windows 95/98

Project budget: Approximately $3 million

Project length: 2.5 years

Team size: 19 full-time developers. Some contractors.

Critical development software: Microsoft Visual C++ 5.0, Watcom C++ 10.6, Opus Make, PowerAnimator, 3D Studio Max, Adobe Photoshop, AntimatorPro, Debabelizer, After Effects, and Adaptive Optics motion-capture processing

Full development began in May 1997 with a team comprised almost entirely of a different group of people from those who started the project. During the following year, the team created a tremendous amount of quality code, art, and design. But by the beginning of summer in 1998, the game could not be called "fun," the team was exhausted, and the project was faced with an increasingly skeptical publisher.

The Looking Glass game design philosophy includes a notion that immersive gameplay emerges from an object-rich world governed by high-quality, self-consistent simulation systems. Making a game at Looking Glass requires a lot of faith, as such systems take considerable time to develop, do not always arrive on time, and require substantial tuning once in place. For THIEF, these systems didn't gel until mid-summer, fifteen months after the project began full development, and only three months before we were scheduled to ship.

When the game finally did come together, we began to sense that not only did the game not stink, it might actually be fun. The release of successful stealth-oriented titles (such as METAL GEAR SOLID and COMMANDOS) and more content-rich first-person shooters (like HALF-LIFE) eased the team's concerns about the market's willingness to accept experimental game styles. A new energy revitalized the team. Long hours driven by passion and measured confidence marked the closing months of the project. In the final weeks of the project the Eidos test and production staff joined us at the Looking Glass offices for the final push. The gold master was burned in the beginning of November, just in time for Christmas.

In many ways, THIEF was a typical project. It provided the joys of working on a large-scale game: challenging problems, a talented group of people, room for creative expression, and the occasional hilarious bug. It also had some of the usual problems: task underestimation, bouts of low morale, a stream of demos from hell, an unrealistic schedule derived from desire rather than reality, poor documentation, and an insufficient up-front specification.

However, THIEF also differed from a number of projects in that it took risks on numerous fronts, risks that our team underappreciated. We wanted to push the envelope in almost every element of the code and design. The experimental nature of the game design, and the time it took us to fully understand the core nature of that design, placed special demands on the development process. The team was larger than any Looking Glass team up until then, and at times there seemed to be too many cooks in the kitchen. Reaching a point where everyone shared the same vision took longer than expected. A philosophy of creating good, reusable game engine components created unusual challenges that didn't always fit well with schedule and demo pressures. The many risks could have overwhelmed the project, if not for the dedication, creativity, and sacrifices of the team.

Throughout the life of the project, more than 50 people worked in one way or another on THIEF—some as part of the CAMELOT project, others as part of the Looking Glass audiovisual and technology support staff, some as helpful hands from other Looking Glass projects. The core team consisted of a number of veterans of previous Looking Glass titles (UNDERWORLD I and II, SYSTEM SHOCK, FLIGHT UNLIMITED, TERRA NOVA, BRITISH OPEN CHAMPIONSHIP GOLF, and the unpublished STAR TREK™: VOYAGER), as well as some new industry arrivals. The project had a number of very talented people and strong wills. Although it took some time for the team to unite as a tight-knit creative force, the final six months were incredibly productive, spirited, and punishingly fun.

What Went Right

1. Designing data-driven tools

Our experience on previous titles taught us that one of the impediments to timely game development is the mutual dependence of artists, designers, and programmers at every development stage. One of the development goals for the Dark Engine, on which THIEF is built, was to create a set of tools that enabled programmers, artists, and designers to work more effectively and independently. The focus of this effort was to make the game highly data-driven and give non-programmers a high degree of control over the integration of their work. Media and game systems were to be easily and intuitively plugged in and edited by the team members responsible for their creation, without requiring the direct involvement of programmers.

The Dark Object System stood at the heart of our strategy. Primarily designed by programmer Marc "Mahk" LeBlanc, the Object System was a general database for managing the individual objects in a simulation. It provided a generic notion of properties that an object might possess, and relations that might exist between two objects. It allowed game-specific systems to create new kinds of properties and relations easily, and provided automatic support for saving, loading, versioning, and editing properties and relations. It also supported a game-specific hierarchy of object types, which could be loaded, saved, and edited by designers. Programmers specified the available properties and relations, and the interface used for editing, using a set of straightforward classes and structures. Using GUI tools, the designers specified the hierarchy and composition of game objects independent of the programming staff. In THIEF there was no code-based game object hierarchy of any kind.

Although the implementation of the system was much more work than we expected, and management of the object hierarchy placed significant demands on lead designer Tim Stellmach, it turned out to be one of the best things in the project. Once the set of available properties and relations exposed by programmers was mature, the Object System allowed the designers to specify most of the behaviors of the game without scripting or programmer intervention. Additionally, the relative ease with which variables could be made available to designers in order to tweak the game encouraged programmers to empower the designers thoroughly.

Concept sketches of Hammer and a burrick.

The second major component of our strategy was our resource management system. The resource management system gave the game high-level management control of source data, such as texture maps, models, and digital sounds. It helped manage the game's use of system memory, and provided the data flow functions necessary for configuration management. Looking Glass's previous resource management system provided similar functionality, but identified resources by an integer ID and required a special resource compilation step. This technique often required recompilation of the game executable in order to integrate new art, and required that the team exit the game when resources were published to the network.

The new system referred to a resource by its file name without its extension, used a file system directory structure for namespace management, didn't leave files open while working, and required no extra compilation step. Developers simply dropped art into their local data tree and started using it. To expose art to the rest of the team, lead artist Mark Lizotte just copied art into the shared project directories. Compound resources were treated as extensions to the file system and were built using the standard .ZIP format. This allowed us to use off-the-shelf tools for constructing, compressing, and viewing resource files.

The system facilitated content development by allowing programmers, artists, and designers to add new data to an existing game quickly. The data-driven approach worked so well that through much of our development, THIEF and SYSTEM SHOCK 2 (two very different games) used the same executable and simply chose a different object hierarchy and data set at run-time.

2. Sound as a game design focus

Sound plays a more central role in THIEF than in any other game I can name. Project director Greg LoPiccolo had a vision of THIEF that included a rich aural environment where sound both enriched the environment and was an integral part of gameplay. The team believed in and achieved this vision, and special credit goes to audio designer Eric Brosius.

As an element of the design, sound played two roles in THIEF. First, it was the primary medium through which the AIs communicated both their location and their internal state to the player. In THIEF we tried to design AIs with a broader range of awareness than the typical two states that AIs exhibit: "oblivious" and "omniscient." Such a range of internal states would be meaningless if the player could not perceive it, so we used a broad array of speech broadcast by the AIs to clue in the player.

Hand-to-hand combat is sometimes necessary.

While very successful for humanoid AIs, we feel the more limited expressibility of non-human creatures is the heart of why many customers didn't like our "monster levels." Second, the design used sounds generated by objects in the game, especially the player, to inform AIs about their surroundings. In THIEF, the AIs rarely "cheat" when it comes to knowledge of their environment. Considerable work went into constructing sensory components sufficient to permit the AIs to make decisions purely based on the world as they perceive it. This allowed us to use player sounds as an integral part of gameplay, both as a way that players can reveal themselves inadvertently to the AIs and as a tool for players to distract or divert an AI. Moreover, AIs communicated with each other almost exclusively through sound. AI speech and sounds in the world, such as the sound of swords clashing, were assigned semantic values. In a confrontation, the player could expect nearby AIs to become alarmed by the sound of combat or cries for help, and was thus encouraged to ambush opponents as quietly as possible.

In order for sound to work in the game as designed, we needed to implement a sound system significantly more sophisticated than many other games. When constructing a THIEF mission, designers built a secondary "room database" that reflected the connectivity of spaces at a higher level than raw geometry. Although this was also used for script triggers and AI optimizations, the primary role of the room database was to provide a representation of the world simple enough to allow realistic real-time propagation of sounds through the spaces. Without this, it is unlikely the sound design could have succeeded, as it allowed the player and the AIs to perceive sounds more as they are in real life and better grasp the location of their opponents in the mission spaces.

3. Focus, focus, focus

Early on, the THIEF plan was chock full of features and metagame elements: lots of player tools and a modal inventory user interface to manage them; multiplayer cooperative, deathmatch and "Theft-match" modes; a form of player extra-sensory perception; player capacity to combine world objects to create new tools; and branching mission structures. These and other "cool ideas" were correctly discarded. Instead, we focused in on creating a single-player, linear, mission-based game centered exclusively around stealth, with a player toolset that fit within the constraints of an extension of the QUAKE user interface. The notion came into full force with two decisions we made about seven months before we shipped.

First, the project was renamed THIEF from the working title THE DARK PROJECT, a seemingly minor decision that in truth gave the team a concrete ideological focus. Second, we decided preemptively to drop multiplayer support, not simply due to schedule concerns, but also to allow us as much time as possible to hone the single-player experience. In the end, some missions didn't achieve the stealth focus we wanted, particularly those originally designed for DARK CAMELOT, but the overall agenda was the right one.

4. Objectives and difficulty

One of the THIEF team's favorite games during development was GOLDENEYE on the N64. We were particularly struck by the manner in which levels of difficulty were handled. Each level of difficulty had a different overlapping set of objectives for success, and missions were subtly changed at each level in terms of object placement and density. Relatively late in the development of THIEF, we decided such a system would work well in our game. Extending the concept, we added a notion that as difficulty increased, the level of toleration of murder of human beings decreased. We also allowed players to change their difficulty level at the beginning of each mission.

The system was a success in two ways. First, it made clear to the player exactly what "difficulty" meant. Second, it allowed the designers to create a very different experience at each level of difficulty, without changing the overall geometry and structure of a mission. This gave the game a high degree of replayability at a minimum development cost.

5. Multiple, narrow-purpose scripting solutions

Although the Object System provided a lot of flexibility, we also needed a scripting language to fully specify object behaviors. Rather than create a single all-encompassing scripting system, we chose to develop several more focused tools for scripting. This tiered scripting solution worked well. In creating our core "high-end" object scripting technology, we wanted to allow designers with moderate programming skill to create complex object behaviors easily. Scripts were event-driven objects attached at runtime to game objects, and contained data, methods, and message handlers. The game provided a election of services to allow the script to query the world state and the game object state, and also to perform complex tasks.

Our goal was to create a scripting language that offered source-level debugging, was fast, and was dynamic. The solution was essentially C++ in .DLLs, compiled by the C++ compiler, using a combination of classes and preprocessor macros to ease interface publishing, handle dynamic linking, and provide designers a clear programming model.

Though used by both programming-savvy designers and programmers, the fact that it was a real programming language prevented widespread use by all of the designers. Most designers were interested in customizing AI behaviors. For the AI we created a simpler scripting system, "Pseudo-scripts," . that were implemented as properties within the Object System. Pseudo-scripts took the burden of coding scripts off of

Stealth is one of your best weapons in THIEF. The game's designers made sure that expert players would have to make effective use of silent weapons such as the blackjack and the bow and arrow.

the designers. The AI provided a stock set of triggers, such as "I see the player near an object" or "I see a dead body;" the designer provided the consequence of the trigger. Each Pseudo-script was edited in a dialog box presenting parameters to tweak the "if" clause of the trigger, and space for a list of simple, unconditional actions to perform when the trigger fired. In this way, the custom behavioral possibilities of the AI at any moment were described by the aggregate of Pseudo-scripts that were attached to that AI.

This approach had three benefits. First, it was simple enough so that designers with no programming experience were comfortable using it. Second, it narrowed the range of triggers a designer could use to a good pre-selected set, rather than giving them an open-ended system that might not have worked as well. Finally, when and how to evaluate AI triggers, a potential run-time expense if not carefully constructed, could be custom built by a programmer.

The final scripting system built into THIEF was the Tagged Schema system. When the game required motions and sounds, it requested them as concepts modified by optional qualifiers, rather than directly. For example, an AI who had just heard the player would request the concept "moderate alert," qualified with an optional tag like "+sense:sound." A potential set of resources was then chosen using a pattern matcher; in this example, it would choose all samples in that AI's voice expressing a generic "something's not right," all samples expressing "I heard something fishy," but no samples expressing "I saw something fishy." From this set, the specific resource was then chosen using a weighted random selection. The tables used were specified by the designers using a simple language. Specifying motion and sound selection this way, designers created an interesting variety of randomized environments and behaviors without changing the code of the game.

What Went Wrong

1. Trouble with the AI

If one thing could be called out as the reason THIEF's gameplay didn't come together until late in the process, it would be the AI. The AI as a foil to the player is the central element of THIEF, and the AI we wanted wasn't ready until late in the spring of 1998. As lead programmer and author of the final AI, I take full responsibility for that.

The original AI for THIEF was designed by another programmer before the requirements of the revised stealth design were fully specified. Six months after it was begun, the project director and overseer of the system left the team, and the most of the programming staff was temporarily reassigned to help ship another game that was in trouble. During the following months, development on that AI continued without any oversight and without a firm game design. Soon after, the programmer working on the AI also left.

While the core pathfinding data structures and algorithms were basically sound, the code that generated the pathfinding database was extremely buggy. The design of the AI decision process was geared towards an action fighting game requiring little designer customization, rather than a stealth game that needed much more customization. Even worse, the high-level decision process in the AI had drifted away from a rigorous design and the code was extremely brittle. The whole situation was a disaster. These might not have been serious issues, except for one key mistake: I didn't realize the depth of the problem quickly enough, and despite concerns expressed by programmer/designer Doug Church, I didn't act fast enough. I think highly of the programmer involved with the initial AI and wanted to avoid the natural but often misguided programmer reaction within myself that I should just rewrite it my way. So, I took the position that, while buggy, the system as a whole was probably sound. Several months and many sleepless nights later, I concluded that I had been sorely mistaken.

By November 1997, I had the basics of a new design and began working on it. But all work had to stop in order to pull together an emergency proof-of-concept demo by the end of December to quell outside concerns that the team lacked a sound vision of the game. This turned into a mid-January demo, followed by an early February publisher demo, followed by a late February make-or-break demo. During this time the only option was to hack features as best we could into the existing AI.

While better than losing our funding, constructing these demos was not good for the project. In the end, work on the new AI didn't begin until mid-March. Despite the fact that our scheduled ship date was just six months away, we threw away four-fifths of our existing AI code and started over. After a hair-raising twelve-week stretch of grueling hours, the AI was ready for real testing. Had I committed to a rewrite two months earlier the previous autumn, I believe the AI would have been ready for real use three to five months sooner.

2. An uncertain renderer

The project was started because of the renderer, rather than the reverse. The basic core of the renderer for THIEF was written in the fall of 1995 as an after-hours experiment by programmer Sean Barrett. During the following year, the renderer and geometry-editing tools were fleshed out, and with DARK CAMELOT supposed to ship some time in 1997, it looked like we would have a pretty attractive game. Then, at the end of 1996, Sean decided to leave Looking Glass. Although he periodically contracted with us to add features, and we were able to add hardware support and other minor additions, the renderer never received the attention it needed to reach the state-of-the-art in 1998.

The possibility that we might not have a point programmer for the renderer weighed heavily on the team. Fortunately, Sean remained available on a contract basis, and other members of the team developed sufficient knowledge of the renderer so that we shipped successfully. In the end, we shipped a renderer appropriate for our gameplay, but not as attractive as other high-profile first-person titles.

This may prompt the question of why we didn't simply license a renderer. When the project started a few months into 1996, the avalanche of QUAKE licenses hadn't really begun and UNREAL was still two years away. By the time licensing was a viable choice, the game and the renderer were too tightly integrated for us to consider changing.

One of the featured weapons is the fire arrow.

3. Loss of key personnel amid corporate angst beyond our control

Midway through 1997, THIEF was just starting to gather momentum. We were fully staffed and the stealth design was really starting to get fleshed out. Unfortunately, Looking Glass's financial situation was bleak. Few emotions can compare to the stress of heading to work not knowing who might be laid off, including yourself, or whether the doors would be locked when you got there. The company shed half of its staff in a span of six months, and while the active teams tried to stay focused, it was hard when one day the plants were gone, another day the coffee machine, then the water cooler.

Some of the THIEF team couldn't continue under these conditions. We lost two programmers, including the former lead programmer, and a designer. When we were forced to close our Austin office, we lost our producer, Warren Spector, as well as some programmers who made valuable technology contributions to our engine. All of these individuals are now on Ion Storm's DEUS EX team. Although it took some months to fully restore the spirit of the rest of the team, we held together and the company eventually rebounded. Perhaps it bestowed a stoicism that comes from knowing that however bad things might seem, you've already seen worse.

4. Undervalued editor

One of the boils never lanced on the project was our editor, Dromed. Although it was sufficiently powerful and provided the essential functionality we needed to ship the game, Dromed was a poorly documented and sometimes disagreeable editor. Dromed was first developed as a demonstration editor when the target platform of the game was DOS. As a demo, it never received the kind of formal specifications and designs one would expect for the central experience of the design team. As a DOS application, it lacked the consistent and relatively easy-to-use user-interface tools of Windows.

An early mistake was our failure to step back and formally evaluate the editor, and then rebuild it based on our experience constructing the demo editor. We also should have designed a proper editor framework, and hired a dedicated Windows user-interface programmer to support it through development. In retrospect, the time lost cleaning up the editor probably would have been saved on the back end of the project.

5. Inadequate planning

Although it is a cliché in the software industry to say our scheduling and budget planning were woefully inadequate, the THIEF project suffered greatly from this malady. There were several elements to our deficient planning. During DARK CAMELOT, and continuing through the first half of THIEF, we staffed the team before the design and technology was sufficiently mature. In THIEF, this led us to rush towards finishing the design, when we didn't necessarily understand the design and technology. With insufficient specifications of both the code systems and mission designs, we ended up doing lots of content that was essentially wrong for the game we were making. Code was written and spaces were built that weren't well-directed towards the goals of the project.

To make matters worse, we failed to reassess core scheduling assumptions carefully once the schedule began to slip. Captives of a series of unrealistic schedules, we didn't leave enough time for the sort of experimentation, dialogue, and prototyping a project like THIEF needs. Late in the winter of 1998, many of our scheduling mistakes had been corrected. Still, during the remainder of the project, the legacy of our earlier missteps required cutting missions that relied on technology we didn't have, and reworking missions not focused on the core gameplay.

Stepping Back from the Project

THIEF was constructed as a set of appropriately abstract reusable game components designed for creating object-rich, data-driven games. Although increasing the cost of development, this approach allowed Looking Glass to leverage various technologies across disparate types of games, from the first-person action game SYSTEM SHOCK 2 to our combat flight-simulator FLIGHT COMBAT. In our next-generation technology, some of the systems, such as the AI and the Object System, will merely be revised, not rewritten.

We intend to continue with this development philosophy in our future games. The next time around, our approach to constructing the engine will differ. The engine will be scheduled, staffed, and budgeted as a project in its own right. The editor will be treated as more of a first-class citizen than was the case in THIEF. Finally, a content development team will not be geared up until the technology is sufficiently mature to allow for an informed game design process.

Oh, and we'll get our schedules right—really.

DreamWorks Interactive's TRESPASSER

by richard wyckoff

> One seldom hears the true story of what happened at the place where the world changed. How it began. What were the reasons? What were the costs?
> —John Parker Hammond

This quote from TRESPASSER'S opening movie serves just as well to open the real story of a game development team's struggle to create a breakthrough dinosaur game as it does to open the fictional story of Hammond's struggle to develop a biotechnological breakthrough and clone dinosaurs.

Back-Story

In the history of game development, TRESPASSER stands as an ambitious but failed experiment. The game is set in the world of Jurassic Park and portrays a young woman named Anne exploring the abandoned island laboratory, learning its secrets and the past of its creator. The vision for TRESPASSER is a game that pushed the envelope in several areas at once. Foremost is the physics-based gameplay that would allow players more flexibility in combat and puzzle-solving and give the game-world a heightened realism. The team also created outdoor environments that broke shooter gameplay out of the rooms-and-corridors mold, as well as innovations in graphics technology and storytelling. In the end, the project proved overambitious but makes for a fascinating case study.

An Ambitious Project

The parallels between the TRESPASSER project and Hammond's cloning project were numerous: ambitious beginnings, years of arduous labor, and an eventual tragic ending. Hammond's diary, as related in the game itself, dwells on the past and never attempts to explain Hammond's future direction now that he has failed so grandly. This postmortem is intended to be much more forward looking.

TRESPASSER was begun by two former employees of Looking Glass Technologies: Seamus Blackley and Austin Grossman. By the time the game was rolling, two more ex-Looking Glass employees would join the team, and our common background was instrumental in setting the direction for the project.

The Concept

The pie-in-the-sky concept for TRESPASSER was an outdoor engine with no levels, a complete rigid-body physics simulation, and behaviorally-simulated and physically modeled dinosaurs.

The underlying design goal was to achieve a realistic feel through consistent looks and behaviors. Having an abandoned island setting was a useful way to exclude anything which did not seem possible to simulate, such as flexible solids like cloth and rope, wheeled vehicles, and the effects of burning, cutting, and digging.

Game Data

Release date: December 1998

Publisher: Electronic Arts

Genre: first person, outdoor physics-based action/adventure

Intended platform: Windows 95/98/NT

Project budget: Estimated $6–7 million

Project length: 32–36 months

Team size: 39 Including a full-time staff of 7 engineers, 5 game designers, and 10 artists.

Critical development hardware: 266MHz Pentium II with 128 Or 256MB RAM

Critical development software: 3D Studio Max 1.2 and 2.5, Photoshop 4.0, Microsoft Visual C++ 6.0, Visual SourceSafe 5.0

The game would play from a first-person perspective, and you would experience the environment through a virtual body to avoid the "floating gun" feeling prevalent in the WOLFENSTEIN breed of first-person games. Combat would be less important than in a shooter, and dinosaurs would be much more dangerous than the enemies in traditional first-person shooters. The point of the game would be exploration and puzzle solving, and when combat happened, it would more often involve frightening opponents away by inflicting pain than the merciless slaughter of every moving creature.

The original plan for TRESPASSER certainly seemed like a good one. It was very ambitious, but the team made tradeoffs on implementation and execution time from the very beginning. For instance, the team wouldn't attempt to do multiple or moving light sources or QUAKE-style shadow generation in order to accommodate arbitrary numbers of moving objects and long, wide-open views. Unfortunately, there is a difference between having a plan and successfully executing it, and the product that we eventually shipped was as disappointing to us as it was to the great majority of game players and game critics.

Some have dismissed TRESPASSER altogether because it was such a visible failure. Respected industry columnists and editors use it as a reason why physics is bad, or make it the butt of their jokes ("at least it wasn't as bad as TRESPASSER!"). However, from a project perspective there were a number of successes. Before we get into the problems which ended up sinking the ship, let's look at these successes.

What Went Right

1. Use of license

Making a new story with someone else's licensed property is often creatively stifling for designers and ultimately disappointing for fans of the original work. The Jurassic Park license could have been an especially limiting one, representing some of director Spielberg's and novelist Crichton's weakest work. However, TRESPASSER's

Hammond diary actually contains lots of interesting tidbits about the early days of characters like Henry Wu (the scientist from the beginning of the first movie) and Dennis Nedry (Wayne Knight's character who basically caused the first disaster), which made the game world a richer environment. The player can also check out locations on the island which imply backstory which isn't explicitly told, like Henry Wu's house with its 1980s executive bachelor stylings, Nedry's office with its poster for the fictional computer game series "Swords of Kandar," and Hammond's lavish mansion.

Concept art for TRESPASSER.

The settings and the diary itself serve to reveal much of Hammond's motivation and personal reactions to the building of Jurassic Park, creating more of a character than exists in either the books or the movies. (Crichton killed Hammond off in the first book, anyway.) The overall plot of our game is as simplistic as most others (the character must find a way to escape a death trap), but the details revealed about the Jurassic Park world extend it in a way which is faithful to the originals.

Although it is quite likely that the next Jurassic Park movie to be released will make TRESPASSER non-canon, for now it stands as the only real extension of the series published. If there are such things as Jurassic Park fanatics and they were able to look past the game play flaws, they hopefully enjoyed our development of the world.

2. Art and music

On an individual basis, the models created for TRESPASSER rank with the best-looking work done for computer games. We limited the largest texture size to 256×256 pixels, and at model import time textures were converted to 8-bit paletted images. But artists worked with their models using 24-bit art in 3D Studio Max, applying the textures using any mapping methods that Max supported. We had the standard limits on visible polygons, so most models were made with as few as possible: dinosaurs ranged from 300 to 500 polygons and trees from 50 to 120, for example. But this still gave our artists more complexity than was standard at the time.

Many of TRESPASSER's artists had never worked on games or done 3D modeling before, and some had never even used computers at all. This was a fairly deliberate decision, in an attempt to achieve a much higher standard of art than we were used to seeing on previous products. The number and resolution of textures we were able to support called for painting skills far beyond the average game-trained artist.

The music is one of TRESPASSER's best accomplishments. Originally, we were slated to use John Williams's score, but the cost proved to be excessive. Fortunately, our sound effects company, SounDelux, put us in touch with one of their stable of composers who specialized in "imitation" music. With very little prompting, he recorded about 30 minutes of music for us which in some parts far exceeds the rather forgettable work Williams himself did for the *Jurassic Park* movies.

Some reviews still accused us of having spotty or inappropriate music, but this was more an implementation problem than a problem with the music itself.

The music was recorded as a couple dozen short sections which were scattered through the world on location-based triggers. Much like the voice-overs, more attention could have been paid to their placement so that they only played at appropriate and regular intervals. Even more desirable would have been a system with the ability to play tension or combat music loops and fade them in and out of the special-event songs to make it seem more like a continuous musical score.

3. Innovative systems

Our artists were able to paint textures with near-total disregard for common memory-conservation practices, thanks to the texture caching system which one of the last programmers to be hired created fairly late in the project. Textures for our game were MIP-mapped by our helper application, GUIApp, as part of the process of building level data (curved bump maps were also created at this time). A level could have a nearly unlimited amount of textures, and once MIP-maps were created, all textures and their MIP-maps were saved into a single swap file. GUIApp automatically organized the swap files into pages based on texture size, with the lowest couple of MIP levels for all textures on a set of pages which were always committed.

As the player moved through the level and objects came into view, the appropriate pages from the swap file were accessed. In any circumstances where an appropriate texture hadn't been loaded in yet, the always-committed MIP-maps could be used until the higher-resolution texture had been loaded. In theory, this could result in a frame or two where an object was textured at a lower resolution than desired, but in practice it rarely happened, even on the most texture-intensive levels.

Another major system for TRESPASSER was its audio system, which we described as "real time Foley" because of its ability to generate collision and scraping effects between differing sound materials in real time. Although the system could have used more sound material data, even with what it had it resulted in some wonderfully immersive sound effects which most other games do not duplicate—things like scraping a board down a concrete surface or hitting an oil barrel with a metal bat sound almost perfect. The system doesn't just play two stock effects but actually chooses from several samples and sets volumes based on the strength of the underlying physics collision, with very natural-sounding results.

Finally, our image caching system, which rendered groups of distant objects into single 2D bitmaps to speed rendering, while responsible for the most disturbing visual anomalies in the game, was also by its own right an amazing piece of work. Image caching allowed scenes with tens of thousands of polygons to be rendered in near-real time, and it is the first technology which has allowed outdoor scenes to have a reasonable fraction of the complexity of the real outdoors.

4. Outdoor level design

When we created our terrain geometry, we were deliberately trying to avoid the "marbles in rubber" look of a lot of bad fractally-generated outdoors. To this end, we decided that we needed to base our island on real-world terrain rather than build it from scratch. Luckily, we had a real-world model to go from: Costa Rica's Cocos Island, the same island which Crichton used as his inspiration for Site B. Unfortunately, no relief maps of sufficient detail existed for the island, so we ended up having our lead artist sculpt a large model of the entire island, had it laser scanned, and did all our final work on it in 3D Studio Max.

Modeling was only the first step to creating a level. After most of the terrain was established, it took significant time to populate the levels with objects. There were 10–15,000 trees, shrubs, and rocks in most levels, and a few thousand man-made objects as well. Every object could be placed individually, but for time-saving reasons we generally used groups of objects for areas off the gamepath and only spent a lot of time hand-placing items in places we knew the player would go. The rolling terrain and a random-delete tool we often ran for optimization generally kept the repetition from seeming obvious.

In the end, although our levels didn't quite fulfill our personal expectations, they usually look more like real environments than previous games. Starting from a real map seemed to be the most useful tactic for this, and looking for a real-world starting point for vegetation placement is the next obvious step for outdoor games.

5. Realistic physics in a first-person perspective

The first discovery we made as our physics simulation was slowly implemented was that it was an engrossing toy. When we finally got support for compound object physics (so that a bench could consist of a top and two legs instead of a single block, for instance), it was possible to spend an hour just dropping the bench onto things to see how it would catch on edges and flip and slide around. Toys do not make games, however, and trying to establish game play that would work with our simulation was our major challenge.

Due to the vagaries of our particular physics simulation and interface, we eventually arrived on game play that primarily involved knocking things over rather than stacking things up. Knocking over will probably be the first application of realistic physics to see widespread use, as it will work even with a less-than perfect physics

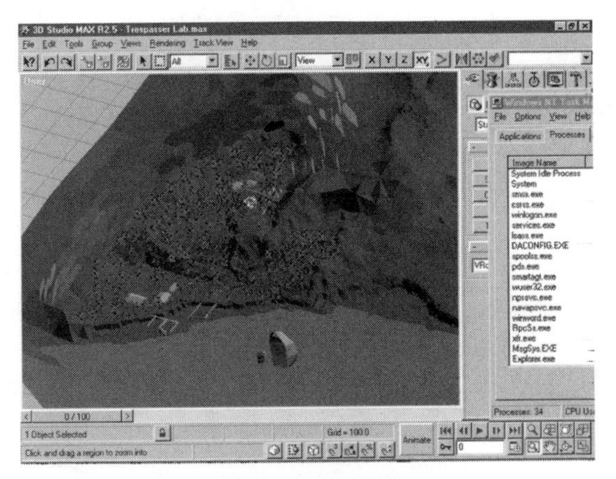

Level design in Max was tolerable, not enjoyable, for the TRESPASSER team.

model (such as TRESPASSER's). It is also a behavior which easily shows off the difference between realistic physics and what we usually referred to as "fake" physics—compare pushing a box off a ledge or hill in any game which actually lets you move boxes to the same action in TRESPASSER.

Since our game play was supposed to revolve around the physics, however, we needed to apply that knocking-over behavior in slightly more sophisticated ways than just using it as eye candy. The best uses that we found in the small amount of time we had involved knocking stacks of boxes down to fill holes, or unbalancing something resting on a high ledge in order to get it or use it as a step. It also quickly became apparent that building even a seemingly simple knocking-down puzzle required a much more highly refined sense of physical laws than many of us had.

What Went Wrong

It might seem as though TRESPASSER deserves more entries in its "what went wrong" section than the usual project postmortem. However, TRESPASSER's failings are actually few in number. Unfortunately, the failings that we did have were serious enough to more than outweigh our successes.

1. Software-oriented renderer

TRESPASSER was begun before the original Voodoo started the wave of 3D hardware popularity. The TRESPASSER engineers set about to create an engine in the old-school manner: they picked some previously-unseen rendering technologies and implemented them, ignoring any issues of compatibility with hardware cards. Our engine's two most incompatible features were its bump mapping (which used a true geometrical algorithm that could take surface curvature into account) and its image caching.

Image caching was intended to allow real-time rendering of huge numbers of meshes, but it was also the system almost solely responsible for the graphical anomalies of popping, snapping trees in the game. The other primary visual artifact of the game was the frequent sorting errors, but this was a result of poorly-constructed levels which continually handed our depth-sort algorithm more polygons than its limit, and not a direct result of image caching itself.

The image cache system worked by rendering distant objects into 2D bitmaps on the fly, and then updating them when the angle or distance changed enough so that the 2D representation was no longer sufficiently accurate. This may sound familiar to those who remember Microsoft's Talisman architecture, and there was a hope at one time that our game would be a "killer app" for Talisman accelerators, but resistance from key figures in the industry and 3dfx's sudden popularity pretty much put an end to Talisman.

TRESPASSER ended up slipping by more than a year, as did many games of its time. Our hardware programmer put in a valiant effort in the last half year of the project, and managed to get much more use out of 3D hardware than we initially thought possible. We ended up with a fairly unique mixed-mode renderer which drew any bump-mapped objects in software and the rest of the scene with hardware. Unfortunately, the large number of bump-mapped objects present in our game, such as all the dinosaurs and nearly every crate, meant that the fill rate advantages of accelerators were often negated.

In addition to being a costly software-only rendering method, our bump mapping was never very evident: we could have used multiple, moving light sources and had the art staff make better use of bump maps in their objects. Many of the bump maps were created by simply converting the original texture to grayscale, an artist's hack that works for rendered images and animations but not in real-time 3D. Image caching was an even bigger problem than bump mapping, because although it was the key technology that we were using to try to improve scene complexity, the game's visual quality was also the source of most people's complaints.

It seems clear in retrospect that we should have made a tradeoff somewhere along the line and either dropped the physics technology and physics game play in favor of the rendering technology, or more likely dropped the rendering technology and the ability to do complex scenes in favor of the physics technology.

2. Game design problems

The biggest indication that TRESPASSER had game design problems was the fact that it never had a proper design specification. For a long time, the only documents which described the game play were a prose-style walkthrough of what the main character would do as she went through the game, and a short design proposal listing the keys which would be used and some rough ideas of what game play might actually be.

Our experiences on TRESPASSER made it clear that it is worse not to have a design specification at all than to have one which becomes out of date and is frequently rewritten. TRESPASSER started and finished weak in the game design, and this affected every other part of the project. When it became clear that the technology was not going to exist to support the initial high-concept design, it would have been best to throw out all our existing notions and reinvent the game.

Unfortunately, our license made it all but impossible to throw out the original TRESPASSER concepts. The only major deviations from the original idea were the change from constructive, stacking-based physics puzzles to destructive, knocking-over puzzles, and an attempt to make combat more prevalent in order to shore up the weakness of the destructive physics puzzles. Since no part of the TRESPASSER code was written to be good at doing first-person shooter game play, this attempt to make shooting a more important feature only ended up flaunting some of the weaker points in the game, like the lack of an inventory system and the slow frame rate.

3. Tools problems

TRESPASSER was built entirely in 3D Studio Max. There was no level editor, only the generically-titled GUIApp, which was the game with a debugging shell—not really a tool at all. Our level creation procedure consisted of arranging 20–25,000 meshes in Max, using dummy meshes to represent game play objects like triggers, and typing trigger code into these objects' "object properties" buffer.

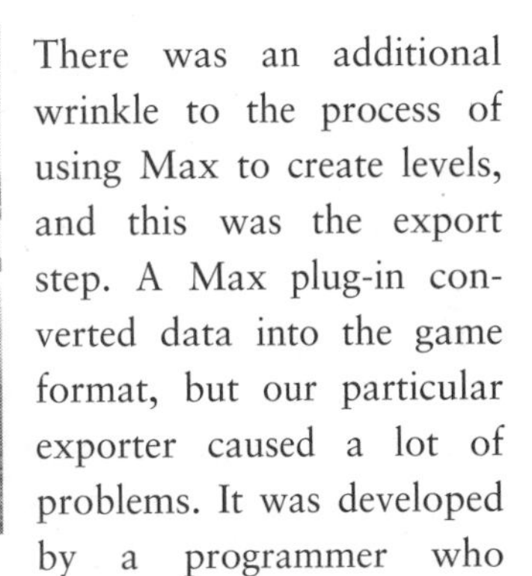

There were two unexpected and incredibly severe drawbacks that we discovered only after it was far too late to change our method of building the game world. The first problem was that Max is basically unfit to work with more than about 5,000 objects at a time. TRESPASSER levels averaged 40MB in size, and could take a couple minutes to load on the systems our designers used (Pentium II-266 with 256MB RAM). When all objects in a level were visible, it could take from 30 to 60 seconds to respond after clicking on an object to select it, making fast work difficult (to say the least).

The second problem with the Max method was our use of the object properties text buffer. The buffer seems to be one of those features which no one ever used before, because we discovered that if more than 512 characters were typed into an object's properties buffer, Max could become unstable. If Max didn't crash outright and a file was saved with one of these bad objects, it would become unloadable. TRESPASSER's technical artist wrote many design tools in MaxScript and also coded warning scripts to guard against problems such as properties buffer overflows, but these solutions only made designing in Max tolerable—not enjoyable.

There was an additional wrinkle to the process of using Max to create levels, and this was the export step. A Max plug-in converted data into the game format, but our particular exporter caused a lot of problems. It was developed by a programmer who worked from home, an hour away from the office, and used a separate code base with unique classes and a different version of the compiler. This was also his first project in 3D, and it became the second-most delayed part of the project after physics. Until the last year of the game, there were significant bugs in the exporter which required time consuming work-arounds.

Important functionality, such as the ability to export object properties, also was not delivered until very late in development, which prevented designers from implementing game play. In the end, the exporter was assigned to another programmer and rapidly brought up to usability, but it had already delayed level building significantly.

4. AI problems

The largest problem with the AI system was that its progress was blocked by a lack of dinosaurs with which to test it. The first time a dinosaur made the transition from a separate test application into the game was in early 1998, with significant missing functionality which prevented the completion of visually important AI behaviors, like howling and glaring. The first quadruped went in around the early summer of 1998, about four months from the then-intended ship date (as it turned out we slipped by about another month). The dinosaur AI was a state-based system, based on the creatures' emotions.

It became apparent once dinosaurs were working well enough to put into levels that the differences between the activity states were not discrete enough. Dinosaurs were governed by a set of emotions which theoretically would prompt them to pick appropriate responses at any time. However, in practice they would end up oscillating rapidly between many activities, sometimes even literally standing still and twitching as they tried to decide what to do. Making a usable dinosaur required disabling all but one or two of their activities. This allowed aggressive dinosaurs to really be aggressive, but it also meant that most dinosaurs were as single-minded as the traditional video game monsters we were trying to one-up.

The AI system suffered from the lack of a clear game design. There are two scenes in the Jurassic Park movies which demonstrate quintessential dinosaur game play: the scene in Jurassic Park where the kids hide from raptors in a kitchen, and the scene in Lost World where Jeff Goldblum deals with several cautious raptors in the ruins of the town. Both of these scenes rely on dinosaurs which can be fooled by ducking behind objects and which can home in on or be distracted by localized noises. Neither of these two fundamental abilities is actually present in the TRESPASSER dinosaur AI.

Instead, the dinosaurs have a simpler and more industry-standard detection radius which doubles as sight and hearing and is not blocked by objects in any way. Without a design specification calling for these kind of behaviors, though, the AI development went in directions which ended up being largely unsuitable for game play. This problem wasn't even discovered until a few months before we shipped, when there was only time to work around it rather than completely rework it.

5. Physics problems

The box model was TRESPASSER's most significant physics innovation: it was intended to be a complete simulation of any arbitrarily-sized box interacting with a number of other boxes. The approach used in TRESPASSER was what is known as the "penalty force" method. In incredibly simple terms, when boxes collide, they are allowed to intersect with each other (mathematically), and then they push each other apart until they are no longer intersecting.

The penalty force model is generally believed to be an unworkable one by the few other people in the industry attempting real-time solids models, but our physics programmer believed he could make it work. There were several notable flaws with TRESPASSER's solids model as shipped: it ended up only working well when used with roughly cube-shaped boxes with dimensions between 0.5 and 1 meter on a side, it did not model friction well, it was extremely slow, and it was not free of interpenetration even within the size constraints.

We were aware that physics would be slow, and that ten boxes at once would represent the practical upper limit, but we had not expected that so much of that physics overhead would be eaten up by the dinosaur body physics, which used five boxes in the worst cases: head, body, tail, and two feet. Although the dinosaur physics boxes executed faster because they did not interact with each other, it turned out that in common cases (like a scene displaying two raptors and the player holding a gun), the physics budget was completely consumed and there were no were no processor cycles left to handle knocking over a stack of boxes.

Physics speed was an issue, but other problems were more severe. The game design depended on boxes of sizes other than small cubes, and we ended up including many objects outside that safe range. Unfortunately, all objects outside the safe range, even large cubes, were more prone to reveal the most egregious problem with the physics system: interpenetration. At best, these interpenetration bugs completely blow the consistency of simulation we tried to set up, and at worst they make the game unplayable. If it was not clear before shipping TRESPASSER, it is clear now: no amount of interpenetration is acceptable, and preventing it absolutely should be the number one concern of any physics coder. TRESPASSER's dinosaurs and the arm itself were inverse-kinematic (IK) systems controlled by physical models. Originally, the dinosaurs were supposed to be full physically-modeled bipeds whose physics actually knew how to use legs to stand, walk, run, and jump. They ended up with more standard game movement physics and an

IK animation system very similar to Looking Glass's TERRA NOVA.

Just like in TERRA NOVA, the dinosaur legs frequently stretched, bent, and popped as the IK system struggled to handle the physically impossible movements that the simplified physics generated. This movement problem was a case of lacking realistic boundary conditions. The joints of the arm never had realistic limitations put on their rotation or even limitations on the distances between joints. A system written by a different programmer sat on top of the underlying arm system and continually tried to make sure it had not moved into an impossible position, but as a separate system it could only be partially successful at best.

The arm as shipped would often go almost out of control for a few frames, stretching or spinning in impossible ways. During this time the fragile feeling of connection between the player and their character would be shattered. The arm suffered not only from its unbounded model but also from bad design choices. Its creator intended it to be wholly context-insensitive. The fact that guns, unlike other objects, get held fairly steadily and away from the body was only a result of some key members of the test staff adding their voices to the cries which had been coming from within the team to fix shooting so that it was easy to hit a desired target. It should have been obvious from the mere fact that a 2D interface was being used to move in 3D space that an even larger amount of context sensitivity was needed.

If a truly successful virtual arm is ever to be implemented, simple mouse movements will have to be translated into complicated arm movements based on what is in or near the hand, or it will be as impossible to use as TRESPASSER's arm. That there was a conscious decision to avoid context sensitivity in our project is indicative of the larger problems with physics in our project. The physics code was largely written in a vacuum and tested in separate applications and non-representational levels, and not enough attempts were made to analyze it from a player's perspective and design it to support game play in every way.

Lessons Learned

How did TRESPASSER end up shipping with the number of problems that it had? TRESPASSER was a project with management problems at all levels. It suffered from being an innovative, technologically ambitious project produced by a team with little previous management experience at a company which had not yet gained institutional experience from publishing significant, less-ambitious projects.

That TRESPASSER shipped at all is a testament to the strength of the individual members of its team. In looking back at my own experience, I find that I learned a lot about game development, and I'm already putting that knowledge to work. Although the game does not fulfill the many high hopes I had for it (or even my base expectations), I am happy with the work I put into it. I also hope that every other person who contributed to the massive effort is equally proud of their work, and that sometime in the future we all have a chance to make a major project that succeeds where TRESPASSER failed.

195

Ion Storm's

DEUS EX

by warren spector

Back-Story

If the mid-90s were the era of stripped-down, no-frills shooters, DEUS EX, released in 2000, is the logical backlash. It features both high-speed action and familiar role-playing elements—plot twists, conversations, inventory, and a large cast of characters. As superagent J. C. Denton, players navigate a complex story of intrigue and conspiracy, traveling the world and changing sides at least once. DEUS EX was designed to support a range of play styles, from full-on assault to stealth, and to allow players to solve problems creatively, using a wide array of gadgets and abilities.

Fictionally, DEUS EX is set in a near-future version of the real world (as it exists if conspiracy buffs are right). For some real shorthand, call it "James Bond meets The X-Files." Conceptually, DEUS EX is a genre-busting game (which really endeared us to the marketing guys)—part immersive simulation, part role-playing game, part first-person shooter, part adventure game.

It's an immersive simulation game in that you are made to feel you're actually in the game world with as little as possible getting in the way of the experience of "being there." Ideally, nothing reminds you that you're just playing a game—not interface, not your character's back-story or capabilities, not game systems, nothing. It's all about how you interact with a relatively complex environment in ways that you find interesting (rather than in ways the developers think are interesting), and in ways that move you closer to accomplishing your goals (not the developers' goals).

It's also a role-playing game in that you play a role and make character development choices that ensure that you end up with a unique alter ego. You make your way through a variety of minute-to-minute gameplay experiences (which add up to a story) in a manner that grows naturally out of the unique aspects of your character. Every game system is designed to differentiate one player-character from another, and to allow players to make decisions that reflect their own biases and express character differences in obvious ways in the game world.

It's a first-person shooter because the action unfolds in real time, seen through the virtual eyes of your alter ego in the game world. To some extent, your reflexes and skill determine your success in combat. However, unlike the typical FPS, DEUS EX doesn't force you to shoot every virtual thing that moves. Also unlike the average FPS, in which gameplay is limited to pulling a virtual trigger, finding blue keys to open blue doors, and jumping to reach seemingly inaccessible locations, DEUS EX offers players a wide range of gameplay options.

And finally, DEUS EX is like adventure games in that it's story-driven, linear in narrative structure, and involves character interaction and item accumulation to advance the plot. However, unlike most adventure games (in which you spend the bulk of your time solving clever puzzles in a search for the next static, but very pretty, screen), DEUS EX asks players to determine how they will solve game problems and forces them to deal with the consequences of their choices.

Game Data

Release date: June 23, 2000

Publisher: Eidos Interactive

Genre: first-person action/role-playing game; science fiction

Intended platforms: Windows 95/98/NT/2000 plus third-party Macintosh and Linux ports

Number of full-time developers: Approx. 20: 1 of me, 3 programmers, 6 designers, 7 artists, 1 writer, 1 associate producer, 1 tech.

Number of contractors: Approx. 6: 2 writers, 4 testers.

Length of development: 6 months of preproduction and 28 months of production.

Critical development hardware: Ranged from dual Pentium Pro 200s with 8GB hard drives, to Athlon 800s with 9GB fast SCSI, and everything in between. More than 100 video cards were cycled through during development.

Critical development software: Visual Studio, Lightwave, Lotus Notes.

Notable technologies: Unreal engine and associated tools such as UnrealEd and ConEdit (our proprietary conversation editor).

DEUS EX combines elements of all of these genres. But more important than any genre classification, the game was conceived with the idea that we'd accept players as our collaborators, that we'd put power back in their hands, ask them to make choices, and let them deal with the consequences. It was designed from the start as a game about player expression, not about how clever we are as designers, programmers, artists, or storytellers. Which leads naturally to a discussion of having clear goals—the first thing I think we did right.

What Went Right

1. A clear high-level vision

It's pretty self-evident that you can't achieve goals if you're not clear about what they are. We knew with a high degree of confidence what kind of game we wanted to make. This was possible for two reasons. First, DEUS EX is a natural outgrowth of work done by and in some cases with the late, lamented Looking Glass Technologies. We were inspired as well by games made at Valve, Origin, and a host of other places.

Many of the things we wanted to do were a reaction to things they (or we) didn't do, didn't do well, or couldn't do at all in earlier games. We weren't building from scratch, but rather building on a foundation already laid for us. Second, and on a personal level, DEUS EX is a game I've been thinking about since right around the time UNDERWORLD 2 shipped. I've tried to get a game like this started several times (as TROUBLESHOOTER at Origin; in some respects, as JUNCTION POINT, for Looking Glass). Those games didn't happen for a variety of reasons, but I never stopped thinking about them and, despite the failure of those games to reach production, they laid much of the conceptual groundwork for DEUS EX. The lesson here is that if there's a game you really want to make, don't give up on it. Someone will be foolish enough to give you the money eventually.

Real-world spaces, such as the Statue of Liberty in New York City, can be compelling game spaces, but offer unique challenges to game developers.

Several years passed. I left Origin to go work for Looking Glass, but TROUBLESHOOTER stayed on my mind. In the fall of 1997, before Ion Storm entered the DEUS EX picture, I drafted a manifesto—a description of an ideal game—and also a set of "rules of roleplaying." Much of that material ended up in an article published in *Game Developer* ("Remodeling RPGs for the New Millennium," February 1999), which is still available online on Gamasutra.com.

The details of DEUS EX—plot, character lists, game system designs and so on—changed radically in the years following the original TROUBLESHOOTER proposal and writing my manifesto and rules list. Conceptually, however, the game still plays much the way I hoped TROUBLESHOOTER would play, and it definitely fulfills most of the ideals I had outlined in that *Game Developer* article.

Quite simply, with a solid concept of what we wanted to achieve in mind, we were able to assess every design decision and every game system specification in light of our ultimate goals.

2. We didn't skimp on preproduction

We spent the first six months of DEUS EX (before we licensed a game engine), with a team of about six, just thinking about how we could turn our high-level goals into a game. We hammered on the setting and decided to move the game into the near future to buy ourselves some room to play around—the real world, as we quickly discovered, was very limiting.

Ultimately, we settled on a conspiracy-oriented background. We did a vast amount of research into "real" conspiracies—the Kennedy assassination, Area 51, the CIA pushing crack in East

L.A., Dwight Eisenhower's UFO connection, and of course Freemasons tunneling below the Denver airport and building abducted-baby cafeterias for alien invaders at George Bush's direction. Only a fraction of this stuff ended up in the game, but it gave us a peek into the minds of conspiracy buffs that was both scary and useful.

We worked on back-story stuff so we'd know what was going on in the world, even in places the player never got to visit. Some of this stuff may come to the forefront in DEUS EX 2 but, for DEUS EX, it was just a way of making sure we knew enough to include the kinds of small details that make a fictional world convincing. We also created a cast of more than 200 characters, many of whom didn't yet have specific roles in the game. Ultimately, this list proved to be both a help and a hindrance to designers as they fleshed out the missions. Characters sometimes suggested missions or subquests, but just as often ended up being filler we were reluctant to cut, even though their missions or story purposes changed during our storyline focusing passes.

We hammered on game systems. We conceived a skill system that didn't depend on die-rolls or tracking skills at a fine level of granularity. We came up with a system of "special powers" (nanotech augmentations) that differentiated the player character from ordinary humans. We designed a conversation system with some cinematic elements and some elements borrowed from console RPGs. We mocked up 2D inventory, skill, and augmentation upgrade screens, map screens, even a text editor so players could take notes. We conceived several player reward systems, including skill point awards, augmentation upgrades, weapon availability timelines and tool/object availability timelines.

By March 1998, we had 300 pages of documentation and thought we knew everything we'd needed to know to make a game. Were we ever wrong. In the time between March 1998 and our Alpha 1 deadline of April 1999, that 300-page document mushroomed into more than 500 pages, much of it radically different from what we thought of and wrote initially.

Clear goals and a detailed script are all well and good, but goals change, thinking changes, and game designs have to change, too. Which leads nicely into the next thing that went right.

3. Recognizing that game design is an organic process

Why did our thinking and goals change? There were lots of reasons. First, new people joined the team, with new ideas. Our staff grew from six people to roughly 20. I hired a bunch of people, of course, but we had the added excitement of integrating an entire art team assigned to us, in Austin, by an art director a couple of hundred miles away in Ion Storm's Dallas office.

As we brought on new people, we found ourselves to be a team of hardcore ULTIMA geeks, hardcore shooter fans, hardcore immersive sim fans, strategy game nuts, and console gamers. Some of our new team members proved to be "maximalists"—wanting to do everything, special-case lots of stuff, and stick as close to reality as possible. Other team members proved to be minimalists—wanting to include fewer game elements but implementing them exceptionally well, in ways that could be universally applied rather than special-cased. Also, we made a point of letting select friends and colleagues play the game at various points along the way. We were interested in well-reasoned opinions from folks who understood the kind of game we were making intimately and who had a handle on the development process that was at least as good as our own.

With all the new folks contributing and all the feedback from our chosen critics, well, let's just say we had some interesting debates at Ion Storm, Austin. Out of those debates new ideas arose, and the game changed as a result. Technology forced design changes, too. It took time to become familiar with the Unreal engine. Months of experimentation were necessary to reveal how best to do things in Unreal and what things not to do at all.

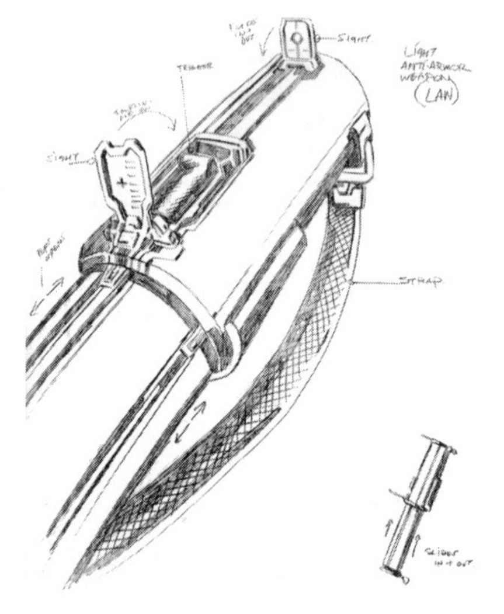

A detailed weapon sketch.

A third area that influenced the changing nature of the game's design was when the game systems didn't work as we intended them to. We quickly found that descriptions of game systems are no substitute for prototypes and actual implementation. We prototyped every game system as it was documented relatively early on. We also built some test missions, not quite early-on enough, but still early. These test systems and missions revealed gaping holes in our thinking, or things that we thought would be true and which turned out not to be true at all.

For instance, once implemented, our augmentation and skill systems proved dry and rather dull, despite looking really good on paper. I thought the tension of standing outside a locked door, not knowing if a guard was going to show up while you picked the lock, would provide sufficient excitement. I thought knowing you could leap across a chasm because you had the Jump augmentation at Tech Level 3, and opening up new paths through maps that were inaccessible to players without that augmentation, would be cool enough to keep players interested.

We took this criticism, and with it in mind, lead designer Harvey Smith revised the skill and augmentation systems pretty thoroughly, increasing the tension level, providing new rewards, and allowing players to think and make informed decisions. None of this would have happened without the prototype missions and some harsh (but fair) criticism they elicited.

Another big reason for changes from our original design document was our realization that the idea of a real-world RPG, with real-world locations and real-world weapons, was cooler in some ways than it turned out to be on the screen. When we started building places like the

Statue of Liberty, a few square blocks of New York City, the White House, Parisian streets, and so on, we found that most of the real world is not all that interesting as a gaming environment. We also found it difficult to live up to people's expectations of places they've actually been.

We created an object-rich environment, only to hear things like, "Hey, why can't I use that telephone to call anyone I want whenever I want?" and had to cut some objects whose real-world functionality we couldn't capture in the game.

Finally, we had to ask ourselves whether human non-player characters (NPCs) are interesting enough to carry an entire game. We were about a year into development when designers and artists balked at a game entirely about human beings. Movies don't need non-humans to be cool but the same cannot be said, apparently, for games. People want monsters and bad guys.

The feeling was so pervasive that it changed my thinking completely. The original design spec called for a couple of robots, but the team demanded that they be made a more important part of the landscape, and we introduced genetically manipulated animals and some alien-looking creatures. (Luckily, our game fiction supported all of this.) The game benefited, but this was a radical change from the original plan.

4. Creating "proto-missions"

It's a truism that milestones should be testable, showing visible progress, whenever possible, and we lived up to that standard. We could always pull a version together, always show off for press or our publisher. Most importantly, we always knew where we were (even if that knowledge was sometimes painful). But the proto-mission idea is something beyond simply visible, testable milestones. The proto-mission is critical in the process of design, as well as in milestone and schedule setting.

One example of where our proto-mission idea was successful was in May 1998, when our milestone was to have prototypes of critical game systems in place and two test maps running, in this case the White House and part of Hong Kong. The maps were crude, the conversations raw, and the game systems hacked, but we could see—and show—the potential.

To our advantage, we resisted the temptation to do just the stuff we knew would work and the stuff that would look the prettiest, and prototyped new, risky stuff first. Conversation, interface, inventory, skills, and augmentations were all at least hacked in so we could see them in action. The White House was likely to prove our toughest map challenge, so we built it first. (Almost unbelievably, I missed what may have been the riskiest, most critical game system in all of our early prototyping, NPC AI. I should have insisted on early prototyping of our AI but I didn't.)

With the proto-mission system, we could immediately see some of the limitations of our technology. For example, we had some serious speed problems with areas as big as the White House and Hong Kong. After this, we knew we'd have to break maps up into small pieces. And we began to suspect, though I couldn't quite embrace the idea, that we'd eventually have to cut maps and missions from the game—most notably the White House.

In May 1999, we had a milestone calling for the delivery of the first two missions of the game, playable start to finish. All of our game systems were implemented (not hacked) as originally documented. You could start a game, create a character, upgrade skills, solve problems in a variety of ways, manipulate inventory, acquire augmentations, talk to NPCs, get and accomplish goals, save your game, and so on. To the team's chagrin, I had a tendency to call this the "Wow, these missions suck" milestone.

The DEUS EX player's alter ego, J.C. Denton, strikes a heroic pose.

Our earlier demos had shown the potential of what we were doing. This demo showed us how far we had to go before we reached that potential. This milestone also benefited us in that it showed us all the steps necessary to create a mission, and revealed the elements that really made the game work. That knowledge allowed us to go through our 500-page design document and cut everything that was extraneous, winnowing it down to a svelte 270 pages. Less game? Not at all. What was left was the best 270 pages—the stuff that worked.

"Less is more" was something Harvey Smith had said over and over, from the day he signed on as lead designer. While some team members resisted this notion outright, I took a middle road, which just frustrated everyone. In the end, we cut a lot, left a lot, and made a game that everyone on the team was happy with (I think). This milestone made it clear that the time had come to make cuts, while giving us enough knowledge to cut intelligently. If we had waited until beta to make cuts, with just a few months to go before our ship date (as many developers do), it would have been a disaster.

5. Licensing technology

We went into DEUS EX hoping that licensing an engine would allow us to focus on content generation and gameplay. For the most part, that proved to be the case. The UNREAL TOURNAMENT code we ended up going with provided a solid foundation upon which we were able to build relatively easily. Dropping in a conversation system, skill and augmentation systems, our inventory and other 2D interface screens, major AI changes, and so on could have been far more difficult. We were able to make what I hope is a state-of-the-art RPG-action-adventure-sim with only three slightly overworked programmers, which allowed us to carry larger design and art staffs than usual.

However, to my surprise, licensing technology didn't save us all the time I'd hoped it would. You'd think cutting a year or more of engine-creation off a schedule would result in an earlier release date. On DEUS EX, that didn't prove to be the case. Time that would have been lost creating tools was lost instead to learning the limitations and capabilities of "foreign" technology.

The biggest downside to licensing was that we were just never going to understand the code as well as we would have if we'd created it ourselves. That led to two distinct kinds of problems. First, there were areas where we ended up treating the engine as a black box. I think it's pretty well documented by now that we shipped DEUS EX with some Direct3D performance issues. Once players started reporting troubles, we were kind of in a lurch—we couldn't very well go in there and mess with the Unreal engine—we just didn't understand it well enough to do that safely. We had built around the edges of Unreal without ever getting too deeply into the nuts and bolts of it.

Second, because we didn't know the code inside out, and because we'd shelled out a fair amount of money for it, we tended to be conservative in our approach to modifying it. There were times when we should have ripped out certain parts of the UNREAL TOURNAMENT code and started from scratch (AI, pathfinding, and sound propagation, for example). Instead, we built on the existing systems, on a base that was designed for an entirely different kind of game from what we were making. It's not that UNREAL had bad AI or pathfinding or sound propagation, but those systems were designed for a straightforward shooter, which was not what we were making.

I guess the fact that we'll be licensing technology for our next round of projects, DEUS EX 2 and THIEF 3, says the price was right. But it remains an interesting dilemma, and we will be able to approach our next licensed engine with the wisdom gleaned from using UNREAL for this project.

What Went Wrong

1. Our original team structure didn't work

You'd think after 17 years of making games and building teams to make games, I'd have a clue about team structures that work and those that don't. Ha! When I started pulling the DEUS EX team together I had a core of six guys from Looking Glass's Austin office. Having tapped Chris Norden to be lead programmer, I needed to find a lead designer and a lead artist. As I started casting about for the right person for the design job, something really good, but ultimately really bad, happened—two guys came along with enough experience to expect a leadership position.

Instead of doing the sensible thing and picking one of them, even if that meant the other chose not to sign on, I got cute. I created two design teams, each with its own lead. I put together two groups of people with differing philosophies—a traditional RPG group and an immersive sim group. We were making a game designed to bust through genre boundaries, and I thought a little competition and argumentation would lead to an interesting synthesis of ideas. I thought I could manage the tension between the groups and that the groups and the game would be stronger for it.

My plan didn't work. The design team was fragmented from the start. We had to name one of the groups "Design Team 1" and the other "Design Team A." (Neither group would settle for "2" or "B.") It became apparent—later than it should have—that I was going to have to merge the two groups and have a single lead designer. When I finally made that change I disappointed some folks, but the game was the better for it, and that's what's important in the end.

A genetically manipulated creature called a "Greazel" was added to DEUS EX in response to the team's feeling that human interaction might not be enough to carry the entire game.

There were also challenges on the art side. DEUS EX suffered dramatically because for over a year, the artists "on the team" worked not for me or for the project, but for an art director in Ion Storm's Dallas office. Don't misunderstand—the art director was a talented guy. But talent doesn't make up for a matrix management structure (wherein resources in a department or pool are "lent out" to a project until they're not needed anymore) ill-suited to the game business, and it doesn't make up for being off-site.

During this time, the art department drifted a bit. It was unclear whether the artists worked for me or for the art director in Dallas. I couldn't hire, fire, give raises to, promote, or demote anyone on the art team. We were assigned some artists who weren't interested in the kind of game we were making. Matrix management may work in some circumstances, at some companies, in some businesses. But I've never seen it work in gaming, and I've seen it attempted at three different companies. It especially doesn't work when one of the department managers isn't on-site.

I argued for a year that matrix management had failed at Origin and at Looking Glass. I had no doubt it would eventually fail at Ion. Eventually I got my way, and things got much better on the art front once the artists were officially part of the DEUS EX team. Still, I can only imagine how DEUS EX might have looked if we'd been one big happy team, including the artists, from the start.

If the experience of DEUS EX taught me one thing, it's the importance of team dynamics. You have to build a team of people who want to be making the game you're making. You have to deal with personnel issues sooner rather than later. And there has to be a clear chain of command. Many decisions can be made by consensus, but there can only be one boss for a project, there can only be one boss for each department, and department heads have to answer to the person heading up the project.

2. Clear goals are great...when they're realistic

We started out thinking very big. That in itself isn't bad—it's necessary to advance the state of the art—but we were unrealistic, blinded by promises of complete creative freedom, and by assurances that we would be left alone to make the game of our dreams. A really big budget, no external time constraints, and a marketing budget bigger than any of us had ever had before made us soft.

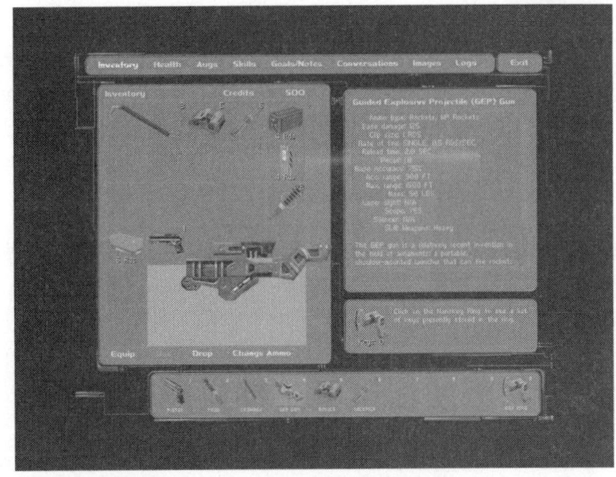

Everything in DEUS EX is about choices—who you are in the world, how do you interact in the world, what are you carrying, and so on. In this case, the player has clearly decided to go through the game as a heavy weapons specialist, despite the fact that this will leave little room in inventory for anything else.

Let me give you some specific examples of ways in which we outreached ourselves in the original design of DEUS EX (before we made significant cuts). For one, there's no way, in a first-person RPG, to stage a raid on a POW camp to free 2,000 captives. Also, there's no way to re-create all of downtown Austin, Texas, with any degree of accuracy. Third, blinded by the power of UnrealScript, many of our original mission concepts depended upon special-case scripting and lots of it. We discovered the need for general solutions rather than special-case solutions later in the project than we should have (this despite much harping on the subject by some team members).

Find your focus early and maintain that focus throughout. General solutions are better than special casing. Give players a rich but limited tool set that can be used in a variety of ways, not a bunch of individual, unpredictable solutions to every problem. Always work within the limits of your technology rather than trying to make your technology do things it wasn't meant to do. Big budgets, lots of time, and freedom from creative constraints are seductive traps. Don't settle for less than greatness, but don't think too big. Balance should be the goal.

3. We didn't front-load all of our risks

In fact, we missed a big one. We were smart enough to realize we'd have to prototype and implement our new game systems early so we'd have time to tweak and refine them sufficiently.

We did our conversation system and our complex 2D interface screens early, which was a good thing, too—they required as much tweaking as we feared. And in the end, they turned out pretty well, I think.

Unfortunately, we missed one huge risk area—artificial intelligence. I don't know how we missed it, but we did. It's not that we didn't spend time on AI. We started thinking about AI early in preproduction. Unfortunately, what that meant was that the AI was, to a great extent, designed in a vacuum, and as is often the case, we didn't really know what the game required with respect to AI until relatively late in development. And that meant implementing AI features early on that ended up being unnecessary later, once our design had evolved into its final form.

In addition, building on the base of UNREAL TOURNAMENT's pure shooter AI meant that, instead of designing a system specifically for our needs, we ended up adding stuff and tweaking until the bitter end, causing NPC behavior to change constantly, right up to the last day of development. We ended up with some pretty compelling AI, but the problem of convincing people they're interacting with real people is immense, particularly when you're talking about characters whose reactions have to run the gamut from fear to friendliness to violent enmity. Our sin was, I think, giving people a hint of what human AI could be in games, but delivering the goods inconsistently.

4. Proto-missions redux

Game Developer's Postmortems typically focus in on things the team clearly did right and things the team clearly did wrong. It sure is nice when things are that clear. Maybe it's just me, but I almost never see things in such black-and-white terms. Most of the time, problems are knotty and solutions are far from obvious or clear-cut, which is where the final two "What Went Wrongs" fall.

As I already mentioned, we recognized the need for proto-missions relatively early on, and built our schedule around the idea. We implemented two such missions, which helped us identify many things that didn't work (and many that did). With proto-missions in hand, we found ourselves at a critical juncture with two possible choices to make, the implications of which I still don't entirely understand.

On one hand, I could have gone off with some subset of the team and tweaked our proto-missions until they were absolutely right and models for all subsequent mission implementation before turning the rest of the team loose on implementation of the rest of the missions. On the other hand, I could have kept the entire team in implementation mode, getting all of the missions to the level of the proto-missions, meaning none of them would be exactly right but we'd be able to see the shape of the entire game and all of the missions would be ready for tuning at about the same time.

The first approach would have left large portions of the team in thumb-twiddling or make-work mode for some unspecified period of time.

This promised to prove that we could create a ground-breaking, compelling game, but could leave us without a finished game to ship. The second approach would have kept everyone productive throughout the project and at least put us in position to decide whether or not to ship the game at some foreseeable point in the future. The question was whether we would be able to turn all of the bare-bones missions into something fun or not.

I chose the latter approach and told everyone to get the game "finished" and playable at a bare-bones level. We'd worry about fleshing out all the missions, making the game as interesting and fun and dense and exciting as it needed to be during the inevitable gameplay tuning, tweaking, and balancing phase at the end. This probably isn't so much of a "What Went Wrong" as it is an open question of whether that was the right call.

I think so, and the plan clearly worked to the extent that we shipped a game that people seem to like pretty well. But it's unclear to me whether using our proto-missions to fine-tune might not have resulted in an even better game.

5. Is it true that any publicity is good publicity?

This wouldn't be a complete or accurate picture of the development of DEUS EX if we didn't take a look at the Sturm und Drang that was Ion Storm. In case you you've been living under a rock, there's been a lot of hype surrounding the company. On the negative side, Ion Storm was heaped with bad press for much of 1998 and 1999. The company did the same things all game companies do, went through the same problems, but because we painted a big ol' "suck it down" target on our chests, the gaming press and a fair number of hardcore gamers went after us with a vengeance.

Not too surprisingly, this had an effect on those of us working away in the Austin office. Morale hits were frequent and problematic. It simply isn't possible to be bombarded by negative press about the company you work for and not take it somewhat personally. Trust me when I say that seeing your personal and private e-mails posted on the Internet is a devastating experience.

Also, recruiting was more difficult than it should have been. We were able to put together an incredibly talented team for DEUS EX, but too many talented people told us that while they would like to work on DEUS EX, they couldn't work for Ion Storm. Eventually, a "we'll show

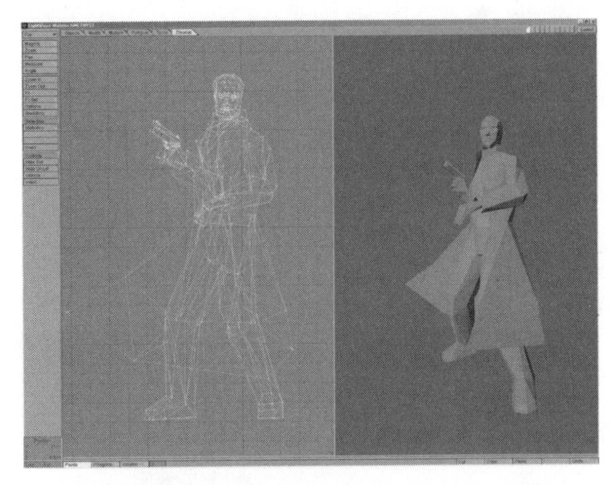

Bringing believable human characters to life is no easy task. The artists, whether working on concept art, 3D models, or texturing, had their work cut out for them.

them" mentality became prevalent in Austin. I don't know that anyone who worked on DEUS EX thought of him- or herself as part of the same company making DAIKATANA and ANACHRONOX up in Dallas. That kind of us-versus-them thinking is rarely good in the long run.

Now that we've shipped, the reviews seem to fall into two categories—those that begin with some statement implying that Warren Spector makes games all by himself (which is silly), and those that begin with some statement proclaiming that DEUS EX couldn't possibly have been made by Ion Storm (also silly). Silly or not, there's a level on which we're still trying to live down our past, at least in terms of the media's perception of our game and the company that paid the bills here.

But, for all the problems, being associated with Ion Storm wasn't all bad—far from it. On the plus side, it isn't as if anyone from *Rolling Stone*, *Entertainment Weekly*, the *New York Times*, the *L.A. Times*, *USA Today*, *Mother Jones*, the *Wall Street Journal*, *Forbes*, *Fortune*, *Time*, *Architectural Digest*, CNN, or the BBC ever banged down the doors at Origin or Looking Glass to talk to me or anyone on any of my teams. In reality, the bad publicity was almost entirely limited to the gaming press. The mainstream media, which barely notice anything about gaming (other than the fact that we supposedly turn normal kids into vicious killers), didn't seem to care about the bad stuff. But they sure did take notice of us. Ultimately, Ion's ability to attract attention to itself, even if it was sometimes in negative ways, probably worked to our advantage. Whether publicity at any cost is good or bad is still an open question for me.

The Bottom Line

Part of the challenge of game development is making the tough decisions along the way, the many difficult junctures when you have to determine that something that can't be done right in the game shouldn't be done at all. It's all well and good to have design goals and an ideal game pictured in your head when you start, but you have to be open to change and realistic about what can and can't be done in a reasonable time frame, for a reasonable amount of money, with the personnel and technology available to you. And if you don't have time to do something right, cut it and do everything that's left so well that no one notices the stuff that isn't there.

I'm not saying we did that perfectly on DEUS EX. We certainly didn't ship a perfect game. But if we hadn't gone into development with the attitude that we'd do things right or not at all, we would have fallen far shorter of perfection than we did. How close we did get is something all of you can decide for yourselves. All I know is we're going to get closer next time.

Naughty Dog's JAK & DAXTER: THE PRECURSOR LEGACY

by stephen white

Back-Story

A flagship title for the PlayStation 2, JAK & DAXTER is the latest in a line of third-person, platform-jumping, item-collecting games featuring charismatic lead characters. To this venerable formula, Naughty Dog brought their experience and prestige as creators of CRASH BANDICOOT, one of the PlayStation's signature titles. JAK & DAXTER features new-generation graphics and, notably, a huge, sprawling world that unfolds continuously rather than in discrete levels.

By the end of 1998, Naughty Dog had finished the third game in the extremely successful CRASH BANDICOOT series, and the fourth game, CRASH TEAM RACING, was in development for a 1999 year-end holiday release. And though Sony was closely guarding the details of the eagerly awaited Playstation 2, rumors—and our own speculations—convinced us that the system would have powerful processing and polygonal capabilities, and we knew that we'd have to think on a very grand scale.

Because of the success of our CRASH BANDICOOT games (over 22 million copies sold), there was a strong temptation to follow the same tried-and-true formula of the past: create a linear adventure with individually loaded levels, minimal story, and not much in the way of character development. With more than a little trepidation, we decided instead to say goodbye to the bandicoot and embark on developing an epic adventure we hoped would be worthy of the expectations of the next generation of hardware.

For JAK & DAXTER, one of our earliest desires was to immerse the player in a single, highly detailed world, as opposed to the discrete levels of CRASH BANDICOOT. We still wanted to have the concept of levels, but we wanted them to be seamlessly connected together, with non-obvious boundaries and no load times between them. We wanted highly detailed landscapes, yet we also wanted grand vistas where the player could see great distances, including other surrounding levels. We hoped the player would be able to see a landmark far off in the distance, even in another level, and then travel seamlessly to that landmark.

It was important to us that Jak's world make cohesive sense. An engaging story should tie the game together and allow for character development, but not distract from the action of the game. The world should be populated with highly animated characters that would give Jak tasks to complete, provide hints, reveal story elements, and add humor to the game. We also wanted entertaining puzzles and enemies that would surpass anything that we had done before.

Game Data

Release Date: December 2001

Publisher: Sony Computer Entertainment

Genre: 3D fantasy platformer/adventure

Platform: Playstation 2

Number of Full-time Developers: 35

Length of Development: 1 year of initial development, plus 2 years of full production.

Operating Systems Used: Windows NT, Windows 2000, Linux

Development Software Used: Allegro Common Lisp, Visual C++, GNU C++, Maya, Photoshop, X Emacs, Visual SlickEdit, tcsh, Exceed, CVS

To achieve these and many other difficult tasks required three years of exhausting work, including two years of full production. We encountered more than a few major bumps in the road, and there were times when the project seemed like an insurmountable uphill battle, but we managed to create a game that we are quite proud of, and we learned several important lessons along the way.

What Went Right

1. Scheduling

Perhaps Naughty Dog's most important achievement is making large-scale games and shipping them on time, with at most a small amount of slip. This is an almost unheard of combination in the industry, and although there is a certain amount of luck involved, there are valid reasons to explain how Naughty Dog has managed to achieve this time and again.

Experience will tell you it's impossible to predict the precise details of what will be worked on more than a month or two in advance of doing it, yet many companies fall into the trap of trying to maintain a highly detailed schedule that tries to look too far into the future. What can't be effectively worked into these rigid schedules is time lost to debugging, design changes, over-optimism, illness, meetings, new ideas, and myriad other unpredictable surprises.

At Naughty Dog, we prefer a much more flexible, macro-level scheduling scheme, with milestone accomplishments to be achieved by certain dates. The schedule only becomes detailed for tasks that will be tackled in the near future. For example, a certain level will be scheduled to have its background modeled by a certain date. If the milestone is missed, then the team makes an analysis as to why the milestone wasn't achieved and changes plans accordingly: the background may be reduced in size, a future task of that artist may be given to another artist to free up more time, the artist may receive guidance on how to model more productively, or some future task may be eliminated.

In the case of JAK & DAXTER, we used the knowledge we'd gained from creating the CRASH BANDICOOT games to help estimate how long it should take to model a level. As we modeled a few levels, however, we soon realized that our original estimates were far too short, and so we took appropriate actions. If we had attempted to maintain a long-term, rigidly detailed schedule, we would have spent a lot of time trying to update something that was highly inaccurate. Beyond this being a waste of time, the constant rescheduling could have had a demoralizing effect on the team.

Extensive character sketches and color key/ concept design work were done in advance of actual modeling.

2. Effective localization techniques

We knew from the start that we were going to sell JAK & DAXTER into many territories around the world, so we knew we would face many localization issues, such as PAL-versus-NTSC, translations, and audio in multiple languages. Careful structuring of our game code and data allowed us to localize to a particular territory by swapping a few data files. This meant we only had to debug one executable and that we had concurrent development of all localized versions of the game. All of our animation playback code was written so that it could automatically step animations at a rate of 1.2 (60fps/50fps) when playing in PAL. We also used a standardized number of units per second so that we could relate the amount of time elapsed in a game frame to our measure of units per second. Once everything was nice and consistent, then timing-related code no longer had to be concerned with the differences between PAL and NTSC.

Physics calculations were another issue. If a ball's motion while being dropped is computed by adding a gravitational force to the ball's velocity every frame, then after one second the ball's velocity has been accelerated by gravity 60 times in NTSC but only 50 times in PAL. This discrepancy was big enough to become problematic between the two modes. To correct this problem, we made sure that all of our physics computations were done using seconds, and then we converted the velocity-per-second into velocity-per-game-frame before adding the velocity to the translation.

3. Seamless world, grand vistas, and no load times

We knew very early on in the development of JAK & DAXTER that we wanted to immerse the player within one large expansive world. We didn't want to stall the game with loads between the various areas of that world. Jak & Daxter's designers had to overcome many obstacles to achieve our open environments. They had to lay out the levels of the world carefully so that levels could be moved in and out of memory without stalling gameplay or causing ugly visual popping. They also had to create challenges that would engage the player and maintain the player's interest, even though the player could roam freely around the world. And they had to tune the challenges so that the difficulty ramped up appropriately, without giving players the impression that they were being overly directed.

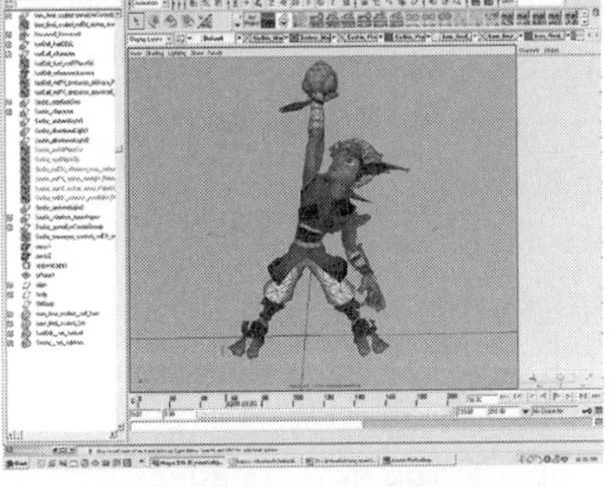

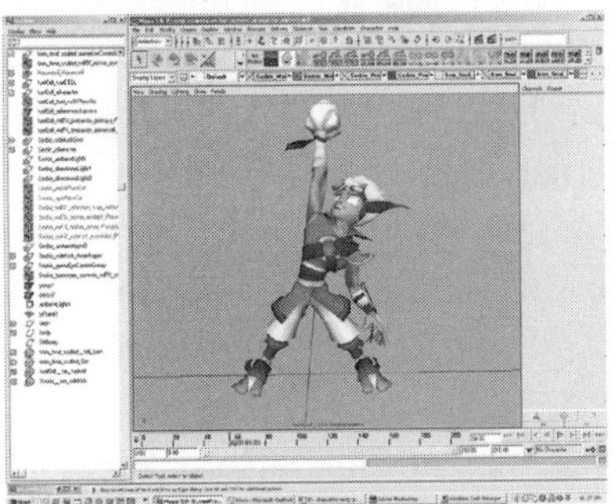

A frame from Jak's victory animation displaced as IK, textured, and textured with color shading.

The programmers had to create tools to process interconnected levels containing millions of polygons and create the fast game code that could render the highly detailed world. We developed several complex level-of-detail (LOD) schemes, with different schemes used for different types of things (creatures versus background), and different schemes used at different distances, such as simplified models used to represent faraway backgrounds, and flats used to represent distant geometry. At the heart of our LOD system was our proprietary mesh tessellation/reduction scheme, which we originally developed for Crash Team Racing and radically enhanced for Jak & Daxter.

The artists had the burden of generating the enormous amount of content for these environments. Their task was complicated by the very specialized construction rules they had to follow to support our various renderers. Support tools and plug-ins were created to help the artists, but we relied on the art staff to overcome many difficulties.

4. Camera control

From the initial stages of Jak & Daxter, we looked at the various camera schemes used in other games and came to the depressing conclusion that all existing camera schemes had serious issues. We suspected that making a well-behaved camera might be an unsolvable 3D problem: How could one possibly create a camera that would maneuver through a complex 3D world while behaving both unobtrusively and intelligently? Only fools would believe that all problems have a solution, so, like idiots, we decided to give it a try.

The resulting camera behaved extremely well, and although it had its limitations, it proved the problem does indeed have a solution. Jak can jump through trees and bushes, duck under archways, run between scaffolding, scale down cliffs, and hide behind rocks, all with the camera unobtrusively keeping the action in view. We wanted the player to be able to control the camera, but we did not want to force the player to do so. Players can use the second joystick to maneuver the camera (rotating the camera or moving it closer to or farther from Jak), but we were concerned that some people may not want to manipulate the camera, and others, such as children, may not have the required sophistication or coordination.

Therefore, we worked very hard at making the camera do a reasonable job of showing players what they needed to see in order to complete the various challenges. We accomplished this through a combination of camera volumes with specially tuned camera parameters and specialized camera modes for difficult situations. Also, creatures could send messages to the camera in order to help the camera better show the action.

This may sound funny, but an important feature of the camera was that it didn't make people sick. This has been a serious problem that has plagued cameras in other games. We spent a bit of time analyzing why people got sick, and we tuned the camera so that it reduced the rotational and extraneous movement that contributed to the problem. Perhaps the greatest success of the camera is that everyone seems to like it. We consider that a major accomplishment, given the difficulty of the task of creating it.

5. GOAL rules!

Practically all of the run-time code (approximately half a million lines of source code) was written in GOAL (Game Object Assembly Lisp), Naughty Dog's own internally developed language, which was based on the Lisp programming language. Before you dismiss us as crazy, consider the many advantages of having a custom compiler. Lisp has a very consistent, small set of syntactic rules involving the construction and evaluation of lists. Lists that represent code are executed by evaluating the items that are in the list; if the head of the list is a function (or some other action), you could think of the other items in the list as being the parameters to that function.

This simplicity of the Lisp syntax makes it trivial to create powerful macros that would be difficult or impossible to implement using C++. Writing macros, however, is not enough justification for writing a compiler; there were features we felt we couldn't achieve without a custom compiler. GOAL code, for example, can be executed at a listener prompt while the game is running. Not only can numbers be viewed and tweaked, code itself can be compiled and downloaded without interrupting or restarting the game.

This allowed the rapid tuning and debugging, since the effects of modifying functions and data structures could be viewed instantaneously. We wanted creatures to use nonpreemptive cooperative multi-tasking, a fancy way of saying that we wanted a creature to be able to execute code for a while, then "suspend" and allow other code to execute. The advantage of implementing the multi-tasking scheme using our own language was that suspend instructions could be inserted within a creature's code, and state could be automatically preserved around the suspend.

Consider the following small snippet of GOAL code:

```
(dotimes (ii (num-frames
idle))
   (set! frame-num ii)
   (suspend)
      )
```

This code has been simplified to make a point, so pretend that it uses a counter called ii to loop over the number of frames in an animation called idle. Each time through the loop the animation frame is set to the value of ii, and the code is suspended. Note that the value of ii (as well as any other local variables) is automatically preserved across the suspend. In practice, the preceding code would have been encapsulated into a macro such as:

```
(play-anim idle
   ;; Put code exe-
cuted for each time..
   ;; through the loop
here.
   )
```

There are other major compiler advantages: a unified set of assembly op-codes consistent across all five processors of the Playstation 2, register coloring when writing assembly code, and the ability to intermix assembly instructions seamlessly with higher-level code. Outer loops could be written as "slower" higher-level code, while inner loops could be optimized assembly.

What Went Wrong

1. GOAL sucks!

While it's true that GOAL gave us many advantages, GOAL caused us a lot of grief. A single programmer (who could easily be one of the top ten Lisp programmers in the world) wrote GOAL. While he called his Lisp techniques and programming practices "revolutionary," others referred to them as "code encryption," since only he could understand them.

Because of this, all of the support, bug fixes, feature enhancements, and optimizations had to come from one person, creating quite a bottleneck. Also, it took over a year to develop the compiler, during which time the other programmers had to make do with missing features, odd quirks, and numerous bugs.

Eventually GOAL became much more robust, but even now C++ has some advantages over GOAL, such as destructors, better constructors, and the ease of declaring inline methods. A major difficulty was that we worked in such isolation from the rest of the world. We gave up third-party development tools such as profilers and debuggers, and we gave up existing libraries, including code previously developed internally. Compared to the thousands of programmers with many years of C++ experience, there are relatively few programmers with Lisp experience, and no programmers (outside of Naughty Dog) with GOAL experience, making hiring more difficult.

GOAL's ability both to execute code at the listener and to replace existing code in the game at run time introduced the problem of memory usage, and more specifically, garbage collection. As new code was compiled, older code (and other memory used by the compiler) was orphaned, eventually causing the PC to run low on free memory. A slow garbage collection process would automatically occur when available memory became sufficiently low, and the compiler would be unresponsive until the process had completed, sometimes taking as long as 15 minutes.

2. Gameplay programming

Because we were so busy creating the technology for our seamless world, we didn't have time to work on gameplay code until fairly late in the project. The situation caused no end of frustration to the designers, who were forced to design levels and creatures without being able to test whether what they were doing was going to be fun and play well. Eventually programmers were moved off of technology tasks and onto gameplay tasks, allowing the designers to play the game and make changes as appropriate. But without our designers' experience, diligence, and forethought, the results could have been a disaster.

3. Audio

We were plagued with audio-related problems from the start. Our first indication that things might not be going quite right was when our sound programmer quit and moved to Australia. Quickly hiring another sound programmer would have been the correct decision. We tried several other schemes, however, made some poor choices, and had quite a bit of bad luck. We didn't recognize until fairly late in development what a monumental task audio was going to be for this project.

Screenshot showing highest level of detail of in-game geometry for the Forbidden Jungle level.

The same shot displayed with textures.

Not only did JAK & DAXTER contain original music scores, creature and gadget noises, ambient sounds, and animated elements, but there are also over 45 minutes of story sequences, each containing Foley effects and speech recorded in six different languages. Our audio issues could be broken up into four categories: sound effects, spooled Foley, music, and localized dialogue. Due to the large number of sound effects in the game, implementing sound effects became a maintenance nightmare. No single sound effect was particularly difficult or time-consuming; however, creating all of the sound effects and keeping them all balanced and working was a constant struggle. We needed to have more time dedicated to this problem, and we needed better tool support.

We used spooled Foley for lengthy sound effects, which wouldn't fit well in sound RAM. Spooling the audio had many advantages, but we developed the technology too late in the project and had difficulty using it due to synchronization issues. Our music, although expertly composed, lacked the direction and attention to detail that we had achieved with the CRASH BANDICOOT games. In previous games, we had a person who was responsible for the direction of the music. Unfortunately, no one performed that same role during JAK & DAXTER.

Dialogue is a difficult problem in general due to the complexity of writing, recording, editing, creating Foley, and managing all of the audio files, but our localization issues made it especially challenging. Many problems were difficult to discover because of our lack of knowledge of the various languages, and we should have had more redundant testing of the audio files by people who were fluent in the specific languages.

4. Lengthy processing times

One of our greatest frustrations and loss of productivity came from our slow turnaround time in making a change to a level or animation and seeing that change in the actual game. Since all of our tools (including the GOAL compiler) ran across our network, we ran into severe network bandwidth issues. Making better use of local hard drives would have been a smarter approach. In addition, we found extreme network slowdown issues related to reading file time/date stamps, and some tools took several minutes just to determine that nothing needed to be rebuilt.

When we compiled some of our tools under Linux, we noticed dramatic improvements in network performance, and we are planning on using Linux more extensively in our next project. We implemented the processing of the lengthy story-sequence animations as a hack of the system used to process the far simpler creature animations. Unfortunately, this bad system caused lengthy processing times, time-consuming debugging, and a lot of confusion.

If we had initially hidden the processing complexity behind better tools, we would have saved quite a bit of time.

We used level-configuration scripts to set actor parameters and other level-specific data. The script processing was done at an early stage in our tools pipeline, however, so minor data changes took several minutes to process. We learned that tunable data should instead be processed as close as possible to the end of the tools pipeline.

5. Artist tools

We created many tools while developing JAK & DAXTER, but many of our tools were difficult to use, and many tools were needed but never written. We often didn't know exactly what we needed until after several revisions of our technology. In addition, we didn't spend a lot of time polishing our tools, since that time would have been wasted if the underlying technology changed. Regrettably, we did not have time to program tools that were badly needed by the artists, which resulted in a difficult and confusing environment for the artists and caused many productivity issues. Since programming created a bottleneck during game production, the added burden given to the artists was considered necessary, though no less distasteful.

We lacked many visualization tools that would have greatly improved the artists' ability to find and fix problems. For example, the main method artists used to examine collision was a debugging mode that colorized a small section of collision geometry immediately surrounding Jak. A far better solution would have been to create a renderer to display the entire collision of a level.

We created plug-ins that were used within the 3D modeling package; however, for flexibility's sake most of the plug-ins operated by taking command parameters and outputting results as text: not a good interface for artists. Eventually, one of our multi-talented artists created menus and other visualization aids that significantly improved productivity. Many of our tools were script based, which made the tools extremely flexible and adaptable; however, the scripts were often difficult for the artists to understand and use. We are replacing many of these scripts with easier-to-use GUIs for our next project.

The Legacy

Creating JAK & DAXTER was a monumental effort by many hardworking, talented people. In retrospect, we were probably pretty foolish to take on as many challenges as we did, and we learned some painful lessons along the way. But we also did many things right, and we successfully achieved our main goals. At Naughty Dog, there is a strong devotion to quality, which at times can border on the chaotic, but we try to learn from both our success and our failures in order to improve our processes and create a better game. The things that we learned from JAK & DAXTER have made us a stronger company, and we look forward to learning from our past as we prepare for the new challenges ahead.

Section IV

Building on a License

A license game is a game based on an existing creative property borrowed from some other medium. A game could be based on nearly anything—we've seen adaptations of books, films, television shows, magazines, dolls, rock bands, comic books, basketball players, and soft drinks. For any work under copyright, somebody holds the interactive rights and may part with them for a price.

The prospect is enormously tempting. What game developer hasn't dreamed of adapting some cherished work, of building their own personal vision of the Mines of Moria or Gormenghast, of Dickensian London, Chiba City, or Neo-Tokyo? It's part of the basic lure of the medium, being able to enter into and interact with imagined worlds.

And why not? It also makes business sense. Economically, licensing games is a method for reducing financial risk. The licenser takes a fee or a cut of the profits, but the combination of name-recognition, added marketing muscle, and an established fan base guarantees a minimum level of sales.

From a production standpoint, the license means you have original content you don't have to develop yourself, most of it probably first-rate. Character design, world design, and story are taken care of. If it's a film or television license, you may be able to pick up actual audio, texture, and voice acting from the original source.

There are downsides to licensing games, however. Of course, whoever owns the license is going to receive a portion of the profits. Licensers can also be extremely protective of their creative property, and not without reason. A creative property can be damaged by improper handling. A licensed game that is poorly done, that fails to convey the spirit of the original creative work, or alters its fictional continuity in some way can change how the public sees that property. All this tends to make the owner of the license quite nervous, quick to demand oversight of the project.

Licensers may set rules and limits on what the project team can do, which may hinder their creative freedom, especially when the licenser is unfamiliar with interactive media. The licenser can even deny access to crucial resources (such as actors for voice acting) or revoke the license entirely.

The flip side of name recognition is high expectations from fans of the original work. People who are genuinely invested in a work may be unhappy to see a video game based on it. People invest emotion in works of art, and they don't like having their emotions messed with. Audiences may not trust interactive adaptations, and there is some justice to that attitude. If you screw up, the potential for backlash is enormous. In any case, the original creative team behind the property may not be participating in the production process, so even if you do a reasonable job, your effort won't bear the seal of authenticity.

Any game released on a license bears the burden of reproducing the thrill of the original work, while adding interactivity. In a sense, they are competing with the license on its home turf. For example, a property that originates in a novel can trade on the strengths of that medium—witty, nuanced dialogue, direct perception of characters' thoughts, large-scale scenes, descriptive language that inspires the imagination. The game version has to give players an equally good rendition of the property, but using totally different tools. Few enough licensed games live up to the challenge—most manage to remind us of the original work, but don't deliver equally. A few—Totally Games' X-WING, Rare's GOLDENEYE—equal or even surpass their source material.

The challenge of adapting works from other media can tell us an enormous amount about our own. When a film or a book or a comic becomes a video game, everything changes, and those changes reflect the nature of the interactive medium itself. Just ask yourself why the game industry hasn't adapted Jane Austen, Shakespeare, E. M. Forster, or Henry James? Their books have been adapted into a number of successful movies recently. They aren't even under copyright, so they're available for free. Why hasn't anyone scooped them up? The fact that the game industry hasn't done so illustrates the weaknesses of interactive media.

Every year computer game graphics improve, but even so, no game has approached the quality of the cinematic image in a real-time interactive format. This is especially true when it comes to the human form—our ability to simulate human faces and body language is primitive compared to what film can do.

Films and novels show characters talking to each other, having intimate, nuanced exchanges—it's one of the basics of those forms, but computer games can't do it interactively, not on the same level. Natural language, facial expressions, and body language are unsolved problems for computers. Real people are too hard to simulate—the best we can do at this point is to produce consistent-looking worlds, stylized and perhaps cartoonish, but successful on their own terms.

Adapting story is almost as big a problem. Novels and films have become the storytelling media par excellence of the twentieth century, with a well-understood body of techniques. Again, it's a basic part of those media, something you don't even think about, but we are still learning how to do it in interactive media. Instead, we stretch out narratives with long episodes of running through sewers or jumping around on ledges, situations we do know how to show extremely well.

We face so many obstacles—the relative clumsiness of character interaction, the difficulty of integrating gameplay with narrative exposition—that our efforts may look clumsy in direct comparison to a film's smooth exterior. How many early licensed games bore almost no resemblance to the original? The grand promises laid out on the back of the box gave way to stilted little cartoons within. What was a vivid and taut action sequence on film, became hours of jumping over boxes on a TV screen. No one is going to forget E.T. on the Atari 2600.

But these failures at least show us how much better we're getting. Along the way we have learned a few things. Aside from the advantages listed above, the main lesson about licensed games is this: there is more than one way to adapt a license, so play to your strengths. You don't have to limit yourself to simply recreating the original—you can use the license in different ways to suit the style of game you're ready to make. You can expand a small part of the fictional world, do a prequel, a sequel, or carve out your own niche in the established universe, far away from the main action.

In a world as expansive and rich as the *Star Wars*™ universe, you don't have to be Luke Skywalker every time. In DUNE 2, Westwood took their license and stripped it down to one essential aspect—desert planet economic warfare—and reproduced it beautifully, while ignoring other aspects of the license, characters' personal stories, that didn't suit their game and were much harder to reproduce in the interactive medium.

Licenses are an important section of the industry. They bring much-needed financial stability to any company's balance sheets. They create links between our industry and other sections of the entertainment world, with film directors and actors and novelists. They bring in new audiences, fans of other media who might otherwise never sit down in front of a computer to be entertained. And, finally, they teach us about our own medium, show us where our strengths and weaknesses are, the things we can't do, and the things we can do better than anyone else.

LucasArts' STAR WARS™ STARFIGHTER

by chris corry

Back-Story

This air- and space-combat game is set in the *Star Wars* universe of *Episode One: The Phantom Menace.* The game's story follows three protagonists—a Rebel pilot, a bounty hunter, and a pirate captain—in a series of missions, tracing a story that interleaves cleverly with the events of the movie.

Work on Project Europa—the internal codename for the development effort that would eventually metamorphose into STAR WARS STARFIGHTER—began in earnest in April 1998. A small crew of programmers, headed up by director Daron Stinnet, began preproduction work on a STAR WARS: EPISODE I PC title that had grand ambitions. As one of LucasArts' great unsung talents, Daron had previously led the DARK FORCES and OUTLAWS teams to much critical and commercial success. Now, following in the footsteps of Larry Holland's X-WING games, Europa was to bolster LucasArts' presence in the space-combat genre and support the new film franchise. While embracing much of the X-WING series's simulation-oriented aesthetic, the team also wanted to deliver the visceral, sweaty-fingered arcade experience that we were starting to see in early builds of ROGUE SQUADRON.

During the early months of 1999, a well-known designer who was in the market for a new lead programmer and lead level designer for his company's overdue project secretly approached two members of our team about the possibility of jumping ship. Although obviously conflicted, the allure of working with a famous industry heavyweight proved too tempting, and within a few short weeks we had lost our main graphics programmer and level designer. Shaken but undeterred, we were determined to make the best of a bad situation, but three months later the project suffered another blow when we lost our second graphics programmer.

This was Europa's darkest hour. The technology development was progressing slowly, and our inexperienced programming staff was still climbing the C++ learning curve. As lead programmer, this predicament was largely of my own making. I had joined LucasArts from outside the game industry, where I was accustomed to a corporate R&D environment that valued solid engineering and extensible software architecture over quick solutions that were perhaps less elegant or flexible. Now, with little to show but a creaky Glide-based graphics engine and no graphics programmer, we were at a loss as to what to do next.

As if things weren't bad enough, we were also floundering on the game design side of the fence. Although we had a lot of excellent concept art, few of us had a clear idea about exactly what type of game we were making. We were painfully starting to discover that while it is easy to characterize a title as being a cross between ROGUE SQUADRON and X-WING, it's another thing completely to describe what that actually means.

Game Data

Release date: February 2001

Publisher: LucasArts

Genre: science fiction, ship-to-ship combat

Platform: Playstation 2

Full-time developers: Approximately 40 at the height of production

Length of development: 30 months

Hardware used: 700MHz Pentium IIIs with 256MB RAM, GeForce 256, PS2 tools

Software used: Windows 2000, Microsoft Visual C++, Metrowerks for PS2, 3D Studio Max, Softimage, Photoshop, Bryce, Visual SourceSafe, Perl, AfterEffects, Premiere

Technologies: Eve level design tool, Miles Sound System, ObjectSpace STL, Macromedia/Secret Level Flash, Planet Blue's Tulip for prerendered cut-scene lip-syncing

Lines of code: 301,000 including tools

At this point two events occurred that I'm convinced saved the project. Our multiplayer programmer, Andrew Kirmse, who had already proven himself as a remarkably capable technologist, teamed up with two of our other programmers to create a graphics-engine "tiger team," a small subteam dedicated to attacking a single task with unwavering focus. In just a few months the three of them delivered a brand-new OpenGL-based engine that was far better than anything we had built previously.

Shortly after the new graphics engine came online we also found the solution to our game design woes. Tim Longo, who had recently helped complete INDIANA JONES AND THE INFERNAL MACHINE, joined the team as our lead level designer. The change was immediate and profound; five other level designers joined the project at about the same time, and now we had the foundation for a thriving, collaborative design process. Daron worked with Tim and the other level designers on an almost daily basis, systematically identifying areas of the game design that were incomplete and working together to come up with concrete solutions.

By the end of 1999 the project had performed a 180-degree turnaround, but there was one more significant twist in the road awaiting us. Sony had turned the game industry on its ear with the formal announcement of the Playstation 2 that year, and every major development house was furiously rewriting business plans to accommodate support for the new platform; LucasArts was no exception. The biggest problem for the company was that we wanted to have a title close to the system's launch, and Europa was the only project far enough along to be a serious candidate. The thought of throwing the PS2 into the mix made many people very uncomfortable, but when we were able to port all of our non-graphics code in a single 48-hour period, senior management became convinced.

The rest of the project was an exciting and manic blur of activity. Early in 2000 we hit the "snowball point," that period when all of a sudden the tech falls into place, the art production paths are running on all cylinders, and the team is seeing exciting new gameplay on an almost daily basis. From then on, STAR WARS STARFIGHTER was indeed like a runaway snowball, picking up momentum and new features almost as fast as we could think of them.

A Naboo Starfighter cruising over an early take on the rolling hills of Naboo.

What Went Right

1. Good team communication

I've read many *Game Developer* Postmortems that blamed failures on a lack of communication, so I'm particularly proud that we got this one right. From the beginning of the project, Daron worked hard to impress on the programmers that it was the level designers and artists that would ultimately secure the success of Europa. As I became fond of saying, programmers build the picture frame, but it's up to the rest of the team to provide the most important part, the picture.

To bring this to fruition, the programming team needed to understand as best we could the way the rest of the team worked. While Andrew worked with lead artist Jim Rice and our world-builders to understand their workflows, Brett Douville, our AI and mission programmer, filled a similar role with the level designers. Brett scheduled regular "LD Days" with each individual member of the level design staff. This gave each designer the opportunity to meet with Brett on a regular basis and show him the specific challenges and problems that they were tackling in their missions.

Europa periodically had full-blown team meetings where we could get together and kibitz about the overall state of the project. However, the most valuable meetings were at the subteam level. Both the programming team and the art teams would meet weekly to discuss the issues of the day, and each of these meetings would have an attendee from the other camp—a role we referred to as the "exchange student." This meant that if questions came up in the art meeting, for example, that required answers or input from a programmer, there would always be someone present that could give an informed opinion. Likewise, as programmers would discuss issues or new features in their weekly meeting, the art or level design representative would be able to disseminate this information among the other team members.

Finally, we relied on an internally maintained Web site as a pivotal communications tool. We tried to make the site as comprehensive as possible, organizing areas along the lines of programming, art, level design, project management, and so on. When artists had questions about how to implement a particular effect, or a level designer

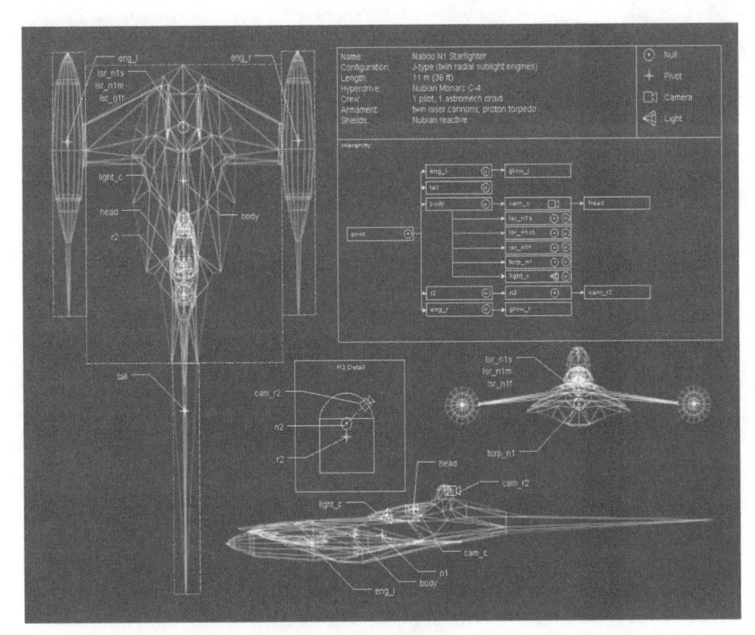

A schematic for the Naboo Starfighter—one of the only elements in the game that was present in both the original design concept and the final product.

needed a refresher on our class-file script syntax, there was usually a web page that they could be directed to that would answer many of their questions.

2. Project discipline

STAR WARS STARFIGHTER was a well-organized project. In the heat of battle it's all too easy to let requirement lists and schedules get lost in the shuffle of the moment. We were determined not to let this happen. As soon as our technology began to take shape, we started to follow an iterative process of milestone planning and execution. These milestones were typically four to six weeks in duration, with no milestone extending longer than eight weeks. Milestones were also required to demonstrate some visual or gameplay aspect of the game.

As a consequence, we had very few milestone tasks that looked like "complete the Foobar class"; instead we would have a milestone task that might read "Explosion smoke trails," and the assigned programmer would know that completing the Foobar class was an implied requirement. By keeping our attention focused on a discrete and relatively small body of work, we were able to avoid the cumulative errors that invariably creep into longer schedules, while still allowing for demonstrable progress.

Most of the milestones were driven by the progress of the technical team. Programmers were solely responsible for estimating the duration of their tasks. We would occasionally adjust these estimates outward but would never change an estimate to be shorter. Tasks were structured so that the shortest scheduled task was never shorter than a half-day. Even if a programmer was certain that a task could be completed in less than half a day, experience clearly showed that the time would be lost elsewhere.

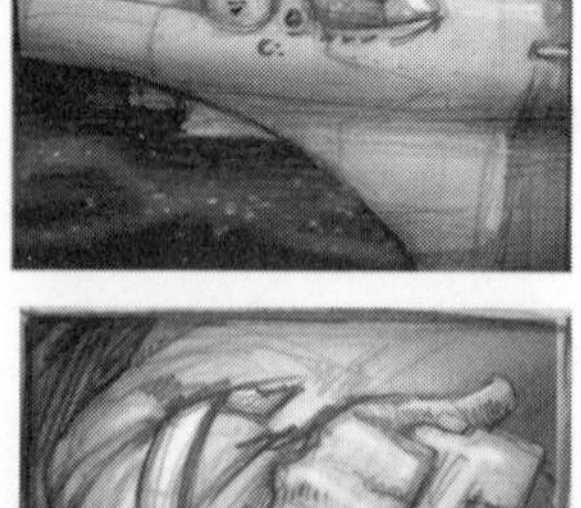

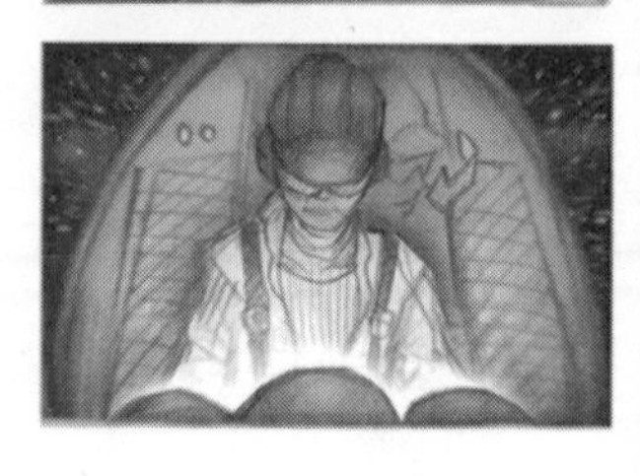

Storyboard depicting Rhys Dallow's ship getting hit.

Using these simple rules of thumb, we were consistently able to build schedules that were fair and accurate. Out of eight scheduled milestones, we never missed one by more than a handful of days. Best of all, most team members completely avoided extended periods of crunch time. Like most game teams as they approach their ship date, everyone was working hard and often into the evenings; however, this period of time was short, and we never had to resort to all-nighters.

We also closely managed the process we used to distribute new binaries to the team at large. Since most of our development occurred on the PC even after making the decision to ship on the PS2, it was important that team members have timely access to stable builds of the game. We accomplished this through weekly public builds. Once a week we would package and distribute the current code as a full-blown InstallShield-compiled install. This provided team members with debug and production versions of the game, along with level design tool and art exporter updates.

Predicting that public builds would become critically important, we tried to be as ruthless as possible about maintaining the build schedule. As we got closer to our ship date, the frequency of these public builds increased until we were performing new builds as often as three times a week. By this point we had a full-time staff member dedicated to managing the public build process and ensuring that the distributed code met quality and functionality expectations.

3. A well-executed PC-to-PS2 transition

Making the decision to move the project to the PS2 could have been a complete disaster. Yet, despite paying little attention to portability during the earliest stages of the project, the Europa code base was well positioned to make the jump to the PS2 platform. With the aid of strong and generally stable development tools provided by Metrowerks, the core port went off without a hitch.

The biggest trick was on the graphics side, because this was clearly where we were most vulnerable. None of our programmers had any console experience, and none of us was up to the task of tackling the PS2's infamous low-level vector units. Enter LECgl. LECgl was the brainchild of Eric Johnston and Mark Blattel, two of LucasArts' most senior console programmers. They had recently shipped STAR WARS: EPISODE I RACER for the N64, and they welcomed the opportunity to tackle a problem temporarily that was one step removed from the day-to-day pressures of a project team. Although Europa was the most immediate recipient of their efforts, Eric and Mark were never officially on the project. Instead they worked in a support role, providing us with regular LECgl library drops and immediate "on-call" PS2 graphics support.

There was another, more subtle problem that we had to conquer when we made the decision to adopt the PS2 as our primary platform. Most of the team members were big PC game players, but very few of us played console games. Intellectually, we knew that there were huge philosophical differences in game design between consoles and the PC. Much of our original game design had used the X-WING games as a conceptual leaping-off point, wandering into the arcade action of ROGUE SQUADRON only when it suited us.

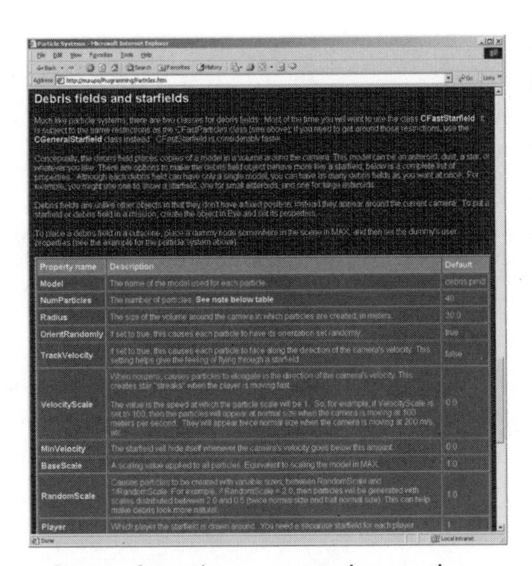

Debris fields and starfields

Much like particle systems, there are two classes for debris fields. Most of the time you will want to use the class **CFastStarfield**. It is subject to the same restrictions as the CFastParticles class (see above); if you need to get around those restrictions, use the **CGeneralStarfield** class instead. CFastStarfield is considerably faster.

Conceptually, the debris field places copies of a model in a volume around the camera. This model can be an asteroid, dust, a star, or whatever you like. There are options to make the debris field object behave more like a starfield; below is a complete list of properties. Although each debris field can have only a single model, you can have as many debris fields as you want at once. For example, you might use one to show a starfield, one for small asteroids, and one for large asteroids.

Debris fields are unlike other objects in that they don't have a fixed position; instead they appear around the current camera. To put a starfield or debris field in a mission, create the object in Eve and set its properties.

To place a debris field in a cutscene, place a dummy node somewhere in the scene in MAX, and then set the dummy's user properties (see the example for the particle system above).

Property name	Description	Default
Model	The name of the model used for each particle	[illegible]
NumParticles	The number of particles. **See note below table**	40
Radius	The size of the volume around the camera in which particles are created, in meters	30.0
OrientRandomly	If set to true, this causes each particle to have its orientation set randomly	true
TrackVelocity	If set to true, this causes each particle to face along the direction of the camera's velocity. This setting helps give the feeling of flying through a starfield	false
VelocityScale	When nonzero, causes particles to elongate in the direction of the camera's velocity. This creates star "streaks" when the player is moving fast. The value is the speed at which the particle scale will be 1. So, for example, if VelocityScale is set to 100, then the particles will appear at normal size when the camera is moving at 100 meters per second. They will appear twice normal size when the camera is moving at 200 m/s, etc.	0.0
MinVelocity	The starfield will hide itself whenever the camera's velocity goes below this amount	0.0
BaseScale	A scaling value applied to all particles. Equivalent to scaling the model in MAX.	1.0
RandomScale	Causes particles to be created with variable sizes, between RandomScale and 1/RandomScale. For example, if RandomScale = 2.0, then particles will be generated with scales distributed between 2.0 and 0.5 (twice normal size and half normal size). This can help make debris look more natural.	1.0
Player	Which player the starfield is drawn around. You need a separate starfield for each player	1

A page from the programming section of the STAR WARS STARFIGHTER internal Web site.

Now that we were on the PS2 we recognized that our design priorities needed to be completely flipped. Instead we would use ROGUE as our primary point of reference and work from there, layering on gameplay elements borrowed from X-WING as needed. As such, I think the final game demonstrates our successful indoctrination into the console mindset. We were having so much fun blowing things up that we had little desire to start adding sim-like features to the gameplay experience.

4. Macromedia Flash

As we approached the end of summer in 2000, we realized that we had a serious problem on our hands. Despite our best efforts, we still had not addressed the issue of our out-of-game user interface. We had a 2D virtual-page system that we were using for our HUD (heads-up display) symbology, and we had always planned to evolve that into something that could be used for what we called the "administrative interface." However, in August, with the quality assurance department nipping at our heels and our ship date looming ominously in the distance, things were not looking good.

Early concept art for the mercenary Vana.

We had heard that a small San Francisco–based company named Secret Level was adapting Macromedia's Flash technology for use in PS2 games. After meeting with company representatives, we were excited by the prospect. The Macromedia content-authoring tools were far more elaborate than anything we could come up with in the same time frame. We also suspected that there was a wealth of Flash authoring expertise available from out-of-house contractors which would help us smooth out the work load. Most importantly, we were very impressed by the intelligence and games savvy of the Secret Level staff.

When we realized that building our user interface in Flash would significantly ease our localization efforts, we decided to take the plunge. Soon afterward we hired a design firm named Orange Design to help us implement our administrative interface in Flash. Orange not only had a ton of experience with Flash, but they also brought a technical perspective to the table. We knew that this technical emphasis would be critical for working with our programming team on integration issues.

Integrating Flash into the Europa engine was not a completely smooth process, however. Performance in the first-generation Flash Player was poor (current generations of the Player are now much faster), and we had to spend a lot of time integrating the user interface Flash movie with the core game systems. That said, the five months that a single half-time programmer spent on this task ended up yielding a user interface that was far beyond what we would have been able to custom-code in the same period of time.

5. Good debugging systems

Our programmers built several tools that greatly helped our pursuit of high-quality code. One of the most instrumental was a Windows-only library that provided detailed stack-tracing information. This library was largely based on the code and concepts covered by John Robbins' "Bugslayer" column published in the *Microsoft Systems Journal*. As is standard practice on many games, we built a custom memory manager that could detect when the application was leaking memory. However, unlike most implementations, when our memory manager detected a leak it could provide a comprehensive stack trace of arbitrary depth, leading directly to the leaking code statement.

This capability represented a significant advantage over other implementations that could only provide the immediate location of the allocation request. If the memory allocation were being made by the Standard Template Library (STL) or one of our widely used utility classes, it was usually not enough to know what part of the STL or which one of our utility classes was the culprit. What we really needed to know was what class called the STL method that caused the leak. In fact, the leak was usually several steps up the call chain. Our stack-tracing library made finding these cases almost trivial.

We also incorporated stack tracing into our exception- and assert-handling systems. When the game encountered a hard crash, we trapped the exception and generated a complete stack trace; a similar process occurred when our code asserted. This information was initially reported back to the user in dialog form. However, we also packaged up this same data and had the game send the programmers an e-mail detailing exactly where the problem occurred. This ended up being an invaluable tool for us. As a matter of practice, the Europa programmers got into the habit of checking the assert mailbox regularly. In addition to appraising the current stability of the code, we could also use this data to spot trends and note when people weren't being diligent about installing new builds.

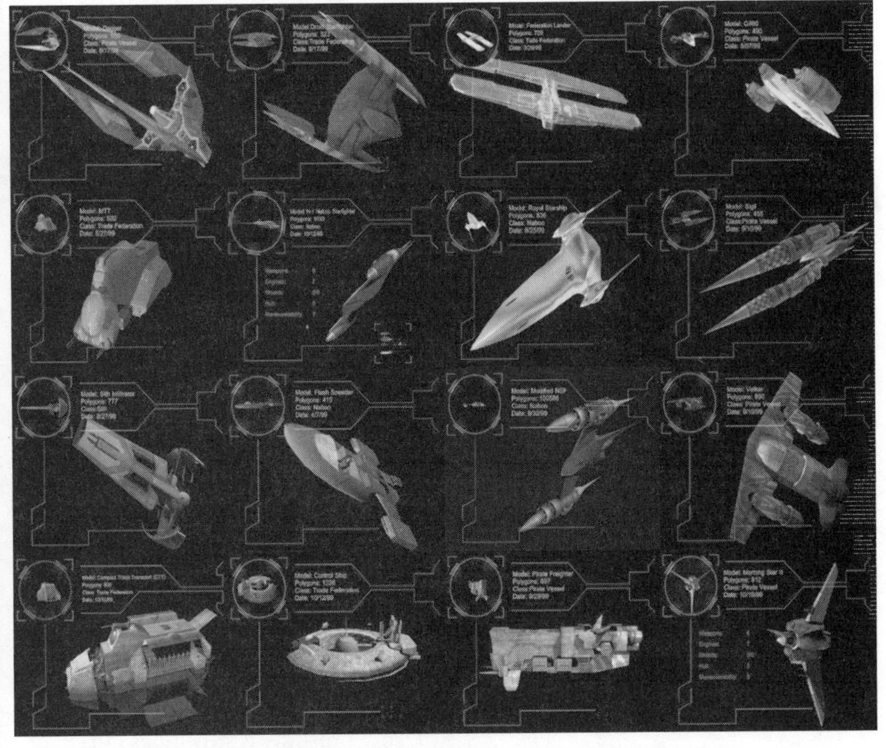

Several of the ship models developed for STAR WARS STARFIGHTER.

In the end, we had an exceptionally smooth QA process because the bugs we did have were generally easy to track down and fix. There were no last-minute "heart attack" bugs that required us to set up camp and track a single problem for hours or days at a time. This made life easier on the programmers, but it also made things easier for the testing team and improved morale across the entire project.

What Went Wrong

1. Staffing

As you can probably tell by now, staffing was easily the biggest problem the project encountered. Try as we did to manage staff retention, the team experienced an alarming amount of turnover, both in the programming and art departments. This invariably made life harder for the people left behind, because the amount of work remained constant, but team members could not be replenished as quickly as they were lost.

This also meant that many of the team's junior staff members missed out on valuable mentoring or experienced spotty supervision by their leads. On the programming team, senior programmers were so busy that we had little time to train new team members. This led to a stressful sink-or-swim mentality which was difficult for new hires. Even relatively simple quality-control procedures such as code reviews were never instituted, since every moment of every day was dedicated to making forward progress on the game.

The staffing issue continued to dog us throughout the project. Even after we had regained some momentum, we still ended up losing two programmers and a handful of artists, all to the same online gaming startup. Although nine programmers contributed to the main code base at one point or another, the vast majority of code was written by the core group of four programmers who stayed with the project to completion.

2. Initial lack of detailed design

Europa was always envisioned as having some sort of *Star Wars: Episode I* tie-in. During much of 1998, however, it was difficult to predict to what degree Lucas Licensing would allow this to happen. One of the barriers we encountered was the intense veil of secrecy that surrounded any Lucas-owned company involved with the movie property. Some of us had access to the script and the occasional rough-cut screening, but particularly during the first half of 1998 it was virtually impossible to learn the important details about the film needed to build a solid franchise title.

Initially we had assumed that the game should stay as far away as possible from the events of the film. Because we were going to be telling one of the first original stories set in the time line of the new film, we had no feeling for where the boundaries were with respect to planets, characters, vehicles, and the like. We were intimidated by the pervasive atmosphere of secrecy and general sensitivity of the Episode I storylines; the first game designs described a pirate war far divorced from the events of the film. In fact, the Naboo Starfighter was one of the only elements that could be found in both the first design and the film.

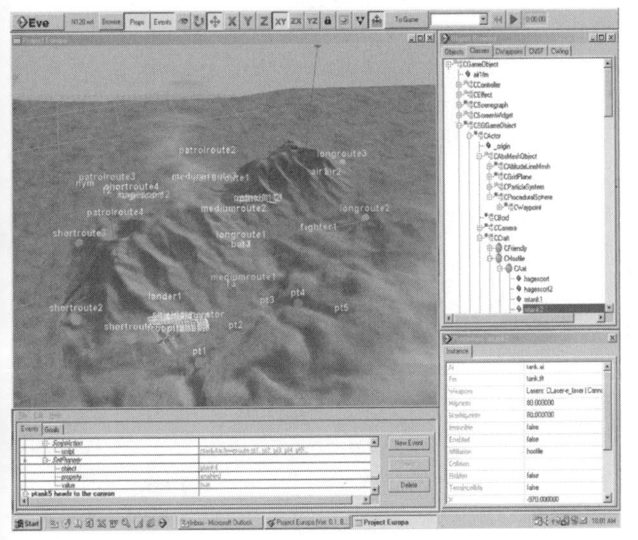

The Eve level design tool was a critical part of STAR WARS STARFIGHTER's success.

As this design started to circulate, however, Licensing contacted the team and explained that the design contained too many pirate elements; they wanted the game to contain more elements from the film. The "moving target" nature of this exchange ended up being very disruptive and effectively paralyzed the design effort for weeks at a time as we wandered from idea to idea, wondering what fit into continuity with the film and what was straying into areas that we should keep away from.

The Europa team also had some pretty big shoes to fill. It didn't take long for us to realize that whatever we did was going to be directly compared to Larry Holland's previous X-WING titles. The Totally Games guys had been making games like for this for the better part of a decade, and they had gotten very, very good at it. Game players could rely on Larry to produce large, sophisticated games with well-designed features and compelling gameplay. This success had, in turn, incubated a dedicated and enthusiastic fan base that we knew would mercilessly scrutinize STAR WARS STARFIGHTER.

Frankly, we were in a no-win situation: if we deviated too far from the Totally Games designs, we risked disenfranchising some of our most loyal fans, but we also didn't want simply to copy Larry's last game either. Fortunately, once we decided to ship on a console, the design shackles fell away and we were free to chart our own path. While we realized that the hardcore X-WING players might not appreciate STAR WARS STARFIGHTER as much as the Larry Holland games, they were no longer our primary audience.

3. Naïve approach to memory usage

As quickly as we were able to get Europa up and running on the PS2, it took the programming team much longer to fully embrace the creed of the console programmer. Since Europa was originally intended to be a PC title and our programmers only had PC experience, it's not surprising that most of the code suffered from a bad case of "PC-itis." I use this term to refer to programming practices that, while potentially portable to a console, are definitely not console-friendly.

Our approach to memory allocation is a perfect case in point. For starters, we relied on the STL for all of our container classes. On one hand we benefited from a bug-free and robust set of standardized collection classes. As an integral part of the C++ Standard Library, the STL contains a powerful toolset for general application development. We're big fans of the STL, and for the most part we can't imagine working on a project that doesn't use it. Unfortunately, depending on what containers you decide to use, the STL is notorious for making many small memory allocations.

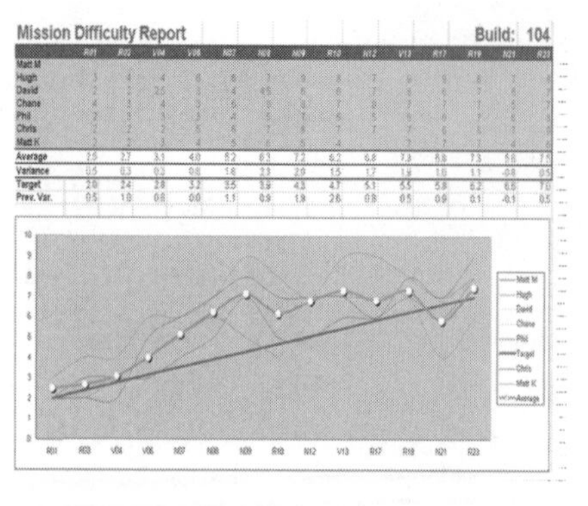

An example of the statistics that Daron tracked during the game's development.

Our STL container usage was paralleled by our use of an uncomfortably large number of ANSI string objects. The ANSI string class is a great little class that makes dealing with character strings much easier than it used to be when we were all writing code in C. Like most STL containers, however, excessive use of the string class also leads to large numbers of small memory allocations. By the time we decided to port to the PS2, most of the damage had already been done.

As I mentioned earlier, our global memory manager's original focus had been memory-leak tracking, but now we needed it to help with our STL problem. We accomplished this by introducing the concept of bins, which were really just a hierarchy of fixed-length memory allocators. When the memory manager received a small memory request, it could very quickly and efficiently satisfy the allocation if the size of the request fell into the range serviced by our bins. We ultimately relied on the bins for both rapid memory allocation services and fragmentation management.

I should also note that we had a pretty rough time with memory fragmentation. Going into the PS2 port we suspected that fragmentation was going to be a problem. On the PC we had made an effort to generally clean up after ourselves in ways that would help reduce fragmentation, but we never made a concentrated effort to eradicate it completely, because we knew that in a pinch we could always rely on the PC's virtual memory system.

One of my jobs during the last six weeks of the project was to build debugging systems that would give us detailed memory maps and then track down each fragmenting memory allocation one at a time. It was every bit as unpleasant as it sounds, and I urge those PC developers making the switch to consoles to take this lesson to heart.

4. Not enough attention paid to performance

There is little question that in the rush to implement features and ship the game on time, performance suffered. Part of this was due to having an inexperienced staff, and part of this was due to the fact that we had ported a PC code base to the PS2, but in truth most of us were so preoccupied with one issue or another that we had little time to revisit code with an eye toward optimization. There was a pervasive attitude among many of us that we could safely ignore code problems until they showed up as hotspots on a profiling run.

There is some merit to this strategy, since premature optimization efforts can be more wasteful than not fixing the code at all. But since profiling can turn up hidden problems in areas of the code that the team had previously thought complete or issue-free, it's important to start profiling much earlier than we did. For example, we had severe performance problems in our collision detection systems that we would have identified immediately if we had profiled sooner. As it happened, by the time we realized that collision detection was working poorly, the best we could do was apply spot fixes instead of the large-scale reworking that the problem actually demanded.

An early version of the Naboo Starfighter passing in front of a nebula in deep space.

Even after we started a fairly regular regimen of profiling late in the development cycle, we still didn't do enough of it. In the end, only one programmer did all of our profiling, and he was responsible for making the rounds and pointing out problems to other members of the programming staff. This was a real shame, because the Metrowerks PS2 profiler is a very nice tool, and most members of the team had uninstalled licenses. I should have made our developers responsible for profiling their own code and doing so at a much earlier stage.

5. Space-to-planet

If there was anything about the original STAR WARS STARFIGHTER pitch that met with widespread enthusiasm, it was the idea of seamlessly transitioning from planetside environments to the depths of space and back again. Dogfighting close to the planet surface certainly has its own appeal, but there is something about the promise of being able to pull back on the stick and blast off all the way into space that is simply very, very cool. This high concept was so exciting to the team that the original game pitch featured this idea predominantly. In fact, in many ways this single feature was to define the game.

Well, it's a bit of a trick to actually pull off. First, there were the technical considerations. A planet is big. I mean really, really big. Even a small planet would require dynamically creating thousands of terrain tiles. Although most of these tiles could be procedurally generated, they would still need to be created and discarded on the fly; depending on the player's location, custom mission-area tiles would have to be streamed in from the hard disk, all while maintaining frame rate.

Of course, since we wanted to allow the player to fly absolutely anywhere on the planet, ordering this data on the disk in a streaming-friendly format was problematic. We exacerbated the situation by requiring even our lowest-resolution terrain height maps to be much higher resolution than they really needed to be. This in turn made higher theoretical demands on the streaming and resource systems. This single feature had introduced a tremendous amount of technical risk to the project, and yet we had blindly charged ahead anyway because of the idea's inherent coolness factor.

The technical issues, however, did not describe the full extent of our problems with this feature. Quite quickly we also came to realize that there were plenty of game design issues implied by the space-to-planet concept. For example, there was the constant issue of player craft speed. We felt pretty sure that our ships should have a top speed of about 450 miles per hour, because dogfighting and bombing ground targets becomes extremely difficult if you move much faster. However, at that speed it would take the player 20 minutes to achieve a low-planet orbit. To circumnavigate a small planet the size of the moon could take as long as 16 hours.

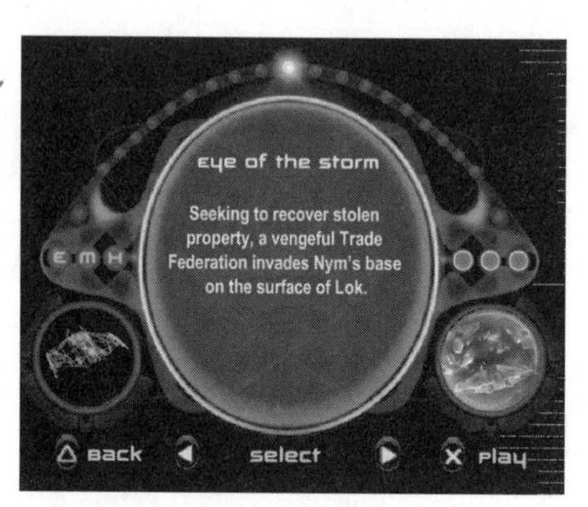

Screenshot featuring the user interface created with Macromedia Flash.

Although we were able to brainstorm several fanciful solutions to this problem, most were time- or cost-prohibitive, and all of our solutions threatened to shatter the illusion that you were in a small fighter craft, engaged in small, intimate battles.

Back to Earth

STAR WARS STARFIGHTER finally shipped in February 2001. While it was a little bit later than we had initially hoped, we burned our first set of master disks in mid-January, within three days of the "realistic" schedule projection that Daron had made a year earlier. While it certainly has its flaws, STAR WARS STARFIGHTER represents the culmination of an effort that involved almost 50 people, and it is a product that we are all very proud of. The lessons leaned over the last few years, both positive and negative, are already starting to be used by other LucasArts teams, ensuring that the project's legacy will be with us long after the last copy of the game has been sold.

Raven Software's
STAR TREK™: VOYAGER—ELITE FORCE

by brian pelletier, michael gummelt, and james monroe

Back-Story

VOYAGER—ELITE FORCE faces special challenges, adapting a traditionally combat-heavy form (first-person shooters) to a license that privileged conversation and character over action. They solved this issue by letting players take command of a special-forces style unit selected from a traditional Starfleet crew. These aren't the only challenges—Raven also faced the problems of convincingly portraying characters and settings familiar to most players and giving players intelligent-seeming crew to accompany them on their missions. The resulting game is an interesting fusion of the first-person shooter into the familiar format and rhythm of a Star Trek episode.

In the summer of 1998, Activision had acquired licensing rights to make games using a number of *Star Trek* franchises. Their goals from the beginning were to create a broad selection of games and show the gaming community that Activision could take the *Star Trek* brand and make high-quality games with it, better than other publishers had in the past. The preliminary game slate was set with a first-person shooter as one of the initial titles. Raven Software had been an external studio of Activision for a year, finishing up work on HERETIC 2 and diving deep into the development of SOLDIER OF FORTUNE.

HERETIC 2 was near completion, and we would soon need another project to work on. With our experience developing shooters and a reputation for making quality games, Activision handed the *Star Trek* first-person shooter project to us.

The game started out being based on an unknown *Star Trek* crew within the Next Generation franchise. For two months work was done on the plot and story line, with a test level of a Defiant-class ship made using the QUAKE 2 engine. The main factor in designing the plot of the game was that it had to be an action game, despite the fact that *Star Trek* isn't known for action. To give meaning to the action, the idea for a Special Forces team soon emerged to drive the action for the game.

Ultimately, because Activision already had two other games using the *Next Generation* license, the setting for our game changed to the *Voyager* franchise. Our excitement level was low at first, with the team feeling that *Voyager* was the least popular of all the *Star Trek* franchises. We soon realized that *Voyager's* plot allowed us not only to make our game with much more creative freedom, but also to create from something no one else had used.

Game Data

Release date: September 20, 2000

Genre: first-person shooter in science fiction setting

Publisher: Activision

Intended platforms: Windows 95/98/NT/2000, Macintosh, Linux, Playstation 2

Number of full-time developers: 20

Number of contractors: 13

Length of development: six months of preproduction, 18 months of production

Project size: Single-player and Holomatch: 919,749 lines of code; 1,679 files. The single-player game was largely controlled by scripting, totaling 112,056 lines of code and 2,236 files.

Project budget: Multimillion-dollar budget

Critical development hardware: Average system: Dell Pentium II 550 with 128MB RAM, 18GB hard drive, GeForce 3D acceleration card, and 21-inch monitor.

Critical development software: Microsoft Visual C++ 6.0, Microsoft Visual SourceSafe 6.0, Borland JBuilder 3.5, 3D Studio Max 2, Softimage 3D, Photoshop.

Notable technologies: Licensed the QUAKE 3: ARENA engine from id Software (using OpenGL); Icarus scripting system, BehaveEd scripting tool, Carcass skeletal system, Bink, and motion-capture data from House of Moves.

This inspired us to open the floodgates, continue on, and eventually realize that *Voyager* was the best setting for what we wanted to do. We quickly adapted the plot we had at that point into the *Voyager* setting. This was much easier than we thought it would be, and the Elite Force, or the Hazard Team, as we called them, actually seemed to make more sense as a by-product of *Voyager's* situation.

In January 1999, full production on ELITE FORCE began with a small team of 15 people that would grow to about 25 core team members, with additional support from the SOLDIER OF FORTUNE team. Our main focus during production was not to think about the game as a *Star Trek* product per se, but rather an action shooter that borrowed from the *Star Trek* universe. This helped us focus more on what would be fun for players.

To our surprise, the Paramount approval process was much easier than we anticipated. We had heard many horror stories regarding Paramount's strictness with their licenses, things like, "You can't do anything new," and, "It's hard to get things approved because they're so protective of the license." What we experienced was the exact opposite. Paramount was more than accommodating in helping us create a fun game, and we were able to bend the rules a little along the way to help accomplish our goal. We created new Starfleet weapons, a *Voyager* SWAT team, used the Klingons, and even added "classic" *Star Trek* to the *Voyager* setting. As long as an element made sense to the story and its presence could be explained, it was no problem.

One of the biggest obstacles we had to overcome was that we would be making an action game that had to appeal to both the hardcore FPS player as well as the average *Star Trek* gamer and fan. This was no easy task, and we spent a lot of time debating over the game style being too much of an action game or more of a *Star Trek* game. Balancing these two aims was a constant battle during the course of production. We knew we had to walk a fine line blending a shooter and a *Star Trek* experience if we were going to both make a successful game and overcome people's perceptions that *Star Trek* games are not good games.

What Went Right

1. Improvements to the QUAKE 3 engine

Raven had worked with id Software's engines since 1992, but this was the first time we had to add a single-player game to an id engine. Normally, we had the luxury of starting with a full single-player code base and just adding things such as breakable brushes, new AI, navigation systems, and so on. But this time we had licensed a multiplayer game and had to put in many systems we took for granted. We needed AI and navigation appropriate for single-player enemies (not multiplayer bots), as well as teammate non-player characters (NPCs) and cinematics. We needed an expanded animation system for all the different animations our cinematics would require, we needed to create a load and save routine from scratch, and the list went on.

One of the things that made this possible was the decision early on to separate the multiplayer and single-player executables. At this time, QUAKE 3 was still about eight months from completion, so we started on single-player and would worry about multiplayer when we got the final code base. We were able to make drastic changes to the single-player game and shortcut the networking, allowing us to get away with a lot of things that would have just done very bad things to networking. With this new freedom, we revamped even more systems. In the end, we actually surpassed our initial ambitions as far as new systems and features were concerned.

For example, our Icarus scripting system was planned from the beginning and ended up working out very well. The initial setup was finished relatively quickly and the remainder of the work was mostly just tying the commands to the game and AI. However, for the first seven or eight months, only a couple of programmers were doing any scripting, as they were still refining the commands and there was no GUI for it yet. It wasn't until the fall of 1999 that we made a GUI and the designers could finally start scripting. The system ended up contributing a huge amount to the detail, uniqueness, and complexity of the game, and without it ELITE FORCE would have been a totally different game.

Another big technology decision we had to make was with Carcass, our new skeletal model format. It was a huge undertaking to switch over to the new format, but it really saved us in the end. At first we were using the same model format as QUAKE 3, but it quickly became apparent that we were surpassing that format's capabilities, so we looked for a solution. id had already laid the groundwork for a skeletal model, which seemed like it would work for us. Starting with that basis, we completed it and developed it into the final format we called Carcass. With it, we reduced tenfold the amount of memory a single model took up. Without the Carcass format, we would have had to cut back many animations, and we would have lost the complex detail in our cinematics.

Another technology that was successful was our lip-synch system, which really added realism to the facial animations. We did some research, looking into phoneme recognition, but finally settled on a quick volume analysis. We planned this system to make it very easy to use. Once the mouth animation art was made for each character, the system used the appropriate frame without intervention. The code automatically scanned for peak volume of sounds when loaded, and compared against that whenever a sound was played on the voice channel. Then the animation system picked up that value to choose the speaking frame. This setup required no extra effort when adding sounds, and would work automatically for any foreign languages used.

Another system we revamped was the cinematic system, which had to be powerful and flexible enough to give our cinematics that *Star Trek* "feel." The camera system itself wasn't that hard to implement, and it worked out well. First, the scripter/designer would set up the blocking of the NPCs through Icarus. Then they could go into the game and let the scripted event play out, pausing it whenever they wanted to save a camera position to a file that could be imported into the map.

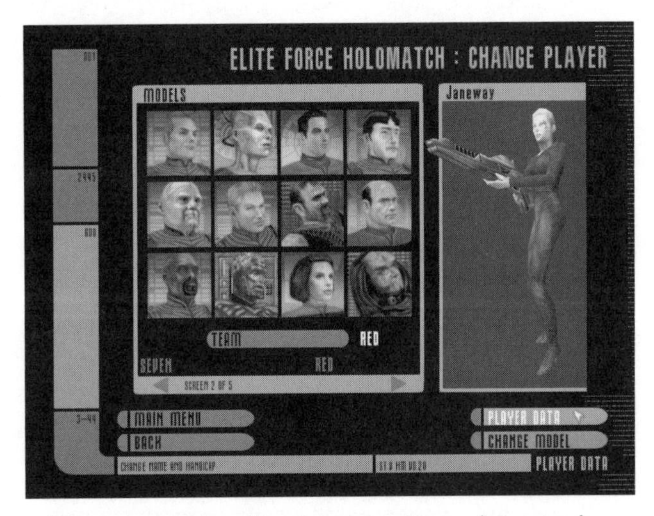

Menu screen for choosing your player character in Holomatch gameplay.

Using Icarus commands, they could make the camera zoom in and out, change the field of view to simulate close-ups and wide shots, move along a track, dynamically follow a subject, fade in and out, shake, and so on. This allowed us to set up our insane amount of cinematics as quickly as possible and still allow for some fine-tuning and detail (such as the "walk and talk" with Tuvok and Munro, and especially all the gestures and expressions the NPCs themselves would do to add to their characterization and the believability of a scene).

Storyboards were created as guides for the in-game cinematics, helping to speed up production of more than 50 cinematic sequences.

2. Complete plot and story right from the start

From the beginning of production, ELITE FORCE had a detailed story line, and every level of the game was written out in story form. We also had standards we had to meet; after all, our game was going to be compared to the *Voyager* TV show, so there was even more emphasis on storytelling. The story had to be engaging and reminiscent of what a *Voyager* episode would be, and we had to make sure our story had a lot of depth and interest for the player, to give them the feeling that they were partaking in an episode of the show.

Since one of our main goals was to have an away-team accompany the player for the missions, it was even more important that the story be solidified up front. A lot of story is conveyed during the missions, so we had to make sure the levels were paced out well and the level designers knew up front what story content their levels contained. We were able to pace the story throughout the game so that players would be continually rewarded with exposition. As they completed more missions, the overarching plot of the game would slowly form in their minds.

With our tight schedule, we wouldn't have time to redo parts of the game if they didn't work out, so it was crucial for all the people involved to work together on the story line toward one common goal. With a complete walk-through of the levels written, the level designers could concentrate on the looks of the level and accommodate for where the cinematics and story segments were going to take place.

Because our story line never changed during production, we were able to proceed forward uninterrupted, and never had to scrap any levels due to plot restructure. This was key, as we had a fairly small team charged with creating a lot of content in a short period of time. The majority of the dialogue was written after all the levels were finished, but this too went smoothly because the walkthroughs were updated from the finalized levels, and then the dialogue was written from them.

3. The dialogue

The team was excited about the concept of playing with a team of NPCs in an FPS. This led to the definition of the different characters of the Hazard Team early on. However, the actual script for the game didn't begin right away, since that had to wait for the final game flow design to be finished. Our writer (also one of our programmers) started in September 1999 and finished the first draft in March 2000. While he was writing the script, we were making all the cinematics and needed some temporary voices. We had employees record the lines and then dropped them into the cinematics to give us a feel for the pacing of each scene. This allowed us to tweak the dialogue while saving us from having to bring the expensive *Voyager* cast back for pickup lines.

The *Voyager* 3D model used in prerendered cinematics is the actual one used for the TV show.

The script finally came together after many revisions and, once it was approved by Paramount, the actors were lined up very quickly and the voice recording was done in about a month. We were then able to put the final lines into each scene, replacing our temporary dialogue without having to adjust the timing or change the scripts. This was due to the fact that Icarus could pause execution of a script until a sound file finished playing, so dropping in a new line of dialogue automatically adjusted the timing of each scene. This also meant that lines would generally flow better in translation, since they wouldn't have to deliver the line too quickly or slowly to match any hard-coded timing.

We also had a system for automatically reading the dialogue script itself and turning it into .PRE files that would let the game precache all the dialogue for a level and simultaneously assign the caption text to it. Included in this was automatic localization and dialogue adjustment for the player's gender.

All of these things together enabled our game to have captioning, localization, gender-specific dialogue, precaching, lip-synching, and almost no pickups. In the end, the dialogue turned out very well and our performances were good (Paramount even let us make final casting decisions on all the ELITE FORCE–specific characters). The story and dialogue added a great deal to the game and contributed heavily to the feeling of actually being in an episode of *Star Trek*.

4. Re-creating the look of the *Star Trek* universe

Raven has always tried to push graphics boundaries and painstakingly create beautiful settings

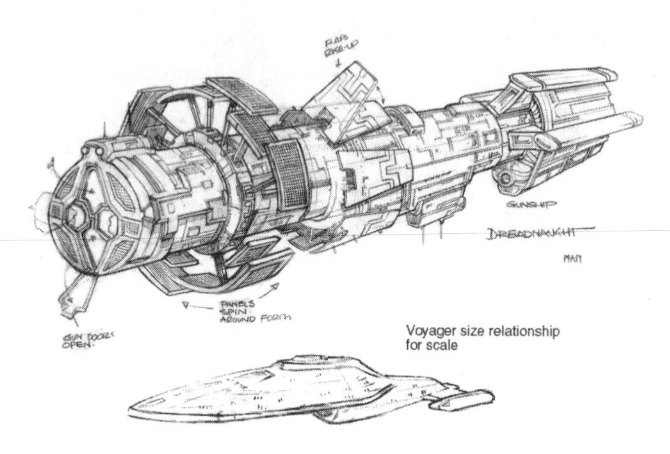

It was important to make highly detailed sketches, since another company was making the models from them.

for our game worlds. STAR TREK was no exception, and challenged us not only to create a beautiful gaming environment but also to create it in a likeness that is known worldwide. It's one thing to make arbitrary-looking levels in a never-before-seen world, but when trying to re-create the look of *Voyager* we came across many difficulties that we hadn't expected. For starters, the QUAKE 3 level editor is made to create levels at a fairly big scale. When we built the bridge of *Voyager*, we were all astounded by the detail that we achieved, but when we put a normal-sized character on the bridge, he was incredibly tiny. The bridge was huge, yet it was built like you would build any normal QUAKE 3 level. We realized that we had to build the levels on a much smaller scale than what we were used to. It took seven attempts at rebuilding *Voyager*'s bridge until we attained the proper proportions between the characters and the level. We tweaked the scale until it looked perfect and the player and other characters could move around with ease. Once the scale of the levels was set as a standard, we continued forward with the other *Voyager* rooms with little rework needed.

The artists spent much time working on the textures for the environments, getting their reference from many sources to make sure everything was exact. Having access to Paramount's *Star Trek* reference library was key in getting reference for carpets, chairs, upholstery, computer panels, and more. We sometimes scanned in the photo references themselves for the textures. Watching episodes of the show on tape was also instrumental in determining what things looked like. We used a total of 1,033 textures to create the look of *Voyager*'s rooms and hallways. Working together, the level designers and artists created the best-looking *Star Trek* environments in any game to date.

Just like the challenges we faced building the environments, creating *Voyager*'s characters and crew presented the challenge of re-creating something that already existed. We used many references from the *Star Trek* reference library to help us re-create these real people. Each actor had a series of photos of him or her as their character, which we used to help get just the right shape of the head, and we even used the photos themselves (with Photoshop touchups) as textures on the polygon heads to achieve the likenesses.

There are limitations to any technology, and working around the limitations is where we succeeded. The heads could only have 150 polygonal faces and the textures for the skins could only be 512×512 pixels. The fine craftsmanship required to work with so little and still achieve the right look for the characters is a testament to our artists' skills. For example, designing the Hazard Suit in the *Voyager* style took many attempts, but we finally got something everyone was happy with and looked natural to *Star Trek*.

5. Creating smart NPCs

To create a *Voyager* game that resembles what you would see in a TV episode, we had to create a working spaceship filled with its busy crew, and make it believable enough so players would feel like they are in a real place. We also had to create an away-team to fight alongside the player. After all, what is *Star Trek* without an away-team?

Voyager's Hazard Team, created by Raven to help accentuate the action for the game.

We created our NPCs using a few different things. The Icarus scripting system allowed us to have precise control over specific actions. The NPC Stats system allowed us to create many characters with various looks. The Squadmate system gave us the tools to enable the teammates to work with the player, and we used a waypoint or pathfinding system to make our NPCs navigate through a complex environment. All of these systems together created the artificial intelligence for our NPCs.

We used scripting with the pathfinding to make the crew of *Voyager* come to life, and we could tell them exactly where to go and what to do without too many unknowns to cause problems. They did exactly what we as designers wanted them to do. The teammates, on the other hand, have to act according to what is happening with the player. Since players can do anything they want while playing the game, this means a lot of unknowns for how the teammates should react. The teammates could have easily been a hindrance to the gameplay, and now we know why no other company has ever tried to make an FPS game with up to five teammates working alongside you throughout entire levels.

In the final stages of developing the teammates, we weren't sure if they were going to work out; they had so many problems, and every time we would fix something another problem would crop up. Just getting them to follow you was no easy task and was something we kept tweaking right up to the final days. Sure, we could get them to follow the player, but the game took place in tight hallways and small rooms so players would bump into them. They wouldn't get out of the way and would constantly get stuck on each other.

Also, having them follow the player everywhere made them seem less like intelligent characters, so sometimes we had them stand their ground or take up a position while the player went exploring. Then we had the constant problem of the team not following players at all, even though they might need them later on. When we did get it working, someone found a new way to break a level with a teammate. Elevators and teleporters added to the risk of teammates being left behind. We were getting worried that we wouldn't even be able to get them to walk through an entire level, and we would have to resort to something drastic. Luckily, we did get them to work in the levels. They may have run funny or jumped down long elevator shafts to catch up with the player, but at least they stayed in formation through the whole level no matter what the player was doing.

Of course, once there were enemies we had to worry about friendly fire. We wanted the team to react intelligently to being shot, but we didn't want to punish the player for shooting them accidentally. After a lot of trial and error, we decided that teammates would retaliate against a player only if the player had shot them repeatedly outside combat. In combat, they'd still react to friendly fire, but couldn't be killed, and would never turn on the player.

Then came the problem of trying to balance the teammates' involvement in combat. Once we put enemies in the levels, we found that the teammates were so good that they killed most of them, leaving little for the player to do. To balance this, we had the teammates shoot less often, but then they got attacked constantly by enemies, turning the gameplay into "shoot the aliens attacking your teammates." Eventually we made the enemies attack the player more, so the player would feel threatened by them, and the teammates helped but didn't do all the work.

It's funny now to hear people say that the teammates were stupid because they hardly killed any enemies, or that the enemies were dumb because they attacked the player more than the teammates. If they only knew how tiresome the gameplay would have been had we not balanced it the way we did.

Save your teammate from the Borg, one of the many multiple outcome events.

1. Not enough programmers

For the first half of development, there was mainly only one programmer working on scripting, enemy AI, teammate AI, pathfinding, and the animation system. This programmer was also writing all the dialogue, and it became necessary for him to relinquish other programming duties in order to finish writing. Unfortunately, we didn't have any extra programmers to help.

Eventually we got a programmer from a different project to start working on game code. He completely rewrote the navigation system, which took time away from creating the AI for all the enemies, which didn't end up being completed until the game itself was done. This created a real lack of cooperation between level design and enemy AI, and forced the designers to rewrite their scripts constantly to match the changes in the underlying game systems.

With more programmers working on AI and navigation early on in the development, these kinds of last-minute changes and back-end design could have (hopefully) been avoided.

Other models were designed by Raven and made by the company making the prerendered movies.

2. From Ghoul models to regular models to skeletal models

It was a big decision to switch to the new skeletal models. In the beginning, we were using what was to become SOLDIER OF FORTUNE's Ghoul system (see "Raven Software's SOLDIER OF FORTUNE," Postmortem on page 259, for more on Ghoul). When we received the QUAKE 3 code, we tried to integrate Ghoul into the new code, but found it to be too different. It just didn't fit in with the new optimized rendering pipeline QUAKE 3 provided. So we switched over to regular QUAKE 3 models.

There was a lot of learning going on at this time. When we get new code, it doesn't come with operating instructions, and it's often not complete. We went through a lot of growing pains adopting the new format and figuring out its requirements. When the option to go skeletal came up, we had to weigh the benefits of the new system versus the risks and time it would take to switch over. While we did the right thing and embraced the new technology, we had to write a new set of tools to handle the new formats and learn new procedures to get our animations out of Softimage 3D and into 3D Studio Max. We had a lot of squashed creatures and bizarrely stretched limbs along the way, but it was well worth the trip.

Unfortunately, by the time we got it working right, we were past our alpha date, and because of all the different changes the models had gone through by that time, we didn't have enough time to fully implement a good AI system for the enemies, and had to settle with what we could do in the time we had.

3. Underestimating the amount of scripting work needed

As we mentioned previously, our Icarus scripting system was a huge plus. But we also encountered a lot of problems with scripting. Not only had no one ever used this system before, none of the programmers behind it had ever written a scripting system before. The designers didn't even get their hands on the scripting system until about eight months before the game was done. They did pick it up quickly, but not without a lot of effort and time involved.

The Klingons' AI allowed them to crouch and run for cover.

One of the major problems designers had when scripting was the constant changes to the underlying systems that the Icarus commands relied upon. They'd script an NPC one way and it would work fine. Then the following week, something in the navigation, AI, or animation systems would change, and the script would be broken. This was a source of major frustration among the designers and definitely impeded their productivity. Ideally, those systems would have been finalized before the designers had to start scripting.

Within Icarus itself, there was one major flaw that should be addressed. Icarus can start a command and wait for completion, but it does not have a built-in system for letting the command (or "task") time-out and continue or take another route. There was no failsafe if, somehow, a command never completed. Given the sheer complexity of our scripting, these kinds of showstopper problems showed up constantly and would completely stop the game in its tracks. Up until the last minute, we were frantically trying to find every case in which a script would just stop execution. In the end, we did manage to catch them all, except for two cases that were caused by people turning their detail levels up too high and causing the game to drop to very low framerates, which could in turn mess up the scripted events.

It turned out pretty well in the end, but all the effort that went into constantly revising the scripts could have been put to other, more productive uses.

4. Adjusting to new QUAKE 3 technology

The biggest level design headache in working with technology that is still being developed is that it's constantly changing. We started building our levels way before the QUAKE 3 engine was near completion, and this caused scheduling problems every time we got a new code build. We built our levels one way with the tools and knowledge we had at the time, and then when a big change was made to the QUAKE 3 code, the level designers had to spend a few days altering each of their levels to keep up with the changes in the code and how it handled surfaces, lights, and architecture.

This happened numerous times during development, and we often went months without new code drops. The level designers would continue to work on levels in order to make progress, and then when we finally received new code, we had to go back to all the levels that had been done and spend a month getting them up to date. This month was not accounted for in the schedule, and therefore a month of designer time was simply lost. This happened more than once and was a big factor in keeping us behind our original schedule.

Fighting aliens in the stasis ship, which was created with 90 percent curved surfaces.

Another part of adjusting to the QUAKE 3 technology was realizing that our levels couldn't be as big as QUAKE 2 levels. When we started building levels, we made them as we did using QUAKE 1 and 2 technology. We had expansive levels that looked awesome and showed off what the QUAKE 3 engine could do. Then, somewhere near the middle of our development, we realized that the file size of most of our levels was huge, running 11 to 15MB each, when they should have been about 6MB. This was a problem, since we'd planned for the file sizes to be 10MB or less out of a total memory budget of 64MB. The levels were the normal game-world size of a QUAKE 2 level, so what was the problem?

It turned out to be the high polygon (or triangle) count used to create a much more intricate and detailed environment. We realized that although QUAKE 3 can handle more polygons in the view at one time, the file size for the level had not increased much from a QUAKE 2 level. We had a dilemma; either we could bring the file size down by taking out all of the detail that made the QUAKE 3 engine superior and keep the physical size, or we could cut the size of the level down, making it smaller yet highly detailed. Since we were making a world that could readily be compared to a TV show, we opted to keep the detailed environments of the *Star Trek* universe and cut the level size down.

We were able to cut most of the levels in half and make two separate levels out of them, but then all the level designers had twice as many levels to work on, and this could have caused some major scheduling problems. Unfortunately, to keep up with the schedule, large parts of the levels were deleted and redesigned, which resulted in much smaller levels that could be traversed quicker, and ultimately made for a shorter game.

5. Mission stats never got finished

The only major thing that didn't get into the game that we originally planned for was our end-mission statistics. The feature made it into the game in the form of basic stats when you died, but it was planned to be much more, and would have really added to the game. The end-mission stats would have improved the replayability of the single-player game and given more emphasis to the interactive and multiple-outcome events.

The main goal with the stats was to grade players' performance when they completed a mission; for example, giving a score of 100 percent for a perfect mission. A number of medals would also be awarded to players based on what they did during the mission. At the end of the game, all the scores and medals would be added up for one final game score. The stats would have made a significant gameplay feature, letting players know at the end of a mission whether they could have saved someone or done something differently to get a better score.

This would have made the interactive events mean something more, emphasizing the fact that they are interactive; events that players didn't even know could be changed would have been presented to them after the mission, making the game world seem that much more alive. With this feature not in the game, the multiple outcome events didn't mean anything more than just a "cool" factor, instead of being intrinsic to the gameplay and adding to replayability.

Final Thoughts

We started out with a lot of great ideas, and almost all of those ideas were implemented in the game with the exception of a couple. That's certainly an achievement in this industry. We made the game we set out to make and are very happy with the end result, so it was hard to think of the things that went wrong. Even though we had many problems, we worked around them and ultimately finished the game, which makes us feel like we did everything right.

Then we heard comments from fans and game reviewers who didn't like certain things about the game, and all the memories of working through all the obstacles came back, and we thought, "If they only knew how many problems we had to work through to get the game to its final state." It's working through those development obstacles that makes a game successful. It's also gratifying to hear from fans and reviewers that the game was successful both as a fun game and as a *Star Trek* game. For us, that means many more things went right than wrong, and the team was talented enough to work through the things that went wrong and make a game that is being enjoyed by thousands of people.

ELITE FORCE was a very difficult project cycle with a really long crunch mode, but what game is any different? Yet we had a lot of extra obstacles to overcome, including the perception that all *Star Trek* games suck and that meant ours would too. It seemed like we were destined to fail before we even started. Working with one of the two biggest science-fiction franchises in the world added to the pressure. But Activision supported us all the way from upper management to a top-notch marketing and PR staff. Paramount was surprisingly helpful and proved to us that they care about the quality of the games made and would do everything possible to ensure that quality. With a dedicated and very talented team of individuals, we met our challenges and succeeded in making what is being called the best *Star Trek* game ever made.

Red Storm Entertainment's RAINBOW SIX

by brian upton

RAINBOW SIX and Red Storm Entertainment both came into being during the same week. When the company was formed in the fall of 1996, the first thing that we did was to spend a weekend brainstorming game ideas. That initial design session generated over a hundred possibilities that we then winnowed down to a handful that we thought had star potential. The only one that we unanimously agreed we had to build was HRT—a game based on the FBI's Hostage Rescue Team.

Back-Story

In RAINBOW SIX, players lead a multinational team of military operatives who intervene in sensitive crises in the post-Cold War world. The game has both tactical and action elements. Players go into battle, but they also manage their squad, choosing equipment and creating a tactical battle plan before going into action. The game has a real-world feel—one shot can kill, and small mistakes can doom an entire mission. Typical missions involve rescuing hostages and assassinating terrorists and criminals, and over time, the missions cohere into a Tom Clancy-style plot arc that takes players all over the globe.

The Concept

It was a long road from HRT to RAINBOW SIX, but along the way, the basic outline of the title changed very little. We knew from the start that we wanted to capture the excitement of movies such as *Mission: Impossible* and *The Dirty Dozen*—the thrill of watching a team of skilled specialists pull off an operation with clockwork precision. We also knew that we wanted it to be an action game with a strong strategic component—a realistic shooter that would be fun to play even without a QUAKE player's twitch reflexes. From that starting point, the title seemed to design itself.

By the time we'd finished the first treatment a few weeks later, all the central game-play features were in place. We expanded the scope of the game (rechristened BLACK OPS) beyond hostage rescue to encompass a variety of covert missions. Play would revolve around a planning phase followed by an action phase, and players would have to pick their teams from a pool of operatives with different strengths and weaknesses. Combat would be quick and deadly, but realistic. One shot would kill, but the targeting model would favor cautious aiming over the running-and-gunning that was typical of first-person shooters.

Ironically, the only major element that we hadn't developed during those first few weeks was the tie-in to Tom Clancy's book. Clancy was part of the original brainstorming session and had responded as enthusiastically as the rest of us to the HRT concept, but he hadn't yet decided to make it the subject of his next novel.

Game Data

Release date: August 1998

Publisher: Ubi Soft

Genre: tactical team-based shooter

Intended platform: Windows 95/98

Team size: 16 full-time and 6 part-time developers

Critical development hardware: 400MHz Pentium II w/64MB RAM and a 3D accelerator

Critical development software: Microsoft Visual C++, SourceSafe, Hiprof, Boundschecker, and 3D Studio Max.

Because we had moved away from doing a strict hostage rescue game, we batted around a lot of different BLACK OPS back stories in our design meetings, ranging in time from the World War II era to the near future. For a while, we considered setting the game in the 1960s at the height of the Cold War, giving it a very Austin Powers/Avengers feel.

We eventually converged on the RAINBOW SIX back story in early 1997, but we didn't find out that we would be paralleling Clancy's novel until almost April. Fortunately, we'd been sharing information back and forth the whole time, so bringing the game in line with the book didn't involve too much extra work. (If you compare the game to the novel, however, you'll notice that they have different endings. Due to scheduling constraints, we had to lock down the final missions several months before Clancy finished writing. One of the pitfalls of parallel development...).

The Production

Originally, the RAINBOW SIX team consisted of me and one other programmer. Red Storm started development on four titles straight out of the gate, and all the teams were woefully understaffed for the first few months. The first RAINBOW SIX artist didn't come on board until the spring of 1997, with a full-time producer following shortly after. With such a small group, progress was slow. During that first winter and spring, all that we had time to do was throw together a rough framework for what was to follow. This lack of resources up front would come back to haunt us later. Because we were so understaffed, we tried to fill the gaps in our schedule by licensing several crucial pieces of technology.

The first was the 3D renderer itself. Virtus Corp., our parent company, was working on a next-generation rendering library for use in its own line of 3D tools. We decided to save ourselves work by building on top of the Virtus renderer, rather than developing our own. At first, this seemed to be an ideal solution to our problem. Virtus had been doing 3D applications for years, and the renderer that its engineers were working on was a very general cross-platform solution that ran well with lots of different types of hardware acceleration.

We also went out of house for our networking technology. We had researched a variety of third-party solutions, including Microsoft's DirectPlay, but we weren't satisfied with any of them. Just as we were on the verge of deciding that we'd have to write our own library, a local development group within IBM contacted us.

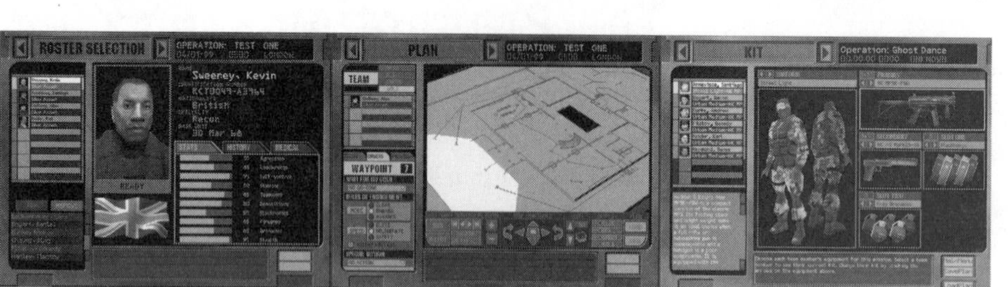

A 2D floor plan, created for the purpose of collision detection, also helped players in both the planning and action interfaces.

The group's engineers were interested in finding uses for their powerful new Java-based client/server technology. The technology, called Inverse, was designed to allow collaborative computing between large numbers of Java applets. The IBM engineers wanted to see how it would perform in a number of different application domains, including games. Inverse supported all of the features that we wanted in a networking solution, such as network time synchronization and reliable detection of disconnects, so after much deliberation we decided to use it for RAINBOW SIX. Eventually, we would come to regret both of these third-party technology decisions, but not until months later in the project.

Over the summer of 1997, we acquired most of the motion capture data that was used for animating the characters in the game. One of the advantages of working with Tom Clancy was that he put us in touch with a wide variety of consultants very quickly. Among the many experts we spoke with to get background information on counter-terrorism were two close-quarters combat trainers who worked for the arms manufacturer Heckler and Koch. When it came time to do our motion capture, these trainers volunteered to be our actors. They spent a couple of days at the Biovision studios in California being videotaped running through every motion in the game. Using real combat trainers for our motion capture data represented one of our better decisions. While a professional actor might have been tempted to overdo the motions for effect, these guys played it absolutely straight—the results are impressive. The game's characters come across as serious and competent, and are twice as scary as a result.

Our crisis came in October of 1997. We'd been working hard all summer, but (although we refused to admit it) we were slipping further and further behind in our schedule. Partially, the delays were the result of my being completely overloaded. Partially, they were the result of the ambitious scale of the project: because the plot of Clancy's evolving novel was driving our level design, we'd committed ourselves to creating sixteen completely unique spaces—a huge art load. And partially, they were the result of the fact that the "time-saving" technology licenses that we'd set up were proving to be anything but.

Inverse was a great networking solution—for Java. Unfortunately, we wrote RAINBOW SIX in C++. Our initial research had suggested that mixing the two would be trivial. However, in practice the overhead involved in writing and debugging an application using two different languages at the same time was staggering. The interface code that tied the two parts together was larger than the entire networking library. It became clear that we'd have to scrap Inverse and write our own networking solution from scratch if we were ever going to get the product out the door. (As a side note, we did continue to use Inverse for our Java-based products: last year's POLITIKA and this year's RUTHLESS.COM. The problems we faced didn't arise from the code itself, but from mixing the two development environments.)

We also had problems with the Virtus rendering library. As we got deeper and deeper into RAINBOW SIX, we realized that if the game was going to run at an acceptable frame rate, we were going to have to implement a number of different renderer optimizations. Unfortunately, the Virtus renderer was a black box. It was designed to be a general-purpose solution for a wide variety of situations—a Swiss Army knife. With frame rates on high-end systems hovering in the single digits, we quickly realized that we would need a special-purpose solution instead.

In early November 1997, we put together a crisis plan. We pumped additional manpower into the team. We brought in Erik Erikson, our top graphics programmer, and Dave Weinstein, our top networking programmer, as troubleshooters. I stepped down as lead engineer and producer Carl Schnurr took over more of the game design responsibilities. The original schedule, which called for the product to ship in the spring, was pushed back four months. The artists went through several rounds of production pipeline streamlining until they could finally produce levels fast enough to meet the new ship date.

Finally, we took immediate action to end our reliance on third-party software. We wrote an entire networking library from scratch and swapped it with the ailing Java code. Virtus graciously handed over the source code for the renderer and we totally overhauled it, pulling in code we'd been using on DOMINANT SPECIES, the other 3D title that Red Storm had in progress at the time. All this took place over the holiday season. It was a very hectic two months. From that point on, our development effort was a sprint to the finish line. The team was in crunch mode from February to July 1998. A variety of crises punctuated the final months of the project. In March, I came back on board as lead engineer when Peter McMurry, who'd been running development in my place since November 1997, had to step down for health reasons.

As we added more and more code, builds grew longer and longer, finally reaching several hours in length, much to the frustration of the overworked engineers. The size of the executable started breaking all our tools, making profiling and bounds checking impossible. In order to make our ship date, we had to cut deeply into our testing time, raising the risk level even higher. On the upside though, the closer we got to the end of the project, the more the excitement started to build. We showed a couple of cautious early demos to the press in March

1998 and were thrilled by the positive responses. (At this point, we were so deep into the product that we had no idea of what an outsider would think.)

The real unveiling came at the 1998 E3 in Atlanta, Ga. Members of the development team ran the demos on the show floor—for most us, that was the longest stretch we'd had playing the game before it shipped. Almost all of the final gameplay tweaks came out of what we learned over those three days.

What Went Right

1. A coherent vision

Throughout all of the ups and downs in the production process, RAINBOW SIX's core game play never changed. We established early on a vision of what the final game would be and we maintained that vision right through to the end. I can't overstate the importance of this consistency. Simply sticking to the original concept saw the team through some really rough parts of the development cycle.

For one thing, this coherent vision meant that we were able to squeak by without adequate design documents. Many parts of the design were never written down, but because the team had a good idea of where we were headed, we were able to fill in many of the details on our own. Even when we had to perform massive engineering overhauls in the middle of the project, a lot of the existing art and code was salvageable. Our vision also did a lot for morale. Many times we wondered if we'd ever finish the project, but we never doubted that the result would be great if we did. It's a lot easier to justify crunch hours when you believe in where the project is going.

2. An efficient art pipeline

The art team tried out four or five different production pipelines before they finally found one that would produce the levels that we wanted in the time that we had available. The problem was that we wanted to have sixteen unique spaces in the game—there would be almost no texture or geometry sharing from mission to mission. Furthermore, instead of creating our own level-building tool, we built everything using 3D Studio Max. Thus, artists had more freedom in the types of spaces that they could create, but they didn't have shortcuts to stamp out generic parts such as corridors or stairwells—everything had to be modeled by hand.

Eventually, the art team settled on a process designed to minimize the amount of wasted effort. Before anyone did any modeling, an artist would sketch out the entire level on paper and submit it for approval by both the producer and art lead. Then the modelers would build and play test just the level's geometry before it was textured. Each artist had a second computer on his desk running a lightweight version of the game engine so he could easily experiment with how the level would run in the game.

3. Tom Clancy's visibility

A good license won't help a bad game, but it can give a good game the visibility it needs to be a breakout title. When we first approached members of the gaming press with demos of RAINBOW SIX in the spring of 1998, they had no reason to take us seriously—we had no track record, no star developers, and no hype (OK, not much hype...). We were showing a quirky title with a less-than-state-of-the-art rendering engine in a very competitive genre. With much-anticipated heavyweights such as SIN, HALF-LIFE and DAIKATANA on the way, having Clancy's name on the box was crucial to getting people to take a first look at the title. Fortunately, the game play was compelling enough to turn those first looks into a groundswell of good press that carried us through to the launch.

The various mission levels called for the creation of sixteen completely unique spaces.

4. Reworking the physics engine

In February 1998, we completely overhauled the RAINBOW SIX physics engine, which turned out to be a win on a variety of fronts. We'd retooled the renderer during the previous month, but our frame rate was still dragging. After running the code through a profiler, we figured that most of our time was going to collision checks—checks for characters colliding with the world and line-of-sight checks for the AI's visibility routines.

The problem was that every time the physics engine was asked to check for a collision, it calculated a very general 3D solution. Except in the cases of grenade bounces and bullet tracks, a 3D collision check was complete overkill. Over the next month, we reworked the engine to do most of its collision detection in 2D using a floor plan of the level. These collision floor plans would be generated algorithmically from the 3D level models.

The technique worked. In addition to getting the frame rate back up to a playable level, it also made collision detection more reliable. The game engine also used the floor plans to drive the path-finding routines for the AI team members. Players would view these same floor plans as level maps in both the planning and action interfaces. By figuring out how to fix our low frame rates, we wound up with solutions to three or four other major outstanding engineering issues. Sometimes, the right thing to do is just throw part of the code out and start over.

5. Team cohesion

Red Storm employs no rock stars and no slackers. Everyone on the RAINBOW SIX team worked incredibly long hours under a tremendous amount of pressure, but managed (mostly) to keep their tempers and their professional focus.

What Went Wrong

1. Lack of up-front design

We never had a proper design document, which meant that we generated a lot of code and art that we later had to scrap. What's worse, because we didn't have a detailed outline of what we were trying to build, we had no way to measure our progress (or lack thereof) accurately. We only realized that we were in trouble when it became glaringly obvious. If we'd been about the design rigorous up front, we would have known that we were slipping much sooner.

2. Understaffing at the start

This point is closely related to the previous point. Because we didn't have a firm design, it was impossible to do accurate time estimates. Red Storm was starved for manpower across the board, and because we didn't have a proper schedule, it was hard to come to grips with just how deep a hole we were digging for ourselves. There were always plenty of other things to do in getting a new company off the ground besides recruiting, and we were trying to run as lean as possible to make the most of our limited start-up capital. Given the circumstances, it was easy to rationalize understaffing the project and delaying new hires.

Additionally, I badly overestimated my own abilities. For Red Storm's first year, I was working four jobs: VP of engineering, lead engineer on RAINBOW SIX, designer on RAINBOW SIX, and programmer. Any one of these could have been a full-time position. In trying to cover all four, I spent all my time racing from one crisis to the next instead of actually getting real work done. And because I was acting as my own manager, there was no one to audit my performance. If one of the other leads was shirking his scheduling duties or blowing his milestones, I'd call him on it. But on my own project, I could always explain away what should have been clear warning signs of trouble.

3. Reliance on unproven technology

Our external solutions for rendering and networking both fell through and had to be replaced with internally developed code late in the development cycle. In both cases, we were relying on software that was still under development. The core technology was sound, but we were plagued with inadequate documentation, changing programming interfaces, misunderstood performance requirements, and heavy integration costs.

Because both packages were in flux, we failed to do a thorough evaluation of their limitations and capabilities. By the time it became obvious that neither was completely suited to our needs, it was too late to push for changes. In retrospect, we would have saved money and had a much smoother development process if we'd bitten the bullet early on and committed ourselves to building our own technology base.

4. Loss of key personnel

Losing even a junior member of a development team close to gold master can be devastating. When our lead engineer took ill in February 1998, we were faced with a serious crisis. For a few frantic weeks, we tried to recruit a lead from outside the company, but eventually it became obvious that there was no way we could bring someone in and get them up to speed in time for us to make our ship date in July 1998. Promoting from inside the team wasn't a possibility either—everyone's schedule was so tightly packed that they were already pulling overtime just to get their coding tasks done; no one had the bandwidth to handle lead responsibilities too.

Ultimately, I wound up stepping back in as lead. This time, however, we knew that for this arrangement to work I'd have to let my VP duties slide. The rest of management and the other senior engineers took up a lot of the slack, and Peter had set a strong direction for the project, so the transition went very smoothly. (After his health improved Peter returned to work at the end of the project, putting in reduced hours to finish off the RAINBOW SIX sound code.)

5. Insufficient testing time

We got lucky. As a result of our early missteps, the only way we could get the game done on time was to cut deeply into our testing schedule. We were still finding new crash bugs a week before gold master; if any of these had required major reengineering to fix, we would have been in deep trouble. That the game shipped as clean as it did is a testament to the incredible effort put in at the end by the engineering team. As it was, we still had to release several patches to clean up stuff that slipped through the cracks.

In the End...

RAINBOW SIX's development cycle was a 21-month roller coaster ride. The project was too ambitious from the start, particularly with the undersized, inexperienced team with which we began. We survived major overhauls of the graphics, networking, and simulation software late in the development cycle, as well as two changes of engineering leads within six months.

By all rights, the final product should have been a buggy, unplayable mess. The reason it's not is that lots of very talented people put in lots of hard work. I'm not going to say that RAINBOW SIX is the perfect game, but it is almost exactly the game that we originally set out to make back in 1996, both in look and game play. And the lessons that we've learned from the RAINBOW SIX production cycle have already been rolled into the next round of Red Storm products. Our current focus is on getting solid designs done up front and solid testing done on the back end—and on making great games, of course.

Raven Software's SOLDIER OF FORTUNE

by eric biessman & rick johnson

The development of SOLDIER OF FORTUNE was rife with questions and uncertainties right from the very beginning. Fresh from finishing up PORTAL OF PRAEVUS, the HEXEN 2 mission pack, Raven was ready to dig in to a full-fledged stand-alone product. Unfortunately, no one at Raven had a solid idea for our next project and we found ourselves floating in a sea of ideas without a solid direction. With a full team ready and willing to go, we needed a project and we needed one fast. It was then that Activision handed us the Soldier of Fortune license.

In the beginning, what was to become the SOF team was focusing on several different story lines and game ideas. One of these was a somewhat real-world, military-style shooter based in a World War II setting. When we decided not to pursue that game, we began looking for new game ideas. We knew that we still wanted to do a real-world military game, but beyond that we didn't have much of an idea. As soon as we got the Soldier of Fortune license, though, the groundwork for the game immediately began to fall into place.

While the license name itself was met with mixed reactions from the SOF team, at its core was everything that we wanted from the game.

Back-Story

SOLDIER OF FORTUNE puts the player in the role of a contemporary mercenary, fighting in locations around the globe for the highest bidder. The game puts a premium on making real-world considerations a part of gameplay, which distinguishes it from other first-person shooters. For example, a noise meter warns players if they are alerting opponents, and wound location and weapon caliber matter in combat. An array of high-tech, but still realistic, gadgetry rounds out inventory possibilities. The game's graphic violence and the detailed anatomical specificity in its damage system raised a few eyebrows on its release, and a non-violent version was released in tandem with the original.

Action, intrigue, political turmoil, and firepower were key elements of the design from the very beginning. Now we needed to find a story that would complement the license and turn it into a great game.

The name SOLDIER OF FORTUNE evokes different images for different people. One thing that we could all agree on was that the title reflected the mercenary life; making money at the risk of death. This was something that we wanted to highlight and focus on dramatically throughout the game. However, focusing on this one aspect tended to blind us to the bigger picture of what we were trying to accomplish, and our first few story attempts failed miserably. We focused too much of the gameplay on making money and not enough on finding something that would truly compel the player throughout the game.

Nevertheless, even without a story set in stone we began the production of the game. This was a decision that we would come to regret many times throughout the rest of the development cycle. The bright side to spending a large portion of development time working on a game without a solid story was that most of it was spent on technology creation. The bad part was that many of the levels that were originally planned and created had to be reworked or removed from the game entirely.

Game Data

Release date: March 2000

Publisher: Activision

Genre: First-person realistic shooter

Platforms: Windows 95/98/NT/2000, Linux

Full-time developers: 20 (on average)

Contractors: 2

Budget: Multimillion-dollar budget

Length of development: 23 months

Hardware used: Dell Pentium 550 with 128MB RAM, 18GB hard drive, and a TNT2

Software used: Microsoft Visual C++ 6.0, Microsoft Visual SourceSafe 6.0, 3D Studio Max 2.x, Softimage 3D, Photoshop

Notable technologies: Licensed the QUAKE 2 engine from id Software (using OpenGL), motion-capture data from House of Moves, force feedback, A3D/EAX 3D sound, World Opponent Network (WON) matchmaking services

Project size: 406,044 lines of code, 602 files

On top of that, Activision was getting a little nervous that they had not seen any solid gameplay from us yet after almost a year of development. This uneasiness itself caused major turmoil in the development and it took a while for us to settle into the game that we would eventually create. Luckily, during this time, all of the core technology was implemented and functioning smoothly. Because of this, once we nailed the story down, we were able to jump head-first into the production and quickly create a solid product.

In order to achieve a strong sense of realism, we decided to talk to a published author about the script and also to a real-life "military consultant" about how a soldier of fortune truly lives his life. This was one of the major turning points in the development and we were finally able to focus the game into its final product. As we settled on an action-movie feel, SOF finally began to take form. We were able to tie together an appealing story line quickly with several twists to keep the player enthralled.

Combining this with the extensive amount of information that our military consultant provided us, everyone on the team was excited about the project again and the true development of the game got underway. In less than ten months, the core of SOF was assembled into a fun, viable product. After the game was released this past March, the rest, as they say, is history.

What Went Right

1. Familiarity with technology plus powerful tools and enhancements

One of the most important pluses for SOF was the team's experience and familiarity with the QUAKE technology. Raven has been using id

Two views of Sergei Dekker, the quintessential bad guy.

Software's technology since its early days of HERETIC and HEXEN. This familiarity allowed us to experiment, create, and use tools that vastly sped up the game's development.

QuakeHelper. One of the first tools that we developed was QuakeHelper. As SOF's development progressed, we realized that all of the options associated with the individual textures for the world were becoming too complex to encode into a parsing file. QuakeHelper was created to allow a visual way to assign all of these properties. This included texture scaling, detail texturing, damage texture (next texture to be shown, and the amount of damage it should take), material properties (sound and visual effects for user interactions), and alternate textures (more detailed and unique textures would be replaced by common textures on video cards with lower texture memory). In the end, SOF had more than 5,000 unique world textures. QuakeHelper saved the artists a tremendous amount of time in preparing the textures for the game and in adjusting and tweaking their properties.

ArghRad. One of the benefits of working in the QUAKE community is that the public has access to most of the source code to the tools. In the beginning of the project, we used QRAD, which was the original tool id developed to calculate the lighting information on the world. Our designers learned of an enhanced version of QRAD that had been developed by Tim Wright. He called the new modified version ArghRad!, which added a Phong-type shading model to the light map calculation, a global sunlight casting point, and several bug fixes. Raven contacted him to arrange to get the source code. In the end, this helped us create better-looking levels by utilizing the wonderful QUAKE community.

DS. DS, or Designer Script, was developed jointly for both HERETIC 2 and SOF. The goal was to provide a simple language for designers to help create more complex scenes and puzzles in the game. Those who designed this language rightfully kept in mind whom the language was for. In other words, it was a language created by programmers for designers. While this may seem like a straightforward concept, often this idea gets lost during the development phase of tools or other items that are supposed to assist the desired recipient. Even though this language did have certain limitations (described under "What Went Wrong," beginning on page 265), it did help meet our goals for both projects. The following two tools helped extend the scripting language in simple yet powerful ways.

ROFF. While one of SOF's designers was playing around with Lightwave to create a complex motion path for an entity, he ended up writing an exporter that created a DS script. The script consisted of a series of move and rotate commands to simulate the complex movement animated in Lightwave. While this accomplished the ultimate goal of importing the entity's animation into the game, it was not very efficient. Exporting the movement into a file and adding a command to the scripting language to play that movement file corrected this. This format was known as ROFF (Rotation Object File Format). SOF used about 500 of these movement files, from the simulation of helicopter movement and exploding crates, to creating a flying bird (although you'll have to look really hard to see that one).

Chimaera. Because of the large amount of animation needed for SOF and the fact that we were going to be using a mix of traditional hand-animated sequences and motion capture sequences, we needed something that would work well with both. All of our motion capture data was taken by House of Moves, a wonderful motion capture house, and sent to our animators. From there, we used Chimaera, a control rig within Softimage that allowed us to tweak both types of animation easily. It also allowed the animators to utilize both inverse and forward kinematics simultaneously, accomplishing

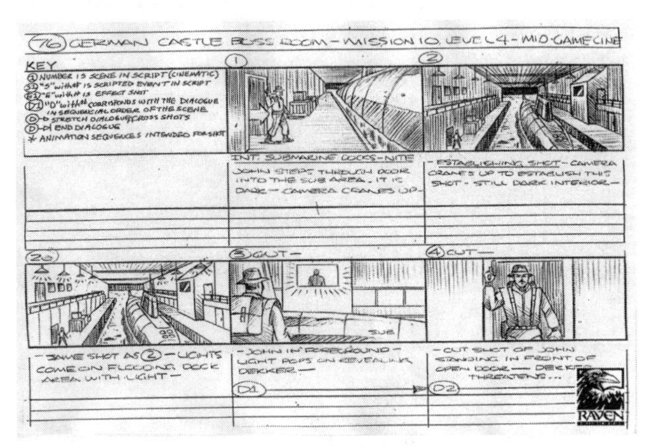

Every cinematic sequence was conceptualized with storyboards first.

this ordinarily complex task with relative ease. One of Chimaera's most important features was that it allowed the animators to apply every animation to any humanoid model, including models not local to SOF. This tool has also been put to good use on our next release, STAR TREK: VOYAGER—ELITE FORCE.

SoFPath. We originally developed SoFPath to create a pathfinding system based on the BSP of a map. During the development of this tool, however, we discovered that the world was broken up too much to provide an effective means of pathfinding. Our early use of .ROFF files also showed that animating entity movement or rotation in a commercial package was difficult without a good representation of the world. Since the SoFPath utility had a good "understanding" of the BSP world, we changed it to export .IFF Lightwave object files. The designers would basically BSP their map (either the full map or a partial region), create the Lightwave file, and import it into Lightwave. They then had a representation of the world, a rough outline of all entities, and could then animate things accurately. Later in the project, we also added the ability to edit these files in 3D Studio Max.

Audio tools. Both dynamic music and ambient sound systems were designed internally to create immersive environments in SOF, but they also allowed the sound designer to add sound assets into the game more easily. Instead of hard-coding the names of the sound files, the tools provided a quick and flexible method of tweaking sonic properties in levels. This process not only took the weight of sound placements off the programmers' shoulders, but also empowered the sound designer with a powerful and creative tool to create unique soundscapes.

2. Taking time to address violence concerns

From its inception, we knew that SOF was going to be a game for adults. Due to its large amount of simulated violence, we wanted to make sure that adults had every opportunity to keep SOF out of the hands of minors while still being able to play the game on their home computers. In order to do this, we implemented several different protective measures for consumers.

First and foremost was creating the SOLDIER OF FORTUNE: TACTICAL NON-VIOLENT VERSION. A totally separate SKU from the regular version of the game, the low-violence option removed all of the gore, limited the number of death animations, and seriously toned down the game in general. This version used the same box as the regular version, but colored red instead of green and stamped with a large advisory that stated that it was different from the regular version.

For the regular version, we added a violence-lock feature to allow users to password-protect the game and change various options to their liking. The consumer could lock out dismemberments, blood, death animations, adult textures, and other adult content, essentially turning the regular version into the low-violence version. To further inform consumers of the violent subject matter, a large warning was placed on the front of the box and the ESRB rating was enlarged for greater visibility. A "mature audiences" warning was also added to the game's bumper and implemented into the menu system so that no one would be surprised by the game's content.

All of these features and functions helped extensively in the end. We widened our sales platform as stores realized they could order the tactical version if they wanted to, and we showed consumers that we listened to their needs and concerns, giving them a broader choice in their purchase.

3. Outside help

Although your team will most likely not be using real-life mercenary John Mullins to help design your game, outside individuals can be an incredible help in product development. Talking and working with a person who has an exhaustive knowledge of your game's subject matter will help refine your project and add a truly cohesive feel to the final product. As a consultant helping us with the military aspect of the game, Mullins gave instant feedback in areas where our knowledge was lacking and helped round out the areas that needed it.

Breaking out the big guns.

He described how trained soldiers would react to attacks. He discussed what sounds you would expect to hear in battle. He advised us on how the weapons in the game should "feel" to the player. In short, he helped us to create the correct atmosphere in which to immerse players. By drawing on the insights and knowledge of someone with first-hand experience of the action we were looking for, we were able to focus the design of the game.

4. "Commando" marketing and buzz words

We knew that in order to keep the QUAKE 2 engine competitive in the FPS realm, we had to add significant technology. Many of the technology improvements we made were centered on new modeling technology, which featured, among other things, a completely new modeling system, compression of animation data, attachment of models (bolt-ons), multiple skin pages per model, and advanced networking. Our lead technology programmer dubbed this new modeling system Ghoul (in keeping with an earlier in-house technology proposal called Specter).

In the public's eye, we associated all of these major changes with the Ghoul name. Without Ghoul, SOF would have been a mere shadow of the final product. It allowed us to throw in all the bells and whistles, including the vast array of enemies and the high degree of gore. As SOF's development progressed, our continued references to Ghoul caused the public to monitor the changes and build up their expectations. Ghoul became an important marketing word for SOF.

Besides normal marketing channels such as magazines and print ads, we decided to try our hand at "commando" marketing. By using our .plan files, giving web interviews, supporting the wonderful fan sites that were popping up, and making ourselves available through e–mail and online chats, we established a strong presence in the Internet community. This proved invaluable for consumer feedback. With the release of the demo and the early OEMs, players gave us instant feedback on what they liked and disliked and we were able to change the game accordingly.

One example where this feedback came in handy was with limited saves. Originally, players were limited in the number of saves that they could make based on their present difficulty level. Many people who played the demo disliked this feature, so we added the ability to customize the number of saves that players could make, thus adapting the game directly to consumers' preferences.

5. Good planning and scheduling

One of SOF's saving graces was that it was planned and scheduled well. The sheer volume of animation, art, programming, and levels forced us to update our schedules on a frequent basis. With a concrete animation naming system, an incredibly large and detailed database for animations, storyboards for every cinematic sequence, and a well-designed QA system, SOF did not suffer much inefficiency. The only area that endured some wasted time was the design due to the various story and game changes.

Once the story was finalized and had the green light, establishing and maintaining good planning and scheduling for the design process helped finish the game in a timely manner. We created total level walkthroughs, with each room and encounter written out. Flowcharts were used to draw the preliminary levels, and concept art was used for key location elements. Perhaps the most important lesson we learned from SOF was that preplanning is the most important aspect of game creation.

What Went Wrong

1. Unfocused design

The single most damaging problem during SOF's early development was that the original game lacked a truly focused design. We knew what the fundamentals of the game would be, but we did not have the specifics that we needed to create a solid, cohesive product. The game's overall story changed five times before it was finalized—at one point we had even changed the basic game concept to a team-based tactical shooter, similar to RAINBOW SIX.

One reason for this indecisiveness was that, at the time, our original marketing team was wondering what the "hook" would be for the game. This was a major roadblock in creating the game because we knew that if marketing wasn't behind the idea, SOF wouldn't get the marketing money that it deserved. On top of that,

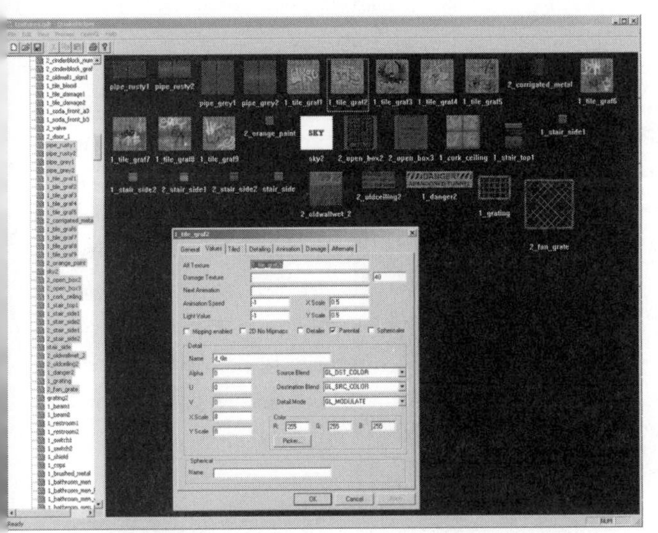

Raven developed QuakeHelper to manage more than 5,000 unique world textures with a visual means to assign properties to them.

without the backing of the marketing division, the senior management at Activision wouldn't get behind the title, either. We had to constantly sell and resell the idea that a high-octane, action-movie-like, real-world combat game would be enough of a hook. At times, it went so far that we were making design decisions not for the fun or betterment of the game, but to find the hook that we felt we were missing.

The last straw came when we found ourselves working on a tactical team-based shooter, a complete 180-degree shift from our original design. We then decided to return to the game's roots and started banging out a new story. Eventually, a new marketing team came on board that recognized exactly what we had been saying all along. SOF had more than enough to stand on its own, and they worked with us to find the right angle for marketing the product. This new team fit right in with the development team and things started to roll.

On top of that, since we urgently needed to nail a story down in a short amount of time, they recommended that we meet with a hot-selling writer (Gonzalo Lira, author of the spy novel *Counterparts*) and John Mullins. Although the full story that Gonzalo Lira wrote for us was never used, some elements of it were, and the process made us realize exactly what we wanted from this game and how to get it. John Mullins contributed an element of realism to the game that we were missing at that time.

In short, working on everything at once was not the way to go. For the projects that we currently have lined up we are designing the entire game from start to finish before we begin physically developing it. The SOF team learned the hard way that a day of preplanning saves a week of rework. Also, getting a green light for everything before starting development saves having to backpedal later on. Both of these lessons will be applied to our future projects.

2. Technology creation took longer than expected to visualize gameplay

A sure way to sell your product is to have a working prototype a tan early stage in its development. Since we had decided to give the QUAKE 2 engine an entire overhaul, we realized that we would really have to come together and work as a team to make sure things were completed on time. One of the major enhancements for SOF was the Ghoul modeling system, which replaced the entire QUAKE 2 modeling system, and turned out to be quite the undertaking. Throughout the entire life of the project, tweaks and changes were made to Ghoul to make it more flexible and powerful. Unfortunately, this also meant that for a substantial part of the early development, we had no game to look at — only individual components. It's one thing to be able to look at a model in a model viewer, or at a level with nothing in it, but it's essential to be able to see the model in the world and interact with it.

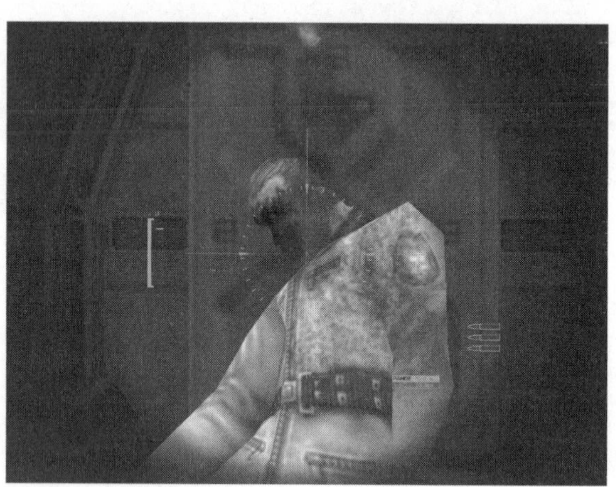

Another problem was the huge number of animations planned for SOF. Since we had so many animations (more than 600 sequences) we had to limit which animations would appear on a specific level due to memory constraints. Limiting the animations on a per-level basis was a nightmare in itself, not only for the animators but also for the AI programmer (who had to make the AI work within the animation constraints) and the designers, who had to create scripted and cinematic sequences using only the animations available for each level. As the game drew nearer and nearer to completion it became increasingly difficult to bring new animations into the game without ruining someone else's work by removing an animation that was already in use.

The final problematic technology was the AI. Developed throughout the entire course of the project, the AI went through many different incarnations. We decided early on that the pace of the game should be fast and furious with a large number of enemies attacking at once. Enemies were to be reactive, but not too intelligent. There were three major areas that caused AI problems: developing the models, developing the intelligence, and working with the scripting language.

The main enemy model for the game was very complex. Incorporating all of the animation sequences and consisting of nearly 4,000 polygons, the model contained every piece for various body builds, coats, and other items that differentiated the enemies. Because of this complexity, we were forced to preprocess enemy sets for each level. These individual enemy sets looked at what enemy pieces and animation frames were needed for the level because we did not have a skeletal system in place. This directly impacted the AI because not every move was now available on every level. In turn, the AI could only call animations that were generic across the levels.

The second area that caused AI problems was the addition of multiple skin pages, bolt-on accessories, gore, and death animations. Although not directly seen by most people as AI, all of these were important features for SOF. One of our main goals from the beginning of the project was to have lots of unique-looking enemies. This meant that our model was composed of many different skin pages into which we could swap different faces or outfits. We also implemented what we termed "bolt-ons": any item or feature that was not originally part of the model. These included Mohawks, canteens, briefcases, and side arms, which helped distinguish different characters. Implementing the gore was also very time consuming. We implemented gore zones that required skin page overlays, bolt-on models of viscera, the ability to remove limbs, and all of the blood pools and spatters that litter the game.

Finally, implementing the various death sequences also hampered the AI. In addition to all of the gore that we created, we also had to play one of several animations when an enemy died. Animations had to be called based on certain circumstances, such as where on the body the enemy was shot and what he was shot with. On top of all of that, adding the violence-lock system that would allow players to lock out the game violence meant that all of the gore and animations had to be able to be shut off if the player wanted.

The third area that caused problems for the AI was its actual development. Along with the problems created by the per-level animation system, the AI also had to work with the game's scripting language. If the AI was tweaked in certain ways, it caused the scripting to break. Many times in the game, enemies had to be "frozen" in place while their script waited to be activated. If a player happened to see one of these suspended enemies before they were triggered, it obviously made the AI appear less intelligent. We had to come up with ways around these problems, and expended considerable time and energy to fix them.

To make matters worse, the AI had a slight unpredictability built into it that caused scripted events to occur differently each time. Although unpredictability is good for gameplay, it had to be removed from the scripting element. Finally, a large amount of time was spent with the designers to build in hints for the areas (such as reactions of the enemies) and to specify which areas the enemies could traverse. At the beginning of the development we had "duck," "hide," "flee," and other commands that eventually were removed and taken over totally by the AI. The AI was in development until nearly the end of the project.

3. Too many OEMs and demos

Something that seemed like a great idea at the time but turned out to hurt us in the end was the decision to make specific OEM releases before the game was truly finished. The main reason for this was that we looked at the revenue that would help the bottom line instead of considering how much it would set back the game. Because there were both regular and low-violence versions of the game, we needed to make several different builds for the different violence levels and test each build accordingly.

In the end, we had roughly 75 QA submissions. While each OEM and demo iteration helped bring more of the game together, it also diverted our attention from the final product. As we were tweaking and fixing the OEM versions, full production would come to a standstill as we focused on getting the smaller versions out the door.

4. No fixed deadlines

Originally, SOF was scheduled to ship in July 1999. Activision wanted to avoid releasing SOF in the "blast zone" of competing FPS titles that were shipping that year, so they extended the deadlines on the game. As our competitors' titles were pushed back, so was SOF. Although within these deadlines we had schedules set up and planned out, this caused a never-ending uncertainty of how much time we had left in the project and how much technology we could add or change within that time.

In March 1999, we realized that with our complex models and the amount of animation we wanted, we needed to address memory concerns. Because we thought that we only had three or four months left of core development at that stage, we concluded that switching to a skeletal system would be too risky for the project. Instead, we created a vertex compression system that mimicked the benefits of skeletal compression in a few ways. Unfortunately, this meant that we were not able to provide all of the animations at once, as we would still be over memory budgets. If we had known that our deadlines would be pushed back another six months, we would have added the skeletal system, saving everyone a large amount of headaches and work.

5. Miscommunication about some technologies

Confusion over project scheduling aside, additional technologies were developed during the course of the project that were never truly planned out appropriately, such as the terrain engine, the in-game effects editor, and the scripting system that we used. All of these technologies served to improve the game substantially, yet they could have worked better if they had been properly discussed between the team members.

The terrain engine, while flexible enough to do various types of visual effects, was never properly coded into the gaming logic. The basic premise of the terrain engine was that the designers would create architecture that represented the portions of the world that the player could interact with. For example, on the train level, the train was created by the designers. The terrain engine would then be responsible for the scrolling polygons, in this case the train tracks and surrounding landscape. When we put this level in, we soon realized that we needed a bunch of special code to handle the various effects, such as when a person falls off a train. We wanted to add more unique kinds of levels like this, but we didn't have time to develop a generic physics system for handling other types of terrain, such as water where bodies might float or sink.

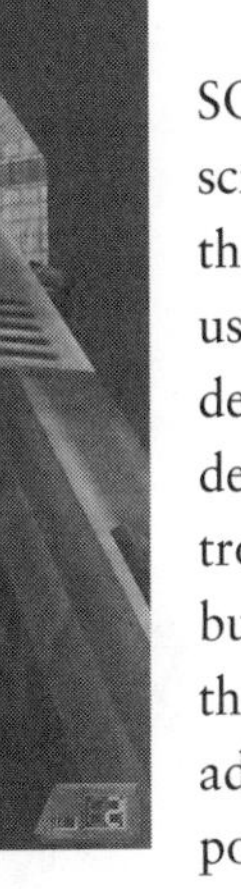

The effects editor was created by one of the programmers to help him create visuals for the weapons. The interface, while functional, was crude. Other people wanted to create visuals, including designers, but were hampered by the editor's interface design since it was never intended to go beyond the programmer who created it. Although the in-game editor allowed someone who knew the tool to create a special effect quickly and efficiently, it had a long learning curve for those not familiar with it. This reduced the amount of control that the artists had over the effects.

SOF shared the same scripting language that HERETIC 2 had used. It was originally developed to give designers more control over their levels, but we soon learned that we would need to add more and more power to the scripting system. SOF's complex scripting soon overwhelmed the scripting language and too much time was spent trying to tweak out sequences. With the addition of in-game cinematics (an unplanned feature not included in the design document), we realized that the way we were using the powerful scripting language was wrong. If we had planned better from the beginning, the scripting would have gone much easier. Unfortunately, since the story was planned so late, we didn't know at the time what would be needed.

A Direct Hit

Originally slated for an 18-month development cycle, SOLDIER OF FORTUNE ended up taking nearly two years, a considerable undertaking that in the end allowed a talented group of developers to really shine. As with all projects, SOF had its problems, but for the most part things went well thanks to the efforts of an incredible team of people, and SOLDIER OF FORTUNE has quickly become one of Raven Software's best-accepted titles. With strong sales to date and a solid Internet community, SOF has exceeded many people's expectations, including our own.

We've been very happy for the large number of good reviews, both in print magazines and on the Internet, and we are helping to support the online community as much as we can. From a development viewpoint, SOF allowed the Raven team to grow and mature, and many lessons that we learned are now being put to use in our next set of products. Of course, no project ever runs smoothly, but with each new game we gain more understanding of what it takes to make the next one better.

SECTION V

The Online Frontier

Online gaming as a large-scale commercial endeavour is clearly a big part of the future of gaming. There is something uniquely thrilling about the experience of sharing a virtual world with other people. The emotional buzz and endless unpredictability of human interaction are irreplaceable.

However, it's still unexplored territory. We are still exploring ways to crystallize that fascination in a mass-market game. Like the Internet, we don't quite know what to make of it or what to do with it; we just know it's huge and interesting and it's not going away. Like 3D graphics, online multiplayer gaming has swept the industry as a technology without providing a clear blueprint for what kind of games should be made using it.

It's just clear there's something fundamentally powerful about it. Single-player games allow players to immerse themselves in dreamlike fictional worlds with the total absorption common to films and novels, with the added experience of interactivity. One downside is that they have a solitary, even solipsistic quality that some find to be lonely or sterile. By contrast, online games are vibrant social worlds, challenging, unpredictable, and occasionally moving. They blur the line between art, game, and community in ways we are still sorting out.

Online gaming—two or more people playing a shared game through a computer—has been with us almost since computer games were invented. As researchers, hobbyists, and entrepreneurs explored the beginnings of the computer game phenomenon, many of those early directions involved multiplayer worlds and networked interactions. In 1978 Roy Trubshaw and Richard Bartle coded the first MUD (Multi-User Dungeon), an online virtual space that players accessed through text interface. Work like this continued through the 1980s and early 90s, largely out of the public eye, until in the mid-90s a few games brought the idea to prominence, showing how much fun and profitable it could be. A few games like AIRWAR and MERIDIAN 59 gained devoted followings, and DOOM introduced the charming neologism "deathmatch" into our collective vocabulary.

In 1997, though, online gaming entered the mainstream with Richard Garriott's ULTIMA

Online, the first massively multiplayer online game, a gigantic implementation of a fantasy world derived from his earlier, genre-founding role-playing series. UO had many supporters and many critics, but over time it proved its concept—its popularity demonstrated the feasibility as well as the profitability of such an enterprise. Large-scale fantasy role-playing is currently the dominant paradigm for online play, but it probably won't remain so—there are too many interesting modes of play waiting to be explored.

As they continue to evolve, online games bring up new questions and raise new challenges for game production. Development teams aren't just creating a piece of software they can forget about once it has been published—they're planning a service that users will subscribe to and keep interacting with, potentially for years. There has to be a business model that will sustain not just the production cycle, but the maintenance and administration of the game once it goes "live" and stays active for as long as it can turn a profit. How do players pay for such a service—by the hour, the month or according to some unit in the game, like territory or titles or troops to control? The live game creates a whole new phase of the production life-cycle, one which probably lasts much longer than development and is equally unpredictable. We are still learning what it looks like, what kind of team structures and roles and skills it involves.

Game design has been equally redefined by the problems of the online space. Is the game's virtual space a place to explore, to conquer, or to build? Do players meet to collaborate, compete, trade, or fight? Do they clear out a given area and move on, or stay in one space to interact? What happens if players run out of things to do? Is the game-world static, or does it change over time? How do we avoid dangers like flash crowds overloading servers, and players disrupting other players' experiences?

The least predictable and least controllable factor in an online game is the players themselves. An online game is partly composed of the people that play it, the community that surrounds it and the culture that forms in the process. But as a developer, how do you influence the nature of the community that comes about, both before and after a game's launch? You can't control what players do in your world, only try to create a system that encourages play. At times, rule-changes feel more like legislation than game design. Community management has become an essential development task. The whole nature of the relationship between game developers and players is changing from vendor-buyer to some amalgam of host-guest, server-client, and government-citizen.

Little enough is known about how to make online games, which makes the few postmortems available in this section that much more interesting. Here are a few tips that can be abstracted from these developers' accounts:

- **Anticipate high demand.**

  Nearly everyone seems to underestimate the number of users who want to play their game.

- **Tools.**

  World-building tools aren't enough; administrators and customer service people need tools to monitor the game and assist players once the game goes live.

- **Get full use out of your public beta.**

  In addition to reporting bugs, experienced and committed players can be help educate new players and set the overall tone and culture of your online community.

- **Don't trust the client.**

  A tried and true observation—players will exploit, hack, or otherwise take advantage of any weakness in the game to gain power or just disrupt the game.

- **Don't rely on existing content to keep players entertained.**

  Players are ravenous for things to do. They will instantly strip bare as many dungeons and hunt down as many monsters as you can make. The lasting interest of your game will always be in strength in players' interaction with one another, in community and competition.

Mythic Entertainment's

DARK AGE OF CAMELOT

by matt firor

DARK AGE OF CAMELOT was the best-selling computer game in the United States for the week of October 7, 2001, and is still comfortably in the top five as I write. This Postmortem is an overview of how this successful title was conceived and developed. My role on the project was as the game's producer. Mythic Entertainment has been developing online games as a company since 1995—forever in this field—but the company's founders had made online games even before then. In fact, as a company, we probably have more experience than any other company in developing online games of all types—over the years we have developed role-playing games, first-person shooters, top-down spaceship shooters, and strategy games.

Back-Story

DARK AGE OF CAMELOT is part of the second generation of massively multiplayer online games to reach the public. The game is set in a mythic British past in the chaos following the death of King Arthur; accordingly, the world is divided into three realms (respectively Celtic-, Norse-, and Arthurian-themed) eternally at war with one another, giving shape and purpose to interplayer conflict. At first glance, it appears cast in the same mold as its predecessors—medieval fantasy adventure—but a host of smaller changes, such as in interface and community-related features, reshape the gaming experience.

When I last wrote a Postmortem in the pages of *Game Developer*, it was back in May 1998 for ALIENS ONLINE, our online first-person shooter based on the well-known *Alien* movies. After ALIENS ONLINE, a nonaccelerated game, we created our first 3D-accelerated game, SPELLBINDER: THE NEXUS CONFLICT. During that project, we developed a relationship with NDL, makers of the NetImmerse 3D engine API toolkit. We learned a lot about 3D engine development over the course of that project and became very comfortable with software and art development in this environment.

We finished SPELLBINDER, which went on to be a mildly successful Internet shooter, and it still has a small but loyal following. After completing the SPELLBINDER project, we decided to create a graphical online roleplaying game to compete with the then new wave of online RPGs such as ULTIMA ONLINE and EVERQUEST, which were taking traditional text-based games and adding a graphical front end, with very successful results.

Over the years, we had developed several non-graphical online role-playing games, including

DRAGON'S GATE and DARKNESS FALLS: THE CRUSADE. Because of our experience developing RPGs, we knew that we had to have a slightly different slant on our new title in order to distinguish it from the RPGs that were already on the market. DARKNESS FALLS: THE CRUSADE (DFC) featured a built-in player-versus-player (PvP) conflict in which three different teams, called Realms, fought each other for control of magical artifacts, known as Idols. We really liked this concept, which served to keep DFC players hooked on the game—especially because no other online game featured such team-based conflict as a core part of the game design. So, in late 1999, we decided to make a graphical version of DFC.

Game Data

Release date: October 9, 2001

Genre: Massively multiplayer, online fantasy role-playing game

Publisher: Mythic Entertainment/Abandon Entertainment/Vivendi Universal Interactive Publishing

Platforms: Windows 98/ME/2000/XP

Number of full-time developers: 25

Number of contractors: 5

Estimated budget: $2.5 million

Length of development: 18 months

Development hardware: 900MHz Pentium IIIs

Development software: 3DS Max, Photoshop, Visual C++, Linux GNU C++, various proprietary in-house tools

Notable technologies: NetImmerse, Linux open-source server and database products

The project was dubbed "Darkness Falls 3D," and we began preliminary work researching client engine and server technology. Right off the bat it was obvious that we had two major factors going in our favor. First, we determined we could use a much-enhanced version of the SPELLBINDER graphics engine as DFC3D's client, just as we were able to use DFC's server code as a platform for the new game's back end. Having such a solid client and server right at the start—with associated client/server messaging—alone saved us at least a year of development.

Second, and even more advantageous, DFC's server came with that game's database of objects, monsters, and weapons. Indeed, we went into the CAMELOT project with a huge head start. We were proceeding along under the DFC3D concept until our president, Mark Jacobs, came up with the idea of basing the game, at least partially, on the Arthurian legends. It was a great idea, since the stories of King Arthur are in the public domain, which meant we could use them with no fear of licensing issues.

Of course, because the game was based on the idea that three Realms were in conflict, we quickly came up with the idea of basing the other two Realms on Norse Viking myths and Celtic Irish legends, respectively. Having the myths and legends of three cultures gives CAMELOT the feel of being three games in one, since each Realm has different races, classes, guilds, terrain, and monsters. Because everyone knows what happened in Arthurian England, we based the game after Arthur's death and developed a back story of conflict among the three Realms. The game was rechristened DARK AGE OF CAMELOT, and around January 2000 we began the project in earnest. A year and a half and untold numbers of Monty Python jokes later, we finished the game.

The initial versions of DARK AGE OF CAMELOT used the rights for a tabletop role-playing game called Rolemaster as a basis for the class and spell systems. Not long into the project, the company that created Rolemaster, Iron Crown Enterprises, filed for bankruptcy, and we lost the rights. This turned out to be good for us, however, because we were no longer required to adhere to a set of rules based on the license—although we did have to scramble for about a week to rename and retune spells and classes and otherwise clear Rolemaster content out of the game.

It all starts with a concept. The troll, a playable race, changed the most over the course of development from a hulking, human-like creature the more mythologically inspired version seen here.

As a company, Mythic had never before been able to devote all of its resources to any one game—we'd never had a project big enough to pay for it. Because of the sheer size and scope of CAMELOT, we wanted to ensure that everyone at Mythic devoted themselves fully to the project. Doing so required an influx of money, and that's where New York's Abandon Entertainment stepped in. Abandon owns a couple of small companies, each of which specializes in different types of entertainment: a film studio, a web company, and a couple of game content development companies. Abandon wanted to become more involved in game development, so it purchased a minority stake in Mythic. This money allowed us to devote everyone on staff to the CAMELOT project, while also expanding and hiring much-needed programmers and artists. Our spreadsheets showed that we had enough money to support exactly 18 months of development starting from January 2000, giving the project a hard end date of September 2001.

By the summer of 2000, we had nearly our entire team in place. We had about 25 developers working full-time on the project—quite a small number compared to other online RPGs, but our existing technology allowed us to reduce substantially the amount of technical programming staff required. We had five programmers, ten world developers, seven artists, and several other people working on the game. Rob Denton, Mythic's vice president and chief technical brain, was responsible for all client and server programming, as well as the client/server messaging that tied the two together. His input was critical during design discussions, as he could tell us whether an idea would work or not. He immediately categorized features into "doable," "not doable," and the dreaded "on the list," which meant that it could be done, but he wouldn't commit to it. Brian Axelson was in charge of server programming as well as design of the game's combat system—a critical component in a PvP-centric game. Jim Montgomery provided CAMELOT's client interface coding and also designed and coded the game's magical spell system.

CJ Grebb and Lance Robertson led the art team. CJ was responsible for the game's look and feel, while Lance handled figure modeling and animations and managed the team's deadlines. Their team used 3DS Max and Character Studio to create CAMELOT's character and monster models and animations. The character models were technically advanced, as each in-game character has several different parts buried in it that can be turned off and on by the game. So, each model can have a helmet head and a regular head (with hair) without having to load in a new model. Mike Crossmire created the game's spells in 3D Studio, tweaking the NetImmerse system to display animated spells with spectacular results.

It was essential to provide players with plenty of player-versus-environment conflict, such as with the forest giant seen here.

The other major group in CAMELOT's development was the world team, led by Colin Hicks. This group was responsible for quests, monster placement, object placement, and just about everything else having to do with creating the world of DARK AGE OF CAMELOT. CAMELOT's economy was designed by Dave Rickey. This economic system ensures that players must continue to spend money as they rise in level, which limits the amount of money that stays in the game. Dave and Mark Jacobs designed CAMELOT's trade skill system, which enables players to make armor, weapons, and other objects in the game—all tied to the economic system.

Among the myriad tasks that I did as a producer (writing, designing, persuading, arguing, and such), my job was to make sure all the teams worked together. I hosted an almost-daily morning meeting (at the wretched hour of 8:30 A.M.) where Colin, Rob, CJ, Lance, and I got together to make sure that we were all on the same page. I was also responsible for maintaining the master game client—all files added to the game had to be given to me, so I could verify they worked and then integrate them with the rest of the game.

For the game's sound and music, we contracted with Womb Music, based in Los Angeles, which had provided music for some of our previous titles. Rik Schaffer, the main guy at Womb, composed a wonderful soundtrack that consisted of several long main scores, as well as many shorter pieces in the style of Celtic, Norse, and old English folk songs, adding a sense of depth and quality to the world.

What Went Right

1. Community management/beta program

From the beginning of the project, we knew we had precious few dollars available for marketing, and that our best chance to capture public attention would be to have a big presence on the various roleplaying fan sites around the Internet.

One, the Vault Network, provided us with some message board space, a news page, and a couple of moderators, and we were off and running. We devoted a lot of time over the year and a half that DARK AGE OF CAMELOT was in development to interacting with the future fans of the game. We hired a community relations manager whose sole job was to read different message boards and report back to us what was happening in the community. From the beginning, we took our fans seriously and made many tweaks and additions to the game based on their commentary and ideas.

2. No bureaucracy

Since the founding of Mythic, we have striven to have little bureaucracy. We have no levels, no directors, and few managers. We have a president, a vice president, and a producer. That's it for management, although for CAMELOT we did have to assign a lead world developer and art co-leads, just to streamline the day-to-day processes of the project. Because of this simple command chain, we experienced no power struggles. We feel this is the best way to make a solid, cohesive game—a small group controls what the game is and how it is presented to the user. Because of this approach, decisions are made quickly, and features can be implemented without an endless line of approvals and politics.

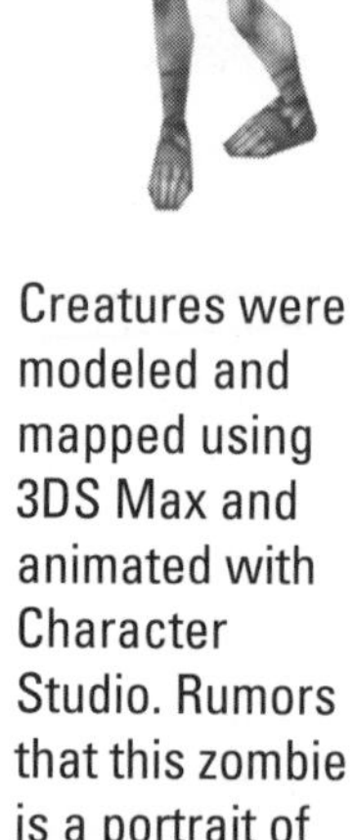

Creatures were modeled and mapped using 3DS Max and animated with Character Studio. Rumors that this zombie is a portrait of the producer after too many meetings are totally unfounded.

3. Smart business decisions

Our close relationship with Abandon Entertainment was a critical factor in the success of the game. Abandon's purchase of a minority interest in Mythic ensured that we had enough money to fund the game from start to completion. Abandon's management was smart enough to realize that we knew more about game development than they, so they largely left us to make game-related decisions ourselves. They were involved in the project, of course—some Abandon employees even became avid beta players of the game, even though most had never played an RPG before.

Abandon's investment meant that we did not have to rely on any outside influence in designing or creating the game, which means that CAMELOT is wholly ours.

With Abandon teaming with us, Mark Jacobs, our president, decided to take a big chance and wait until the game was almost complete before looking for a distributor. In most cases, game companies seek out publishers, which typically have a hand in the design and production of the game and then distribute the game to the retail chain. With Mark's gamble, we produced the game ourselves (with critical financial help from Abandon and business advice from our business development person, Eugene Evans) and then looked only for a retail distributor. This gamble could have placed us at the end of the project with a great game but no way to get it into the hands of our customers. It all worked out in the end, of course, with Vivendi Universal stepping in and distributing—but on our terms.

4. Sweet serendipity

The CAMELOT project was helped immensely by factors completely out of our control—in other words, blind luck. Several high-profile online RPGs that were slated to launch at about the same time as CAMELOT were either pushed off (SHADOWBANE) or canceled outright (DARK ZION, FALLEN AGE). Also, the week we launched was originally scheduled to be the same week as the launch of WARCRAFT III, which will almost certainly be a huge seller. That project was also delayed, which ensured that CAMELOT launched as the only large-scale game, and the only online RPG, when it debuted on October 9, 2001. This little bit of good fortune gave the game a big initial boost, as there was little direct competition from other new products.

In addition to designing CAMELOT's many outdoor areas, Mythic's world development team had to populate those areas with interesting encounters and dynamic quests—no small task, considering they had not one but three distinct Realms to accommodate, as well as a finite amount of creatures available to them. Work on this content is ongoing, with new updates added to the game on a regular basis.

5. The joys of open source software and stability

Long ago, during the development of our early titles, we decided to use Linux wherever possible as our server back-end OS, and we kept to this same practice when creating DARK AGE OF CAMELOT. We have extensive Linux experience in-house, and it made sense for us to stay with a platform that we knew could handle the task and also was, well, free. Because running CAMELOT would require a considerable amount of data management, we initially planned on using Oracle to store account and character information. However, Oracle's quoted license fee of more than $900,000 quickly removed them from contention.

Once we got over our shock and amusement at Oracle's pricing, we turned to a Linux-based freeware solution, MySQL, to manage CAMELOT's data storage, which so far has worked admirably. Everyone developing games should at least investigate open source solutions for their servers. It's saved us a pile of money and has been stable and reliable.

In fact, prior to CAMELOT's launch, it was axiomatic that MMORPGs were unstable and prone to crashing during their first month or so. From the outset, we were determined to buck this trend. We co-located our servers directly at UUNET, on the network backbone, which ensured a wide network pipe to the Internet. With this Internet connection, we can increase our bandwidth with just a few hours' notice to UUNET.

With the combination of reliable server code and a stable Internet connection—all running on open source software—CAMELOT went live on October 9, 2001, with virtually no problems. That first night, the game went down for about an hour and a half due to a database configuration problem, but since then, the game has been remarkably solid and stable. As of this writing, it hasn't been down due to server error for more than a few minutes ever since the first night.

What Went Wrong

1. Development of customer service tools

We really tried to avoid the customer service problems that are characteristic of some recently launched online games. One of the most important factors in keeping customer service reasonably effective was a smooth launch. Obviously, giving players fewer problems results in fewer calls to customer support. We did an excellent job with the launch—it went very smoothly.

However, we could have better foreseen other parts of our customer service plans. First, we had a lot more players in the first week after CAMELOT went live than we ever could have forecast—1,000 boxes were sold in the first four days alone. Our forecast numbers called for a much smaller number, and we hired our customer service staff based on this smaller number.

Also, we put off creating customer service tools until much too late in the development cycle—some had yet to be developed when the game went live. These missing tools really hurt the customer service staff and added to the time it took to help each player with in-game problems. Eventually, wait times became much too long, and customer support as a whole suffered because of it. As I write, we still are trying to work ourselves out of this hole.

2. Lack of a cohesive marketing plan

We went into the CAMELOT project with a lot of experience in developing software, but no real experience in creating a marketing plan. We got a lot of help with advertising from Abandon Entertainment, but there was no overall project plan. Basically, we took out ads in magazines that we thought were important and tried to keep on top of the Internet community. We didn't regularly issue press releases nor attempt to do a press tour or invite reporters to the Mythic offices to show off the game.

It's difficult to gauge just how much this hurt us. Our focus on Internet marketing gave us strong support among fans of the genre, but our lack of commercial marketing kept our company profile low, and we never received much mainstream media coverage because of it. Fortunately, we made up for our slow start, and then some, by our successful presence at E3. Abandon funded, designed, and staffed a large booth for us at the show, complete with medieval motif and lots of giveaways.

3. O Dungeons and Cities, where art thou?

The first major update we made to CAMELOT's graphics engine to differentiate it from SPELLBINDER was to put in the rolling terrain system that makes the world so lifelike. We spent a long time making the outdoor areas of the game beautiful and well stocked with monster encounters. The ease with which we did this gave us a false sense of security when it came to developing our dungeon/city technology.

These areas in the game required a large number of models and characters in a much smaller space than the outdoor terrain, so creating dungeons and cities proved to be a much more difficult job than we thought. Because we put off doing the technical designs for the interior spaces for so long, in the end we simply didn't get enough of them done. The game launched with only three capital cities (one per Realm) and about 15 dungeons.

4. We have a great game but no servers!

In a great "Why didn't they tell us about this in college?" situation, we went into the final months of the project with no credit rating. Mythic Entertainment has been around for a long time, but we simply hadn't ever borrowed any money, and so we didn't have a credit history. This turned out to be a problem when we went out to lease our servers from Dell and were flatly denied. We pointed out that we had plenty of money in the bank, but to no avail. Dell simply wouldn't lease us the computers until we had a credit history.

In the end, we were forced to purchase the servers outright from Dell, which obviously had a much greater impact on our bottom line.

5. Postrelease fan communication

As good as our communication with CAMELOT's fan base was during the game's design and beta periods, it began to suffer soon after the game's release. The community simply grew too large to communicate with in the manner we had during beta, when we simply went out to Internet message boards and posted our thoughts and plans. With the game live, it was obvious we needed a much more coherent way to communicate with our fans, one that would not send them to numerous different fan sites to sift through literally thousands of messages. This situation grew into a big problem when players became extremely frustrated by what they perceived as a lack of communication from us.

About six weeks after release, we realized that we needed to create our own Web site to publish information about the game: release notes, plan files, server status, Realm War status, and many other little things that we knew but our players didn't. This Web site, dubbed "Camelot Herald," launched the following week and so far has been a great success. Fans of the game can now go to one Web site to get all the information about the game in one place and with no interference.

For the Ages

It was a great pleasure to create DARK AGE OF CAMELOT, as it is the first big title that Mythic Entertainment has ever worked on. It was a wonderful thrill to see our names on top of the best-seller lists for those couple of weeks in October 2001, and we hope to be working on the game for a long time to come. As long as players are interested in playing the game, we'll be there adding content and updating it.

Multitude's FIRETEAM

by art min

Our goal with FIRETEAM was to create a complete online game experience. The Internet gives game designers the ability to take multiplayer gaming one step further by creating a community, something that wasn't possible before online games came about. Multitude wanted to take the next step in gaming evolution by making the community a significant part of our product. In other games, such as DIABLO or QUAKE, the players were creating communities themselves, mostly through their own Web sites. Multitude, on the other hand, devoted significant development time to creating tools that would help the community. We spent as much time on FIRETEAM's lobby and community web pages as on the game engine itself. Our goal was to create a game that would make people say, "Wow, this is what I've wanted from an Internet game."

FIRETEAM is an online-only gaming experience. The actual game play is a squad-based tactical combat. Players can communicate with other members of their team using Multitude's voice technology. Each player controls one character in the battlefield. The game uses an isometric, three-quarter view 2D graphics engine. There are four different FIRETEAM scenarios, and each game session is ten minutes long. The scenarios are very sports-like in their design to help promote team play.

Back-Story

FIRETEAM's approach to online play is distinctive, a series of game modes that are half futuristic sport, half squad-based tactical combat. Players sign on as part of small teams rather than massive worlds and let teammates chat by voice rather than text to create camaraderie and a more intimate social environment. Although FIRETEAM hasn't persisted, it's an interesting case study, contrasting with the dominant massively multiplayer approach to online play.

Equally important to the FIRETEAM experience is the lobby, where players can view other players' statistics, chat between games, and find squad mates and enemies for their games. The last component of FIRETEAM is the community web pages, which display players' complete statistics and provide support for FIRETEAM Companies (which are similar to QUAKE Clans). On the community web pages, players can create companies, add/kick members, and access private Company bulletin boards.

Brief History

FIRETEAM evolved dramatically over its first year of development. Multitude was originally founded to create the "ultimate online game," which was to be a large persistent science fiction world. We knew that there would be some competition because ULTIMA ONLINE had already been announced, although Origin hadn't yet performed any alpha or beta testing. We spent months writing and planning for a massively multiplayer online game set in a futuristic world. The project was to have a server team of around 10 people and a game team approximately double that size.

Game Data

Release date: December 1998

Publisher: Cryo Interactive Entertainment

Genre: online tactical team-based sports game

Target platform: Windows 95/98

Team size: 14 full-time developers. Some number of contractors.

Budget: Approximately $2.5 million

Time in development: Two and a half years

Tools: Microsoft Developer Studio 5.0, Microsoft SQL Server, Microsoft IIS, 3D Studio Max, Microsoft Interdev 6.0, Microsoft Chat Service, and Windows NT

As we were designing around our original concept for the game, our desire to make a persistent-world game work as well as a single-player game presented us with many hard technical and design problems. On the good side, it was during this process that we finalized the design spec for our combat engine. The combat engine was inspired by X-COM: UFO DEFENSE, emphasizing squad combat with features such as line-of-sight.

We soon realized that our new company's financing was coming along very slowly and that we needed a much more easily attainable goal (due to lack of resources, both financial and human) that would still showcase the unique voice technology that we'd developed. We looked at the combat engine specification, our voice technology, and the Internet technology that we were designing and realized that we could make a great tactical team game. So at that point, we decided to abandon the large persistent world and make team play the essence of the game.

Designing a multiplayer game is very different from designing a single-player game. I've heard that in many games, the multiplayer component was added on only because marketing had requested the feature; this approach can make the multiplayer experience less than ideal. In a single-player game, the player is the hero and the focus of the game experience. The player should be able to win 100 percent of the time (with some effort). In a multiplayer game, a player should win 50 percent of his or her games against an equivalently skilled player. The thrill of a multiplayer game shouldn't be in the winning, but more in the process and the actual competition. Team play gives players a deep gaming experience, even if they lose.

Our efforts to create engaging multiplayer game play were made even more effective by our voice technology, which allowed players to hear the emotions of their fellow players.

FIRETEAM's Components

FIRETEAM's network architecture is client/server-based. We chose a client/server architecture because of the benefits that it offered us in the areas of performance (especially with the voice technology), cheat prevention, and centrally located statistics. The clients all run on Windows 95/98 and the servers run on Windows NT boxes, where we use Microsoft Chat services to do the intercommunication between our server processes. We also have a Microsoft web server running the community web pages, with a Microsoft SQL server maintaining the database. Our servers are at one location, our ISP, Globalcenter, in Sunnyvale, California.

FIRETEAM uses the Elemedia SX2.0 Voice Codec to do its voice compression and decompression. Multitude's proprietary software wraps around this voice codec and interfaces with the Windows sound system for both input and output. The game mixes multiple voices on the client side rather than the server side. Clients simply send voice packets to the server, the server then routes them on to the appropriate teammates.

In the future, spectators or enemies will be able to listen in on the voice chatter. Our voice software handles both DirectSound and non-DirectSound drivers because some sound cards work with DirectSound in full duplex. Full duplex means recording from microphone and playing sound at the same time.

Who Worked on FIRETEAM

Ned Lerner and I started Multitude and began working on the original project in April 1996. The development team grew gradually over the course of the project. Jim Morris was brought on during the summer of 1996 to be the chief technical officer, and his first project was to develop the voice technology. Alan Murphy was brought on to provide art for the prototype and eventually was named art director. Conroy Lee, Harvey Smith, and Harry Schaffer were brought on in early 1997 to help take FIRETEAM from a prototype to the real game that we showed off at E3 1996. Bill Money, James Poelke, and David Reese came on in late 1997.

The team has a very diverse group of products to its collective credit. Lerner and Morris were two of the first people to work on 3D in the game industry. Murphy's art credits include GALAXIAN, PAC-MAN, DEFENDER, TAZ, and X-MEN. The others have worked on games such as SYSTEM SHOCK, TERRA NOVA, MAGIC SCHOOL

BUS, ULTIMA VIII, and FRONT PAGE SPORTS: BASEBALL.

What Went Right

1. Combining team play and voice together

FIRETEAM's design focus was on team play. Just as we've seen in team-oriented sports, the cooperative nature of playing as a member of a team has proven to be a very addicting and powerful gaming design. FIRETEAM's cooperative nature was a symbiosis of our voice technology and team play design. We needed to give people a reason to talk to strangers on the Internet.

Team play was that reason; it gives people the ability to say "Watch out behind you!" or "Good job!" Teammates can share the joys of victory or the agonies of defeat. Because there is no button to push to transmit your voice (it transmits automatically when you talk), players can hear the spontaneity of teammates yelling and laughing. Emotion comes across very clearly with voice and is definitely preferable to typing in ALL CAPS or emoticons. The ease of vocal interaction brings the team together.

In a fast-paced tactical game such as FIRETEAM, players don't have time to coordinate movements with the keyboard. Without voice, you limit team communication to select macro keys (or players who can type very fast). In FIRETEAM's Basetag scenario, for example, teammates protecting the base can give instant information on where the enemy is making its attack. Over the course of their lives, people have already learned how to talk; it's an interface they understand. Vocal communication doesn't require a key card list for communication hotkeys, just a microphone to talk into.

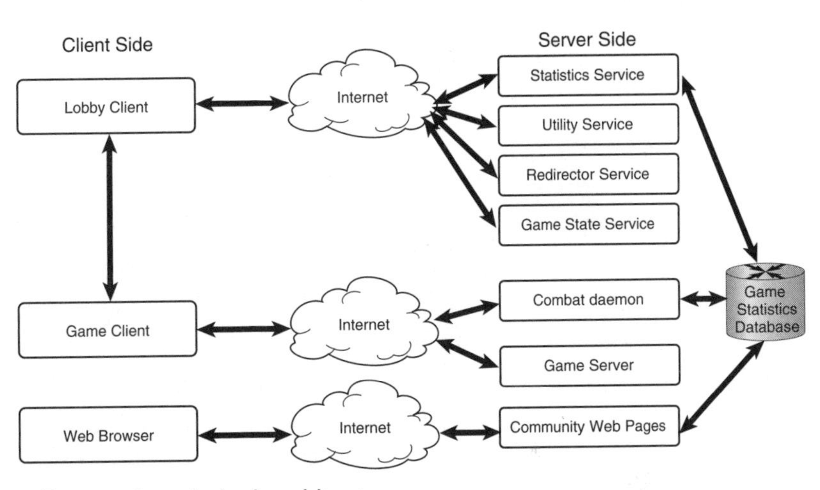

FIRETEAM's technical architecture.

2. Designing the project around constraints

Multitude was founded to do a game for the Internet. The Internet offers many problems that we had to solve in order to make a fun game. The biggest technical problem was Internet latency. Fundamentally, latency causes each player to have something different on his or her screen, so there is always a delay between a

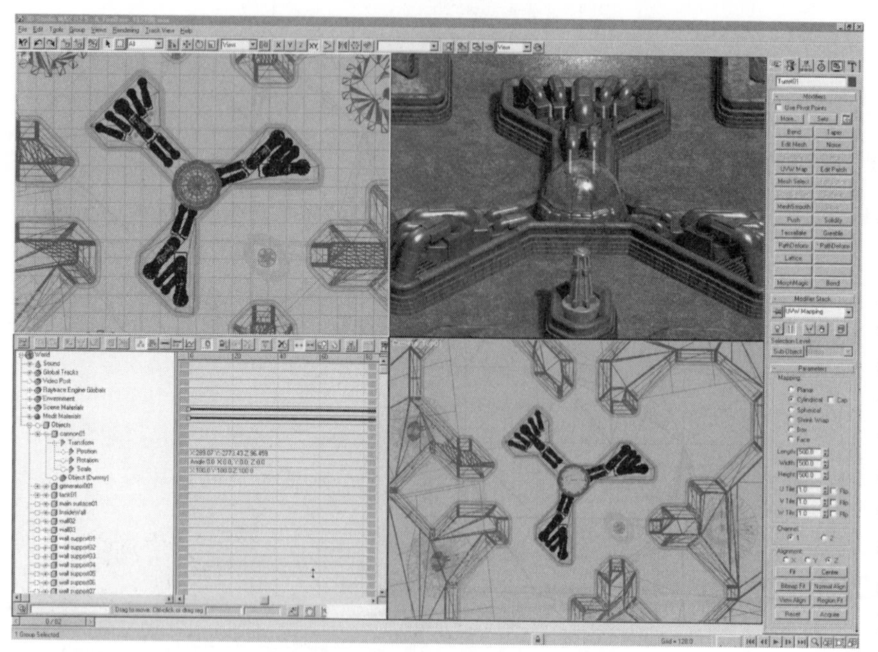

A 3D Studio Max layout of one of the maps. Our artists take the game-tested layout from Tile Edit to create backgrounds for each map.

player performing an action and the other players seeing that action carried out.

For example, we decided early on that we wanted the game to respond as quickly as possible. When you shoot at something during a FIRETEAM game, you'll see instantly whether or not you hit your target. The actual damage will take a small amount of time to be applied to the target. So it's possible that you'll see someone get shot, walk a bit, and then die. The game cannot provide a perfect view of the world to each player; that's not possible given the limitations of the Internet. So we decided not to show players their opponents' health. If you can see that your opponent has only a sliver of health and that one shot could kill him or her, then you would expect that player to die instantly with the next shot you made. By hiding opponents' health from our players, we hide the perception of lag.

A project's constraints can also be exploited to the project's benefits. Because the constraint was that we needed to be on the Internet, we created the community web pages to give players the ability to look at their statistics and create FIRETEAM Companies. We wanted a strong community for FIRETEAM, and the community web pages were an easy way for people to have an identity in this community and to join a group of other players.

3. Spending sufficient time to develop tools

We used several proprietary tools to create FIRETEAM's game environments. Early on, we spent a lot of time building easy-to-use tools that allowed us to create content rapidly. Our internal testers used these tools to create new arenas for FIRETEAM. And because FIRETEAM is an online game, we were able to test new maps very quickly with our beta testers.

With an online game, game balance is crucial. Players will find any competitive edge and map imbalance they can and exploit it. Especially in an online game with a lobby, word of cheats or advantages spreads very fast. Your tools must allow you to tweak your maps, so you can quickly fix any small problems. Many of our maps changed during the course of testing as our testers would point out weaknesses that they found.

I can recall a particular controversy over whether Gunball (a FIRETEAM scenario similar to combat football) was balanced enough. Many of the advanced players were complaining that Gunball's offense was too hard. Using our Tile Edit tool, we quickly created a few maps with two endzones for each team (Gunball maps normally only have one endzone). Through testing the new maps, we discovered some of the problems with Gunball were unrelated to the maps themselves, but that the offense simply had a disadvantage when trying to score. So instead of redoing all of our map designs, we tuned the Gunball game by giving the Gunball carrier a protective drone.

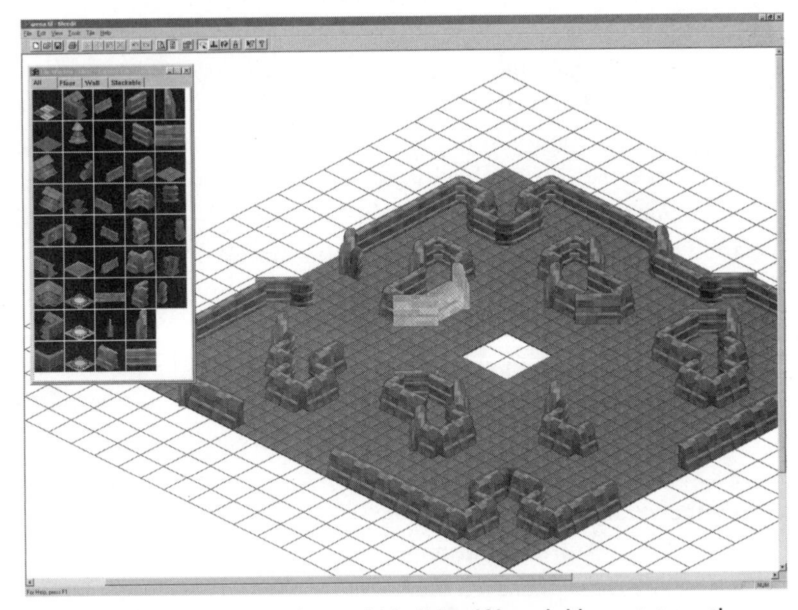

This is Tile Edit, our basic world builder. We quickly prototype the physical layout of the maps with this tool. It's very easy to move walls around to achieve the right game balance.

An added bonus of easy-to-use tools is that you can make them available to the public and let your players customize the game and create their own content. We haven't yet taken that last step, because we're not sure how we want to store the maps on our servers and present them to the community.

4. Managing risk: voice technology

The biggest risk in developing FIRETEAM has been the voice technology. Many smart people initially said it was impossible, but we knew that the game's design objective was a cooperative team game, and voice was very important to accomplishing the goal. So FIRETEAM's first technical project was to determine whether or not voice on the Internet was even possible. Once we had the technology running over the Internet, we still faced the possibility that it wouldn't work with the wide spectrum of sound cards in the market.

We tried to minimize the problems that voice would cause by providing users with a tool that would configure the sound card and microphone during installation. Multitude was very aware (almost scared) of the fact that FIRETEAM would represent most users' first use of voice technology on their computers. So we had to make sure that it worked on as many sound cards as possible and that it was very easy to use. We eventually released FIRETEAM as two executables—one for systems with DirectSound and one for systems without it. One feature that we explicitly did not put into the game was the ability for players to talk to their opponents. We wanted players' first experience with voice to be a positive one. We didn't think a 12-year old telling you where to put your gun in his shrieking voice would convince people that voice is a wonderful addition to gaming. Similarly, people asked for the ability to eavesdrop or steal another team's radio and listen to the other team. This feature would impel team members not to talk if they believed they were being monitored. These types of behavior would weaken the voice feature.

5. Promoting community

If you're going to design an online game, you cannot ignore the community. Any online game, from FIRETEAM to Poker on AOL to ULTIMA ONLINE, will have a community because the players will be able to communicate with each other.

Online game developers should take advantage the fact that their product inherently has a community. Most online games go through alpha and beta online tests mostly to test the software, but few deliberately create or test the community aspects of a product.

Players are not only a source of revenue for a project, but they are a feature of your game. In an online environment, the players' game experiences are dictated by their teammates and the opponents against whom they play. You want the players to follow guidelines and really care about the game and the community. If your population is full of a bunch of player killers, then that's the experience that the players will get.

Multitude succeeded in developing community-enabling tools. We spent significant time and discussion on our lobby and community web pages. Given FIRETEAM's team nature, we wanted players to feel a sense of belonging so that they would want to save each other's lives. The FIRETEAM product is not just the game itself. The game is an important piece of the FIRETEAM experience, but it's only a piece. The community plays a large part of the whole experience.

What Went Wrong

1. Misjudging market conditions

When Multitude was founded in April 1996, there was a lot of buzz in the online game space. Mpath and Ten had big plans. ULTIMA ONLINE was about to go through testing. We believed that an online-only game, sold directly to customers via the Internet, would be acceptable to the market when we eventually shipped. What we've discovered is that the online game market has not matured to the level that we expected. Very few online-only games have been released, with ULTIMA ONLINE being the only clear success.

We made two decisions early on that should have been reexamined when it became clear that customer acceptance of an online-only game was not a foregone conclusion. FIRETEAM would have been more willingly accepted by the market if it contained some artificial intelligence (AI). With such an implementation, players could practice using the interface by themselves and, more importantly, players could practice as a team against AIs. With computer-controlled opponents in place, players could play offline or possibly on a LAN against computers opponents. Many users are intimidated by having to learn a new game while playing against other more experienced human players. AIs would have helped ease players into the online-only part of the game, providing a feature that many players expect to find in games today.

FIRETEAM also should have had a demo available on day one. As an online game, providing a demo presented an interesting problem because of the server issues. With a traditional game, developers can hand out a million demo disks and never think about the problems their users might experience. If we gave out a million demo disks, then we would need to have enough servers to support all those people that actually play the demo. We didn't create an infrastructure to support a demo mode of FIRETEAM. FIRETEAM is a new type of game—people aren't yet accustomed to online tactical team games with voice technology. We should have made some extra promotional effort to get potential users to make that initial leap and try out the game.

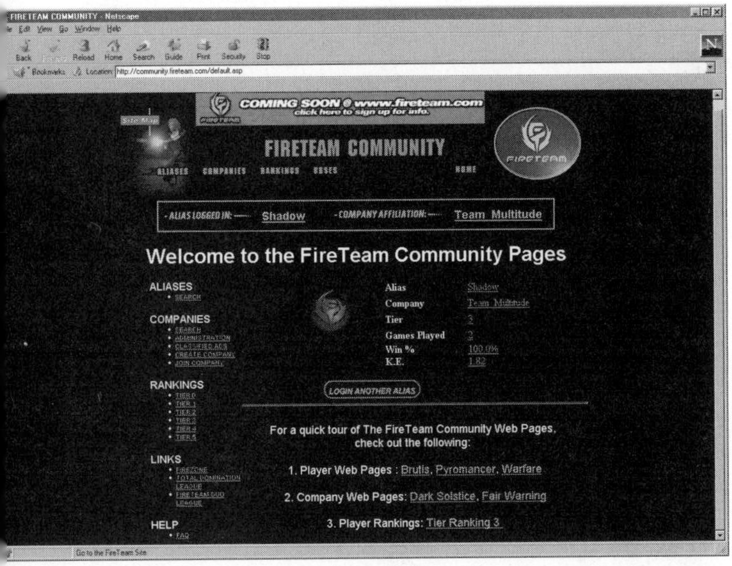

The home page for the community web pages. Players can access a wealth of information about their statistics or other players' statistics.

2. Managing contractors

FIRETEAM was a large and extremely challenging project. We had to look outside of our own company for help with certain parts of the project. Our mistake was in assuming that these experts held the same priorities as the rest of the development team. These groups have their own objectives and aren't expected to understand the big picture or know how to create fun games. We realized that when working with contractors, we needed to give those contractors a very precise and clear specification. Because a good game design evolves over the course of a project, a project manager must constantly make certain that the contractors are following the latest version of the specification.

As we were developing FIRETEAM, our attention was also focused on growing our new company. We found that it was easy to forget what the contractors were doing and how they fit into the project. We made the naïve assumption that they would be willing to work with an evolving specification. However, when a project is fix-bid, an external developer will only do so much tuning and reworking of code before he or she starts charging you for it. If you don't manage this relationship closely, these costs add up very quickly.

For example, the cost for developing the community web pages doubled from the original quote because the design evolved. The final version of the community web pages was great, but a more thoughtful initial design specification and better management of the process would have saved Multitude significant money and time.

3. Internet technical issues

The Internet poses significant problems for developers. Although we did our best in designing the game around the limitations of the Internet, we did have some technical problems. We originally designed FIRETEAM around TCP/IP because it's a reliable transport protocol for net-

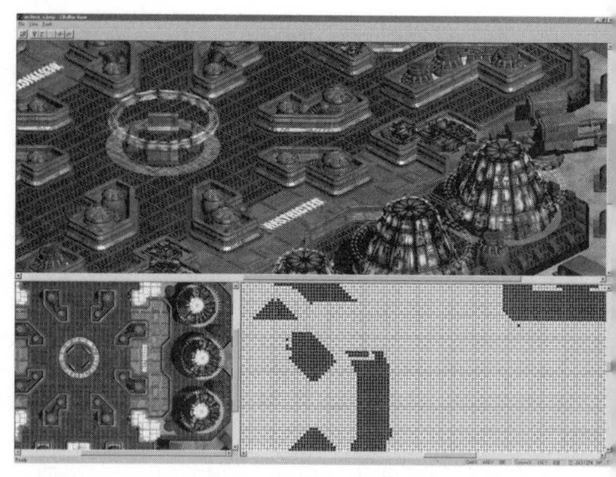

We take the output from 3D Studio Max (with our plug-ins) and, with our proprietary ZHMPView tool, convert the files to a format that FIRETEAM can read.

work traffic. However, the reliability comes at a very high cost: retransmission times. If a packet is lost on the Internet (which happens a lot), it takes some time for the machines on both ends to realize this and resend the data. TCP/IP guarantees that all packets are in order; therefore, all of the packets after the lost packet will be delayed until the lost packet is sent again. In a fast-paced game such as FIRETEAM, lost packets can really cause problems.

As soon as we started doing real Internet tests, we realized that we needed to start sending some packets unreliably via UDP. These packets could get lost, be out of order, or even duplicated, but they wouldn't be delayed by other packets. We learned that different packets require different sets of reliability and timeliness, and that developers should use all the tools available to them, both TCP/IP and UDP. We initially labored under the idea that only one protocol should be used for the sake of simplicity, but it's best to use the appropriate tool for each job.

Packet loss and high ping times are simply part of the reality of dealing with the Internet. You do your best to deal with these issues, but they'll still cause you endless headaches as routers over which you have no control go down throughout the country. Many online games come with a little utility that does a trace on the route the packets take between a player's machine and the servers. The information that the utility returns can help the player and his or her ISP determine where the bad connection is along that route. Developers should be aware that while they cannot fix the Internet infrastructure, it's important to understand its limitations and deal with them as best they can.

4. Server spaghetti

FIRETEAM is a very complicated project with many processes running on both the client and the server. Add in the complication of the Internet, and you can get one confusing mess (Figure shows just how complicated the FIRETEAM architecture is). We tried to break our server components down into smaller, more manageable pieces, each with its own function. We hired some experts in various disciplines to help us better understand parts of the server technology that were new to us. Our mistake was in thinking that these experts could just come in and solve our problems. As we busied ourselves with other parts of the project, it was easy for us to say to ourselves, "They know what they're doing."

In the end, however, the development team needs to understand the whole picture and how the pieces really fit together. One of FIRETEAM's unique properties is that its server-side components run remotely at an ISP's facilities. In order to debug something as complicated as our server architecture remotely, our key programmers—not just the client/server experts—needed to understand the whole system.

5. Coping with the community

As I mentioned previously, when you create an online game, you need to embrace the community. At the same time, a direct connection with a community of testers who aren't 100 percent aware of your objectives is something that needs to be managed very carefully. The testers will always want something different. When is the last time you played a game and said, "This is perfect"? I've often said that even my favorite game would be better if it had feature X.

Most beta testers are young people who have a lot of time on their hands; that's great for finding bugs, but it can also be a problem because some of them lack perspective. All players have an equal voice in the FIRETEAM lobby, so we had to watch over the lobby constantly because a few testers could ruin the fun for others, even to the point of instigating a mini-online-riot.

From what I can tell, some online game companies simply ignore their testers' constant demands. After the experience of developing FIRETEAM, I must admit that this is a possible solution, though not an optimal one. Many of us on the development team spent many hours justifying our design decisions in order to educate the testers on why we were doing things a certain way. While this education does make them better testers, it takes up a lot of time. And it's a dangerous black hole that you can be sucked into if you're not careful.

I believe that the true balance is to pay attention to your community, but sometimes to sacrifice the battle in order to win the war. You should involve your intended community in the evolution of your game, but don't let it take over your design process or time.

Evolving Right Along

In building FIRETEAM, we as developers accomplished our goal of providing a complete online gaming experience with true team play, innovative voice technology, and extensive community building tools. The Internet offers brand new gaming experiences; game players can compete in ladders such as battle.net or tournaments such as the PGL. Also, an online game lets players meet new friends with whom they can share true social gaming experiences.

However, the Internet introduces a lot of negatives to the gaming experience. Instead of lightning-fast LAN connections, players must now tolerate latency. Instead of a small group of friends, a player's opponents may be complete strangers who aren't polite and may even be cheaters.

Because of the newness of this market, FIRETEAM may be ahead of its time. Or it may not have exactly hit the sweet spot that online multiplayer gaming should be. But FIRETEAM has helped online game evolution along by demonstrating that voice technology does work and that team play and community are compelling elements that don't have to be accidental.

Turbine's
ASHERON'S CALL

by toby ragaini

Back-Story

ASHERON'S CALL is the third massively multiplayer persistent online world to reach the market, although it was developed in parallel with ULTIMA ONLINE and EVERQUEST. Like its competitors, it is set in a heroic-fantasy world, but with crucial differences. It offers a fealty system that creates formal links and hierarchies between players and rewards cooperative play. It also offers episodic narrative content, periodic new quests, and events that visibly affect the entire world.

ASHERON'S CALL is a statistical anomaly. In an industry where cancelled games and dashed hopes are the norm, this project seemed one day away from certain failure for nearly its entire history. And yet, thanks to the visionary foresight of a handful of people, a healthy dose of luck, and incredible conviction from both the development team and publisher, it made it to store shelves and has received a great deal of critical acclaim.

In May 1995, I walked into a small suburban home in southern Massachusetts and met my new co-workers. Having left my previous job at a genetics lab, I expected nothing more than an interesting summer project as "A Game Writer." Little did I realize what was in store for me and this start-up company called Turbine. Having filled every nook of a residential home with PCs, an enterprising group of about ten developers was already busy working on the game that would one day become ASHERON'S CALL. Although not a single one of them had professional game development experience, I was immediately impressed with their enthusiasm and dedication. After introductions, I was told to scrounge around for a desk. Upon securing an end table and a plastic lawn chair, I sat down and started meeting with various team members to figure out just what this game was all about.

What was described to me was something that nearly every computer game geek is by now familiar with: a 3D graphical MUD. A persistent fantasy environment where hundreds of players could explore the land, defeat monsters, form adventuring parties, delve into dungeons, and complete quests. I'm not sure why anyone thought it was possible. We had no office, no technology to speak of, and no publisher. And I was being paid $800 a month. Yet from these humble beginnings, something truly wonderful was created.

The development team was divided into functional departments. Tim Brennen, a Brown University dropout who had helped develop

Windows NT as a Microsoft intern, led the engineering team and would go on to design the server, networking, and character database. Chris Dyl, a former physicist turned programmer, would develop the 3D graphics engine and server-side physics. Andy Reiff, also a Brown alumnus, would later round out the engineering leads as the game systems programmer, responsible for implementing all of the game rules systems and functional interactions in the game world. All of the game's code would be developed from scratch. At the time, this was a fairly easy decision, since licensable game code was pretty much nonexistent in 1995.

Game Data

Release date: November 1999

Publisher: Microsoft

Genre: Massively multiplayer, online fantasy role-playing game

Intended platform: Windows 95/98

Project budget: multimillion-dollar development budget

Project length: 40 months plus 8 months of beta

Project size: approximately 2 million lines of code.

Team size: 30+ full-time developers, including 6 artists, 4 game designers, 15 software engineers, and 5 QA testers.

Critical development hardware: Intel Pentium PCs

Critical development software: Microsoft Visual C++ 5.0, Visual SourceSafe 5.0, Lightwave 5.5, Photoshop 4.0, RAID

On the art team, Jason Booth, a music student with experience using Lightwave, would take on the title of lead technical artist. In this role, Jason bridged the gap between the art and graphics teams, ensuring that the art asset pipeline ran smoothly. Sean Huxter brought his substantial animation and modeling experience to the team as the lead artist. My own contributions to the team were in the area of game design. As the project grew in scope, my role changed to become that of lead designer. Soon realizing the amount of work required to design a game with the scope of ASHERON'S CALL, I put together a team of designers that envisioned and documented the characters, monsters, history, and timeline of a fantasy world called Dereth. In addition, the design team spec'd all of the game rules and systems necessary to RPGs.

Although the team had no professional game development experience, one invaluable thing that the team did have was experience playing MUDs and similar text-based Internet games. Although these games were comparatively simple, the game-play dynamics created in a massively-multiplayer environment are extremely different from a single-player game. MUDs proved to be a very useful model for multiplayer gaming patterns.

ASHERON'S CALL was initially designed to support just 200 simultaneous players, each paying an hourly fee. Turbine would host the servers, which were originally going to be PCs running Linux. Although in today's market, this sounds ludicrous, in 1995 this was in fact the standard premium online game model. Games using similar models, like Genie's CYBERSTRIKE and America Online's NEVERWINTER NIGHTS, were quite successful at the time. Based on this goal, the original schedule had ASHERON'S CALL shipping in the fourth quarter of 1997.

What Went Right

1. Staying true to our original vision of the game

ASHERON'S CALL was a ridiculously ambitious project for an unproven team. Yet despite this naïveté (or more likely because of it), the final product is frighteningly close to the original goal of the project. Of course during that time, Turbine learned lessons in feature cutting, scheduling risks, and compromise. But despite all the missed deadlines, all-nighters, and other disappointments, we are able look back on our shared vision and take pride in that we achieved what we set out to do.

Typically, there exists a master document that describes the overall game concept and goal. Although the documentation at the inception of the game was in fact very sparse, what little that did exist described the fundamental architecture of the game, including its client/server model, dynamic load balancing capabilities (described later), and 3D graphics. In addition, gameplay details such as the allegiance system, magic economy, and the emphasis on social game play are in my notes going as far back as 1995. The team internalized these goals, and a form of oral tradition maintained them in meetings.

Although we didn't know it at the time, ASHERON'S CALL would debut as the third massively-multiplayer online RPG amidst two strong competitors, ULTIMA ONLINE and EVERQUEST. We're often asked if we made any dramatic changes in response to the release of these two titles. In all honesty, the answer is no. If anything, these two products proved to us that our initial technical and game design decisions were correct. Clearly, social game play helped drive the success of these games. This made our game's social systems such as allegiance and fellowships all the more important. It was also obvious that immersion was critical. Instability and pauses were the bane of massively-multiplayer games. In theory, the dynamically load-balanced servers would prevent many of these problems.

In an industry that can be driven by holiday deadlines, marketing hype, and cutting corners, it's refreshing to know that ambitious goals can still be rewarded. But it's more than that. While we certainly could have created a less ambitious game, I believe it would have been a detriment to Turbine's competitiveness as an independent development studio. ASHERON'S CALL might have shipped earlier had it been a LAN game or a series of connected arenas, but we would not have the innovative technology and game design experience that today puts Turbine in such a desirable competitive position in the industry. In this way, our team's unwavering vision was handsomely rewarded.

2. Securing a publishing agreement with Microsoft

In mid-1996, representatives from the newly-formed MSN Gaming Zone were booed by the audience of the first Mpath Developer Conference. Their crime was the prediction that hourly fees were dead and that flat monthly rates would become standard. Our business plan at the time counted on an hourly model, but we recognized the truth to the Zone team's statement. At that year's E3, we relentlessly pursued Jon Grande, product planner on the Zone, in order to pitch him our game proposal and show him our technology demo.

At that time, the demo consisted of two PCs connected to each other. One was running the client software, complete with 3D graphics. The other was the server executable. The Zone team was very impressed, and scheduled a visit to our office (we'd since moved into an actual office space south of Boston). Soon after the visit, Microsoft agreed to enter into a publishing agreement with Turbine, secured initially with a letter of intent. The actual contract arrived six months later, but the letter of intent granted us an initial milestone payment and enough certainty to schedule the milestone deliverables.

This was the start of a long, sometimes tumultuous, but ultimately fruitful alliance. After we secured the contract, the division of labor was discussed. As the developer, Turbine was to design the game, engineer and implement all of the code, generate all art assets, create a QA plan, and perform testing on all game content. With its pre-existing Zone platform, Microsoft was responsible for code testing, billing, and ongoing server operations. Fundamentally, this meant that while Turbine would create the game, the day-to-day operations of the ASHERON'S CALL service would be entrusted to Microsoft.

One thing that Turbine successfully negotiated for was the rights to our source code. Besides the team, we knew that our massively-multiplayer technology was going to be our single most valuable asset. In addition, we agreed to a one-title deal that gave us the flexibility to pursue other development deals as opportunities arose. In this way, we ensured that Turbine would remain independent and effectively in control of our own destiny.

In many respects, Microsoft proved to be an ideal partner for Turbine. Like Turbine, the Zone was a start-up organization, and was eager to prove itself. The Zone was pioneering a new type of business, with a business model new to Microsoft, and this placed the managers of the Zone in a position where they could afford to take risks. And while ASHERON'S CALL ultimately validated Microsoft's belief in Turbine, at that point Turbine was certainly a risk.

Besides the obvious funding issue, Turbine benefited from its partnership with Microsoft in other ways. We had free access to Microsoft development tools like Visual C++, Visual SourceSafe, and a bug-tracking database called RAID. We learned a lot about professional software development from Microsoft as well, such how to create an efficient build process, manage code source trees, and organize effective test cycles on the daily builds.

Finally, we gained prestige by working with one of the most respected software companies in the world. Having Microsoft as a partner gave us a lot of credibility and put us in a much better position to pursue funding and make critical hires, two incredibly important objectives for a small startup company.

3. Reusable engine and tools

Massively-multiplayer games require a fundamentally different architecture from that of single-player games, or even multiplayer LAN games. Beyond the graphics engine, user interface, and other elements of a typical game, persistent massively-multiplayer games generally require a centralized server, networking layer, user authentication, game administration tools, and a host of other technologies.

Early on, Turbine recognized that many of these technologies would be required by any massively multiplayer game, and could perhaps be generalized enough that they could be reused in different massively-multiplayer titles. At the time, this was an unusual premise for a game developer; typically, source code was thrown out at the end of a project, and the idea of licensing a 3D engine like QUAKE was still a long way off. From our perspective it just made good business sense to leverage our R&D as much as possible.

Since so much of our development budget was devoted to creating these key technologies, we made every effort to keep the technology modular and data-independent. This modular architecture has since proven to be a tremendous win for Turbine. We've been able to prototype new game concepts rapidly by changing data while keeping the server executable nearly unchanged. Not only has this helped us get new business, it has also proven to be extremely useful for in-house play testing and constructing proof-of-concept demos.

Currently we are investigating the potential of licensing our technology. While we continue to advance the code base, we have placed some emphasis on productizing the Turbine engine. From a business perspective, this is a very desirable source of revenue. We can leverage our R&D efforts and development costs, while advancing the engine that our own future products will use.

In addition to the ability to reuse code, Turbine's modular emphasis extended to the way content is created for the game world. As development on ASHERON'S CALL progressed, we quickly came to realize that populating a game world the size of Dereth was going to be a monumental task. By this time, we knew our competitors were hiring teams to design individual levels and create content manually. This seemed less than optimal to us, and furthermore we didn't have the resources to hire a large content team.

Instead, we created a series of world-building tools to maximize our efforts. The first kind of tool allowed artists to create vast chunks of game environment (represented as a grayscale height map) with each stroke of their brush. Random monster encounters and terrain features such as trees and butterflies could also be placed using this method.

We also developed a tool called Dungeon Maker to create subterranean environments such as dungeons and catacombs. Early on, Jason Booth got sick of hand-modeling the complex level designs he was getting from the design team, so he and user-interface programmer Mike Ferrier created a level-building tool that used an intuitive drag-and-drop interface. This allowed nontechnical designers the ability to create and instantiate dungeons quickly without taking up the art team's valuable time.

An offshoot of Dungeon Maker, World Builder, became a much more advanced tool by the time ASHERON'S CALL shipped. Using World Builder, a content designer could wander around the game world placing houses, decorations, and monster encounters, and even raise and lower the terrain. This proved to be an incredible timesaver, and the amount of landscape content we were able to generate easily quadrupled. This kind of tool modularity allowed us the ability to update the game world easily with new content, such as new monsters, quests, items, and adventure locations.

Thanks to monthly content additions, ASHERON'S CALL "events" can propel an overarching story forward and involves players in all areas of the games. So far these events have proved to be a huge success. Players feel like they are part of a living, breathing world, and are more likely to stay involved in the game for longer periods of time.

4. Painless launch

When the first few thousand players began pouring onto the production servers, we were certain that there would be all sorts of catastrophes. We had watched our competitors suffer similar calamities, and we had resigned ourselves to accept this rite of passage. To our surprise, nothing went wrong the first day. We were delighted by just how stable and uneventful the retail launch was. Everything went without a hitch. This stability was due to effective beta testing, intelligent project management, and insightful data-center equipment deployment.

Here's how it worked. During beta, both Microsoft and Turbine testers submitted bugs into RAID. In addition, user-submitted bugs were tracked by the Microsoft team and were added into RAID if they were deemed important. Server performance metrics were one of the key goals towards meeting our shipping requirements. Each server had to maintain a minimum level of performance, given a concurrent user base of 3,000 players. To meet this metric, a few changes were in order. The server-side physics was modified to use a more simplified collision model. In addition, a faster "clean-up" cycle for objects dropped on the landscape was implemented.

Having made these changes, we were able to meet the aggressive server metrics and our server software has since proved to be nearly bulletproof. In fact, for the first several weeks, the server software did not crash once, which was a major accomplishment, considering the technical problems evident in other massively-multiplayer games.

Our retail launch was a staggered affair. Initially, only two "enthusiast-oriented" retail chains received shipments of ASHERON'S CALL boxes. This allowed our die-hard fans from the beta testing program to get copies, but prevented the deluge that would have occurred had we been in the larger, more mainstream retail stores. While it would have been exciting to see massive sales on day one, I believe that this gradual approach was a smart move.

5. Seamless environment using dynamically load-balancing servers

One the most impressive features of the Turbine engine is the continuous outdoor environment. This is made possible thanks to dynamic load balancing, which is a scalable server-side architecture. The easiest way to appreciate the need for dynamic load balancing is to consider the following scenario. Imagine a hypothetical game world that is divided into four servers, each of which corresponds to a geographic area in the game world. With a static server architecture, if everyone in the game world decides to go to the same area, that one server's performance would be dramatically impaired, while the three remaining servers would effectively be idle, completely unaware of their overtaxed brother.

Dynamic load balancing solves this overloaded server problem. Instead of assigning a static geographic area to each server, the individual servers can divide up the game world based on the relative processor load of each server. In the previous example, instead of remaining idle, all four servers would divide the load equally among themselves, ensuring the most efficient use of the hardware's processing capacity. Dynamic load balancing allows a very free-form environment where players can travel wherever they want with very few hard-coded limits.

But in order for the graphics engine to accommodate the seamless nature of the server, we couldn't allow the "level loading" pause typical in many 3D games to interrupt the game play. To avoid level-loading, the geometry team headed by Chris Dyl engineered a unique rendering engine that constantly loads data in the background, and draws objects at far enough distances so as to minimize obvious "popping" effects and without having to rely on a fogging effect to hide the clipping plane.

What Went Wrong

1. Poor scheduling and communication

For most of its early history, ASHERON'S CALL was the victim of poor project management. During the last year of development, a management reorganization took place that salvaged the project. Depending on how far back you look at the schedules, ASHERON'S CALL was either one to two years late. This is attributable to a number of reasons, some of which I will explain momentarily.

When Microsoft and Turbine entered into the development agreement, neither side had any idea of the scope of the project. An initial list of milestones was drawn up by the Microsoft product manager and our development leads. Unfortunately, after the second milestone, deadlines were consistently missed. A lot of this was due simply to underestimating the time required for development tasks. This created a domino effect as we continually played catch-up, trying desperately to make up for lost time.

This schedule free-fall continued into 1997 and forced us to re-evaluate the feature set. Unfortunately, feature cuts were made without considering the impact on the playability of the game. Ultimately, most of these features were added back into the game anyway, which took additional time due to the reallocation of team resources. The lesson here concerns the value of effective scheduling. Identify the risky areas in your schedule early, figure out the dependencies, and make sure you pad the time estimates for tasks.

Communication between Microsoft and Turbine was also a major factor. The teams were separated by about 3,000 miles and three time zones. Although weekly conference calls were scheduled, they lacked the collaborative mentality necessary for maintaining a successful relationship. E-mail threads were either ignored or else escalated into tense phone calls, and in some cases the bug-tracking database (RAID) was not used effectively. Clearly, everyone would have benefited from more face-to-face time. E-mail—and even conference calls—are poor media for managing new and sensitive corporate relationships, especially ones between companies with such different corporate cultures.

From a developer's perspective, it's always easy to blame the publisher for unrealistic expectations and bureaucracy. What's important to realize is that it is everyone's obligation to communicate expectations and problems before they escalate to the point of being a crisis.

2. Inexperienced development team

None of the senior developers at Turbine (including me) had ever shipped a retail PC game. None. Many of the employees were students immediately out of college, or even college students completing a work-study program. This obviously was the source of several severe problems in the development of ASHERON'S CALL. It was nearly impossible for team leads to give realistic schedule estimates for tasks, since few of us had experience in professional software development. It was also initially difficult to get different teams from the programming, art, and design departments to communicate regularly with each other.

The collegiate atmosphere made it very difficult for decisions to be made; meetings would happen and resolutions would seemingly be agreed upon, only to have those same questions asked in a subsequent meeting. No one likes unnecessary bureaucracy and giving up creative freedom, but ultimately one person needs to be given the authority to make a decision and hold people to it. A good supervisor takes into account the opinions of everyone involved; design by committee simply does not work.

Obviously, having a seasoned and experienced development team has innumerable advantages. While it's not critical that everyone on the development team have professional experience, at the very least team leads should have some form of professional experience. As it was, Turbine had to get by with raw talent, unabashed enthusiasm, and simply not knowing any better.

3. No feature iteration during development

Many weaknesses of ASHERON'S CALL at launch stemmed from the methodology we followed for feature completion. Features were scheduled by milestone and were expected to be completed in their entirety before other features were worked on. While this approach may work for more typical software applications, PC games rely on a host of interrelating systems that cannot be implemented in a vacuum.

An example of this involved our melee combat system. This game feature was completely spec'd and implemented long before magic spells worked within the game, under the misguided assumption that it saves developer and test resources not to have to revisit completed features. Clearly, these two game systems needed to be tested and balanced in stages alongside each other, not independently.

Another example of this problem occurred during beta testing. A massively-multiplayer game cannot be considered adequately tested until thousands of players have participated in the game world for at least a few months. The first time ASHERON'S CALL was exposed to this many users was when it went into beta testing. Unfortunately, we were placed in a code freeze situation during the beta test, and only the most serious bugs were fixed.

Both Microsoft and Turbine recognized many serious game balancing problems during beta, but at that point it was extremely difficult to make changes. This can be attributed to our tight schedule, but earlier beta tests would have accelerated the bug-finding process and resulted in a better balanced game. On future projects, Turbine is deploying a more iterative implementation process where rapid prototyping and early play-testing is encouraged.

4. An ambitious project lacking fundamental underlying technologies

As one of the first massively multiplayer 3D games, ASHERON'S CALL was a bold undertaking. Several core components were still theoretical when the project was planned. Things like dynamically load-balanced servers and continuous, uninterrupted outdoor environments were still unproven concepts when we committed to them for ASHERON'S CALL. Furthermore, we had to create our own 3D graphics engine, a latency-friendly network layer, and physics and game rule systems that would all work within a client/server model.

We learned very quickly why there hadn't been a game like ASHERON'S CALL before us: It was damned hard to develop such a game. I don't

think committing to a less aggressive feature set was the right solution, though. Instead, we should have acknowledged up front that R&D efforts are fundamentally hard to schedule, and been more flexible with our development schedule. With this in mind, we could have created more realistic estimates and done a better job managing expectations within and outside Turbine.

5. No documented high-level feature statement

Because ASHERON'S CALL had such a long and evolving development cycle, it was difficult to keep all the documentation up-to-date. To compound the matter, the project never had an official feature set as part of the development contract with Microsoft. The technical design document process and high-level feature overviews were basically skipped. This created severe problems when it came to prioritizing which features were important. We constantly had to justify features, and we had no documentation to fall back on to resolve our discussions.

Without a high-level vision statement it was also very difficult to educate new employees about the game. There was a sort of oral tradition to initiate new employees that had been passed down for so long that it just became part of our company's culture. This was partially possible because the concept of a 3D graphical MUD intuitively made sense to a lot of people. Unfortunately, it was very difficult to explain what ASHERON'S CALL was about to people who didn't understand this concept or had their own ideas about how things should be done. Having a documented vision statement and a description of the high-level feature set is absolutely essential for any title.

A Unique Company Résumé

ASHERON'S CALL was a tremendous learning opportunity for Turbine and Microsoft. Despite all the problems and setbacks, ASHERON'S CALL is a success story. The game has been well received by PC game enthusiasts as well as the majority of the game industry press. The fan support for ASHERON'S CALL is overwhelming, and players routinely spend more than six hours a day logged into the game world. In addition, Turbine is now in a very desirable position, being one of only a handful of developers (and the only independent studio) that has successfully created a massively-multiplayer title. Industry analysts predict that online games will be the fastest growing segment of entertainment software. With its reusable architecture, robust toolset, and (now) experienced developers, Turbine intends to remain at the forefront of massively-multiplayer gaming.

AFTERWORD

Independent Game Development

By now it's a commonplace observation that the game industry has become more conservative, that games have become less interesting, more stereotyped, less original, less willing to take risks. This development coincides with a trend towards consolidation: large publishing conglomerates have bought out many of the small independent developers. These conglomerates make money by cranking out sequels and copycat products rather than truly interesting and innovative creations. As a result, each year E3 is crammed with the same old games with new names and the latest graphical bells and whistles.

One response has been to look for freshness and inspiration outside the corporate environment, from independent game developers, hobbyists, students, and mavericks who can try out new ideas without focus groups or corporate bureaucracy. A clear analogy exists to the resurgence of independent filmmaking in the 90s that popularized the Sundance Festival and created a sense of an independent movement, a rough, edgy, original style to counteract the big-budget slickness and comfortable predictability of mainstream Hollywood productions. This style then filtered back into mainstream moviemaking and helped revitalize the medium. It's one of the venerable Romantic myths of art—Outsiders vs. The Man, creative renewal from the margins—and additionally it's often true. We've seen it in music (think of the punk, DIY, and grunge movements) to painting (*salon des refusés*) to literature (the Beats).

Can independent game development do the same? No reason why not—the video games industry is still in pretty close touch with its hobbyist roots. Independent game development is proceeding on any number of fronts. Indie game development happens all the time, although it doesn't always get the attention it deserves. Alone or in groups, students, hobbyists, and coders crank out shareware and freeware games, either for money or in response to some burning interior impetus. Some games, such as NETHACK (http://www.nethack.org), have existed for decades. NETHACK was born in the age of university-based mainframes and has grown by accretion over the years, as people add new features to this sprawling, rich dungeon game. Most exist virtually unknown or with underground fan bases. A few games, such as PONTIFEX (http://www.chroniclogic.com), have won cult followings, even within the game industry itself, but cannot be said to have had a widespread influence.

One problem for the indie scene is that with rising standards in production values, indie games can't match the lavish graphics and sound and programming finesse of mainstream games. Even when they have solid, original game mechanics, they can look clunky next to the latest multimillion-dollar fantasy epic. Tools such game editors, Shockwave, and Director have made it possible to produce professional-level work on a relatively independent basis, but it remains to be seen whether digital gaming will become a medium too expensive to support an indie sector.

A prominent sector of indie game development that has undoubtedly influenced the mainstream is the mod community—game fans who tinker with existing games, creating new levels, objects, characters, and rules, downloading editing tools or writing their own. This phenomenon began in the first days of computer gaming and took root in the fertile soil of the Internet, especially for games such as DOOM where the multiplayer component encouraged community and peer-to-peer exchange rather than solitary play. Industry powerhouses, such as id Software, led the way in providing tools for the mod community to change and expand the games they wrote, while websites, such as Blue's News and Planet Quake, became gathering places for fans to trade tools and new game levels. Plenty of ideas, such as Capture the Flag and other team-based games, have made their way from mod community web sites into shipping products. Likewise, fans who began by making their own levels for their favorite games have ended up with game-industry jobs.

The Interactive Fiction movement has taken the text-adventure, which is now extinct commercially, and made it a thriving amateur concern. Text adventures aren't competitive in the market because they don't display any pretty moving pictures, but this doesn't mean they aren't artistically powerful or outmoded. Dozens of new text adventures appear every year. The medium has numerous advantages for indie development—it's a stable technology, costs little to produce, and new works can be written, revised, and released in relatively little time by a single author. As a result, the IF movement has a thriving avant-garde that puts the mainstream industry to shame.

The game industry has begun to reach out actively to the independents. The annual Game Developers Conference now showcases the finalists of the Independent Games Festival (http://www.igf.com), an annual Sundance-like event for games developed outside the ranks of the major publishers, with a separate category for student work. The results are typically low-budget affairs but based around a solid original conception, and the event is getting bigger every year. Another sign of interest is the Indie Game Jam (http://www.indiegamejam.com), an annual event begun in 2002 that brought 14 professional developers together for four days to hack together as many different games as possible based on a single piece of technology, the idea being to encourage originality and brainstorming outside the usual corporate production process. The first Jam was a success—12 wildly different games resulted and were displayed the following week at GDC as part of the Experimental Games Workshop. As a movement and an ethos, independent game development is beginning to exist.

That having been said, it would be premature to abandon hope for mainstream game production—to point to an independent scene as the only source of creative renewal is too simple an idea. The line between indie and corporate is blurrier than the romantic myth would make it. Like a shape-shifting alien on *Star Trek*, the game industry has two sets of cultural DNA, partly corporate, partly devoted amateur, which is one of our great strengths. Our medium had its genesis among amateurs and entrepreneurs, and that generation is still part our industry, making it hard to tell who is definitively indie and who isn't. The industry has only very recently become big and static enough to make people worried—until a few years ago, there wasn't enough of a mainstream to warrant an idea of an independent scene.

The medium is still changing too rapidly to declare the death of all originality. We're constantly adjusting to a dozen new ideas at once. The Internet, the trend toward licensed middleware, massively multiplayer gaming, and the overall breakneck pace of technological change are still transforming gaming faster than we can follow. We can't tell if we're in a downward spiral or just a temporary retrenching.

The independent scene is a place from which to draw inspiration and ideas to reform our work and our production processes, a source of ideas rather than a magic bullet. It's important to remember that great work can come from anywhere—we have only to look at classic Warner Brothers cartoons and Golden-Age Hollywood film (to say nothing of Shigeru Miyamoto's oeuvre) to find examples of brilliant work that came from the mainstream. They came from people who loved their work and also understood their art form and how to work together to produce it. Like them, we're in the incredibly fortunate position of being part of the next great entertainment medium. By learning from one another, examining our successes and failures, and never being satisfied with the status quo, we have the opportunity to do as well.

APPENDIX A

GAME DEVELOPMENT TEAM ROLES

The age of the single-author game is more or less over, and game production has been split into discrete jobs. As an industry, we have invented terminology to describe the different members of a development team. This has turned out to be a devil's bargain—job titles are great because they tell you who's responsible for what kinds of tasks, but they also tend to give people the misconception that everything outside their job description is none of their business. One of the lessons that repeat throughout the postmortems is how important it is for the entire team to understand what the game is and be able to contribute ideas on any subject. Otherwise, the abilities of the team aren't really being put into play.

Every one of these descriptions is an oversimplification. In practice, game development jobs shape themselves to the needs of the project and the skills of the person doing them. The sharp lines within art, programming, design, audio, writing, and management that seem to exist on a spreadsheet, don't exist at all—every one of these jobs has technical, artistic, and game-design areas. That said, here is a rundown of current industry job titles and what they, basically, mean:

Artist

This is the broad category of workers who create the graphical content for a game. It can include anything from a concept artist to a 3D animator to an architectural consultant; from artists make cut-scenes, walking animations, 3D furniture, wall-textures, landscape geometry, fake newsreel footage, and a thousand other things. Although technical expertise is always a plus, the actual requirements vary. A concept artist might work only with paper and pencils, whereas a technical artist might spend 90% of their time hacking file formats and writing custom plug-ins for a commercial graphics package.

As with all game industry jobs, this one blurs into the others. Designing natural-looking terrain geometry and realistic architecture blurs into level design; creating interface buttons blurs into interface design; writing 3D Studio plug-ins blurs into tools-programming; crafting textures to look correct in a 3D world requires understanding rendering algorithms; and so on.

Audio

Long neglected, audio is now one of the fastest-growing areas in game production. Two reasons are that exciting new audio technologies are emerging and people are paying attention to games as complete entertainment experiences rather than just graphical displays. Sound and music are tools for giving virtual worlds richness, character, and emotion—tools we're just starting to take advantage of.

Audio departments divide roughly into sound engineers and composers. Sound engineers design the audible world of a game—the voice of a character, the chunky click of a weapon reloading, the tread of a shoe on dry leaves or cold marble, much as a foley engineer in the film world. They supervise recording sessions and engage with emerging audio technologies, such as 3D sound and voice synthesis. Composers score the game, working inside the technical constraints of the computer and the formal constraints of interactive media. If emotion is a problem area for computer games, music might be one of the most powerful solutions.

Designer

This job is the hardest to pin down and the most variable between different projects, companies, and designers. It is perhaps most correct to say broadly that game designers craft the player's interactive experience using tools that artists and programmers make—they make the fun. Typical design tasks include laying out the game interface, building the level maps, designing puzzles, balancing units' abilities to create a game that is both fair and challenging. Designers often double as the game's writer for story and in-game dialogue and text, although increasingly this profession is becoming separate.

In some teams, the lead designer is like an auteur film director. They have the initial vision for the game; they write the overall design document and the story. Later in the development process, this initial game concept is a touchstone for determining priorities. Other designers work as a kind of caretaker for a group vision of the game—they hear all the suggestions, record them, and turn them into a full design document for the game. They make the final decision on some issues, but the design doesn't start with them. The design starts from a company's overall strategy decision, an existing game engine, or a team vote.

Designers often have specialized skills in a related field, such as writing, graphic design, or programming, and this issue shapes how they mesh with the rest of the team. Some technical knowledge is always necessary, so that the designer understands the tools of their trade and what a computer can and can't do.

Producer

Producers are the ones who manage project teams as a whole. They are in charge of project management issues, such as schedules, budget, morale, and coordinating different sections of a project team. They host meetings, facilitate communication, resolve problems, and accept responsibility for the product as a whole.

Leadership styles vary. Some producers view themselves purely as administrators—they make sure the schedule and budget work correctly, and coordinate the team's efforts, but leave the creative vision to a project leader or the design, art, or programming lead. Other producers are the keepers of the product's overall concept and serve as creative director and final decision-maker on the product's feel.

Producers also serve as a liaison to company management and publisher concerns. They make sure a given product meshes with overall company strategy and integrate marketing and localization efforts into the project team's work. Likewise, they represent the team's progress and needs to upper management—if the project is late or there's a problem with working conditions, the producer brings the news up the chain of command.

Programmer

Programmers write the software that comprises the game engine and the tools the team uses to produce the product. Game programmers often specialize in a game subsystem, such as graphics, networking, audio, or AI, or on tools programming, creating things, such as game editors and exporters.

It's easy to see programmers as pure technicians, but as much artistry exists on the programming side as anywhere else—any truly great game is a marriage of creative vision with technical decision-making. An AI programmer creates one of the core elements of the game experiences—the opponent or ally who shares the world with players, who competes or fights or bonds with them. Likewise, coding a good game editor means understanding designers' needs and priorities, as well as the designers themselves. Programmers have to make decisions daily that require an overall understanding of the game vision.

The earliest games were entirely programmer-written, and some programmers see this time as the golden age—games created by people who thoroughly understood the limitations and strengths of the machine and the programs that ran it. That era is past, but programmers now are still the team members who can convey that understanding to the team as a whole.

Quality Assurance

The quality assurance (QA), or playtest department, tests the finished product (or work-in-progress) to see that it works the way it's intended to. Sadly, this job frequently puts the team members in the position of bearers of bad news—"don't shoot the messenger" might be the unofficial motto of every QA department in existence.

The official QA mandate is to make sure the product does what it's supposed to do. They check, in excruciating detail, every feature and every level of the game, in every combination imaginable. This process includes checking in every language the game ships in and on every reasonable configuration of hardware and operating system, in PC products.

The unofficial QA role is that they tend to know the game better than anyone else on the team—no one else is in contact with the actual product, 40 or 60 or 80 hours a week. QA often has the best view of what's actually happening to a product and is best qualified to comment on intangibles: is the game fun and does it correspond to the initial vision. In the best case, QA can become creative collaborators rather than just bug-reporters, reporting on how the game feels and plays, rather than just working from a checklist.

Glossary

cut-scene a non-interactive animated presentation, played back from prepared data rather than generated dynamically; usually used as introduction and conclusion for a game, also for providing narrative exposition and, as a graphic spectacle, rewards for accomplishment.

data game content, such as terrain geometry or spoken dialogue, as distinct from the software used to manipulate and display it; contrast engine.

DDA Dynamic Difficulty Adjustment; a game's ability to react to player performance by increasing or decreasing the level of challenge.

deathmatch a charming neologism coined for player-versus-player modes in first-person shooter games; later broadened for use in other genres, such as real-time strategy games.

E3 Electronic Entertainment Expo; the annual trade show for the game industry, held in late June; games often get their first public showing at E3, hence the importance of the E3 demo in marketing a game.

engine core systems that, taken as a group, display the game environment and enact its basic functions; as distinct from data.

exploit particularly in online games, a flaw in the game that players can use to gain disproportionate advantages and rewards.

first-person shooter popular genre of game, in which players navigate a 3D world full of enemies; players view the world through a camera set at head height (hence the name), which also serves as a gunsight. Id Software's CASTLE WOLFENSTEIN 3D is perhaps the first example.

first-person sneaker term coined to designate games in first-person perspective, where stealth is more important than combat in achieving player goals. Looking Glass Studios' THIEF series is perhaps the prime example.

gameplay vague word denoting what players do in a game, the activities and challenges, as distinct from the technology and artwork that support these.

GDC Game Developers Conference; an annual meeting of game developers to present and discuss their experiences in game creation.

level a unit of game data usually corresponding to one stage of a game, or a virtual location (e.g., a floor of a building); also, a game character's rank in a graded scale of power.

MMPOG Massively Multiplayer Persistent Online Games; multiplayer games involving thousands of players, whose characters are recorded and change over time.

motion capture a technique of recording animation from a real-life source.

patch a piece of software that fixes problems in a product that has already been shipped, correcting bugs and adding missing features.

renderer software that draws a scene procedurally from a set of data, rather than replaying frames of animation.

RPG Role-Playing Game; an early term for paper-and-dice-based fantasy games, later translated into a genre of computer games retaining the conventions of the original; as exemplified in, for example, the ULTIMA and WIZARD series of games. Alternately an acronym for rocket-propelled grenade.

RTS Real-Time Strategy; a genre of game that depicts large-scale military conflicts in continuous-running action, as contrasted with turn-based games; Westwood's DUNE II was the founding example.

sandbox a game whose interest derives from the amusement value of a complex, dynamic simulation, which relies on player creativity rather than pre-set goals or narrative.

texture a 2D piece of artwork, applied to the surface of a rendered polygon to give it added detail and color; often called a skin when applied to a character model.

turn-based divided into discrete rounds that advance when certain conditions have been met (for example, all players have moved their pieces).

waterfall development model a software production process that works by first assessing the required functions, then breaking them into modular subsystems, writing them, integrating them, testing that they fulfill the specified functions, and shipping. Generally held to be good for large, well-understood systems but less effective for projects requiring high efficiency and functional innovation.

Index of Game Titles & Developers

A

B

C

D

E

O

P

Q

R

S

T

U

V

W

X

Index

Be sure to also use the Index of Game Titles & Developers beginning on page 319.

Symbols

Numerics

A

B

C

D

E

F

G

H

I

J

K

L

M

V

W

X

Z